Units 7 and 8

Management of Costs, Value and Resources

Study Pack

Technician (NVQ Level 4)

Published August 1999 by Financial Training, 10–14 White Lion Street, London N1 9PE

Copyright © 1999 The Financial Training Co Ltd

ISBN 1 85179 778 5

This pack has been published by Financial Training, one of the leading providers of training in accountancy and finance. Although it is aimed at students on the Education and Training Scheme of the Association of Accounting Technicians (AAT) it is not published or approved directly by the AAT. Any queries on the Education and Training Scheme and AAT Administration should be addressed to Student Services at AAT, 154 Clerkenwell Road, London EC1R 5AD (0171 837 8600), or emailed to Student.services@aat.org.uk.

Publisher's note

Financial Training study materials are distributed in the UK and overseas by Stanley Thornes (Publishers) Limited. It is another company within the Wolters Kluwer group and can be contacted at Stanley Thornes, Ellenborough House, Wellington Street, Cheltenham GL50 1YD. Telephone: 01242 228888. Fax: 01242 221914.

We are grateful to the Association of Accounting Technicians for kind permission to reproduce tasks from the central assessments.

All business entities referred to in this publication are fictitious. Any resemblance to any actual organisation, past or present, is purely coincidental.

Contents

Chapter 4   Budget Preparation

Chapter 5   Budgetary Control and Responsibility Accounting

Chapter 6   Standard Costing

Chapter 7   Variance Analysis

Chapter 8   Performance Indicators

Chapter 9   Presentation of Reports

Chapter 10   Cost Reduction, Quality and Value Enhancement

Chapter 11   Answers to Chapter Questions

Chapter 12   Practice Central Assessments

Central Assessment Pack

Introduction

1 What are Units 7 and 8 about?

Unit 7

'This unit is concerned with collecting and analysing cost information to assist in highlighting trends in costs and making suggestions for the reduction of costs and adding value. The unit requires the candidate to obtain information from a variety of internal and external sources and monitor performance indicators and movements in prices over an appropriate timescale.'

(Lead Body for Accounting Standards, July 1998)

Unit 8

'This unit is concerned with producing forecasts of income and expenditure, producing budget proposals and monitoring performance against budgets. The unit requires that the candidate is responsible for ensuring the budget has taken all relevant data into account and that the appropriate people have been consulted.'

(Lead Body for Accounting Standards, July 1998)

2 Element to study for Units 7 and 8

There are two elements to study for Unit 7 and three for Unit 8. Each is broken down into performance criteria, all of which should be studied in the context of the range statement. Each performance criterion is cross–referenced below to the chapter(s) in which it is covered in the Study Pack.

Unit 7

Element 7.1: Collect, analyse and disseminate information about costs

Performance criteria

		Chapter(s)
7.1.1	Valid, relevant information is identified from internal and external sources	2, 3
7.1.2	Trends in prices are monitored for movements and analysed on a regular basis and potential implications are identified	2
7.1.3	Standard costs are compared with actual costs and any variances are analysed	6, 7
7.1.4	Forecasts of trends and changes in factor prices and market conditions are consistent with previous experience of factor prices and market conditions	2
7.1.5	Relevant staff in the organisation are consulted about the analysis of trends	2
7.1.6	Reports highlighting significant trends are presented to management in an appropriate form	9

Range statement

1   *Information:* movements in prices charged by suppliers; movements in prices charged by competitors; movements in prices charged by providers of services; general price changes.

2   *Methods of presenting information:* report; table; diagram.

3   *Variance analysis:* Materials variances: usage, price; Labour variances: rate, efficiency; Fixed overhead variances: expenditure, volume, capacity, efficiency.

Element 7.2: Make recommendations to reduce costs and enhance value

Performance criteria

		Chapter(s)
7.2.1	Routine cost reports are analysed, compared with other sources of information and the implication of findings are identified	3, 7
7.2.2	Relevant performance indicators are monitored and the results are assessed to identify potential improvements	8
7.2.3	Relevant specialists are consulted to assist in the identification of ways to reduce costs and enhance value	10
7.2.4	Exception reports to follow up matters which require further investigation are prepared	7, 9
7.2.5	Specific recommendations are made to management and are explained in a clear and appropriate form	9

Range statement

1   *Performance indicators to measure:* productivity; unit costs; resources utilisation; profitability; quality of service

2   *Recommendations:* efficiencies; modifications to work processes

Unit 8

Element 8.1: Prepare forecasts of income and expenditure

Performance criteria

8.1.1	Relevant data for projecting forecasts is identified	2
8.1.2	Relevant individuals are given the opportunity to raise queries and clarify forecasts	5
8.1.3	Forecasts are produced in a clear format with explanations of assumptions, projections and adjustments	4
8.1.4	The validity of forecasts is reviewed in the light of any significant anticipated changes	4, 5

Range statement

1   *Forecasts:* income; expenditure

2   *Data:* accounting information; wage and salary information; market information; general economic information

Element 8.2: Produce draft budget proposals

Performance criteria

		Chapter(s)
8.2.1	Draft budget proposals are presented to management in a clear and appropriate format and on schedule	4
8.2.2	Draft budget proposals are consistent with organisation objectives, have taken all relevant data into account and are agreed with budget holders	4
8.2.3	Annual budgets are broken down into periods in accordance with anticipated seasonal trends	4
8.2.4	Discussions with budget holders are conducted in a manner which maintains goodwill	4, 5

Range statement

1   *Types of budgets:* budget for current expenditure; resource budget; capital budget

2   *Data:* accounting information; wage and salary information; market information; general economic information; strategic plans

Element 8.3: Monitor the performance of responsibility centres against budgets

Performance criteria

8.3.1	Budget figures are checked and reconciled on an ongoing basis	4, 5
8.3.2	Actual cost and revenue data are correctly coded and allocated to responsibility centres	5
8.3.3	Variances are clearly identified and reported to management in routine reports	7, 5
8.3.4	Significant variances are discussed with managers and assistance is given to managers to take remedial action	5

Range statement

1   *Types of budgets:* budget for current expenditure; resource budget

2   *Variances:* actual; potential

3   *Responsibility centres:* expense centres; profit centres

3   Central assessment

3.1   General format

Units 7 and 8 are each assessed by one central assessment of three hours plus 15 minutes reading time.

For the central assessment you will be provided with a question booklet and a separate answer booklet into which you should write your answers. Usually this answer booklet contains just blank pages for your answers, but there may be proforma statements for you to fill in.

3.2   What will be covered?

The central assessment will test a selection of performance criteria plus the related aspects of knowledge and understanding. The format and content are expected to be similar to past sittings.

The assessment is likely to be divided into two sections, each with a number of tasks. It is in a case study format, with some initial data given concerning a particular organisation to which some or all of the tasks will be related.

The tasks will assess your ability to apply basic management accounting techniques in simple business situations. Examples of such tasks would include:

For Unit 7

♦   Preparation and presentation of standard costing reports.

♦   Calculation of materials, labour and overhead variances, and discussion of possible causes and/or responsibility.

♦   Analysis of accounting information, including index numbers, general price changes and the analysis of trends.

♦   Accounting ratios and performance indicators (calculation and interpretation).

♦   Use of published statistics and other sources of information about external costs and revenue trends.

♦   Cost reduction, quality improvement and value enhancement.

For Unit 8

♦   Preparation and presentation of forecasts of income and expenditure, including allowance for price changes

♦   Preparation of budgets

♦   Flexible budgeting

♦   Co-ordination of the budgeting system

◆ Reporting to budget holders, including budgetary control statements incorporating basic variances

Relevant underpinning knowledge as defined in the standards will also be tested, including a basic understanding of the following topics.

For Unit 7

◆ Activity-based costing

◆ Time series analysis

◆ Total quality management

For Unit 8

◆ Types of budget

◆ Sources of data for budget forecasts

◆ Time series analysis

◆ Key factors

◆ The effect of budgetary control systems on the motivation of managers

3.3 Analysis of recent Central Assessments

See Central Assessment Pack Question

Unit 7 (previously Unit 11)

December 1998 (Unit 7)

1	Variance analysis: exchange rate differences	⎫
2	Variance analysis: fixed overheads	⎬ Mock Central Assessment
3	Performance indicators: calculation and explanation	⎭

June 1998 (Unit 11)

1	Standard costing: marginal costing and variance analysis	⎫
2	Variance analysis: performance report	⎬ 11.3
3	Quality costs	⎭
4	Performance indicators: calculation and decision making	8.8

December 1997 (Unit 11)

1	Variance analysis: fixed overheads	⎫
2	Variance analysis: explaining fixed overhead variances	⎬ 11.2
3	Forecasting: using seasonal variations	⎭
4	Performance indicators: calculation and decision making	8.7

3.4 Common problems with recent central assessments

The assessor has made the following comments on the performance of candidates in recent central assessments.

'Presentation is a problem for some candidates. In numerical tasks this can make it difficult to follow a candidate's logic. At one extreme, this can be because there are no workings or, at the other extreme, because there might be several pages of uninformative jumbled calculations. Clear presentation is essential if a candidate is to be given credit for a valid approach even if the final answer is not correct. Equally clear presentation is required when writing memos or other forms of reports. Too often, these kinds of tasks are answered by simply repeating listings from manuals. Little or no credit can be given when that happens. To be judged competent, it is essential that answers should (i) address the requirements of the task, (ii) relate to the data in the case, and (iii) demonstrate analysis.'

'An inability to relate existing techniques to slightly different circumstances suggests that some candidates are still relying on mechanistic recall rather than on understanding.'

'Too many candidates choose to regurgitate listings from manuals without considering the data in the case or the task requirements.'

'Many (answers) ... came out with vague generalisations despite the task specifically asking candidates to use the data in the case to justify any limitation.'

'The overall impression from the candidates' answers ... was that they displayed strong ability in answering numerical tasks but that they were much weaker when non-numeric (discursive) tasks were set. A problem that a significant number of candidates experienced was an inability to answer the task set or to justify their proposals, with many candidates simply restating the data given in the task and not challenging it.'

'The main weakness in the discursive answers was again that of not answering the task set. Another problem which arose was that of using the data provided in the central assessment as the answer to the task without any development of it.'

'A substantial number of candidates derived their solutions in note form or rough workings and then repeated these in the formal answer to the tasks. This is unnecessary. Provided rough workings are clear, and clearly identified, the formal answer can refer the assessor back to these workings.'

'Many candidates do not read the detailed task requirements. Instead, having identified the general area of the task, they then commit to paper every thought they may have had about the task being assessed.'

'Candidates seem to experience difficulty in understanding what words such as 'explain' mean and in answering the task set, ie 'give one reason' and 'identify four weaknesses'. The poorer candidates supplied several instead of one and over five instead of four.'

'Presentation was also a problem for some candidates in that the requests for letters and memos were often ignored.'

What the assessor is looking for

From the above comments on the performances of past candidates, it can be seen that the assessor places importance upon the following factors.

A high level of basic costing knowledge

Before addressing the more advanced topics, such as activity-based costing or value analysis, you must ensure that your knowledge of basic costing topics studied in earlier units is sound.

Relevant answers

If you do not know the answer to the question being asked, do not give an answer to a question you do know about! It will not earn you marks and will waste time.

Ability to explain

At Technician level it is not enough simply to get the calculations correct. You need to be able to demonstrate a clear understanding of the principles, assumptions and limitations of the techniques upon which the calculations are based.

Ability to interpret results

Once you have calculated your answers you need to be able to make sensible comments on what they show and their relevance to the particular management function being addressed.

You must make your comments specific to the particular situation, rather than list out all possible interpretations whether they are likely to apply or not.

Answering all the requirements

No matter how good your answer is to part (a) of the task, if you ignore part (b) you cannot expect to earn full marks. Watch out for several requirements being included in one sentence.

Good presentation

You should aim to present your work as if it were to be submitted to management. However, if you do make mistakes, do not use correcting fluid, but cross them out neatly.

If you are required to prepare a statement or schedule, think about its layout before starting work. Put any detailed computational workings on a separate page and cross-reference them to the main answer.

3.5   How to tackle the central assessment

Always read all the instructions before starting

Although it is likely that you will be required to complete all tasks in the assessment, always check that this is the case.

Ensure you note the advised amount of time to spend on each section, given at the start of the assessment.

Allocate your time sensibly between sections and tasks

The timings given at the start of the paper indicate the relative importance placed upon them by the assessor. Do not overrun these times significantly – leave unfinished tasks at the end of the time and move on, but do allow yourself some time at the end to return to them and complete them as far as possible.

Work through the paper in the order set

Although each section will be largely self-contained, it is quite likely that there will be some link (for example, they may all involve the same organisation). Some of the tasks in later sections may relate to information given or computations from earlier sections. So work through the paper in the order it is set.

Read the data and requirements for each task carefully and fully before starting work

Note all details given of the business with which you are dealing to ensure that your answers are tailored to its particular business and circumstances.

Ensure that all parts of the requirements are addressed in the required format (schedule, table, statement, memorandum, etc.) and comply with the requirement to explain, discuss, comment, suggest, etc.

Consider using examples from previous tasks to illustrate explanations; you must, of course, do this if it is specifically required.

If asked for *four* causes/actions/examples, etc. comply with this exactly – extra ones will not earn you extra credit; they will just be ignored.

4 Using this Study Pack

Whatever your previous experience, you are encouraged to work through this Study Pack as completely and as methodically as you can, paying attention to the areas which are most relevant to you. Here is a short explanation of the aim of each aspect of this Study Pack.

♦ **Study Pack Chapters 1–10.** These contain study material, examples and questions (with answers in Chapter 11) on a particular topic to help you to learn the required techniques. Performance criteria covered are identified at the beginning of each chapter, as is a list of what you should actually be able to do once you have completed your studies of the chapter. There is also a summary at the end.

♦ **Study Pack Chapter 12 Practice Central Assessments.** These formed the Specimen Central Assessments distributed by the AAT when the Standards were last revised in 1998, and so represent a fair example of what you will have to face. Both have full answers.

♦ **Central Assessment Pack Chapters 1–10.** These contain additional questions, most of which come from recent Central Assessments set by the AAT. All have full answers.

♦ **Central Assessment Pack Chapter 11.** This contains six Case Study questions (again mostly from recent Central Assessments). They are more extensive than the questions in Chapters 1–10 which cover discrete topics, and they help you to build up your confidence to tackle full, integrated Central Assessment papers. All have full answers.

♦ **Central Assessment Pack Chapter 12 Mock Central Assessments.** These are the December 1998 actual papers, for you to try as far as possible under timed conditions. Both have full answers.

You should try to make sure that you attempt all questions and central assessments in the Study Pack without looking at the answers. It is only by doing this that you get full value from the Study Pack. By peeking the only person you are cheating is yourself!

FTC Training Centres

Birmingham	Leicester	Manchester	Wokingham
1st floor	3rd Floor	6th Floor	Swift House
Centre City Tower	Beckville House	St James Building	Market Place
7 Hill Street	66 London Road	Oxford Street	Wokingham
Birmingham	Leicester	Manchester	RG40 1AP
B5 4UA	LE2 0QD	M1 6FQ	
Tel: 0121 644 4747	Tel: 0116 285 6767	Tel: 0161 233 2018	Tel: 0118 977 4922
Cardiff	Liverpool	Newcastle	Hong Kong
5th floor	3rd Floor	Provincial House	24th Floor Wyndham
Market Chambers	Coopers Building	Northumberland	Place
5-7 St Mary's Street	Church Street	Street	44 Wyndham Street
Cardiff	Liverpool	Newcastle upon Tyne	Central
CF1 2AT	L1 3AA	NE1 7DQ	Hong Kong
Tel: 01222 388 067	Tel: 0151 708 8839	Tel: 0191 232 9365	Tel: (852) 2526 3686
Glasgow	London (AAT, ACCA, CIMA)	Nottingham	Kuala Lumpur
91 Mitchell Street	7-13 Melior Street	3rd Floor Alan House	1st Floor Wisma Alma
Glasgow	London	5 Clumber Street	2-4 Jalan Manau
G1 3LN	SE1 3QP	Nottingham	50460 Kuala Lumpur
		NG1 3ED	Malaysia
Tel: 0141 248 8080	Tel: 0171 407 5000	Tel: 0115 853 3600	Tel: (603) 274 8884
Hull	London – ACA	Sheffield	Mauritius
Suite R	10-14 White Lion Street	Pegasus House	Coopers & Lybrand
The Shirethorn	London	463a Glossop Road	Training Centre
Centre	N1 9PD	Sheffield	3rd Floor, Astor Court
Prospect Street		S10 2QD	George Guidert
Hull			Port Louis
HU2 8PX			Mauritius
Tel: 01482 620578	Tel: 0171 837 0700	Tel: 0114 266 9265	Tel: (230) 208 7945
Leeds	London – Financial Markets	Southampton	Singapore
49 St Paul's Street	New London House	32 Castle Way	107A Sophia Road
Leeds	6 London Street	Southampton	Singapore 228 172
LS1 2TE	London	SO14 2AW	
	EC3R 7LQ		
Tel: 0113 388 9320	Tel: 0171 265 1011	Tel: 01703 220852	Tel: (65) 333 1877

THE FINANCIAL TRAINING COMPANY

AAT DIVISION

E Mail: aat@financial-training.com

http://www.financial-training.com

A MEMBER OF THE WOLTERS KLUWER PROFESSIONAL TRAINING GROUP

CHAPTER 1

Management Accounting and Information

Objectives

This chapter explains the purpose and nature of management accounting and cost accounting. It also describes the role of the management accountant and the role of the cost accountant.

When you have completed this chapter you should understand the following.

♦ The need for management accounting information as well as financial accounting information within a business.

♦ The nature of a management information system.

The purpose and nature of cost and management accounting

Management accounting vs financial accounting

Accountants have to provide **information** to very diverse groups. The specific needs of each determine whether these can best be served by the financial accounting or the management accounting function of the business organisation. The main **differences between financial accounting and management accounting** are as follows:

♦ Financial accounting provides information to **users** who are external to the business; management accounting is usually concerned with internal users of accounting information such as the managers of the business.

♦ Financial accounting draws up financial statements, the **formats** of which are governed by law and accounting standards for limited companies; management accounting reports can be in any format which suits the user and may differ considerably from one company to another.

♦ Financial accounting reports on past transactions; management accounting records historic transactions, compares actual figures to budget figures and hence makes **predictions for the future**.

Cost accounting

Cost accounting is normally a large part of the management accounting role. It is primarily concerned with ascertainment of costs and it was developed to a great extent within a manufacturing context where costs are most difficult to isolate and analyse. In such a business there are two things which the financial accountant's profit and loss account will not disclose:

♦ the amount of profit **attributable to each unit of a product** or service;

♦ the amount of cost and/or revenue **attributable to each manager**.

This is one aspect of cost accounting.

Although cost accounts are drawn up on established double-entry principles, they nevertheless differ from financial accounts in several important respects. This will become apparent as you work through these units.

The information provided by the cost accountant will be part of the **management information system** (MIS) of the business (often the major part). We shall first consider the nature of the MIS overall.

Management information systems (MIS)

A **management information system** (MIS) is a system using formalised procedures to provide managers at all levels with appropriate information from all relevant sources (internal and external to the business) for the purposes of planning and controlling the activities for which they are responsible.

A MIS has been defined as 'a system in which defined data are collected, processed and communicated to assist those responsible for the use of resources'.

Each MIS will be determined by:

♦ the type of organisation or business;

♦ the products or services offered;

♦ the principal markets;

♦ the principal objectives;

♦ the organisation structure and reporting relationships;

♦ the principal users of information; and

♦ the use to which the information is put.

The information systems will operate within **different levels**, from the board of directors down to shop-floor supervisors, and within different functions (for example, production, marketing and finance).

Management information

Why is information needed?

Information is mainly needed:

◆ to assist management in *planning* the most effective use of resources, such as labour and materials;

◆ to assist management in *decision-making* (ie. choosing between alternative courses of action), for example whether to make a product or purchase it from an outside supplier;

◆ to aid management in *controlling* day-to-day operations, for example by comparing actual results with those planned.

The functions – such as planning and controlling – involved in managing an organisation therefore require knowledge that is relevant to the particular situation. How often is it said, 'If only I had known that at the time'? Managers' judgements will be greatly enhanced by receiving the **appropriate information** on which to base their decisions.

A manager will use resources in the light of the information available to him. Furthermore, the whole complex process of management can be broken down into manageable sections or problems. The problem facing the chairman of a large group might be to decide how much funds to allocate to a particular activity, whereas a foreman in the machine shop might be deciding which machine to use and which operators should be asked to operate it to turn out a particular job. Information is necessary at each level to **guide decisions** and, in due course, to **measure the effectiveness** of the action taken.

Requirements of management information

A successful business needs management capable of making decisions. In turn, a successful business manager has the responsibility and authority to make those decisions. Irrespective of whether these decisions may dictate the future long-term policy or conduct of the business or simply its day to day routine operation, management must be equipped with **adequate and timely information**.

Management information may be of two types, as follows.

◆ Information about the past results of the type of action envisaged – **historical information**.

◆ Information about the future effects of decisions – **forecast information**.

Three basic types of information have been identified.

(a)   *Scorekeeping* – The accumulation of data to enable both internal and external parties to evaluate organisational performance and position. This embraces internal reporting for use in planning and controlling non-routine operations. To some extent this also embraces external reporting to shareholders, government and other external parties.

(b)   *Attention-directing* – The reporting and the interpretation of information which helps managers to focus on operation problems, imperfections, inefficiencies and opportunities. This aspect of accounting assists managers with the provision of important data about the operations enabling timely decision making, whether on a long-term or a short-term basis. Attention directing is frequently associated with current planning and control and with the analysis and investigation of recurring, routine and non-routine internal accounting reports.

(c)   *Problem-solving* – This *ad hoc* aspect of accounting involves the concise quantification of the relative merits of possible courses of action, often with recommendations as to the best procedure. In this it is seen that the cost accountant is a very vital part of the management team.

Attributes of information

Since management at all levels must perform a certain amount of planning, decision-making and control, it is vital that the manager has the necessary information to perform his tasks. There are four fundamental attributes of information.

(a)   *Relevance to the scope of responsibility.* A production manager will primarily be concerned with information about stocks, production levels, production performance and machine loads within his department. He will not be interested in the shortcomings of other departments unless they specifically affect his area. Indeed, he may well only be interested in one part of the manufacturing environment, for example, the manager of the machine shop will not be concerned with an assembly shop in another part of the plant.

(b)   *Relevance to any particular decision.* This is a difficult one. Management have to be able to identify the decisions that need to be made. This requires information that directs attention to specific problems. However, having identified the decisions, the information that enables the right decisions to be made needs to be acquired.

(c)   *Production in time.* This is an area of great conflict for manager and accountant. Two of the most desirable attributes of the accountant's work are accuracy and timeliness. Of course, information to satisfy the requirements already outlined, must be accurate, but to be of use in the business it must be presented quickly. The demand for information in business is like the demand for news, and it is about as perishable. A beautiful, well written, superbly accurate report, covering and analysing all the facets of a particular problem and all the possible solutions and their consequences is useless if it cannot be prepared in time for the decision to be taken, or is delivered after the problem has been resolved.

(d)   *Value.* This value may be assessed by the resulting change in the planned course of action. If no change takes place then the information had no real value; if a change takes place then the value is represented by the benefit in changing. The information also has a cost and the cost of obtaining information must be compared with the potential benefit arising from it. Even cost accounting must be cost-effective!

The accounting information system

The major objective of most commercial organisations is **to make profits**. Consequently, the accounting system is the most important information system, providing the basis for the process of budgetary planning and control and linking together the other information systems within the organisation created by the functions of research and development, production, personnel, etc.

The purpose of a MIS is to determine, and to provide as efficiently, effectively and economically as possible, **what management need to know**. Since most of the information within any business is handled by the accounts department, the accountant, and particularly the cost accountant, is thus in a very important position.

The role of the management accountant

The accountant's skills

The chief role of the accountant was traditionally 'stewardship'. He began as the custodian of the firm's assets and the faithful recorder of their movement. Because profit is the net increase in asset values, stewardship gradually developed so that the emphasis fell on the **calculation of the organisation's profit**.

Stewardship involves the careful, effective and efficient use of assets, and so the management accountant is concerned with the pursuit of efficiency and of productivity in the use of the firm's resources, as well as with the generation of profits.

The tool of the management accountant is **figures**. He must be able to collate them according to logic, fully understand what they tell him, and to know how to help management to understand the significance of his information. In other words, he collects all the available data; records, collates, and analyses it, and then reports his findings to the company's management.

The functions of a management accountant

The management accountant assists management in the following areas:

♦ *Planning* – Primarily through preparation of a short-term annual budget, but also through long range strategic planning.

♦ *Organising* – Planning enables all departments involved to be organised and avoids lack of goal congruence, ie individual managers seeking good results for their department but with a bad overall effect on the company.

♦ *Controlling* – Comparing actual results with the budget helps to identify where operations are not running according to plan. Investigation of the causes and subsequent action achieves effective control of the business.

♦ *Communicating* – Liaising with departments and reporting relevant information on a timely basis.

♦ *Motivating* – A tight but attainable budget communicated effectively should motivate staff and improve their performance. If the target is too difficult, however, it is likely to demotivate and is unlikely to be achieved.

Management accounts will therefore serve a variety of purposes; it is no surprise then that they take a variety of forms. There is no set format; management accounts should include information relevant to their purpose.

Cost accounting and MIS

The scope of cost accounting

The role of the cost accountant is intimately involved with the business information systems. Originally, traditional cost accounting referred to the ways of accumulating and assigning historical costs to units of product and departments, primarily for the purposes of stock valuation and profit determination.

Nowadays, cost accounting embraces a much wider function. Cost accounting is used as a means of **gathering and providing information as a basis for making all kinds of decisions**, ranging from the management of resources within an operation to the formulation of non-recurring strategic decisions and major organisational policies.

Definition of cost accounting

Cost accounting may be defined as 'the application of accounting and cost accounting principles, methods and techniques in the ascertainment of costs and the analysis of savings and/or excesses as compared with previous experience or with standards'. The key factor is the *ascertainment of costs*. Meaningful comparisons cannot be made or analysed until costs have first been ascertained by applying certain accepted principles, methods and techniques.

Cost accounting aims to give the required information for management, whether on a routine or on an *ad hoc* basis, to enable management to perform the functions of **planning, control and decision making**. To that end, cost accounting is concerned with the following.

(a)   The **determination of costs and profit** during a period.

(b)   The value of **stocks** of raw materials, work in progress and finished goods and control stock levels.

(c)   Preparation of **budgets, forecasts** and other control data for a forthcoming period.

(d)   The creation of a **reporting system** which enables managers to take corrective action where necessary to **control costs**.

(e)   The provision of **information for decision-making**.

Items (a) and (b) are traditional **cost accounting** roles; (c) to (e) extend into **management accounting**.

Cost accounting is no longer confined to the environment of manufacturing, although it is in this area that it is most fully developed. **Service industries, central and local government**, and even **accountancy and legal practices** make profitable use of cost accounting information. Furthermore, it is not restricted purely to manufacturing and operating costs, but also to administration, selling and distribution and research and development.

The cost accountant's role

Since cost accounting is a vital element of the MIS, the cost accountant has a vital role within the management team, generating the essential information required. In his relationship with the various levels of management the cost accountant is required to provide information on the following.

(a)   **Past performance** and the results of past decisions.

(b)   **Implications of current and future decisions** through forecast information.

(c)   Information relating to current decisions regarding choice of methods and expected results – what systems analysts call *feedback*.

Chapter 3 will examine the focus and organisation of cost accounting in more detail.

Behavioural and organisational aspects

It is important to take account of the impact of any management decision or action on the **behavioural aspects** of the business.

Decision-making impacts on people involved in the organisation at all levels. The method of generating information on which those decisions are to be based will therefore impact on those people and may consequently influence their behaviour patterns. Therefore the management accountant must always bear in mind **how employees may react to different policies**.

This aspect will be examined further in Chapter 5, in the context of budgetary control.

The management accountant must also be aware of the impact of his role on the **organisational structure** of the firm. A suitable organisational structure must be implemented to allow effective delegation of information-gathering roles and decision-making responsibility. This must allow for a chain of authority and information flow, and also to enable responsibility to rest at the appropriate level in the corporate hierarchy.

Question

Attributes of management accounting information

Management accounting information should comply with a number of criteria including verifiability, objectivity, timeliness, comparability, reliability, understandability and relevance if it is to be useful in planning, control and decision-making.

(a)   Explain the meaning of each of the criteria named above and give a specific example to illustrate each.

(b)   Give a brief explanation of how the criteria detailed in (a) might be in conflict with each other giving examples to illustrate where such conflict might arise.

Summary

The cost accountant is mainly concerned with the proper recording and analysis of costs incurred in a business in a manner that will enable management to control current operations and plan for the future.

Information for decision-making is a key aspect of the cost accountant's function.

The management accountant's role is essentially that of internal planning and control. Effective communication with the workforce and management is vital and will be achieved via the following.

(a)   A suitable organisational structure

(b)   A variety of forms and reports together with accounting statements produced on a timely basis; these will form part of the MIS.

CHAPTER 2

Forecasts and Trends

Objectives

In order to control costs and to prepare budgets it is necessary to predict future events. This chapter explains the techniques involved in forecasting and covers the following performance criteria.

7.1.1 Valid, relevant information is identified from internal and external sources.

7.1.2 Trends in prices are monitored for movements and analysed on a regular basis and potential implications are identified.

7.1.4 Forecasts of trends and changes in factor prices and market conditions are consistent with previous experience of factor prices and market conditions.

7.1.5 Relevant staff in the organisation are consulted about the analysis of trends.

8.1.1 Relevant data for projecting forecasts is identified.

When you have completed this chapter, you should be able to:

♦ understand the sources of information that can be used for preparing forecasts and budgets

♦ select relevant information on which to base a forecast

♦ forecast future prices and costs by isolating trends in historical information and by adjusting information for seasonal variations

♦ use indexes to forecast future prices.

Introduction

Long-range plans are often based on estimations of the future from extrapolations of the past to find **trends**, a method which can be fairly accurate **in the short term**. However, using data and relationships derived from past behaviour is limited in that such data cannot forecast something which has never happened before, nor can it forecast very far ahead.

If a company were to rely solely on *forecasting* rather than *long-range planning*, it would need to operate in a very predictable environment. **Planning is an attempt to control outcomes whereas forecasting is a more passive attempt to predict outcomes,** making educated guesses about the future.

Long-range planning is concerned with deciding which courses of action the organisation should take for the future. Corporate long-range planning does not attempt to minimise risks as, usually, the greater the risk the higher the return, but it helps to ensure that the organisation takes the right kind of risks with the best possible knowledge of the consequences.

Forecasting economic change

Forecasting changes in the external economy is an area fraught with problems and there are various conflicting views on the appropriate model to use. However, it is still essential for a company to be aware of likely trends in, for example, gross domestic product *per capita*. To this end, many large organisations have their own models or adapt the findings of other models to reflect their requirements. Whatever the applicability of the models for forecasting likely effects on a particular organisation, it would be foolish to ignore **trends in consumer incomes and expenditure, and sources of long-term finance**.

Sources of information for assessing economic change influencing industries

♦   Government publications such as the *Monthly Digest of Statistics*

♦   Government reports on particular industries

♦   Reports prepared by international bodies, such as UNO, OECD and EU

♦   Commercial publications dealing with economic matters of particular industries

♦   Publications by trade and professional organisations

♦   Bank reviews

♦   Stockbroker reports

♦   Statistics from advertising agencies

♦   Special sampling surveys

More detail on both internal and external sources of information is included later in the chapter.

Other forecasting considerations

Government action

As a result of government intervention the plans of undertakings laid down some time ago can suffer **dramatic changes**. The government's task is to keep the economy in balance and this may well result in a stop-go type of policy, particularly towards the end of the life of a parliament. Management must therefore be prepared to rethink drastically and immediately should the situation arise.

The effective business can act in the manner of a detective and by keeping track of party political publications try to predict likely governmental changes and when they will occur. Remember that policies can change drastically with a change of government, sometimes even going into reverse.

Social and environmental responsibility

Regularly in the media there are examples of companies that are considered to lack **social responsibility** because they fail to protect the area surrounding their factories from the hazards of their product (eg the disaster at Flixborough where a massive fire and local damage was caused by the explosions at a chemical factory), or because they treat their staff or members of the public shabbily. Society today is far more socially aware and will not accept hazards which can be avoided. This developing awareness has resulted in change in the attitudes of companies.

Awareness of the activities of **pressure groups** can be of critical importance to business planning. Often items that start off as aspects of consumer pressure can lead to legislative controls.

Indicators

Indicators of likely change in the wider environment can be identified. Thus for example problems which are occurring currently may indicate major changes, such as late payment from a customer highlighting possible trading difficulties or potential bankruptcy. Current political changes within a country may indicate future problems for the supply of raw materials and availability of markets. The 'Asian crisis' of 1998 caused a considerable disruption to trading conditions which will continue for some time.

The degree of influence suppliers, markets etc have on the organisation will determine the priority which should be given to these indicators in the planning process.

The importance of trends

It is important to be able to identify **trends in market competition**. Increasing competition can provide the threat of likely takeover or the need to merge with another organisation in order to obtain from larger production units any economies of scale available. It is also important to realise that increasing competition, perhaps even within the context of a diminishing market, may present an **opportunity**. An efficient organisation should be capable of successfully competing, and where organisations go into liquidation this will free sections of the market previously served by the liquidated enterprises.

SWOT analysis

Before any long–term planning decision can be made, four factors have to be taken into consideration: the organisation's **strengths** and **weaknesses,** and the **threats** and **opportunities** presented to the organisation by its environment (**SWOT analysis**)

- Internal appraisal is the assessment of the strengths and weaknesses of an organisation.

- External appraisal is the assessment of threats and opportunities.

Note that the strengths and weaknesses defined by an organisation are peculiar to that organisation alone (it cannot be a strength if it is shared equally by other competitors). However, opportunities and threats are open to all participants in the industry concerned.

Internal appraisal – strengths and weaknesses

The object is to **ascertain the company's strengths** and areas where improvements can be made, and to **forecast what the results may be** if the company continues as it is, in the light of information at present available to it. The review should be organised and co–ordinated throughout the company and carried out in a way that motivates management to face up to the true issues and think constructively and not defensively.

Such a review should include the following.

(a)   a comprehensive review of the **company's results**

(b)   an investigation to ascertain the **strengths** of the company (the areas in which it has exclusive skills or does well as compared with competitive standards) and areas where significant improvements are needed. The word *improvements* is used instead of 'weaknesses' because people are reluctant to confess to weaknesses and are likely to make a better contribution if they are asked to suggest how they think improvements can be made

(c)   **comparisons with competitors,** and other industries where useful. It is this feature which gives the internal appraisal its alternative title of **'competitive audit'.**

The main areas considered in a strengths and weaknesses survey would include the following:

◆   **Products**

Age, life span and current position in product life cycle
Quality comparisons with competition
Profitability, price sensitivity

◆   **Marketing**

Market size and share, presence in target segments
Success of promotions and advertising campaigns
Quality of customer service, both actual and perceived

◆   **Distribution**

Delivery promise performance
Depot location, delivery fleet condition and capacity

◆   **Production**

Age, condition and capacity of plant and equipment
Valuation of assets
Production scheduling

◆   **Research and development**

Number of commercially viable products
Costs and benefits of past/current projects
Relevance of current/proposed projects to overall plan

◆   **Human resources**

Adequacy of manpower plans for future
Skills and utilisation of existing workforce
Strength of management team
Training and recruitment
Level of morale

◆   **Finance**

Availability of cash, short– and long–term finance
Risk exposure
Contribution levels
ROCE and other accounting ratios

Presentation

A summary should be made of the major strengths and weaknesses revealed by this survey. **Weaknesses** indicate areas of 'vulnerability'; for example, a company could be vulnerable to adverse conditions if:

◆ its products were becoming obsolete, and could be replaced by competitors' developments

◆ it was short of liquid resource

◆ particular markets (for example, overseas) ceased to be available

◆ the strength of competition was augmented by amalgamations or mergers

◆ selling prices were being forced below an economic level.

The company's current **strengths** may relate to similar areas, and should be highlighted as a means by which the company can increase its profits.

Need for continuous reviews

The absence of an objective analysis of the organisation's strengths and weaknesses may result in the selection of a strategy which is totally inadequate or inappropriate. Circumstances change rapidly and it is therefore necessary to see the process of internal appraisal as a continuous monitoring of critical aspects of the business. A single snapshot of the organisation is only relevant for one point in time and consequently continual review is essential.

External appraisal – opportunites and threats (PEST analysis)

There are three main ways in which an organisation is affected by its **environment**.

(a) The organisation **imports goods and services from the environment.** Labour, public services, materials, finished goods, professional services etc are bought in by the company, and the organisation exports goods and services to other groups in the environment.

(b) **Outside groups can make demands** upon the organisation and can impose constraints. Such groups are customers, government, employees, shareholders, general public etc. These constraints can be mandatory (eg safety requirements imposed by law) or self–imposed (eg maintaining clean factory areas, restricting noise levels).

(c) The environment contains **opportunities** and **threats** for the organisation. A change in market may create an opportunity for a new product or it may hasten the demise of an existing product. An oil crisis in the Gulf will affect all companies' transport costs but will have more serious repercussions in a company which uses petroleum products in its manufacturing processes.

Opportunities and threats could be expected to arise in five main areas and **will be available to all companies in the industry:** economic, Government, social aspects, competitors and technology. External analysis is often referred to as PEST analysis because it focuses on Politics (Government), Economics, Social policy and Technology. To this we have added **competition**.

Economics

General economic conditions and trends are critical to the success of an organisation. Wages, price changes by suppliers and competitors, and government policies affect both the costs of producing products or offering services and the market conditions under which they are sold.

Common economic indicators measure national income and product, savings, investment, prices, wages, productivity, employment, government activities, and international transactions. All these factors vary over time, and managers devote much of their organisation's time and reosurces to forecasting the economy and anticipating changes.

There are two types of economic change: **structural** and **cyclical**.

♦ **Structural changes** in the economy are major alterations, whether permanent or temporary, in the relationships between different sectors of the economy and key economic variables; such changes challenge our basic assumptions about how the economy works. The shift from an industrial to a service economy and the rise in energy costs relative to the cost of other raw materials are examples of structural changes.

♦ **Cyclical economic changes** are periodic swings in the general activity. Some examples are the rise and fall of interest rates and inflation. Cyclical changes have far different implications for organisational strategies than structural changes, because they are a function of normal economic volatility. The real problem lies in distinguishing cyclical and structural changes from one another.

Government

Environmental legislation, concerning the control of pollution and health hazards, can affect the future plans of a company. The banning of the use of a particular substance (eg asbestos) will initially represent a threat to the manufacturers and to suppliers of goods that use it, but it will also present an opportunity for the development of new replacement products.

Full use needs to be made of government grants and tax concessions available in the industry. Plans for the levels and directions of government spending must be monitored carefully for business opportunities and threats.

Social aspects

Changes in demographic variables – such as age, sex, family size, income, occupation, education, nationality and social class – can have major effects upon the organisation.

People's attitudes and values are an important consideration and are reflected in their lifestyles. In recent years, change rather than stability has become the norm for lifestyle in the UK. For example, families account for a shrinking proportion of UK households and fewer of these families include married couples; households consisting of single adults and one–parent families are becoming more numerous.

Other lifestyle changes include a trend towards better education. Smaller cars, diet and paid household help are only a few examples of new consumption patterns. Physical fitness has experienced a big surge in popularity, and other home–centred activities – notably satellite TV and video recorders – are more and more prevalent as households distribute their leisure time.

All these factors will have an effect, favourable or adverse, upon businesses in the consumer sector.

Competitors

It is argued that competition in an industry is rooted in its underlying economics, and competitive forces exist that go well beyond the established combatants in a particular industry.

Competitors will therefore be concerned with the degree of rivalry between themselves in their own industry and the degree of potential rivalry or threat of entry from others.

The degree of rivalry between organisations already operating within the market is likely to be based on:

◆ whether there is a dominant organisation(s) – generally the most stable markets have dominant organisations

◆ whether the market is growing or declining – generally when markets are entering a 'maturity' phase and firms are trying to establish themselves as market leaders, competitive rivalry will be high

◆ whether the product or service can be differentiated between competitors – generally if products and services can be clearly differentiated then competitive rivalry will be lower

◆ whether the economy is in recession or booming – generally as an economy goes into recession competitive rivalry will intensify in an attempt to 'survive'.

The 'degree' of potential rivalry depends on the extent to which firms are making profits and the effectiveness of any barriers to entry. Typical barriers to entry are as follows

(a) *Financial or capital requirement of entry.* The amount of capital required may not be the major barrier to entry but rather the availability and cost of raising finance.

(b) *The patterns of distribution or access to distribution channels.* The soft drinks industry in the UK for example, is dominated by two companies because brewers such as Bass and Whitbread own the soft drinks companies and the distribution outlets (ie the public house). This pattern of distribution, however, has been forced to change with recent government legislation restricting the number of public houses that can be owned by brewers.

(c) *Government legislation* and changes in such legislation obviously have a major affect on barriers to entry. Deregulation and privatisation has meant that extensive barriers to entry have now been lowered in an attempt to make markets contestable.

(d) *The 'learning curve' phenomenon* could put new entrants at a cost disadvantage. Initially, in the early stages of entry, new firms would probably be operating at higher average costs than existing firms until they have 'learnt' from experiences to operate in a more efficient manner.

There are other barriers to entry such as advertising, patents and trade secrets, but it is not possible to state which are the most important. What is important is the recognition that barriers to entry have a major impact on the threat of potential entry.

Technology

The level of technology in a particular industry determines to a large extent what products and services will be produced, what equipment will be used and how operations will be managed.

Technological development begins with basic research, when a scientist discovers some new phenomenon; other researchers then examine the breakthrough for its potential. If further development leads to a workable prototype and engineering refinements make commercial exploitation practical, then the technology is finally put to use and may be widely adopted. Government institutions, independent research establishments, universities, and large corporations all carry out basic research. Independent entrepreneurs, business firms, and some government agencies carry the developments out of the laboratory and into the marketplace.

Businesses must be aware of the research currently being undertaken either to take the opportunity of its exploitation or to prepare for the threat from competitors who do.

Primary data collection

In order to keep track of economic change, social attitudes and other indicators, the business needs to have up-to-date, relevant information. It may seek this out itself (*primary data*) or it may make use of existing sources (*secondary data*).

How difficult it is to collect primary data will depend upon the nature of the report or forecast for which it is required.

A lot of forecasts will be based on the analysis of sales, costs and other **internal data** that will already be available from the financial and cost accounting systems, and thus will be easy to gather.

Other forecasts may involve information that is **external** either to the monetary accounting systems (eg customer preferences, satisfaction, etc) or to the business (eg information concerning market or industry volumes, trends, averages, etc).

In these latter cases, information consisting of primary data will need to be collected by survey or from external sources, often by use of sampling from an appropriate population.

Population and sample

Before setting out on an exercise involving collection of data, we must decide what data or figures we wish to collect:

(a)   decide what the aim is in collecting the data

(b)   determine what people or companies or other sources we need to collect data from. The whole group of items or people we are concerned with is called the **population**. As it is unlikely that we could collect data from all the members of a population, we gather data from a **sample** of members of the population.

Suppose we wish to establish average earnings per month of college lecturers, we might go to one or two colleges and ask those lecturers we meet what their monthly earnings are. In this situation the **population** would be all college lecturers and the **sample** would be those college lecturers who actually told us their monthly salary.

Alternatively, suppose we wish to find the average contents of bottles stored in a warehouse. As there are several thousand crates of bottles within the warehouse we decide to measure the contents of a few bottles chosen at random from some of the crates. In this instance the **population** is every bottle in the warehouse and the **sample** is the group of bottles whose contents we actually measure.

Sampling methods

How do we select our sample within the limitations of cost, time and required accuracy?

First we need a list of the population to be investigated. This list is called the **sampling frame**. It is not always easy to establish but, if we assume such a list is available, how do we secondly decide which members of the population to sample? There are a number of options as follows.

(a) *Simple random sampling:* every member of a population has an equal chance of being chosen in the sample. This is normally done by computer. Random sampling of some sort is necessary to get a fair sample, but the simple form is costly and time-consuming.

(b) *Stratified random sampling:* the population is split into appropriate sub-groups and a random sample is taken from the different sub-groups. It is usual for the sample size for each sub-group to be in the same proportion as the size of the sub-group to the population. This is the most reliable method of sampling.

(c) *Multi-stage sampling:* a few areas at random are selected from the population as a whole. We then take a random sample of these areas. Finally we pick a random sample of items in sub-groups in those areas. This should reduce the time and cost involved in collecting the data required but we lose some of the reliability of our results as a consequence.

(d) *Cluster sampling:* we state that certain areas are representative of the population as a whole and we sample everyone in these areas, rather than take a random sample.

(e) *Quota sampling:* we set a quota for how many people or items within a certain group we want to sample and then collect our data from anyone or anything that fits the required category until the quota is filled. This method is widely used by interviewers encountered in town centres; it is also the least accurate of sampling methods.

(f) *Systematic or interval sampling:* the first item or person is picked at random then subsequently each 10th or 100th or 834th (or any other *interval* we want to use) is sampled. This is a method widely used in *quality control* of items produced and in auditing.

Survey design

What do we ask of items or people we have chosen to form our sample? There are basically two approaches we can use: **direct measurement** or **questioning**.

Direct measurement

Where the information we require can be measured or counted we take the necessary measurements directly. This method has the distinct advantage that accurate measurements can be obtained.

Questioning

This is usually based on a formal questionnaire and it is important that it is designed properly. A questionnaire can be administered personally, by post or by telephone.

♦ *Personal questionnaires.* An interviewer has a set of questions that he or she asks selected individuals. It has the advantage that the results can be obtained quickly and reliably.

♦ *Postal questionnaires.* This involves sending the respondent a questionnaire which he or she then completes and returns. This method, although cheaper than using personal interviews, has a problem in that the response rate is usually quite low. Also, there can be problems if the respondent fails to understand the questions or simply does not answer some of the questions.

♦ *Telephone questionnaires.* This method, if used at off peak rates, can be cheaper than the postal questionnaire and usually gives a higher response rate. There is, however, one major consideration with this method which should not be overlooked. Not everyone has a telephone, so the population you are trying to reach should be those who have telephones, otherwise the sample can be unrepresentative.

Great care must be taken in the design of questionnaires.

♦ Ask as few questions as you can while still obtaining the information you require.

♦ Make the questions themselves as short as possible.

♦ Make the questions as simple as possible.

♦ Avoid ambiguous questions.

♦ Do not ask questions leading to a certain answer.

♦ Do not use questions which use emotive language.

♦ Do not ask personal questions.

♦ Make sure the questions being asked are relevant to and can be understood by the person answering them.

♦ Whenever possible give people a set of answers to choose from. This will minimise the problems you will encounter when categorising answers. You should, however, allow people the opportunity to give an answer other than those you specify, should they wish to.

♦ Make the questionnaire look simple and interesting so people will want to answer the questions.

Sources of secondary data

What are the potential sources of secondary data we may need in putting together a forecast? The first distinction to make is between **internal** and **external sources**.

Where possible, a management accountant will want to make the most of **internal sources** as follows.

(a) *Production and material control*

    (i)   Forward-loading plans for production cycles

    (ii)   Machine capacity forecasts

    (iii) Departmental operating statements

    (iv) Stock and work-in-progress reports

    (v)   Wastage reports

    (vi) Labour utilisation reports

    (vii) Productivity reports

(b) *Marketing including distribution*

    (i)   Market surveys

    (ii)   Sales surveys

    (iii)   Order reports by product and geographical area

    (iv)   Discount trends

    (v)   Transport and warehouse cost statements

    (vi)   Salesman performance and expenditure

    (vii)   Product service and support costs, including advertising and promotion

(c) *Personnel and administration*

    (i)   Numbers employed by category

    (ii)   Overtime hours

    (iii)   Sickness, absence, lateness

    (iv)   Training requirements

    (v)   Career development plans

    (vi)   Recruitment policy

    (vii)   Job descriptions

    (viii)   Costs of maintenance

    (ix)   Postage costs

(d) *Financial and management accounting*

    (i)   Annual statutory accounts

    (ii)   Budgets and forecasts

    (iii)   Sales and contribution analyses

    (iv)   Cash, management and working capital evaluation

    (v)   Capital project appraisal

    (vi)   Standard cost and variance analysis reports

    (vii)   Returns to government departments (eg VAT)

    (viii)   Cash in hand

    (ix)   Bad debts

    (x)   Loans held

External sources are obviously extremely varied (we saw the sources of information on economic change earlier). A key distinction is between those generated by **central government** and those from **other sources**.

Examples of the latter include the following.

(a) *Trade/professional reports* – reports from trade and professional associations (eg *CBI News*) on particular industries or groups of industries.

(b) *Bank of England Quarterly Bulletin* – reports on financial and economic matters.

(c) *Company reports* (usually annual) – information on performance and accounts of individual companies.

(d) *Labour research* (monthly) – articles on industry, employment, trades unions and political parties.

(e) *Financial Times* (daily) – share prices and information on business.

(f) *The World Wide Web (Internet)* – information on financial and economic matters, government policy and performance of individual businesses.

Central government sources include the following.

(a) *Monthly Digest of Statistics* – a collection of the main series of data from all government departments.

(b) *Annual Abstract of Statistics* – similar to *Monthly Digest* but containing more series and over longer periods of time.

(c) *Social Trends* – a collection of key social and demographic statistics, presentation using colour charts and tables.

(d) *Economic Trends* from the Office for National Statistics provides a broad background to trends in the UK economy, presented via commentary, tables and charts.

(e) *National Income and Expenditure 'Blue Book'* – detailed estimates of the national accounts, including consumer expenditure; produced by the Office for National Statistics.

(f) *Employment Gazette* – from the Department of Employment this includes articles, tables and charts on manpower, employment, unemployment, earnings, labour costs and stoppages due to disputes.

Using secondary data

Secondary data – from both internal and external sources – was originally collected for a purpose other than that for which the company is now to use it.

We would naturally prefer to use primary data if this is possible since data collected for specific purposes is likely to be better. Some **problems with secondary data** are listed below:

♦ **The data has been collected by someone else.** We have no control over how it was collected. If a survey was used, was a suitable questionnaire used? Was a large enough sample taken (was enough data collected)? Was it a reputable organisation that carried out the data collection?

♦ **Is the data up to date?** Data quickly becomes out of date, for example, people's consumer tastes change and prices may fluctuate wildly.

♦ **The data may be incomplete.** Certain groups of people are sometimes omitted from the published data. For example, do you know which groups are included in the unemployment figures?

♦ **Is the information actual, seasonally adjusted, estimated or a projection?**

♦ **The reason for collecting the data may be unknown.** Statistics published on motor cars may include or exclude three wheeled cars, vans and motor caravans. We need to know which categories are included in the data.

If we are to make use of secondary data we need to have answers to these questions. Sometimes the answers will be published with the data itself or sometimes we may be able to contact the people who collected the data. If not, we must be aware of the **limitations** of making decisions based on information produced from secondary data.

Time series analysis

The process of forecasting will inevitably involve some **analysis of historic data** (sales, costs, share prices etc) in order that **future values may be predicted**.

The data may concern the **economy** as a whole, the **particular industry** with which the organisation is involved (or wants to be) or **the organisation** itself.

Time series analysis takes such data and breaks it down into component parts that are easier to **extrapolate** (predict future values of). In particular, it will isolate the **underlying trend**.

Definition: time series

A **time series** is a set of values for some variable (eg monthly production) which varies with time. The set of observations will be taken at specific times, usually at regular intervals. Example of figures which can be plotted as a time series are:

♦ monthly rainfall in London

♦ daily closing price of a share on the Stock Exchange

♦ weekly sales in a department store.

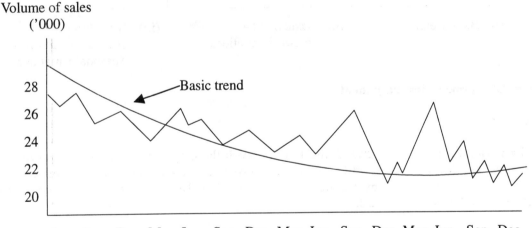

Figure 2.1   Volume of sales by month in a department store

In such a graph time is always plotted on the horizontal x axis. Each point is joined by a straight line hence the typically 'jagged' appearance. Don't try to draw a smooth curve which will pass through all the points on a time series graph. You will find it practically impossible and, in any case, it is incorrect to do so. The only reason for joining the points at all is to give a clearer picture of the pattern, which would be more difficult to interpret from a series of dots.

On this figure you will see that, having completed the time series graph, we have sketched in a 'basic trend' line. But what does it tell us? We need to look in more detail at what factors are at play in a time series.

Characteristic time series components

Analysis of time series has revealed certain characteristic movements or variations, the **components of the time series**. Analysis of these components is essential for forecasting purposes.

The four main types of component are as follows.

♦　　basic trend (long-term)

♦　　cyclical variations (not so long-term)

♦　　seasonal variations (short-term)

♦　　irregular or random variations (short-term).

To illustrate these features, Figure 2.2 shows the graphs of the components of a time series as they are built up into the graph of the complete time series.

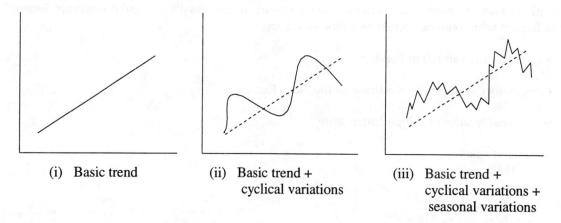

　　　(i)　Basic trend　　　　　　(ii)　Basic trend +　　　　　(iii)　Basic trend +
　　　　　　　　　　　　　　　　　　　　　cyclical variations　　　　　　　cyclical variations +
　　　　　　　　　　　　　　　　　　　　　　　　　　　　　　　　　　　　　　seasonal variations

Figure 2.2　Time series components

Basic trend

The **basic trend** refers to the general direction in which the graph of a time series goes over a long interval of time once the short-term variations have been smoothed out. This movement can be represented on the graph by a basic trend curve or line. Three of the most common basic trends are as follows in Figure 2.3.

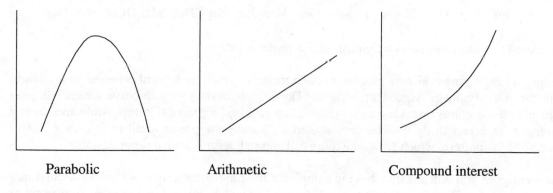

　　　　Parabolic　　　　　　　　　Arithmetic　　　　　　　　　Compound interest

Figure 2.3　Common basic trends

Cyclical variations

Cyclical variations refer to long term oscillations or swings about the basic trend. These cycles may or may not be periodic; they do not necessarily follow exactly similar patterns after equal intervals of time. In business and economic situations movements are said to be cyclical if they recur after time intervals of more than one year. A good example is the **trade cycle**, representing intervals of boom, decline, recession, and recovery.

Seasonal variations

Seasonal variations are the identical, or almost identical, patterns which a time series follows during corresponding intervals of successive periods. Such movements are due to recurring events such as the sudden increase in department store sales before Christmas. Although, in general, seasonal movements refer to a period of one year, this is not always the case and periods of hours, days, weeks, months etc may also be considered depending on the type of data available.

Random variations

Random variations are the sporadic motions of time series due to chance events such as floods, strikes, elections etc.

By their very nature they are unpredictable and therefore cannot play a large part in any forecasting but it is possible to isolate the random variations by calculating all other types of variation and removing them from the time series data. It is important to extract any significant random variations from the data before using them for forecasting. Random variations will not concern you in your assessment.

Analysis of a time series

The analysis of a time series consists of:

◆   breaking the series down into trend, seasonal and cyclical variations;

◆   extrapolating each characteristic into the future;

◆   adding together all the individual extrapolations to arrive at one forecast figure.

The analysis which follows concentrates on isolating only the basic trend and seasonal variations. As already stated, random movements are not usually included in analysis and, although cyclical movements may be treated in the same way as seasonal variations, they repeat over such long intervals of time that masses of historical data are required before the pattern becomes evident.

There are many methods of analysing time series, some sophisticated, others simple. The method considered here are known as the additive and the multiplicative models. The additive model is the best known and most commonly used although, admittedly, it is not the most sophisticated.

Isolating the trend

Sketching a basic trend line

A basic trend line was drawn in on the time series graph in Figure 2.1. Indeed one way of isolating the trend is simply to draw it in freehand on the graph.

This is actually a very helpful method. Once a time series has been prepared as a graph, it is usually a fairly simple matter to sketch in a basic trend line which manages to echo the overall long-term trend of the time series. There are some advantages to doing it this way.

♦   It is **quick and easy**

♦   It allows one to **interpolate** a value easily. If you have monthly data for, say, Months 1, 3, 5, 7, 9 and 11 only, plotting those values and sketching a trend line will allow you to see what the likely value for the even-numbered months might have been. On Figure 2.4 you will see that we have interpolated the values of £125,000 for Month 6 of 19X4, and £170,000 for Month 12 of 19X4.

♦   It is possible to **extrapolate** a figure past the end of the data available (see the dotted line on Figure 2.4 below). We shall look at extrapolating the trend in more detail later on. It is always worth bearing in mind, however, that data cannot be extrapolated very far ahead. Common sense suggests, for instance, that the trend line in Figure 2.4 is unlikely to continue in a horizontal line for very long – it is bound either to rise or fall. So the extrapolation of £170,000 for Month 7 in 19X5 is not unreasonable, but it would not be helpful to extrapolate the line and make the same prediction for, say, Month 1 of 19X6.

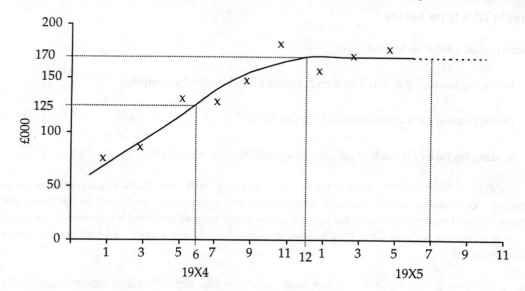

Figure 2.4   Interpolation and extrapolation using a basic trend line

Three other common methods for isolating the trend are as follows:

♦   using **moving averages;**

♦   calculating the 'line of best fit' using **regression analysis** (for a linear trend); and

♦   **exponential smoothing**

We shall consider the first of these in more detail.

Moving averages

By using moving averages, the effect of any seasonal variation in a time series can be eliminated to show the basic trend. This elimination process will only work if the moving average is calculated over the correct number of values (being the number of values in one complete cycle). For instance, if a seasonal variation present in a time series is repeated every fourth period, then moving averages with a cycle of four should be used.

This will become clearer as you follow through this simple example.

Example: moving averages

The following time series (column A) shows a set of values which are clearly increasing; at first sight, however, this increase appears to be quite erratic. This is because the time series is made up of two components:

1   A basic trend (column B)

2   A seasonal variation which repeats every fourth value (column C)

Time series		Basic trend		Seasonal variation
(A)		(B)		(C)
3	=	3	+	0
5	=	4	+	1
5	=	5	+	0
5	=	6	+	1
7	=	7	+	0
9	=	8	+	1
9	=	9	+	0
9	=	10	+	1

How did we determine the basic trend and seasonal variation within the time series? It is necessary to calculate a number of moving averages for various numbers of values as shown below:

Time series	2 values	Moving averages 3 values	4 values
3			
	$4\left(\dfrac{3+5}{2}\right)$		
5		$4\frac{1}{3}\left(\dfrac{3+5+5}{3}\right)$	
	5		$4\frac{1}{2}\left(\dfrac{3+5+5+5}{4}\right)$
5		5	
	5		$5\frac{1}{2}$
5		$5\frac{2}{3}$	
	6		$6\frac{1}{2}$
7		7	
	8		$7\frac{1}{2}$
9		$8\frac{1}{3}$	
	9		$8\frac{1}{2}$
9		9	
	9		
9			

The moving average of 4 values (the last column) is the only one which captures the steadily increasing basic trend. It is therefore important to **examine** the figures before choosing which order moving average to use.

[It will usually be fairly obvious which is the appropriate order in an assessment question due to the way in which the data are presented, eg in 'quarters' (order 4) or days of working week (order 5).]

Note the positioning of the moving averages in the above table. Each average has been written **exactly opposite the middle of the figures from which it has been calculated**. This results in the moving averages for *even* numbers of values (2 or 4 in this case) being suspended halfway between two of the original figures.

Where you have a moving average for an even number of values, it is necessary to realign the moving averages so that they fall opposite the original values by calculating a **centred moving average** for every *two* moving average values.

Original time series	Moving average (4 values)	Centred moving average Order 4
3		
5		
	$4\frac{1}{2}$	
5		5
	$5\frac{1}{2}$	
5		6
	$6\frac{1}{2}$	
7		7
	$7\frac{1}{2}$	
9		8
	$8\frac{1}{2}$	
9		
9		

As you can see by the centring process, the **centred moving average** is the original basic trend (although with some data missing). In this case it was rather a circular computation but, since one of the main purposes of time series analysis questions is to identify the trend, it would not normally be known to start with! This example is to show that the technique does in fact give us the right answer.

Example: TS Limited

The following data for TS Limited will also be used to demonstrate the various techniques in the subsequent paragraphs.

	Quarter			
	1	2	3	4
Year 1	74	100	94	127
Year 2	84	106	120	141
Year 3	94	112	130	147
Year 4	112	118	148	169
Year 5	138	140		

First, the trend can be isolated by moving averages.

Note: An alternative method of finding the centred moving average is shown here. Instead of averaging the four quarter moving totals then taking the average of each adjacent pair as in the previous illustration, the averaging is left to the end. The *totals* of each adjacent pair are shown in column (d) and this is then averaged by dividing by eight. Either method gives the same answer.

Year	Qtr (a)	Value (b)	4 quarter moving total (c)	8 quarter moving total (d)	Trend (T) (d)/8 (e)
1	1	74			
	2	100			
			395		
	3	94		800	100
			405		
	4	127		816	102
			411		
2	1	84		848	106
			437		
	2	106		888	111
			451		
	3	120		912	114
			461		
	4	141		928	116
			467		
3	1	94		944	118
			477		
	2	112		960	120
			483		
	3	130		984	123
			501		
	4	147		1,008	126
			507		
4	1	112		1,032	129
			525		
	2	118		1,072	134
			547		
	3	148		1,120	140
			573		
	4	169			
5	1	138			
	2	140			

Disadvantages of moving averages

♦ Values at the beginning and end of the series are **lost** – therefore the moving averages do not cover the complete period.

♦ The moving averages may **generate cycles** or other **variations** that were not present in the original data.

♦ The averages are strongly affected by extreme values. To overcome this a **'weighted' moving average** is sometimes used giving the largest weights to central items and small weights to extreme values.

Finding the seasonal and cyclical variations

Having isolated the trend we need to consider how to deal with the **seasonal variations.** We will look at two models – the additive model and the multiplicative model.

The additive model is the simplest model and is satisfactory when the variations around the trend are within a constant band width. If, as is more usual, the variations around the trend increase as the trend itself rises, it is better to use the multiplicative model. Figure 2.5 demonstrates the idea of **band width.**

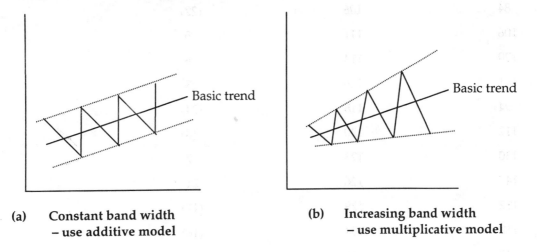

(a) **Constant band width**
     – use additive model

(b) **Increasing band width**
     – use multiplicative model

Figure 2.5   **Band width of variations around the trend**

The additive model – finding the seasonal variation

The additive model we will use expresses variations in absolute terms with above and below average figures designated by plus and minus signs.

The four components of a time series (T = trend; S = seasonal variation; C = cyclical variation; R = random variation) are expressed as absolute values which are simply **added together** to produce the actual figures:

Actual data (Time series) = T + S + C + R

For unsophisticated analysis over a relatively short period of time cyclical variations (C) and random variations (R) are ignored. Random variations are ignored because they are unpredictable and would not normally exhibit any repetitive pattern, whereas cyclical variations (long-term oscillations) are ignored because their effect is negligible over short periods of time. The model therefore simplifies to:

Actual data = T + S

The seasonal variation is therefore the **difference** between the computed trend figure and the original time series figure.

Example: TS Limited

Using the same data for TS Limited from the list table produced in the answer, the seasonal variations can be extracted by subtracting each trend value (using the moving averages method) from its corresponding time series value:

Original time series	Underlying trend	Seasonal variation (S)
(b)	(e)	(b – e)
94	100	(6)
127	102	25
84	106	(22)
106	111	5
120	114	6
141	116	25
94	118	(24)
112	120	(8)
130	123	7
147	126	21
112	129	(17)
118	134	(16)
148	140	8
169	146	23

Average seasonal variations

One of the purposes of extracting seasonal variations is to enable forecasts to be made for future time periods by extrapolating the figures. If we have more than one period's seasonal data we have a problem in deciding which variation to use.

Obviously, if we are making a prediction for a quarter 2 of a year in the future, we will use a quarter 2 variation, but we may have three of these in the data, all different, if we have three years' data.

One way to get a representative seasonal variation, if no obvious pattern exists, is to average out the seasonal variations for each quarter.

	Quarter			
	1	*2*	*3*	*4*
Year 1	–	–	(6)	25
Year 2	(22)	5	6	25
Year 3	(24)	(8)	7	21
Year 4	(17)	(16)	8	23
Total	(63)	(19)	15	94
Average (rounded)	(21)	(6)	3.75	23.50

Deseasonalisation of data

Having isolated the seasonal variations, we could now 'deseasonalise' the original data by removing these variations.

Note that, for example, quarter 1 has a generally *below* trend value (negative average seasonal variation) while quarter 4 is generally *above* trend. Thus in adjusting the original data to eliminate effects of seasonal variations ('deseasonalising'), the quarter 1 data is *increased* by 21 whereas quarter 4 data is *reduced* by 23.5.

After data have been deseasonalised they still include trend, cyclical and random movements. The trend has already been found and can now be removed from the deseasonalised data to leave only cyclical and random movements (residual variations).

Year + Qtr		*Original data*	*Average seasonal variations*	*Deseasonalised data*	*Trend*	*Residual variations (cyclical & random)*
1	3	94	3.75	90.25	100	(9.75)
	4	127	23.50	103.50	102	1.50
2	1	84	(21.00)	105.00	106	(1.00)
	2	106	(6.00)	112.00	111	1.00
	3	120	3.75	116.25	114	2.25
	4	141	23.50	117.50	116	1.50
3	1	94	(21.00)	115.00	118	(3.00)
	2	112	(6.00)	118.00	120	(2.00)
	3	130	3.75	126.25	123	3.25
	4	147	23.50	123.50	126	(2.50)
4	1	112	(21.00)	133.00	129	4.00
	2	118	(6.00)	124.00	134	(10.00)
	3	148	3.75	144.25	140	4.25
	4	169	23.50	145.50	146	(0.50)

The multiplicative model – finding the cyclical variation

With this more sophisticated model, it is assumed that the four components of a time series (T, C, S and R) are **multiplied together** to produce the actual figures.

Actual data (time series) = T x C x S x R

The multiplicative model would most often be used where there is annual data over a long period of time. Seasonal variations will not be an issue, so the model will be:

A = T x C x R

Example: Donner & Company

Donner & Company have the following annual results:

Year	Results £000	Year	Results £000
19X0	900	19X8	1,600
19X1	1,000	19X9	1,800
19X2	1,100	19Y0	1,300
19X3	1,200	19Y1	1,600
19X4	1,300	19Y2	1,900
19X5	1,000	19Y3	2,200
19X6	1,200	19Y4	2,500
19X7	1,400		

Required

What is the trend of these results, and what are the cyclical variations (use the multiplicative model)?

Solution

With the multiplicative model, ignoring S, the time series is as follows:

$$A = T \times C \times R$$

If we can isolate T, then we will know (by manipulating the equation) that:

$$A/T = C \times R$$

We can see that the figures dip every five years, so we shall draw up a five point moving average to get T, then remove this from the actual data to isolate the cyclical and random variations.

Year	Period of moving average	Results (A) £000	5 year moving total	5 year moving average = trend (T)	C x R (=A/T)
19X0	1	900	-		
19X1	2	1,000	-		
19X2	3	1,100	5,500	1,100	1.00
19X3	4	1,200	5,600	1,120	1.07
19X4	5	1,300	5,800	1,160	1.12
19X5	1	1,000	6,100	1,220	0.82
19X6	2	1,200	6,500	1,300	0.92
19X7	3	1,400	7,000	1,400	1.00
19X8	4	1,600	7,300	1,460	1.10
19X9	5	1,800	7,700	1,540	1.17
19Y0	1	1,300	8,200	1,640	0.79
19Y1	2	1,600	8,800	1,760	0.91
19Y2	3	1,900	9,500	1,900	1.00
19Y3	4	2,200	-		
19Y4	5	2,500	-		

To get rid of the random variations, the average cyclical factor for each period is then found by drawing up a table:

	Period 1	Period 2	Period 3	Period 4	Period 5
	–	–	1.00	1.07	1.12
Cyclical variations	0.82	0.92	1.00	1.10	1.17
	0.79	0.91	1.00	–	–
Totals	1.61	1.83	3.00	2.17	2.29
Average cyclical variation	0.80	0.91	1.00	1.08	1.14

Thus we know that, depending on where in the 5 year cycle a particular year falls, it is affected by a cyclical variation factor of between 0.8 and 1.14

Forecasting a time series

At the beginning of this section, we noted that the analysis of a time series into its component parts would make **extrapolation** easier for forecasting future values for planning purposes.

In general, for short-term forecasts, only the trend and seasonal variations will be used; the cyclical variations will only have a significant effect over quite a long period of time and the random variations are, by their very nature, unpredictable.

Thus the approach to forecasting will be to:

♦ extrapolate the trend to the appropriate future time, and

♦ adjust the extrapolated trend value by the appropriate seasonal variation

We will use the analysis carried out for TS Limited to illustrate the approach.

Extrapolating the trend

There is no unique method for **extrapolation** of the **basic** trend, as it will very much depend upon its particular shape (if, indeed, it has a discernible one).

In practice, computers will be of great help in producing various possible equations for the trend, which can be rapidly tested against the data available to determine which fits best.

If the **moving averages method** has been used, a certain amount of judgement will be necessary. Possible approaches include the following.

♦ **Plot the trend values on a graph and extrapolate by eye.** (In fact, an initial sketch graph can be useful anyway to get a visual impression of the trend, before using one of the following methods to predict it.)

♦ Look at the increments between each trend value for any approximate **pattern** (eg roughly equal, which makes the trend approximately linear or steadily increasing) and continue this pattern to the future time required.

♦ If the increments appear to vary randomly, **an average increment** for the period may be calculated and used in the forecast.

♦ If the pattern of the trend appears to **change** significantly over the period, you may restrict your prediction technique to later data values only, as being more representative of future values.

The trend values obtained by moving averages for TS Limited have been plotted on a graph (unless specifically required, it is unlikely that you would have time to do this in an assessment).

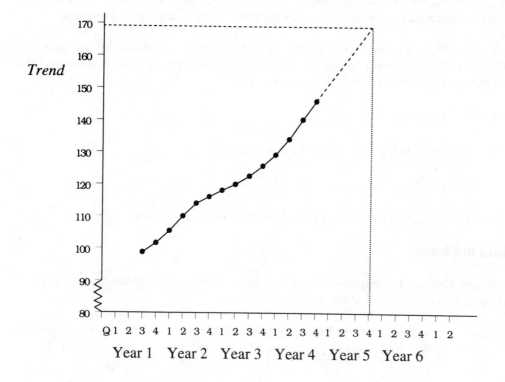

Figure 2.6   Trend line

The graph shows an upward sloping trend, very approximately linear, but which becomes increasingly steep.

Now suppose we wish to extrapolate a trend value for Year 5, quarter 4.

If we were to use the graphical approach to extrapolation, it is perhaps best to extend the line using the later, steeper gradient (although it should be noted that the earlier part of the curve shows that this may, in fact, revert to a shallower gradient). This is shown as a dotted line on the graph, and produces a result of approximately 169.

Now consider the increments (the differences between each successive pair of trend values). Note that you do not need to work these out exactly; they will just be used to detect any pattern or change.

| *From previous quarter to* | | | *Approximate* |
Year	*Quarter*	*Trend*	*increment*
1	3	100	–
	4	102	2
2	1	106	4
	2	111	5
	3	114	3
	4	116	2
3	1	118	2
	2	120	2
	3	123	3
	4	126	3
4	1	129	3
	2	134	5
	3	140	6
	4	146	6

There is no clear pattern, so some average increment may be used.

The average increment over the whole period is $(146 - 100)/13 \cong 3.6$

Note: Divide by the number of increments, not trend values; we're averaging the 'gaps'.

This would result in a forecast trend value for year 5, quarter 4 (which is four increments on from the last trend value) of 146 (the last trend value) + (4×3.6) = 160.

If we confine ourselves to the latter values, say from year 3, quarter 4, the average increment is now $(146 - 126)/4 = 5$, giving a forecast trend value of $146 + (4 \times 5) = 166$.

So we have a range of predictions between 160 and 169.

Adjusting trend prediction for seasonal variations

This is a lot more straightforward! We already have the average seasonal variations for each quarter, the relevant one here being that for quarter 4: +23.5

This means that, on average, quarter 4 values are 23.5 above the trend value. Thus, seasonally-adjusted predictions for quarter 4, year 5 would be:

160, 166 or 169 + 23.5 = 183.5, 189.5 or 192.5

depending upon which trend value were used.

In an assessment, you should only make one prediction, justifying the approach used. There will rarely be one 'correct' way, so do not spend too long deciding how you are going to do it.

Index numbers

As part of the forecasting process, an organisation may make use of published indices that indicate the trend in economic/industrial factors, such as inflation.

An **index number** is a statistic used to reduce a series of data to some common level so that we can make comparisons of variations between items or groups of items. They are used to describe changes in prices, output, income, etc and can be divided into three types:

♦   **price index numbers**, which measure changes in price

♦   **quantity index numbers**, which measure changes in quantity

♦   **value index numbers**, which measure changes in the value of services or activities or goods.

If an index number is constructed from figures for a single item it is known as a **simple index** or **relative**. If a combination of figures relating to a group of items is used then the index number is known as a **complex index**. Many indices are produced by Government departments. The most important in everyday life is the retail price index (RPI), which is used widely as a measure of inflation.

Base period

The **base period** is the time to which all comparisons are made. It may be a single date, a month or a year. The length of the base period usually depends on the interval at which the index number is to be calculated. The index number for the base period is given the value 100 and this might be allocated to:

(a)   a year – 19X5 = 100

(b)   a month – August 19X5 = 100

(c)   a single date – 16 August 19X5 = 100

For an index number to be a reasonable reflection of change, the base period should be chosen to be as **normal a time** as possible. It should be a time which is **not too far in the past.**

One item index numbers or relatives

If we have the price of an item recorded at different times, then an index number can be constructed to show changes in price.

Year	Cost of car service
19X0	£36.50
19X1	£39.20
19X2	£44.70
19X3	£51.40
19X4	£52.50

If we use 19X1 as base year it has index number = 100. The index number for 19X0 is calculated as:

$$\frac{36.50}{39.20} \times 100 = 93.1$$

Similarly, for 19X2 we calculate:

$$\frac{44.70}{39.20} \times 100 = 114.0$$

and if the other years' index numbers are calculated we have:

19X0	$\frac{36.50}{39.20}$	$\times$	100	=	93.1
19X1				=	100.0
19X2	$\frac{44.70}{39.20}$	$\times$	100	=	114.0
19X3	$\frac{51.40}{39.20}$	$\times$	100	=	131.1
19X4	$\frac{52.50}{39.20}$	$\times$	100	=	133.9

The figures obtained are often called **price relatives**. All the figures are calculated as percentages of the figure for 19X1 and so they show percentage changes from 19X1 (eg the price for 19X3 is 31.1% higher than that in 19X1).

However, you cannot say the percentage rise from 19X3 to 19X4 is:

$133.9 - 131.1 = 2.8\%$

It is in fact:

$$\frac{52.50}{51.40} \times 100 = 102.1$$

so a 2.1% increase. Using the index numbers we work out the ratio of the appropriate index numbers as:

$$\frac{133.9}{131.1} \times 100 = 102.1 \text{ (as before)}$$

The idea of a relative or single item index is not limited to prices. Suppose we know how many cars were serviced at a garage. Then, an index with base year 19X1 is calculated as:

Year	Number of cars serviced					Index number
19X0	2,138	$\frac{2,138}{2,210}$	×	100	=	96.7
19X1	2,210				=	100.0
19X2	2,356	$\frac{2,356}{2,210}$	×	100	=	106.6
19X3	2,199	$\frac{2,199}{2,210}$	×	100	=	99.5
19X4	2,056	$\frac{2,056}{2,210}$	×	100	=	93.0

This is called a **quantity index**.

Changing the base period

Index numbers regularly have their base periods **changed** in order to keep them current. Unfortunately this means that some values of an index number cannot be directly compared to other values of the same index number. Suppose we have an industrial production index worked out with 19W8 as base year to start with, which is then changed to 19X2 as base year.

Index of industrial production

	(19W8 = 100)	(19X2 = 100)
19W8	100.0	
19W9	105.6	
19X0	104.8	
19X1	103.1	
19X2	105.7	100.0
19X3		99.6
19X4		99.2

If we wish to compare 19W9 with 19X2 then this can be done directly using the index with base year 19W8 but if we wish to compare 19W9 to 19X3 we cannot do it directly. We must first convert the 19X2 base period figures (the second column) so that they have 19W8 as their base period. This conversion can only be done if the indices have an overlap period. Here, the overlap is 19X2. Take the index values with base period 19X2 and multiply them by the ratio of the index numbers for the overlap period.

Converting the 19X3 index to 19W8 base year gives:

$$99.6 \times \frac{105.7}{100} = 105.3$$

Similarly, the 19X4 index converted to 19W8 base year is:

$$99.2 \times \frac{105.7}{100} = 104.9$$

The combined list for the index is now as follows.

Year	Index (19W8 = 100)
19W8	100.0
19W9	105.6
19X0	104.8
19X1	103.1
19X2	105.7
19X3	105.3
19X4	104.9

with base period 19W8. We can now compare 19W9 and 19X3 directly. The index has dropped from 105.6 to 105.3, ie is at:

$$\frac{105.3}{105.6} \times 100 = 99.7\%$$

of its level in 19X3 that it was in 19W8, a drop of 0.3%.

Example: changing the base period

An index of savings is given as follows.

Year	*Index of savings* *(19W6 = 100)*	*(19X1 = 100)*
19W7	106.7	
19W8	113.9	
19W9	127.2	
19X0	136.7	
19X1	149.2	100.0
19X2		101.6
19X3		103.2
19X4		105.7

Required

(a) Change all the index values to base year 19W6.

(b) Create a new set of index numbers for the first five years, using 19X0 as the base year.

(c) What proportional change in savings occurred from 19X2 to 19X3?

Solution

(a) To convert the 19X1 base figures to 19W6 base we must multiply by:

$$\frac{149.2}{100}$$

This gives an index as follows.

Year	*Index (19W6 = 100)*
19W7	106.7
19W8	113.9
19W9	127.2
19X0	136.7
19X1	149.2
19X2	$101.6 \times \dfrac{149.2}{100} = 151.6$
19X3	$103.2 \times \dfrac{149.2}{100} = 154.0$
19X4	$105.7 \times \dfrac{149.2}{100} = 157.7$

(b)   For the figures to have base year 19X0 we must multiply the 19W6 base figures by:

$$\frac{100}{136.7}$$

This gives the following.

Year	Index (19X0 = 100)
19W7	$106.7 \times \dfrac{100}{136.7} = 78.1$
19W8	$113.9 \times \dfrac{100}{136.7} = 83.3$
19W9	$127.2 \times \dfrac{100}{136.7} = 93.1$
19X0	$136.7 \times \dfrac{100}{136.7} = 100.0$
19X1	$149.2 \times \dfrac{100}{136.7} = 109.1$

(c)   The proportional rise from 19X2 to 19X3 was $\dfrac{103.2}{101.6} \times 100$ (using 19X1 base figures) $- 100$ = 1.6%. Any base can be used to give the same result. This is known as a **chain base index** giving the proportional changes from one year to the next.

Questions

1   Time series example

Give an example of a time series and explain how the four characteristic movements would be caused in the example that you have chosen.

2   Your organisation I   (AAT CA D94)

Your organisation is about to commence work on the preparation of the forthcoming year's annual budget.

As assistant management accountant, you have been asked to assist budget-holders and to respond to any queries which they may raise in the course of submitting their budget proposals.

Your organisation's sales analyst had made some progress in preparing the sales forecasts for year 5 when she unexpectedly needed to take a holiday for personal reasons.

She has left you the following memo.

MEMORANDUM

To: Assistant Management Accountant   Date: 12 December 19X4

From: Sales Analyst

Subject: Sales forecasts for year 5

In preparing the sales volume forecasts for year 5, I have got as far as establishing the following trend figures and average seasonal variations.

	Quarter 1 units	Quarter 2 units	Quarter 3 units	Quarter 4 units
Year 3 – Trend figures	3,270	3,313	3,358	3,407
Year 4 – Trend figures	3,452	3,496	3,541	3,587
Average seasonal variation	(50)	22	60	(32)

As a basis for extrapolating the trend line, I forecast that the trend will continue to increase in year 5 at the same average amount per quarter as during year 4.

Sorry to leave you with this unfinished job, but it should be possible to prepare an outline forecast for year 5 with this data.

Required

(a) Briefly explain what is meant by the following:

    (i)   seasonal variations;

    (ii)   extrapolating a trend line.

    Use the data from the memorandum to illustrate your explanations.

(b) Prepare a forecast of sales volumes for each of the four quarters of year 5, based on the data contained in the analyst's memo.

3 Transport company I (AAT CA J94)

The company directors of a transport company are concerned by the increase in expenditure on fuel over the last few years. Fuel costs have increased although there were no changes in the number of vehicles and negligible changes in the number of miles driven each year.

The company accountant has gathered information on the fuel costs and has also established a price index for fuel as follows.

Year	Expenditure on fuel £	Fuel price index
1	18,000	100
2	19,292	106
3	21,468	120
4	23,010	128

Required

Use the index numbers to express all fuel costs in terms of year 4 prices. All figures should be rounded to the nearest £.

Comment on the results you have obtained.

Summary

In this chapter we have looked at forecasts and trends. Forecasts of future events are normally based on historical information. Information may be available from a wide variety of sources both internal and external to the business.

Primary data is data collected for the specific purpose of the forecast. Secondary data is data that was originally collected for another purpose (often taken from a source external to the business). It is not always possible to use primary data, but you should be aware of the limitations of any secondary data that you use.

Time series analysis and the use of index numbers help with the isolation of trends, although these still may not be easy to extrapolate into the future. Remember that you are using historic data which will not reflect future economic and environmental changes.

CHAPTER 3

The Principles and Techniques of Cost Accounting

Objectives

This chapter explains the basic principles and terminology of cost accounting. It covers the following performance criteria.

7.1.1 Valid, relevant information is identified from internal and external sources.

7.2.1 Routine cost reports are analysed, compared with other sources of information and the implications of findings are analysed.

When you have completed this chapter you should be able to:

♦ understand what is meant by the terms 'cost unit' and 'cost centre'

♦ understand the different ways of classifying costs

♦ estimate future costs from past results using regression

♦ apportion overheads between cost centres

♦ understand and use total absorption costing and marginal costing

♦ understand and apply activity based costing·

Cost accounting

The need for cost accounting

Historically, financial accounts have reflected the transactions of a business entity in its relationships with the outside world: customers, suppliers, employees, shareholders and other investors. To this end, financial accounting has been geared up to the preparation of annual and other periodic accounts, with the emphasis upon statutory requirements.

A typical **profit and loss account statement** follows the following general layout (in summary).

Profit and loss account for the period ended ...

	£
Turnover	500,000
Cost of sales	(370,000)
Gross profit	130,000
Expenses	(80,000)
Profit on ordinary activities before taxation	50,000

Typically the profit and loss account will include a subjective analysis of expense according to category either by **function** (distribution/administrative) or by **nature** (materials/staff costs/depreciation). Despite some recent changes, financial accounts do not readily disclose:

(a)   profit performance by individual products, services or activity; but more importantly

(b)   the responsibility of individual **managers** for performance.

Thus they can only provide 'scorekeeping' statistical information, rather than information that will form the basis of decision-making or control. The provision of this additional detail is one of the functions of cost accounting: *cost-finding*.

Cost-finding means taking the transactions which make up the financial accounts and analysing them to turn data into information which will be more helpful to the managers of the business. This will be an 'objective' analysis, matching the expenses to the purposes for which they were incurred. This analysis may be done on a purely memorandum basis, the results being reconciled with the financial records, or it may be sometimes incorporated into the general bookkeeping system of the company.

Whichever procedure is adopted, cost accounting has two important effects on business documentation:

(a)   **Additional internal documents** will be needed to identify which products or departments are affected by various transactions.

(b)   **Additional data regarding transactions** will be needed to assist accurate classification and analysis.

Example: product cost analysis

Assume that the profit and loss account illustrated above related to a company marketing four different products.

From his analysis of the source documents (purchase invoices, payrolls, petty cash vouchers and so on), the cost accountant is able to provide the following detailed report.

	Product A	Product B	Product C	Product D	Total
Sales					
Quantity	315,000	32,500	80,500	28,100	–
Price per unit	£0.50	£2.50	£1.50	£5.00	–
Amount	£157,500	£81,250	£120,750	£140,500	£500,000
Costs	£	£	£	£	£
Materials	50,000	40,000	75,000	85,000	250,000
Wages	40,000	30,000	20,000	30,000	120,000
Expenses	22,000	25,500	17,500	15,000	80,000
Total	112,000	95,500	112,500	130,000	450,000
Net profit/(loss) before tax	45,500	(14,250)	8,250	10,500	50,000

From this **'product profit and loss account'**, the managers of the business can see that the total profit of £50,000 resulted from profits on products A, C and D, offset by a loss on product B, and that product A alone yielded 91 per cent of the company total. We do not know at this stage whether the information will lead them to take any decision to change things for the future, because we do not know whether the above result is in accordance with a deliberate plan or not. Nor can we be sure without further information whether it would be a good thing to discontinue product B since such a decision might involve some further analysis of the costs incurred, and some forecasts of future developments.

Both **comparisons against plan** and the preparation of **special analyses for decision purposes** fall within the scope of the cost accounting function.

The cost accounting department

Data required for reports

A company's requirements for historical information include three main types of data.

(a)   Data from the normal **financial accounts** of the business: the balance sheet and profit and loss account with their supporting notes and schedules, and the cash flow statement.

(b)   Data obtained by **analysing the accounts of the business**, identifying items with cost units and cost centres: in other words the work of the cost accounting department (details of stockholdings would come from this source).

(c)   Data derived immediately from **source documents** without evaluation, such as statistics on labour efficiency, material usage, sickness, absenteeism and machine breakdowns.

In addition, most reports will include comparisons with budgets, standards, targets or estimates, and the explanations of variances based on detailed investigation and close knowledge of the data used in budget preparation.

Organisation

The accounts department, therefore, comprises a **financial accounting segment**, a **costing segment** and a **budgetary control segment**. The extent to which these are separate departments within the organisation depends on the number and diversity of the transactions to be handled and on the management organisation of the business, including the extent of divisional autonomy. All these factors affect the required number of accounting staff and the consequent need for specialisation of effort.

Cost accounting record-keeping

The cost department is responsible for maintaining the **cost accounting records**. To be effective these records should:

(a)   analyse production, administration and marketing costs to facilitate cost and profit computations, stock valuations, forecast and budget data and decision-making data;

(b)   enable the production of periodic performance statements which are necessary for management control purposes;

(c)   permit analysis of:

   (i)   past costs for profit measurement and stock valuation;

   (ii)   present costs for control purposes;

   (iii)   future costs – forecasts, targets, budgets and decision-making.

Because his job is to interpret physical facts into money values, the cost accountant is in an excellent position to ensure that all types of report are **integrated** and are prepared on a consistent basis. Although inevitably other departments will wish to report on their own activities, the cost accountant should maintain close liaison and **build a good relationship** with them so that:

(a)   the information he provides can **assist** them in interpreting the results of their own activities;

(b)   there is **no conflict** on questions of fact between reports prepared by, for example, the sales manager or the production manager and the information emerging from the costing system.

Whilst records can be maintained manually, **computer-based data** concerning sales and production quantities, stock levels, costs, etc will assist the cost accounting function in the following ways.

(a)   Reports and cost accounts can be prepared quickly.

(b)   Information for decision-making will be more plentiful and be available more speedily than would be the case with manual data.

(c)   Large volumes of data can be stored and manipulated with ease.

The benefits of cost accounting

The benefits of cost accounting can be identified as:

(a)   **disclosure of profitable and non-profitable activities** (as might appear in the product profit and loss account already illustrated). This data would also be modified to identify locations which are unprofitable;

(b)   identification of **waste and inefficiency**, particularly in relation to usage of materials and labour;

(c)   **analysis** of movements in profit;

(d)   assistance in the determination of **selling prices**;

(e)   valuation of **stocks** (there are auditing and taxation implications here);

(f)   development of **planning and control information**;

(g)   evaluation of the **cost effect of policy decisions**.

Cost units

Have a look at the costing profit and loss account illustrated earlier. This showed the sales quantity of various products (A–D) and the total cost of those sales under the headings materials, wages and expenses.

The following additional calculations could be made from that example.

Calculation of cost per unit for month ended ... 19X...

	Product A £	*Product B* £	*Product C* £	*Product D* £
Materials	0.16	1.23	0.93	3.02
Wages	0.13	0.92	0.25	1.07
Expenses	0.07	0.78	0.22	0.53
Total cost per unit	0.36	2.93	1.40	4.62

We have taken the total costs attributable to each product in a month (any other period could have been used) and arrived at the average cost per unit of each product, rounded to the nearest penny, by dividing the totals by the numbers of units involved. The 'cost unit' in this instance is the unit of product sold.

The cost unit might have been a piece, a pack, a kilogram, a litre or any other measure appropriate to what was being produced.

Average unit costs

In practice the business would probably have produced more units that it sold in the period, the unsold quantity being taken into **stock**. In such a case, the costs of production would have been collected and divided by the number of units *produced* to give the average unit cost. This would have been applied to the number of units sold to give the **cost of sales**, and to the number of units remaining to give the **costs of the residual stock**.

This **average unit cost** approach is used whenever production is continuous and leads to uniform product units, as in the case of many chemical plants, food processors or extractive operations such as mining and quarrying.

Job costs

Some businesses, however, undertake **special jobs** for their customers. A workshop making tools and jigs does this; and so on a much larger scale does the contractor building bridges or putting up a factory. In such cases, costs are first analysed between the various jobs or contracts, and then the costs of the jobs invoiced will be gathered together into the periodic summary profit and loss account. For such businesses, in other words, the 'cost unit' is the job or contract.

Batch costs

In the manufacture of mechanical or electrical components or products, which are customarily made in batches of say 1,000 or 10,000 items, according to the circumstances of the case. In this type of business, the cost of each batch is determined and the **batch is the primary 'cost unit'**. Thereafter it is possible, if desired, to calculate the average cost per item in the batch.

Non-manufacturing cost units

The above examples have concentrated on cost units for production or manufacturing processes. Examples of cost units for **service industries**, or non-manufacturing activities within a business are as follows:

Service industry/activity	*Cost unit*
Accountants	Chargeable hour
College	Student enrolled
Hotel	Bed-night
Hospital	Patient-day
Transport department	kg-mile
Credit control department	Customer account
Selling	Calls made
Maintenance department	Man-hours

Note that some of these are in fact **composite cost units**, where a cost is considered to be dependent upon two main factors. For example, if the manager of a chain of hotels wanted to compare costs between two of the hotels, calculating costs per bed would not take account of the differing levels of occupation of the beds of the two hotels. Thus the cost can be calculated per bed-night (ie the cost of one bed per night of occupation).

Definition: cost unit

A **cost unit** is a quantitative unit of product or service in relation to which costs are associated; the purpose of product costing is to arrive at the cost of the cost unit appropriate to the business concerned.

Cost centres

Definition: cost centre

A **cost centre** is a location, function or item(s) of equipment in respect of which costs may be ascertained and related to cost units for control purposes.

A cost centre therefore is used as an initial **collection point for costs**; once the total cost of operating the cost centre for a period has been ascertained, it can be related to the cost units that have passed through the cost centre.

The location, function or item of equipment referred to in the definition can be directly related to production, to a service department or to a business.

Examples of cost centres

Production	Assembly line
	Packing machine
Service department	Stores
	Canteen
	Quality control
Service	Tax department (accountants)
	Ward (hospital)
	Faculty (college)

Responsibility for cost centres

Control can only be exercised by people, and for every cost somebody must be responsible; so whether a cost centre is impersonal or personal there must always be a manager in whose sphere of **responsibility** that cost centre is included.

Overhead costs, therefore, will always be identified with cost centres; and because cost centres are the responsibility of particular functional managers one will find overheads classified according to the main functional divisions of the business.

Definition: profit centre

A **profit centre** is a location, function or item(s) of equipment in respect of which costs and revenues may be ascertained for the purposes of control of the resulting profit.

Cost classification

Types of cost classification

Costs can be classified (**collected into logical groups**) in many ways. The particular classification selected will depend upon the purpose for which the resulting analysed data will be used.

Purpose	*Classification*
Cost control	By nature – materials, labour, overheads, etc.
Cost accounts	By relationship to cost units – direct/indirect costs, etc.
Budgeting, contribution analysis	By behaviour – fixed/variable costs
Decision-making	Relevant and non-relevant
Responsibility accounting	Controllable and uncontrollable

You will come across these classifications in more detail as you work through the Study Pack. At this stage, we will revise the basic classification terms used in cost accounting.

Direct and indirect costs

For cost accounting purposes, the costs of the business will be classified in quite a different way from the analysis required by a financial accountant for the published accounts.

The basic classification of costs may be illustrated as follows.

	£	£
Direct costs		
Direct materials		250,000
Direct labour		120,000
Direct expenses		10,000
		―――
Prime cost (= *Total of direct costs*)		380,000
Indirect factory costs		25,000
		―――
Production cost		405,000
Administration overhead	20,000	
Selling and distribution overhead	25,000	
	―――	
		45,000
		―――
Total cost		450,000
		═══

Direct costs

These are costs which can be related **directly to one cost unit**.

Example: Considering a cost unit of a chair, direct costs will include the cost of wood and screws used (direct material cost) and the cost of manufacturing labour hours per chair (direct labour costs).

In a non-manufacturing context, the direct costs relating to, say, a student enrolled at a college would include the costs of books provided, individual tuition and marking costs.

Indirect costs (overheads)

These cannot be identified directly with a cost unit and are often referred to as *overheads*. For **stock valuation purposes** distinction needs to be made between overheads incurred in the production process (factory costs, eg factory rent and rates, power etc) and non-production costs.

Non-production costs are indirect costs involved in converting finished goods into revenue, comprising:

(a)   administrative overhead costs (eg executive salaries and office costs); and

(b)   marketing, selling and distribution, overhead costs.

These costs are *not* included in stock valuation since they are not costs of making a product, but costs of selling it. **Stock on hand at the end of a period is valued at total *production* cost only,** including overheads (in a total absorption costing system). We shall return to this point later in this chapter.

With the same cost unit of a chair, the salaries of the salesmen who promote and sell the chairs to retail outlets would be a selling overhead.

Indirect costs associated with a college would include premises' running costs, lecturers' salaries and administrative staff costs.

Cost behaviour

The nature of costs

We mentioned earlier the need for cost classification by behaviour for budgeting purposes. In order to make predictions of future cost levels, we must determine the basis of the charge.

As an example, consider the cost of direct materials expected next month. The charge would depend on the amount used and the cost per unit. The amount used would depend, in turn, on the production anticipated for the period.

In order to estimate this cost therefore we must estimate the following.

(a)   Production levels   10,000 units

(b)   Usage of materials per unit

        Material A   2kg

        Material B   1kg

        Material C   0.2kg

(c)   Costs per unit

        Material A   30 pence per kg

        Material B   25 pence per kg

        Material C   50 pence per kg

Estimate

		£
Material A	20,000kg @ 30p/kg	6,000
Material B	10,000kg @ 25p/kg	2,500
Material C	2,000kg @ 50p/kg	1,000
Total estimated material cost		9,500

Mathematical modelling

What have we done? We have set up a simple mathematical model which will, for any level of production, usage and unit cost, enable the level of cost in a future period to be predicted. The **direct materials** example was perhaps the easiest to use and, in practice, we may wish to deal with other variables which affect the cost such as wastage rates thus producing a slightly more complex model.

Direct labour costs may tend to vary due to changes in productivity and other factors in addition to the more obvious variables such as grade and rate of payment. A certain amount of estimation will still be required; if payment is on a production related basis we would expect a cost which, like materials, will vary in line with the volume of production.

At this stage, therefore, we have come to the rule-of-thumb guide that direct material, labour and expenses will probably vary roughly in line with anticipated production levels or the level of activity (**variable costs**).

This will not be the case with all costs. If we take the cost of rent and rates, for example, the charge is not determined on the basis of the intensity of usage of the premises but rather on the basis of time used (**fixed costs**). Labour paid on a time basis would also fall under this heading. How then can we predict the cost of such expenses for next month? Well, there is no difficulty in doing this as all we have to do is consult our rental agreement and the rates notice and we can forecast with complete certainty what these costs will be for the month.

Once budgeted costs have been prepared for next month they can be used for **control purposes** by comparing the actual costs incurred during next month with those set as the target.

Differences between actual and budgeted costs can be investigated to determine the cause(s) and responsibility can be assigned to managers to **improve future control**.

Classification of costs by behaviour

The above example illustrates the need for cost behaviour classification. For cost prediction purposes, we must make a distinction between costs which vary with production or activity levels (**variable costs**) and those which do not (**fixed costs**). There also exists a type of cost which moves in sympathy with production levels but contains an element which does not, such as an electricity charge which contains a minimum standing charge plus an element which relates to the usage of the period. Such a cost would be described as **semi-variable** or **mixed**.

Definitions: variable, fixed and semi-variable costs

Variable costs are those that vary (usually assumed in direct proportion) with changes in level of activity of the cost centre to which they relate (eg output volume). **Example**: the raw material used in a product. It should be noted that the variable cost per unit may not remain constant over a wide range. It may be possible, for example, to obtain discounts for large purchases of material, reducing the cost per unit.

Fixed costs are those that accrue with the passage of time and are not affected by changes in activity level; they are therefore also known as *period* costs. **Example**: rent of premises.

Stepped costs are fixed over a range of output and then suddenly increase in one big jump. **Example**: a staffing level of up to 20 people may only require one foreman but, if the staff level is more than 20, an extra foreman will be needed.

Semi-variable (mixed) costs contain both a fixed and a variable element. When output is nil, the fixed element is incurred, but they also increase, like variable costs, as output increases. **Example**: telephone charges where there is a fixed rental to which is added the charge for calls made.

Graphical illustrations

Various **cost behaviour patterns** are illustrated graphically by way of the example following.

(a)   **Variable cost**: direct materials, the purchase price per unit being constant

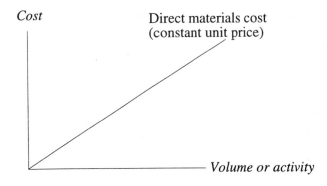

Figure 3.1:   Variable cost

(b)   **Fixed cost:** rent of factory payable under a long-term lease

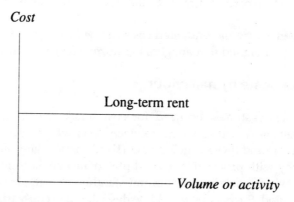

Figure 3.2:   Fixed cost

(c)   **Stepped costs**

(i)   Canteen cost where additional assistants are required as increases in activity result in larger numbers of factory personnel

(ii)   Rent of premises, additional accommodation eventually being required.

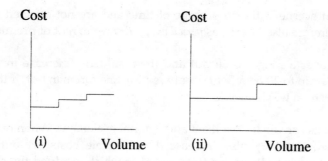

Figure 3.3:   Stepped costs

(d)   **Semi-variable costs**

(i)   Direct materials cost (trade discount at higher levels of activity)

(ii)   Salesmen's remuneration with added commission from a certain level of activity

(iii) Electricity charges comprising fixed standing charge and variable unit charge

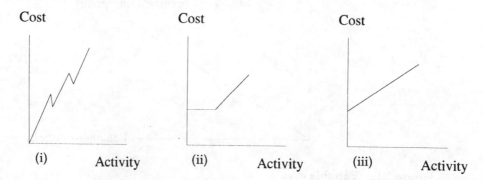

Figure 3.4:   Semi-variable costs

The common approach is as follows.

(a) Treat as **variable** those costs which **change by regular steps**.

(b) Treat as **fixed** those costs which **only change at wide intervals of activity**; this recognises that review will be required if there is a permanent change in the normal level of activity.

Cost estimation

Some costs may have both **fixed and variable elements**. These will need to be identified for budgeting purposes.

If it is not easy to do this directly (as it is in the case of the telephone cost, where the bill clearly shows the fixed charge and rate per unit), then an analysis of past cost and volume data will need to be carried out.

It is assumed that there is a linear relationship, ie:

Total cost = Fixed cost + (Variable cost per unit × Units produced)

and that the total fixed cost and the variable cost per unit are constant at all levels of production unless told otherwise.

Possible techniques include the *high-low method* and *linear regression*.

The high-low method

This is a simple method of **estimating future costs from past results**. It takes the costs for the highest and lowest activity levels, and assumes that a linear relationship covers the range in between.

Example: high-low method

Widgets are produced by a process that incurs both fixed and variable costs.

Total costs have been recorded for the process for each of the last six months as follows.

Month	Output (units)	Total cost £
1	4,500	33,750
2	3,500	30,500
3	5,100	34,130
4	6,200	38,600
5	5,700	38,000
6	4,100	31,900

Required

(a)   Formulate an equation that relates cost to output.

(b)   Plot output against total cost on a graph.

(c)   Predict total cost at the budgeted activity level for month 7 of 6,000 units.

Solution

Select the months with the highest and lowest output levels as follows.

	Output	*Total cost*
		£
Lowest output	3,500	30,500
Highest output	6,200	38,600
	————	————
Increase	2,700	8,100
	═══	═══

For an increase of 2,700 units, cost has increased by £8,100. If we assume that the fixed cost element remains constant, this cost increase must represent a change in variable costs only.

Assuming a straight-line relationship, then the variable cost per unit $\dfrac{£8,100}{2,700} = £3$ per unit

Note that the factor determining which values to choose is the total cost at the highest output level and the total cost at the lowest output level. These are not necessarily the highest and lowest costs. The high/low observations are always based on the independent variable (in this case, output).

We can now substitute back into either of the two output levels to obtain the fixed cost.

At the 3,500 units level:

	£
Total cost	30,500
Variable cost (3,500 × £3)	(10,500)
	————
Fixed costs	20,000
	═══

As a check on the accuracy of the calculations, at the 6,200 unit level:

	£
Total costs	38,600
Variable costs (6,200 × £3)	18,600
	————
Fixed costs	20,000
	═══

Now answering the questions set.

(a)   If we let x =   Production level in units

                              y =   Total cost in £

Then Total cost   =   Fixed cost + (Variable cost per unit × Production level)

ie y =   20,000 + 3x

(b)   We can now plot the original data on a graph of cost against output, along with the line given by the equation in (a) as follows.

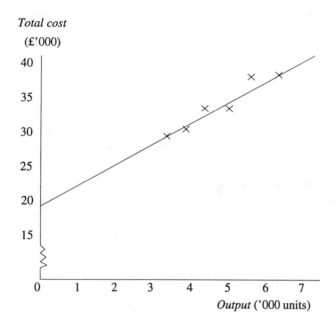

Figure 3.5   Linear equation

(c)   At an output level of 6,000 units, the equation would predict costs of:

$$y = 20,000 + (3 \times 6,000) = £38,000$$

Advantages of high-low method

♦   Simple to operate

♦   Easy to understand

Disadvantages of high-low method

The problem with the high-low method is that it could give a **completely inaccurate result**. This is because we are only considering two sets of data, and ignoring all of the others. It is possible that the points we have chosen are completely unrepresentative of the rest of the data. This is a distinct possibility since we have chosen the two points at the extreme ends of the activity range. At these levels it is more likely that operating conditions will be atypical compared with more normal output. One way around this problem is to choose the 'next to highest' and 'next to lowest' figures, but this destroys some of the simplicity of the model.

Linear regression

The regression line

The graph in Figure 3.5 of cost against output shows that the points lie more or less on a straight line. Such a graph is called a **scatter diagram**, for obvious reasons.

One could draw a straight line through the points by eye, but there is an equation for the line which statistically fits the points most closely – the **regression line**.

The **regression line** (the *line of best fit* or *least squares line*) is the line which minimises the sum of the squares of the *vertical* distances of the scatter points from the line. In other words, if you take each scatter point, measure how far above or below the line it lies, square each of the distances and then add them up, the regression line is designed to give you the smallest possible total.

The equation of the regression line is as follows.

$$y = bx + a$$

where x is output for the period (in units) and y is total cost.

Values for 'a' (fixed cost for the period) and 'b' (variable cost per unit) are calculated using a formula. You will not be expected to do this in your assessment. Instead you will be given the equation.

The equation for the regression line has been calculated for the data in the widgets example earlier in the chapter. It is

$$Y = 19,300 + 3.13x$$

The variable cost per unit is £3.13 and the fixed cost for the month is £19,300.

Interpolation and extrapolation

Now use the regression line to estimate costs for different output levels. For example:

- What is the expected cost for output of 4,900 units?

y = $19,300 + (3.13 \times 4,900) = £34,637$

- What is the expected cost for output of 8,200 units?

y = $19,300 + (3.13 \times 8,200) = £44,966$

At first glance there may seem to be little difference between the two computations we have just performed. Look more carefully at the value of x (output).

For the first example, the activity level is within the range covered by the data. This is known as **interpolation**.

For the second example, the output level is above the range of data. What happens if the production capacity is limited to, say, 7,500 units? In order to produce 8,200 units additional machinery would need to be purchased and extra workers engaged, which would make the cost far higher. It is for this sort of reason that extending beyond the data (**extrapolation**) can be very misleading.

Just because a linear relationship has been established within the range of data examined, it does not follow that the same relationship will persist beyond that range.

Measurement problems

In determining the values for use in regression or for plotting on a scatter diagram, we would generally use **historic cost analysis** obtained from the accounting records of the firm.

This gives rise to a number of potential problems such as:

♦   **Timing differences** – The relationship between output levels and costs could be obscured if costs are recorded after the output levels. For example, we would expect maintenance costs to increase as machinery is used more, but the increased costs may not be recorded in the same period as the output, if the maintenance work is deferred until after the peak period is past.

♦   The **accounting treatment** of some costs may obscure true cost behaviour. A common example here would be the allocation of fixed overhead costs to production departments. If the objective is to determine the cost behaviour pattern in a single department, then only those costs incurred within the department should be included.

♦   It is **too simplistic** to assume that it is only output level that affects costs. Other factors that will affect costs are as follows.

   (i)   Technological changes.

   (ii)   The impact of learning effects.

   (iii)   Inflationary effects (we can compensate for this by discounting all costs to a common time period).

   (iv)   Extraordinary circumstances in any given period(s).

The assumptions of regression analysis

Regression analysis is based on **sample data** and if we selected a different sample it is probable that a different regression line would be constructed. For this reason, regression analysis is most suited to conditions where there is a relatively stable relationship between cost and activity level.

Assumptions we are making:

♦   The relationship is a linear one.

♦   The data used is representative of future trends.

Linearity

In the majority of cases, management will rely on linear models to relate costs to output levels.

This in itself makes certain assumptions:

♦   Each unit of output uses the same physical quantity of inputs.

♦   Unit prices of inputs remain constant regardless of the quantity used or purchased.

Management must carefully assess a range of output levels over which such assumptions are likely to hold good. Preliminary assessments as to linearity can be made by considering a scatter diagram.

Representativeness of observations

Where the data includes **one unusual observation**, then **regression analysis** gives a great deal of weight to that individual observation. For example results for a single period could have been distorted by a strike or material shortage, keeping costs artificially high compared with output level. In such circumstances we may be justified in eliminating such an outlying observation from our analysis, since it is wholly unrepresentative of our normal operating conditions.

Consider Figure 3.6 below.

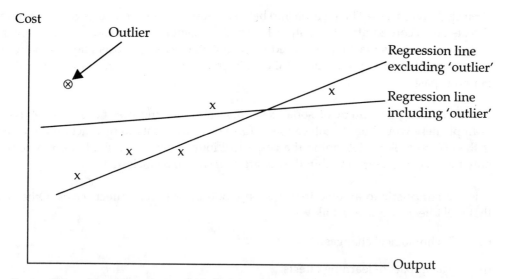

$\otimes$ = *outlying observation that could be validly excluded from regression analysis*

Figure 3.6   Excluding outliers from regression analysis

But we must not simply exclude observations just to get a line of good fit! There must be a valid reason for exclusion of any given data.

Accounting for overheads

We have discussed the idea of the collection of costs: initially in cost centres and then attributing them to the cost units passing through those cost centres. But should all costs eventually get attributed to (absorbed by) cost units?

Two points should be noted regarding the **absorption of costs** into cost units:

♦   *Production/selling costs* – In a manufacturing context, we have already seen that stocks of finished goods will *never* include an element of selling costs. The **stocks will be valued at production costs only** (including overheads). However, for pricing or profitability purposes, the cost of units sold may well include a selling cost element.

♦   *Fixed/variable costs* – Whether or not all production costs will be absorbed into cost units for stock valuation will depend upon the particular system being used.

   (i)   A **total absorption costing (TAC)** system absorbs **all production costs** (direct or indirect, fixed or variable) into cost units.

   (ii)   A **marginal costing (MC)** system only absorbs **variable costs** (direct and indirect) into cost units. Fixed costs are treated as period costs, and deducted as a 'lump sum' from the profits of the period concerned.

The following example illustrates the differences between total absorption and marginal costing.

Example: total absorption versus marginal costing

Tivoli Limited has produced the following budgeted figures for a new product it hopes to launch.

Direct material	£10 per unit
Direct labour	£5 per unit
Variable production overheads	£8 per unit
Fixed production costs	£27,000 per month
Budgeted output	9,000 units per month
Sales price	£30 per unit

	Month 1	*Month 2*	*Month 3*
Production	6,500	9,000	10,000
Sales	5,000	8,500	9,500

Required

Prepare a profit statement for each of the three months on each of the following bases.

(a)   Marginal costing

(b)   Absorption costing

Reconcile the difference in profits for each month.

Solution

(a)   *Marginal costing*

Cost of production (per unit)

	£
Direct materials	10
Direct labour	5
Variable production overheads	8
	23

	Month 1		Month 2		Month 3	
	£	£	£	£	£	£
Sales @ £30		150,000		255,000		285,000
Opening stock	–		34,500		46,000	
Cost of production @ £23	149,500		207,000		230,000	
	149,500		241,500		276,000	
Closing stock @ £23	(34,500)		(46,000)		(57,500)	
Variable cost of sales		(115,000)		(195,500)		(218,500)
Contribution		35,000		59,500		66,500
Fixed costs		(27,000)		(27,000)		(27,000)
Profit		8,000		32,500		39,500

(b)   *Absorption costing*

Fixed costs are allocated to units of production based on the budgeted rate of activity, ie 9,000 units per month. Therefore the fixed cost per unit is £3 (27,000/9,000).

Cost of production (per unit)

	£
Direct materials	10
Direct labour	5
Variable production overheads	8
Fixed production costs	3
	26

However, actual production levels are not known until the end of the period, by which time each product has been charged with standard fixed costs per unit.

So an adjustment for over or under absorption of overheads has to be made at the end of each period, as follows.

Month 1   (9,000 – 6,500) x £3 = £7,500 under absorbed.

Month 2   Production is equal to budget, so no adjustment necessary.

Month 3   (9,000 – 10,000) x £3 = £3,000 over absorbed.

	Month 1		Month 2		Month 3	
	£	£	£	£	£	£
Sales @ £30		150,000		255,000		285,000
Opening stock	–		39,000		52,000	
Cost of production @ £26	169,000		234,000		260,000	
	169,000		273,000		312,000	
Closing stock @ £26	(39,000)		(52,000)		(65,000)	
Fully absorbed cost of sales		(130,000)		(221,000)		(247,000)
Gross profit		20,000		34,000		38,000
(Under)/over absorption		(7,500)		–		3,000
Profit		12,500		34,000		41,000

Reconciliation between marginal and absorption profit

	Month 1		Month 2		Month 3	
Marginal profit		8,000		32,500		39,500
Change in stock level (units) x £3	6,500 – 5,000 = 1,500 x £3	4,500	9,000 – 8,500 = 500 x £3	1,500	10,000 – 9,500 = 500 x £3	1,500
Absorption profit		12,500		34,000		41,000

For the remainder of this section, it is assumed that a TAC system is in operation (we shall return to marginal costing in the next section). We shall consider how, in particular, all production overheads are allocated, apportioned and absorbed into cost units.

Allocation, apportionment and absorption

We have already identified two types of costs that make up the full production cost of a unit:

(a) **Direct costs** are those that can be uniquely identified with an individual cost unit (eg direct materials, direct labour, direct expenses).

(b) **Indirect costs** (overheads) are costs incurred in production, not easily 'traced' to individual units, eg machine power (variable), factory rent (fixed), heat and light (semi-variable).

The problem we are considering here is how to divide indirect costs between cost units, in order to prepare a **'standard' cost card** for budgeting stock valuation and pricing purposes.

Standard cost card

	£
Direct materials	X
Direct labour	X
Direct expenses	X
Prime cost	X
Variable production overhead	X
Marginal cost	X
Fixed production overhead	X
Total production cost per unit	X

The method used to divide overheads between production units is made up of three processes: *allocation, apportionment* and *absorption*. Before commencing these processes, it is necessary to split the factory up into separate cost centres, because the first step in the process is to collect these indirect costs via cost centres.

Cost allocation

Certain cost items will be **incurred entirely by one cost centre**. Allocation deals with this type of cost and simply allots it to the cost centre which has incurred the cost.

Cost centre	*Allocated cost*
Canteen	Tea bags
	Spaghetti
	Chef's wages
Packing department	Cardboard
	String

Cost apportionment (primary)

More frequently, however, the benefit of an item of cost will be **shared** by a number of cost centres. The overhead will be split or apportioned between the relevant cost centres on an 'equitable' basis.

The rent of buildings, for example, can relate to the total floor space occupied by a number of different departments and it is usual to allot the rental charge to those departments in proportion to the floor space they occupy.

Nature of cost	*Possible bases of apportionment*
Rent and rates	Floor area occupied by various departments
Lighting and heating	Cubic capacity of locations or metered usage
Insurance of stocks	Value of stockholdings in various locations

Cost apportionment (secondary)

After completing the allocation and primary apportionment stages, you should have assigned all costs to cost centres.

Some cost centres, however, will not have production units passing through them; these cost centres are called *service departments* (eg quality control department, works canteen). Before the final stage of absorption into cost units can be carried out, it is necessary to perform a further type of apportionment whereby the total costs of the service cost centres are reassigned to production cost centres. This is known as **secondary apportionment**. This should be done on a fair basis to reflect the benefit derived from the service centre.

Absorption

Having collected all indirect costs in the production cost centres via overhead allocation and apportionment, the cost has to be **spread over the output of the production cost centre**.

The allotment of accumulated overhead costs to cost units is called **overhead absorption**. The absorption rate is normally calculated at the start of the period and therefore based on budgeted quantities. Various methods of absorption exist and the one most fitting should be chosen.

The following are the most common methods you will encounter.

Rate per unit

The simple unit rate is obtained by **dividing total overheads by the number of units produced**. However, where more than one product is produced, this is an unsatisfactory basis for absorbing overheads as it will not reflect the relative demands of each product on the production departments through which they pass.

Alternative bases of absorption

There are a number of bases commonly used as an **alternative** to the simple unit rate:

(a)   rate per direct labour hour;

(b)   rate per machine hour;

(c)   percentage of material cost;

(d)   percentage of wage cost;

(e)   percentage of prime cost.

It is important to appreciate, however, that whichever method or combination of methods is used, the result will only be an approximate estimate of what that product actually costs.

In practice, many businesses use a **'direct labour hour rate'** or **'machine hour rate'** in preference to a rate based on a percentage of direct materials cost, direct wages or prime cost, as it may be possible to associate some overheads either with labour time or with machine time.

Notes

1   It may be possible to analyse the total overhead apportioned to each production department into fixed and variable elements. In this case a variable overhead rate per unit and a fixed overhead rate per unit can be calculated.

2   The absorption rates will normally be calculated at the beginning of a period and hence be based on budgeted costs and production levels. This can lead to problems when actual costs and volumes are not the same as budgeted (see over- and under-absorption in a later session).

Example: allocation, apportionment and absorption of overheads

The following illustration covers all stages of overhead allocation, apportionment and absorption summarised above. Work through it carefully to ensure you have fully revised this area.

SB Limited has two production departments (Assembly and Finishing) and two service departments (Maintenance and Canteen). The following costs are expected to be incurred.

	£
Indirect materials	20,000
Rent	15,000
Electricity	10,000
Machine depreciation	5,000
Building depreciation	10,000
Direct labour	55,000

The following information is available.

	Assembly	Finishing	Maintenance	Canteen
Area (square metres)	1,000	2,000	500	500
Kw hours consumed	1,000	4,000	Nil	5,000
Machine value	£45,000	£35,000	£11,000	£9,000
Number of staff	20	30	10	–
Indirect materials consumed	7,000	8,000	3,000	2,000

The maintenance department spends 60% of its time servicing equipment for the assembly department and 40% of its time servicing equipment for the finishing department. The canteen equipment is serviced by outside specialist contractors.

Required

(a)   Calculate overheads in each cost centre.

(b)   Reapportion the service centre costs to production cost centres.

Solution

(a)

Overhead	Total £	Basis of apportionment (note)	Assembly £	Finishing £	Maintenance £	Canteen £
Indirect materials	20,000	Allocate (i)	7,000	8,000	3,000	2,000
Rent	15,000	Area (ii)	3,750	7,500	1,875	1,875
Electricity	10,000	Kw hours (iii)	1,000	4,000	–	5,000
Machine depreciation	5,000	Machine value (iv)	2,250	1,750	550	450
Building depreciation	10,000	Area (v)	2,500	5,000	1,250	1,250
Direct labour	55,000	– (vi)	–	–	–	–
Total			16,500	26,250	6,675	10,575

Total overhead = £60,000

Notes

(i)   We are given the amount of indirect materials used by each cost centre. This allows us to allocate the cost straight to each cost centre.

(ii) Rent is something that is shared by the whole factory and therefore the cost must be apportioned between the cost centres. The first thing to decide is what basis to use. Since rent is related to area, floorspace would be a sensible basis to use (the bigger the area of a cost centre the more rent will be apportioned to it).

There are two techniques for apportioning overheads, and you should use whichever you are happier with.

The first technique is to use proportions. For the rent we need to divide up the rent of £15,000 in the proportions 1,000 : 2,000 : 500 : 500.

The second method is as follows.

♦   Calculate the total floor area for the factory.

♦   For each cost centre calculate what fraction of the total floor area this represents.

♦   Multiply this fraction by £15,000.

In the present case this would be as follows.

Total floor area – 1,000 + 2,000 + 500 + 500 = 4,000 square metres.

Assembly is 1,000 square metres, ie 1,000/4,000 of the total area. Assembly is apportioned £15,000 x 1,000/4,000 = £3,750.

Similarly, finishing is apportioned £15,000 x 2,000/4,000 = £7,500 and Maintenance and Canteen are apportioned £15,000 x 500/4,000 = £1,875 each.

(iii) The most appropriate basis for apportioning the electricity between the cost centres will be the Kw hours consumed since these are a measure of the amount of electricity used.

The total Kw hours consumed = 1,000 + 4,000 + 0 + 5,000 = 10,000. Assembly will be apportioned £10,000 x 1,000/10,000 = £1,000 etc.

(iv) Machine depreciation will be based on the value of the machinery and again needs to be apportioned between the cost centres.

The total machine value is £2,250 + £1,750 + £550 + £450 = £5,000. This results in Assembly being apportioned £5,000 x 2,250/5,000 = £2,250 etc.

(v) Since the whole building is being depreciated, building depreciation should be related to the area of each cost centre. It does not matter that we have already used area once. There is no restriction against using it again if it is the most appropriate basis for apportioning this cost.

(vi) You may have thought that using number of employees was a good way to share out the direct wages bill, but remember that we are only interested here in *overheads*. Direct wages will already be included in the costs of the products that are made by the company. (Similarly direct materials are ignored for overheads.) If the question had included *indirect* labour then that would be included as an overhead and could be apportioned using the number of people working in each cost centre.

(b)

A suitable basis for sharing out canteen costs is the number of employees. A suitable basis for sharing out the maintenance costs is the time spent servicing equipment.

First re-apportion canteen costs since the canteen provides services for maintenance but maintenance do not work for the canteen. Then re-apportion the maintenance work, which include a share of the canteen.

Overhead	Basis		Assembly £	Finishing £	Maintenance £	Canteen £
Total from above			16,500	26,250	6,675	10,575
Canteen	Personnel	20:30:10	3,525	5,288	1,762	(10,575)
Sub-total			20,025	31,538	8,437	
Maintenance	Time	60:40	5,062	3,375	(8,437)	
Total			25,087	34,913		

Total overhead = £60,000

Activity-based costing (ABC)

Criticisms of traditional approach to overhead absorption

Historically a direct labour rate for absorption of all fixed overheads was a very common method, as production tended to be highly labour-intensive in the past. It was reasonable to assume that the more labour time spent on a product, the more production resources in general were being used. Thus the product should be charged with a higher share of the overheads.

However, nowadays, production is far more mechanised. This has two impacts as follows.

(a)   A higher proportion of the overheads is accounted for by **machine-related costs** (power, depreciation, maintenance, etc).

(b)   The amount of **labour time** spent upon a unit is far less representative of its final significance in the use of production resources.

To take a simple example, Product A may use 9 machine hours and 1 labour hour, whilst Product B requires 4 labour hours and 1 machine hour. The traditional approach would charge B with four times as much production overhead (including machine costs) as A, even though it takes half the time overall.

In this example, one solution would be to use machine hours as a basis. However, this still tries to relate all overhead costs, whatever their nature, to usage of machines. This would not necessarily be appropriate for, say, costs of receiving and checking materials going into the production process. This will be more likely to depend upon the number of times an order of material is received into stores for a particular product.

Activity-based costing (ABC) approach

Professors Robin Cooper and Robert Kaplan at the Harvard Business School have developed a costing system called **activity-based costing** (ABC) which avoids the problems experienced by traditional costing methods. If management are keen to control costs, then it is vital that they should know the activities that cause costs to arise. Those activities that are the significant determinants of cost are known as **cost-drivers**. For example, if production-scheduling cost is driven by the number of production set-ups, then that number is the cost-driver for the cost of production–scheduling. The cost-drivers represent the bases for charging costs in the ABC system, with a separate cost centre established for each cost-driver.

The following example contrasts a traditional product costing system with an ABC system and shows that an ABC system produces **much more accurate product costs**.

Example: ABC

Mayes plc has a single production centre and has provided the following information for the period just ended.

	Product A	Product B	Product C	Total
Production and sales (units)	40,000	25,000	10,000	75,000
Direct material cost	£25	£20	£18	£1,680,000
Direct labour hours	3	4	2	240,000
Machine hours	2	4	3	210,000
Number of production runs	5	10	25	40
Number of component receipts	15	25	120	160
Number of production orders	15	10	25	50

Direct labour is paid £8 per hour.

Overhead costs in the period have been as follows:

	£
Set-up	140,000
Machine	900,000
Goods inwards	280,000
Packing	200,000
Engineering	180,000
	1,700,000

A traditional costing approach would cost each product as follows:

	Product A	Product B	Product C
	£	£	£
Direct materials	25.00	20.00	18.00
Direct labour (@ £8 per hour)	24.00	32.00	16.00
Overhead(@ £7.08 per hour)	21.24	28.32	14.16
	70.24	80.32	48.16

Overhead recovery rate $= \dfrac{£1,700,000}{240,000} = £7.08$ per direct labour hour

An ABC system needs to investigate the cost determinants for the indirect overheads not driven by production volume. Assume that these are as follows.

Cost	Cost-driver
Set-up	Number of production runs
Goods inward	Number of receipts
Packing	Number of production orders
Engineering	Number of production orders

The machine overhead of £900,000 is likely to be related primarily to production volume, so it will be recovered on the basis of machine hours used.

The cost per activity for each of the other cost centres is as follows.

$$\text{Set-up cost} \quad \frac{£140,000}{40} = £3,500 \text{ per set-up}$$

$$\text{Goods inward} \quad \frac{£280,000}{160} = £1,750 \text{ per receipt}$$

$$\text{Packing} \quad \frac{£200,000}{50} = £4,000 \text{ per order}$$

$$\text{Engineering} \quad \frac{£180,000}{50} = £3,600 \text{ per order}$$

An ABC approach would cost each product as follows.

	Product A £	Product B £	Product C £
Direct materials	25.00	20.00	18.00
Direct labour	24.00	32.00	16.00
Set-up	0.44	1.40	8.75
Machine	8.57	17.14	12.86
Goods inwards	0.66	1.75	21.00
Packing	1.50	1.60	10.00
Engineering	1.35	1.44	9.00
	61.52	75.33	95.61

It can be seen that product C is significantly under-costed under the traditional system, while products A and B are over-costed. This situation arises because the large proportion of costs driven by product C is not picked up under the traditional costing system. Since it is the cost-drivers identified in the ABC system which generate the costs in the first place, the ABC system must produce a more accurate final analysis.

Marginal costing

In the section on overheads we compared TAC with marginal costing (MC), where only directly attributable variable overheads are absorbed into cost units. The key reason for using MC is to assist in **decision making**. If a decision has to be made it is sensible only to take into account those costs which will actually be affected by the decision. Since most overheads are fixed the decision to make one extra unit of production will not affect that cost, so it should be ignored. **Only the marginal cost of making one extra unit should be considered in decision making and therefore be absorbed into cost units.**

This approach to costing has two key uses:

♦ It affects **stock valuation** (stock valued under an MC approach is generally of lower value than that under TAC since fewer overheads have been absorbed – we shall see this again in Chapter 6).

♦ It enables us to make decisions when there is a scarcity of resources, that is when the shortage of one resource means that that resource limits the entire capacity of the operation: it is the **limiting factor**.

Single limiting factor

A company may have two products, each requiring materials and labour. There may be a limit as to the amount of labour or materials that is available for the coming month. How can the company make the most possible profit subject to such a constraint?

Since fixed costs are independent of production they are **irrelevant** (they will have to be paid however many units of each product are manufactured). The above problem therefore requires us to maximise **contribution** taking into account the limiting factor.

Example: limiting factor

Barbecue Limited manufactures two products for which the following details are available.

	Product X		*Product Y*
Selling price	£38		£38
Direct materials 8 units @ £1	£8	4 units @ £1	£4
Labour 4 hours @ £2	£8	6 hours @ £2	£12
Variable overhead 4 machine hours @ £3	£12	3 machine hours @ £3	£9
Fixed overheads	£5		£7

Maximum demand for X is 2,500 units.

Maximum demand for Y is 2,000 units.

Required

Calculate the optimum production plan for Barbecue in each of the following two situations.

(a)   Labour in the next period is limited to 16,000 hours, with no limit on machine hours.

(b)   Machine hours in the next period are limited to 12,000 hours, with no limit on labour hours.

Solution

We would like to produce Xs and Yx up to the point where maximum demand is reached. (There is no point producing beyond this, because customers do not want any more.) So ideally we would like to produce 2,500 X and 2,000 Y. To do this we would require the following resources.

	Labour hours	Machine hours
2,500 X	10,000	10,000
2,000 Y	12,000	6,000
	22,000	16,000

If labour is limited to 16,000 hours we will not have enough labour hours to achieve this. Similarly, if machine hours are limited to 12,000 our production will be restricted.

To tackle this problem we begin by calculating the contribution earned per unit of each product.

Contribution for each unit of X = £ (38 – 8 – 8 – 12) = £10 per unit

Contribution for each unit of Y = £ (38 – 4 – 12 – 9) = £13 per unit

(a)   Labour is limited so we calculate the contribution earned per labour hour for each product.

X = £10/4 = £2.50 per labour hour

Y = £13/6 = £2.17 per labour hour

You get more contribution per labour hour for X than for Y so make as many Xs as possible.

Available hours = 16,000

2,500 Xs require 10,000 hrs

The remaining hours are all used to make as many Ys as possible.

Remaining Ys will take six hours each to make so produce 6,000/6 = 1,000 Ys.

Contribution = (2,500 x £10) + (1,000 x £13) = £38,000

(b)   In this case, machine hours are the scarce resource so we calculate contribution per machine hour.

X = £10/4 = £2.50 per machine hour

Y = £13/3 = £4.33 per machine hour

Now it is better to make Ys. Making 2,000 Ys requires 2,000 x 3 = 6,000 machine hours. That leaves us a further 6,000 machine hours for making Xs.

6,000 remaining hours for X means making 6,000/4 = 1,500 Xs.

Contribution = (1,500 x £10) + (2,000 x £13) = £41,000.

Note that in the assessment, if you are told maximum demand for a product it is a big hint that this method should be used.

Questions

1   AB Limited I (AAT CA J94)

You have been asked to give a short talk to new employees who are attending your company's trainee induction programme. The talk will be entitled *The importance of understanding cost behaviour*.

You are now in the process of preparing materials for your talk.

Required

(a)   You have decided that you will use sketch graphs to demonstrate cost behaviour patterns. In preparation for your talk, produce sketch graphs which will demonstrate the way in which the following costs behave in relation to the level of activity:

(i)   fixed costs

(ii)   variable costs

(iii)   semi-variable costs

(iv)   fixed cost per unit

(v)   variable cost per unit

Note: You do not need to use graph paper because only sketches will be necessary. However, it is important that you should draw clear diagrams with correctly labelled axes. For ease of explanation, you decide to assume that all costs are linear.

(b)   For each of the graphs in (a), prepare brief notes for your talk which explain the shape of the graph. Also note down **two** examples of **each** of costs (i), (ii) and (iii) above so that you can give them to your audience if requested.

(c)   Prepare a further brief set of notes for your talk which explains why an understanding of cost behaviour patterns is necessary for effective planning and control in an organisation.

2   Luda Limited

Luda Limited manufactures three products: P, Q and R. Each product is started in the machining area and completed in the finishing shop. The direct unit costs associated with each product forecast for the next trading period are as follows.

	P £	Q £	R £
Materials	18.50	15.00	22.50
Wages			
Machining area @ £5 per hour	10.00	5.00	10.00
Finishing shop @ £4 per hour	6.00	4.00	8.00
	34.50	24.00	40.50

There are machines in both departments and machine hours required to complete one of each product are:

	P	Q	R
Machine area	4.0	1.5	3.0
Finishing shop	0.5	0.5	1
Budget output in units	6,000	8,000	2,000
Fixed overheads			
Machine area		£100,800	
Finishing shop		£94,500	

Required

(a)   Calculate the overhead absorption rate for fixed overheads using:

    (i)   a labour hour rate for each department;

    (ii)   a machine hour rate for each department.

(b)   Calculate the total cost of each product using:

    (i)   the labour hour rate;

    (ii)   the machine hour rate;

    as calculated in (a) above.

(c)   Set out your comments to the factory manager who has suggested that one overhead rate for both departments would simplify matters.

3   Lorus Limited

Lorus Limited makes cupboards. This involves three production departments (Sawing, Assembly and Finishing) together with two service departments (Maintenance and Materials Handling).

Last year 4,000 cupboards were made.

Costs incurred:

	Sawing £	Assembly £	Finishing £
Materials	120,000	80,000	20,000
Wages	50,000	25,000	40,000
Overheads	75,000	50,000	20,000

Materials Handling wages: £9,000

Maintenance wages: £15,000

Consumable stores: £5,000 (Maintenance)

The benefits derived from the service departments are estimated to be as follows:

	Sawing %	Assembly %	Finishing %	Materials Handling %
Maintenance	30	40	20	10
Materials Handling	50	20	30	

Required

(a)   Prepare a memorandum to the managing director, copied to each production head, showing the overheads allotted to each production department.

(b)   Calculate the unit cost of a cupboard.

4   Costing methods

The traditional methods of cost allocation, cost apportionment and absorption into products are being challenged by some writers who claim that much information given to management is misleading when these methods of dealing with fixed overheads are used to determine product costs.

Required

Explain what is meant by **cost allocation**, **cost apportionment** and **absorption** and describe briefly the alternative approach of **activity-based costing** in order to ascertain total product costs.

Summary

This chapter has revised several fundamental cost accounting topics from your earlier studies including the following.

♦   The derivation and use of cost units for different types of activities and businesses.

♦   The techniques for splitting semi-variable costs.

♦   The treatment of overheads, including:

–   allocation/apportionment/absorption

–   service departments

–   over-/under-absorption

–   activity-based costing approach

–   marginal costing

♦   Decision making with scarce resources.

CHAPTER 4

Budget Preparation

Objectives

This chapter explains how budgets are prepared and covers the following performance criteria.

8.1.3 **Forecasts are produced in a clear format with explanations of assumptions, projections and adjustments.**

8.1.4 **The validity of forecasts is reviewed in the light of any significant anticipated changes.**

8.2.1 **Draft budget proposals are presented to management in a clear and appropriate format and on schedule.**

8.2.2 **Draft budget proposals are consistent with organisational objectives, have taken all relevant data into account and are agreed with budget holders.**

8.2.3 **Annual budgets are broken down into periods in accordance with anticipated seasonal trends.**

8.2.4 **Discussions with budget holders are conducted in a manner which contains goodwill.**

8.3.1 **Budget figures are checked and reconciled on an ongoing basis.**

When you have completed this chapter, you should be able to:

♦   understand how budget preparation is co-ordinated

♦   understand the significance of the limiting or key factor in budget preparation

♦   prepare budgets for income and costs.

The approach to budgetary control

One commentator has suggested that 'Budgets are a means of attaining organisational control, that is the achievement of organisational objectives'. Within this context, he then went on to consider the various functions which a budget may fulfil.

♦   **Authorisation**

A budget may act as a formal authorisation to a manager to spend a given amount on specified activities. If this is applied to an operating budget, however, it must be appreciated that over-strict enforcement would not be in the best interests of the business.

◆ **Forecasting**

Forecasting refers to the prediction of events over which little or no control is exercised. Some parts of all budgets are, therefore, based on forecasts. Budget figures may also be used by one part of an organisation to forecast the likely effect on it of the activities of other parts.

◆ **Planning**

Planning is an attempt to shape the future by a conscious effort to influence those factors which are open to control.

◆ **Communication and co-ordination**

Budgets communicate plans to managers responsible for carrying them out. They also ensure co-ordination between managers of sub-units so that each is aware of the others' requirements.

◆ **Motivation**

Budgets are often intended to motivate managers to perform in line with organisational objectives. The problem in this area is that when budgets are made relevant and designed to act as motivational devices, the attitude of managers using them tends to be negative.

◆ **Evaluation**

The performance of managers and organisational units is often evaluated by reference to budgetary standards as these are quite possibly the only quantitative reference points available. The way in which performance is evaluated will be a dominating influence on how a manager behaves in the future and is therefore worthy of separate consideration.

Prerequisites of budgetary control are the definition of **objectives** and the existence or creation of an **organisational structure** through which plans may be put into effect. In particular, forecasts on which budgets are based should be made available to operational departments in a clear, easily understood format with explanations of assumptions, projections and adjustments.

The objectives of the business will be defined in the **long-term strategic plan** and any short-term budget must be framed in such a way as to contribute towards the achievement of these objectives.

The budget, therefore, will incorporate its own **short-term objectives**, probably expressed in the form that a financial analyst would use when interpreting the final results as follows (we shall look at these ratios further in Chapter 8).

◆ Rate of return on total capital employed

◆ Net profit percentage (ie net profit: sales)

◆ Asset turnover ratio (ie sales: capital employed)

◆ Rate of growth in sales value

◆ Liquidity and asset management ratios supporting the above

The administration of budgetary control

Budget centres

The organisational structure through which control will be exercised so that budget objectives are achieved must be based on **manager responsibilities**.

It is only when the functions to be carried out by each manager have been defined that it becomes possible to define the following:

♦   the **output** he should achieve

♦   the **resources** he can justifiably employ

♦   the **costs** he is expected to control.

The particular segments of the business for which individuals are allocated budget responsibility are known as **budget centres** or **responsibility centres**.

Some budget centre managers will be responsible for profitability, either profit in relation to output or profit in relation to capital employed under their control. These centres are known as **profit centres** or **investment centres**, depending upon the amount of autonomy given.

Issue of budget instructions

Budgets need to be prepared by all managers on a consistent basis in a form which facilitates combination into the master budget. The information needed includes the following.

♦   The **organisational structure** of the business, setting out clearly the responsibilities of each manager and the limits of his authority.

♦   The **classification and coding** of the various items of income and expenditure to be covered by the budget.

♦   A statement of the **period to be covered by the budget** and of the shorter accounting periods into which it is to be subdivided (or 'phased') for purposes of control.

♦   Copies of the **forms to be used** in submitting budgets.

♦   **Instructions** on what is to be shown on the various forms, and the manner in which particular items are to be calculated. Examples of practical points to be clarified are:

(i)   whether 'sales' are to be budgeted initially on the basis of order intake or of invoiced amounts

(ii)   when costs are expected to increase, whether uniform percentages for particular items are to be used

(iii)   what rates of salary increase, if any, are to be budgeted by managers

(iv)   what types of cost are to be budgeted centrally and not included in departmental budgets.

♦ The **timetable** for the preparation of the budgets. In particular, draft budget proposals, presented in a clear and appropriate format, must be completed and submitted to management on schedule to allow the budget-setting process to proceed in a timely manner.

Instructions which are to be binding on all managers must clearly be issued on the authority of the managing director or chief executive; but somebody must be responsible for drafting them, explaining them when necessary, and ensuring that they are being complied with as the work of budgeting progresses.

The budget officer

The term *budget officer* is used to describe a role which must be played by somebody in the organisation to get the budget processed to completion (even if he or she is actually called something else). This will involve the following duties:

♦ the issue of the **budget instructions**

♦ the **co-ordination** of the budgets

♦ **checking and reconciling** the budget figures on an ongoing basis

♦ **valuing and combining** the various departmental budgets

♦ **submitting the final company budget** to the board.

After the budgets have been approved, he will continue the task of **budgetary control**.

In a **large business** all these activities may be brought together under a budget officer or 'controller' having equal or senior status to the chief accountant.

In the **smaller company** a chief accountant may be responsible directly to the managing director, and have under his control all the functions outlined above, including budgetary control.

To facilitate the budget-setting process, it is important that all discussions with budget-holders are conducted in a **manner which maintains goodwill**.

Co-ordination of budgets

So that an acceptable master budget can be prepared, the various subsidiary budgets must be **co-ordinated**. The most obvious example of this is the need to ensure that the quantities which the sales department are forecasting that they will sell are in line with the quantities which production are budgeting to produce.

Co-ordination of activities can be carried out by a **budget committee** which can include the main function managers under the chairmanship of the budget officer.

Approval of budgets

Budgets must be approved ultimately by the **board of the company**. The management accountant or MD will recommend approval by the board. Before doing so, however, he will need to be satisfied that all budgets have been properly co-ordinated and that the budgets are in line with the company's objectives.

To ensure that this is achieved from the outset the draft budget proposals agreed with budget-holders must be **consistent with organisational objectives** and must be **potentially achievable**.

After being prepared, the individual draft budgets will therefore pass through the following stages before being finally approved by the board:

♦ approval in principle by the **manager** of the function to which the budget relates

♦ examination by the **budget controller** who will ensure that the principles laid down for preparation of the budgets have been adhered to

♦ consideration of the budget in the light of all the other budgets by the **budget committee** before it recommends to the managing director that the master budget should be submitted to the **board for approval**.

Budget preparation

Limiting factors on budgets

The level of activity at which a business can operate will very seldom be unlimited. **Limitations** may be imposed, for example, by:

♦ market demand for its products or services

♦ the number of skilled employees available

♦ the availability of material supplies

♦ the space available either as a working area or for the storage of goods

♦ the amount of cash or credit facilities available to finance the business.

Therefore, when a manager starts to prepare a budget he should review the elements in it and identify where *limiting factors* (or *governing factors*) exist.

They will not all be equally significant; but where one particular limitation is of major importance it may be necessary to budget for that item first and to construct the rest of the budget around it. This can happen not merely in one department but for the company as a whole, when the item concerned may be referred to as the *principal budget factor* or *key factor*.

Quite commonly, the **rate of growth in sales** is the principal budget factor and this would have to be forecast before any other budget plans were made.

It is essential to identify the principal budget factor and any other limiting factors at an **early** stage in the budgeting process so that management may consider whether:

♦ it is possible to **overcome the limitation** which they impose (eg by finding new markets for sales or by obtaining alternative supplies or substitute raw materials)

♦ the limitations imposed must be **accepted** and the business's budgets must be produced within those limitations.

Types of budget

What budgets will be produced? For a manufacturing company, these will typically comprise the following:

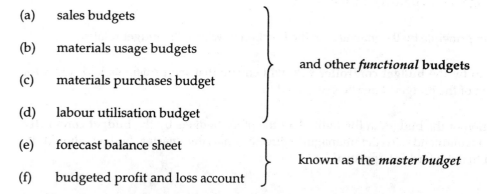

(a)   sales budgets

(b)   materials usage budgets

(c)   materials purchases budget   and other *functional* budgets

(d)   labour utilisation budget

(e)   forecast balance sheet   known as the *master budget*

(f)   budgeted profit and loss account

This example illustrates the preparation of the functional budgets, starting with projected sales information, and shows how they combine to give a budgeted profit and loss account.

One of the most important points illustrated by this example is how the budgets are **inter-related**.

It is a simple example and you should be aware that in practice budgeting can be more than simply an arithmetical exercise. The **practical problems** are discussed later.

Example: budget preparation

There is a continuing demand for three sub-assemblies – A, B and C – made and sold by MW Limited. Sales are in the ratios of A 1, B 2, C 4 and selling prices are A £215, B £250, C £300.

Each sub-assembly consists of a copper frame onto which are fixed the same components but in differing quantities as follows.

Sub-assembly	Frame	Component D	Component E	Component F
A	1	5	1	4
B	1	1	7	5
C	1	3	5	1
Buying-in costs, per unit	£20	£8	£5	£3

Operation times by labour for each sub-assembly are as follows.

Sub-assembly	Skilled hours	Unskilled hours
A	2	2
B	1½	2
C	1½	3

The skilled labour is paid £6 per hour and the unskilled £4.50 per hour. The skilled labour is located in a machining department and the unskilled labour in an assembly department. A five-day week of 37½ hours is worked and each accounting period is for four weeks.

Variable overhead per sub-assembly is A £5, B £4 and C £3.50.

At the end of the current year, stocks are expected to be as shown below but because interest rates have increased and the company utilises a bank overdraft for working capital purposes, it is planned to effect a 10% reduction in all finished sub-assemblies and bought-in stocks during period 1 of the forthcoming year.

Forecast opening stocks

Sub-assembly		Copper frames	1,000
A	300	Component D	4,000
B	700	Component E	10,000
C	1,600	Component F	4,000

Work-in-progress stocks are to be ignored.

Overhead for the forthcoming year is budgeted to be production £728,000, selling and distribution £364,000 and administration £338,000. These costs, all fixed, are expected to be incurred evenly throughout the year and are treated as period costs.

It is expected that a total of 45,500 sub-assemblies will be sold in the forthcoming year and that one-thirteenth of this will be sold in period 1.

Required

(a)   Prepare budgets in respect of period 1 of the forthcoming year for:

     (i)   sales, in quantities and value

     (ii)   production, in quantities only

     (iii)   materials usage, in quantities

     (iv)   materials purchases, in quantities and value

     (v)   manpower budget (number of people needed in the machining department and the assembly department)

(b)   Prepare a detailed budgeted profit and loss account for period 1.

Solution

(a)   ***Functional budgets***

    (i)   *Sales budget*

Strictly, this is not a budget, but a forecast. Once sales quantities of each product have been estimated, production quantities can be budgeted, which in turn will dictate materials and labour requirements, etc.

The last paragraph tells us that the total expected sales for the period are:

45,500/13 = 3,500

The first paragraph states that the ratio in which this will be split between the three products is: 1:2:4, or 1/7:2/7:4/7. So individual sales quantities will be:

A: $1/7 \times 3,500$ =   500
B: $2/7 \times 3,500$ =   1,000
C: $4/7 \times 3,500$ =   2,000

The sales budget can now be prepared, using the price information in the first paragraph. A tabular/columnar format is advisable for all budgets, as it is a clear and efficient layout.

Product	A	B	C	Total
Quantity	500	1,000	2,000	3,500
Price	£215	£250	£300	
Sales value	£107,500	£250,000	£600,000	£957,500

    (ii)   *Production budget*

This is the key budget. All production costs will be based upon the quantities to be produced within the period.

This will follow on from the budgeted sales quantities, but we need to take account of required changes in stock levels of finished goods. For example, if we want more stock at the end of the period than at the beginning, we will need to budget to produce more than we sell. The relationship is described as:

Production   =   Sales   +   Closing stock   –   Opening stock
                                            (finished goods)   (finished goods)

Your budget should incorporate this structure for each product. The opening stocks are given to us under 'forecast stocks at current year-end' – here, we are concerned with finished goods stocks (ie the sub-assemblies). Prior to these figures, we are told that the closing stock requirements are 90% of these levels. The resulting production budget can be drawn up as follows.

Product (units)	A	B	C
Sales [as in (i)]	500	1,000	2,000
Add: Closing stock			
(90% of opening)	270	630	1,440
Less: Opening stock			
(given in question)	(300)	(700)	(1,600)
Production	470	930	1,840

Note that in this case production quantities are lower than sales, as stocks are being reduced.

(iii)   *Materials usage budget*

This shows the amounts of each type of material that will be used in the period. This will depend upon the quantities of each product to be produced (as in the production budget) and how much material is used within one unit of each type of product (given near the beginning of the question).

Materials usage = Usage per unit × Units produced

Again, incorporate this information within your answer to give a clear explanation of where your figures come from.

Product	A	B	C	Total
Production	470	930	1,840	
Frames				
Usage per unit	1	1	1	
Total usage	470	930	1,840	3,240
Component D				
Usage per unit	5	1	3	
Total usage	2,350	930	5,520	8,800
Component E				
Usage per unit	1	7	5	
Total usage	470	6,510	9,200	16,180
Component F				
Usage per unit	4	5	1	
Total usage	1,880	4,650	1,840	8,370

(iv)   *Materials purchases budget*

This shows the amount of each type of material that will be bought in the period, along with the purchase costs.

This is linked with the materials usage budget, but again needs to take stock movements into account – this time, stocks of materials are relevant. Again, as stocks are to be reduced by 10%, the amounts of material purchased in the period will be less than the amounts used. The relationship is as follows:

Materials purchased	=	Materials used in production	+	Closing stock (raw materials)	–	Opening stock (raw materials)

The budget will look very similar to that for production, except that it analyses by material type rather than product.

Material (units)	Frame	Components D	E	F
Usage [from (iii)]	3,240	8,800	16,180	8,370
Add: closing stock (90% of opening)	900	3,600	9,000	3,600
Less: opening stock (given)	(1,000)	(4,000)	(10,000)	(4,000)
Purchases (units)	3,140	8,400	15,180	7,970
Purchase cost	£20	£8	£5	£3
Purchases	£62,800	£67,200	£75,900	£23,910

Total purchases = £229,810

(iv)   *Manpower budget*

This will be based upon the information given concerning operation times. We will start by producing a 'labour utilisation budget' – very similar to the materials usage budget. In some questions, you may in fact be required to produce this budget in its own right.

Once the total hours needed in each department are known, we can use the information about hours per week and weeks per period to determine the number of employees needed.

	A	B	C
Units produced	470	930	1,840
Machining hours required/unit	2	1.5	1.5
∴ Machining hours required	940	1,395	2,760
Assembly hours required/unit	2	2	3
∴ Assembly hours required	940	1,860	5,520

Total machining hours required = 940 + 1,395 + 2,760 = 5,095 hours

This is in respect of a four-week period, in which each employee works 37½ hours, so the number of employees needed in the machining department is as follows.

$$\frac{5,095}{4 \times 37.5} = 34 \text{ people}$$

Similarly, the total assembly hours required are as follows.

940 + 1,860 + 5,520 = 8,320 hours

Number of employees needed in the assembly department is as follows.

$$\frac{8,320}{4 \times 37.5} = 56 \text{ people (rounding up to the nearest person)}$$

(b)   *Budgeted profit and loss account*

Most of the information for this can be taken from the budgets previously prepared. The additional information needed is as follows:

♦   opening and closing stock values (finished goods and raw material)

♦   labour cost [from the manpower budget in (iv)]

♦   variable overhead cost

♦   production overheads and non-production costs (given in question for a year)

Finished goods valuation – standard cost cards

This requires the production of a 'standard cost card' for each product. We shall assume a marginal costing approach and that opening and closing stocks are valued at the same unit cost.

The information is all taken from the question, with the exception of the closing stock units, which can be taken from the production budget.

	A Quantity	A £	B Quantity	B £	C Quantity	C £
Unit costs						
Frame	1	20	1	20	1	20.0
Components D (@ £8)	5	40	1	8	3	24.0
Components E (@ £5)	1	5	7	35	5	25.0
Components F (@ £3)	4	12	5	15	1	3.0
Labour						
Skilled (@ £6)	2	12	1.5	9	1.5	9.0
Unskilled (@ £4.50)	2	9	2	9	3	13.5
Variable overhead		5		4		3.5
Total variable costs		103		100		98.0

Opening stock

	A	B	C
Units	300	700	1,600
Value	£30,900	£70,000	£156,800

Total opening stock = £257,700

Closing stock

	A	B	C
Units	270	630	1,440
Value	£27,810	£63,000	£141,120

Total closing stock = £231,930

Raw materials stocks – valuation

This is simply the stock levels (from question and materials purchases budget) multiplied by the buying-in costs (given in question).

		Components		
Material	Frame	D	E	F
Buying-in price	£20	£8	£5	£3
Opening stock				
Units	1,000	4,000	10,000	4,000
Value	£20,000	£32,000	£50,000	£12,000

Total opening stock = £114,000

Closing stock

Units	900	3,600	9,000	3,600
Value	£18,000	£28,800	£45,000	£10,800

Total closing stock = £102,600

Labour costs

The utilisation budget in (iv) showed that 5,095 machining hours and 8,320 assembly hours were needed for the period's production.

The cost of these, using the rates given, will be:

Machining (skilled):   5,095 × £6   =   £30,570

Assembly (unskilled):   8,320 × £4.50   =   £37,440

Total cost = £68,010

Variable overhead cost

This is given in the question as a unit cost for each product. The total cost will be the production levels multiplied by these unit costs:

Product	A	B	C	Total
Production	470	930	1,840	
Variable overhead rate	£5	£4	£3.50	
Cost	£2,350	£3,720	£6,440	£12,510

We can now draw up the profit and loss account.

Budgeted profit and loss account for Period 1

		£	£	£
Sales				957,500
Cost of sales				
Opening stocks	- raw materials		114,000	
	- finished goods		257,700	
			371,700	
Materials purchased			229,810	
Labour			68,010	
Variable overheads			12,510	
			682,030	
Closing stock	- raw materials	102,600		
	- finished goods	231,930		
			(334,530)	
				(347,500)
				610,000
Budgeted contribution				
Fixed overheads				
Production (728,000 x 4/52)			56,000	
Selling and distribution (364,000 x 4/52)			28,000	
Administration (338,000 x 4/52)			26,000	
				(110,000)
Budgeted profit				500,000

Make sure you are quite clear where all the figures come from.

Practical aspects of functional budgets

Sales budgets

The **sales income budget** is uniquely difficult to prepare because it involves forecasting the actions of people outside the business (the potential customers).

The extent to which **sales forecasting** is necessary will depend on the period covered by the outstanding order book and on the consistency of the conversion rate from enquiries to orders. If there is a well-filled order book for some months ahead then less reliance will need to be placed on forecasting techniques.

Forecasts may be made in a variety of ways. The method used will depend on the nature of the business and the amount of information available, but a **generalised formal procedure** might be as follows.

♦ **Review past years' sales** for whatever period is appropriate to the company's business cycle.

♦ **Analyse the time series** to identify seasonal, cyclical and random fluctuations (see Chapter 2).

♦ **Extrapolate from past years' figures**, assuming no changes in products or prices.

♦ Adjust the extrapolation for **proposed changes which are controllable** by the company, such as price alterations, changes in marketing effort, the introduction of new products, and the discontinuance of existing products (the products' life cycles).

♦ Adjust for market changes due to **external factors**, such as government controls, action of competitors or social changes affecting demand. In particular, appropriate adjustments should be made for changing price levels or seasonal trends.

♦ Check that the resultant quantities are **compatible** with the quantities that can be purchased or produced.

♦ Check **acceptability of forecast** to sectional sales managers. In addition, other personnel who might contribute towards making realistic forecasts of trends should be consulted.

♦ Check **consistency of forecast with long-term corporate plans**.

The forecasting method outlined above depends on the existence of a 'time series' of figures from which extrapolation can be made and is mainly applicable to items in continuous demand. For other types of business, the sales forecast will be based on some form of **market survey** or on subjective estimates by people familiar with the market concerned.

Whichever forecasting method is used, the forecast should take account of **significant anticipated changes in circumstances** which would affect the validity of any statistically derived calculations.

Cost budgets

Budgeting for costs, in the same way as budgeting for sales, begins with facts. What facts they are will depend on the nature of the business; but every business will employ people, and most businesses will use **materials** of some kind. A manufacturing business will use tools and probably machinery. Floor space will be needed, also office equipment and perhaps motor vehicles.

All these requirements will be related in some way to the **output** of the business – its sales and any changes in stocks or work in progress.

In practice there are a wide range of different ways to budget for costs, as follows.

♦   If **standards for cost units** are available, then there may be computer programs to identify the material and labour standards relative to a given output. It then remains for departmental managers to budget for material wastage or spoilage, labour efficiency and idle time.

♦   In a business carrying out **long-term contracts**, cost units (contracts) may be identical with cost centres (each contract having its own controller).

♦   In some businesses it may be sufficiently accurate for the budget for direct materials cost to be an **extrapolation from past total figures**, without any attempt at detailed justification or analysis.

Use of standards in budgeting

Budgeting will inevitably make use of standard costs, as in the worked example above, and you should ensure you are familiar with the techniques and principles involved in their determination (see Chapter 6).

However, budgeting will generally extend beyond the simple multiplication of planned production levels by the standard usages and costs for each product for the following reasons.

♦   Different ranges of output levels will often lead to **changes in unit variable costs** (eg materials discounts, learning effects, etc).

♦   Some variable costs will not vary neatly with production and will need to be estimated for **each particular activity level** (eg wastage, idle time, production set-up costs).

♦   Fixed costs are independent of production levels, although they may be **stepped**.

♦   A large proportion of a business's costs will **not be directly involved in the production process** (eg administration, marketing, capital expenditure, etc).

The following sections describe the common problems encountered in budgeting for the most common cost elements: labour, materials and overheads.

Budgeting for numbers and costs of employees

When budgeting for people to be employed, the starting point must be to assess **the work to be done by people with various skills** and this is equally necessary for manual, clerical and managerial activities.

Having defined what work is to be done, the establishment of budgets for the employment of people falls into two main stages:

♦ planning the **number of** people needed

♦ calculating the **relevant costs**.

In defining the productive workload for the budget year it will be necessary to balance the requirements of the sales budget against the **productive capacity** available. If there is excess capacity over the year as a whole then a decision will be needed whether to operate below full capacity or to use the excess capacity in making goods for stock or getting ahead with work in progress for the following year.

If the sales budget does not provide a steady workload month by month, then in phasing the budgets it may be decided to keep productive output constant and to balance out the short-term differences by fluctuations in **work-in-progress** or **finished stock**.

The degree of precision possible in budgeting for numbers of people employed will depend on the type of work involved and the extent to which work measurement is possible.

Budgeting for the cost of materials

Considerable effort can be involved in preparing detailed budgets of quantities and purchase prices of materials. Whether this effort is justified will depend on the **significance of materials in relation to total costs**, and the extent to which effective control can be exercised.

The starting point for materials budgeting is the **quantity of material** to be used during the budget year, whether in retail sales or in production or for indirect use.

The **form of the materials usage budget** will depend on the nature of the business. Where repetitive operations are carried out it will be possible, and worth the effort, to set standards for the usage of the various items of material, and these standards can be associated with the production forecast to build up the total material requirements.

The **purchase prices** to be applied to the usage of the various items may be obtained from stock ledger records or recent purchase invoices, subject to adjustment for forecast price changes.

In budgeting for **indirect materials** (such as small tools, machine coolants and lubricants, fuel, cleaning materials and office stationery) the common practice is to budget merely for a total cost extrapolated from past experience. It will be important for control purposes, however, that the budget working papers contain as much detail as possible about anticipated usage, even though the individual items may not be evaluated separately.

Budgeting for overheads

The nature of overheads will depend on the type of business, but common categories are as follows:

(a)   premises charges

(b)   costs of plant, motor vehicles and other fixed assets

(c)   communication expenses

(d)   travelling and entertaining

(e)   insurances

(f)   discretionary costs

(g)   financial policy costs

(h)   random costs.

Permanent budget record

For every type of revenue or cost it is highly desirable that a **permanent budget record** be prepared, giving the detailed calculations from which the budgeted amount has been derived. In particular, the data relevant to projecting forecasts of income and expenditure must be identified. This will not only impose a discipline on the budget preparation but will also:

♦   facilitate the eventual **explanation** of any differences between budgeted and actual results

♦   provide a **starting point for budget revisions** or for the preparation of budgets in future years.

The important features of such a record are as follows.

♦   Details of the budget calculation.

♦   Comparison with the actual figures for the previous year.

♦   Basis of variability, noting how the amount is related to such factors as levels of output or numbers of people employed.

Capital expenditure budget

All short-term operating budgets are in effect abstracts from a **continuously developing long-term plan**. This, however, is particularly true of the capital expenditure budget because the major items included in it will not be completed within the bounds of any one budget year.

The main purpose of the capital expenditure budget, therefore, is to provide a **forecast of the amount of cash likely to be needed for investment projects** during the year ahead. It also indicates what items of plant, equipment, vehicles and so on will be needed for the purpose of implementing the profit and loss (or operating) budget; and therefore it must be submitted for approval at an early stage in the budgeting timetable.

Any **capital expenditure budget** would include the following:

♦ a brief descriptive title for the project

♦ the total required expenditure

♦ an analysis of the costs over various time periods

♦ where appropriate, expenditure to date on the project

♦ estimates of future benefits from the project

♦ investment appraisal calculations including details of assumptions made

♦ intangible benefits from the expenditure.

The master budget

The master budget for approval by the board will take the form of a **budgeted profit and loss account** (as seen in the previous example) and a **forecast balance sheet** as at the year-end. These will be supported by such summaries of the various functional budgets as may be required, and by calculations of the key ratios which indicate conformity with the objectives for the year.

The standards for Unit 7 and Unit 8 are largely concerned with budgets for income and expenditure forming the budgeted profit and loss account, and you do not need to be concerned with the detailed preparation of the forecast balance sheet. The following provides an overview.

The forecast balance sheet

In arriving at the forecast balance sheet, it will be necessary to take account of the following.

♦ The **capital expenditure budget**

♦ **Changes in stock levels and work in progress** (as calculated in connection with the budgeting of material and labour costs). If work in progress and finished stocks are valued on a TAC basis, then it will be necessary to calculate **overhead recovery rates**.

♦ **Changes in debtor balances**. Subject to any special delays in collection, the closing debtor balances will be calculated by applying the company's normal credit terms to the phased budget of sales.

♦ **Changes in creditor balances**. In theory, the closing creditors will be calculated by applying a normal credit period to the phased budgets of material purchases, subcontracted work and any other relevant items. In practice, it may be necessary to review the budgeted cash flow before finalising a decision on the credit to be taken.

♦ **Changes in cash balance**. Initially, the closing cash balance may be taken as the balancing figure on the balance sheet, but at some stage this should be validated by building up a cash budget itemised from the other budgets. This is discussed in the following section.

The cash budget

The purposes of the **cash budget** are as follows.

♦   To ensure that the various items of income and expenditure budgeted departmentally, and subject to the normal credit policy of the business, will result in cash flows which enable the company to pay its way at all times; in other words, to ensure that there is a **practical plan**.

♦   Where the cash flow over the year as a whole is satisfactory but there are intermediate periods of **difficulty in financing operations**, to give a basis from which the timing of particular items can be replanned.

♦   Where cash proves inadequate to finance the plan as originally envisaged, to give the financial controller an opportunity to **seek sources of additional capital**.

   (If the budget cannot be financed as it stands, then a **revised budget** will have to be prepared.)

♦   Like any other budget, to provide a basis for control during the forthcoming year.

(Note: The preparation of cash budgets is not within the scope of the standards for Unit 7 and Unit 8.)

Budgeting for changes in prices

Unless frequent budget revisions are to be made, it is essential to take account of **anticipated significant changes** in prices and costs when establishing budgets. If this is not done, particularly when the costs of the various revenue and capital expenditures are increasing at different rates, then the assumptions on which it is based and accepted may prove to have been completely wrong.

The methods of incorporating price changes into budgets may be considered under three alternative circumstances: specific price changes, uncertain price changes and general inflation.

Specific price changes

Where specific changes in costs or in selling prices can be forecast with reasonable certainty, then they should be **incorporated into the budget** as from the forecast date of implementation, and the phased budget figure should be adjusted accordingly.

Examples are pay awards payable in accordance with published scales such as 'birthday' increases payable to junior employees.

Uncertain price changes

Where it is reasonably certain that costs will change but the timing and amount will not, then the **best possible estimate** should be made and incorporated into the master budget. It may be undesirable, however, to include such estimates in the detailed budgets for departmental or product costs control since they will give rise to uncontrollable variances needing continued explanation.

Examples of changes of this nature are forecast wage claims negotiable with trade unions, and fluctuations in commodity prices.

General inflationary changes

Some of the effects of general price level changes may have been dealt with already as specific changes under the two preceding paragraphs, and no further adjustment would then be necessary.

For items of expenditure not dealt with in this way (particularly the cost of services), an **estimated rate of inflationary increase** should be prescribed by the budget controller and be included in the detailed budgets of the items concerned.

Probabilistic budgets

The adjustments outlined above result in the normal kind of budget with a particular set of sales, cost, volume and profit targets. Such budgets do not show any indication of **the likelihood that the budget will be attained**. From a planning perspective, management may wish to try and build into the budget an expression of the probability of certain things occurring, eg a price change or a level of demand. Probabilistic budgets, as they are usually called, can be developed in three main ways, which vary as regards their degree of sophistication:

(a)   Three different budgets are prepared reflecting **pessimistic, most likely** and **optimistic results**. The pessimistic budgets will combine together the less favourable assumptions about all the budgeted variables. Although relatively crude, such an approach does make managers consider risk explicitly, and avoids the need to assign definite probabilities to the estimates.

For example, suppose the sales levels and fixed overhead costs for a budget are particularly subject to uncertainty. The three estimates have been made for these and can be combined into the three levels of budget.

	Pessimistic	*Most likely*	*Optimistic*
Sales – Volume (units)	10,000	16,000	20,000
– Selling price	20	20	20
	£	£	£
– Value	200,000	320,000	400,000
Variable costs (@ £10 per unit)	(100,000)	(160,000)	(200,000)
Contribution (@ £10 per unit)	100,000	160,000	200,000
Fixed overheads	(120,000)	(100,000)	(90,000)
Profit/(loss)	(20,000)	60,000	110,000

(b) Alternatively, three estimates of each budget variable (or a single limiting factor if this was felt sufficient) can be made, and **definitive probabilities assigned to each estimate**. The joint probabilities of different levels of profit can then be calculated. This is obviously a more complex exercise than (a), but perhaps imposes a greater discipline on management thinking. Expected profit can be calculated from the various profits and their probabilities.

Using the example in (a) above, suppose the three sales levels (and thus contributions) and fixed overhead costs are assigned probabilities:

Sales levels (units)	Contribution £	Probability	Overheads	Probability
10,000	100,000	0.25	120,000	0.4
16,000	160,000	0.50	100,000	0.5
20,000	200,000	0.25	90,000	0.1

As before, the results will vary between a loss of £20,000 and a profit of £110,000 but these and many other possible results can now be assigned probabilities. The following table shows just some of the figures:

Sales level (units)	Contribution (£)	Overheads (£)	Profit/(loss)	Probability		
10,000	100,000	120,000	(20,000)	0.25 × 0.4	=	0.100
10,000	100,000	100,000	–	0.25 × 0.5	=	0.125
⋮	⋮	⋮	⋮	⋮		
16,000	160,000	100,000	60,000	0.5 × 0.5	=	0.250
16,000	160,000	90,000	70,000	0.5 × 0.1	=	0.050
⋮	⋮	⋮	⋮	⋮		
20,000	200,000	100,000	100,000	0.25 × 0.5	=	0.125
20,000	200,000	90,000	110,000	0.25 × 0.1	=	0.025
						1.000

This analysis can be used to ascertain the probability of profit reaching particular targets. For example, the probability of not exceeding break-even:

= Probability of £20,000 loss or £Nil profit

= 0.1 + 0.125 = 0.225

The expected profit can be obtained by calculating expected contribution and subtracting expected overheads.

		£000
Expected contribution (£000)	$(100 \times 0.25) + (160 \times 0.5) + (200 \times 0.25)$	155
Expected overheads (£000)	$(120 \times 0.4) + (100 \times 0.5) + (90 \times 0.1)$	(107)
		———
Expected profit		48
		———

(c) The approach explained in (b) can be applied by developing a **computer simulation** of the expected budgeted profit. Rather than carrying out the restricted numerical analysis in (b), a random sampling program is employed to facilitate the calculation of profit and associated joint probability. The results are shown as a probability distribution for profit.

Questions

1   Your organisation II (AAT CA D94)

Your organisation is about to commence work on the preparation of the forthcoming year's annual budget.

As assistant management accountant, you have been asked to assist budget-holders and to respond to any queries which they may raise in the course of submitting their budget proposals.

The following notes are extracts taken from your organisation's budget manual.

'The key or principal budget factor in our organisation's budgetary process is sales volume ... The need for co-ordination in the budgetary process is paramount ...'

The marketing manager is a budget holder and she has approached you with a number of queries concerning the above extract.

Required

Prepare a memo for the marketing manager, which provides brief answers to the following queries.

(a) What is meant by the term *key factor* and why is the determination of this factor so important in the budgetary process?

(b) How can co-ordination be achieved?

2   Master budget

A master budget is created by the integration of many individual budgets.

(a) Outline what preliminary steps are necessary, before the preparation of budgets is commenced.

(b) Detail the main budgets you would normally expect to find in a manufacturing business.

(c) Give reasons why managers may be reluctant to participate in setting budgets.

3 Tiger plc

The managing director of Tiger plc is concerned that his company is not trading efficiently and is therefore losing profits. The company currently has no formal budgeting procedures. The financial accountant and production manager have produced the following information for the first six months of 19X5.

1 *Sales*

The company has one product, the CAT. Sales are seasonal with sales in the months of March, April and May being twice the amount sold in other months of the year. Tiger plc expects to sell 45,000 CATs in the first half of 19X5.

The current selling price is £25 per unit; there will be a price increase of 20% in April 19X5.

2 *Production*

Each CAT uses 10 kg of raw materials. Tiger plc has a contract with the raw material supplier for monthly deliveries at a fixed price of £60 per 100 kg. This contract expires at the end of April 19X5, when it is expected that the price will be increased by 25%.

Tiger has two categories of labour. Each CAT requires one hour's work by a skilled employee and two hours' work by an unskilled employee. The current wage rates are £5 per hour for skilled workers and £3 per hour for the unskilled.

Production overheads are estimated to be £5 per CAT.

3 *Stocks*

To keep the production line running smoothly, it is necessary for Tiger plc to hold enough raw material stocks to meet 80% of the following month's production quota.

To satisfy customer demand, the company holds enough stocks of finished goods to meet 50% of the next month's sales.

Expected stock levels

	1 January 19X5	30 June 19X5
Raw materials	40,000 kg	40,000 kg
Finished goods	2,500 units	2,500 units

Stocks of finished goods are valued at full production cost.

Required

(a) Prepare the following functional budgets for the six-monthly period to 30 June 19X5 for:

   (i)   material usage (in kg only)

   (ii) material purchases (in kg and £)

   (iii) labour utilisation, skilled and unskilled (in hours and £).

(b)   Prepare a budgeted profit and loss account for the six months to 30 June 19X5.

(c)   Write notes for a meeting with the managing director where you will have to explain why Tiger plc should introduce a budgeting system.

4   Loamshire County Council I

The information given below relates to the library services operated by the Leisure Services Committee of Loamshire County Council.

Loamshire County Council – Library Services – annual budget for the financial year 19X3/X4

	A	B	C	D	E
	Budget 19X2/X3 £000	Policy variations 19X3/X4 £000	A + B £000	Inflation allowance 19X3/X4 £000	Budget 19X3/X4 £000
Employees					
Professional	1,200	24	1,224	24	1,248
Clerical	2,100				
Other	305				
Premises	550	–	550	16	566
Supplies and services					
Book fund	1,700				
Cassettes and CDs	160				
Other	70	–	70	2	72
Transport	120	(10)	110	3	113
Establishment expenses	210				
Debt charges	550				
	6,965				
Income from fees, charges and trading	400	80	480	–	480
Cash allocated to the Library Service	6,565				6,565

Notes

1   The committee has approved the following policy variations on the 19X2/X3 budget:

♦   A 2% increase in salaries for all staff

♦   A reduction of £10,000 in the transport budget

♦   A reduction of £20,000 in CDs and cassettes

♦   Debt charges to be increased by £20,000

♦   See below for the treatment of the Book Fund

♦   There are no other policy variations

2   Inflation allowances for 19X3/X4 allowed on the base budget (Column A) and the policy variations (Column B) are as follows.

♦   2% for all employees

♦   4% for the Book Fund, CDs and cassettes

♦   3% for all other expenditure except debt charges for which there is no inflation allowance

3   Income to rise by 20% in 19X3/X4 cash terms

4   It has been decided that the amount of cash allocated to the Library Service in 19X3/X4 will be exactly the same as in 19X2/X3. Any shortfall after allowing for other policy changes will be met by a reduction in the Book Fund.

Required

(a)   As assistant accountant, you have been asked to draft a budget for the financial year 19X3/X4 to give effect to the decisions which have been taken by the Committee by completing the columns in the above table. Work to the nearest £000. Some entries have been already been given to start you off. (**Hint:** Work out the budgets for all remaining items leaving the calculation of the Book Fund till the last; the 19X3/X4 Book Fund budget will be the balancing figure in column E.)

(b)   What is the budgeted percentage reduction in the Book Fund in real terms?

5   Product Q (AAT J95)

Product Q is another product which is manufactured and sold by Henry Limited. In the process of preparing budgetary plans for next year, the following information has been made available to you.

1   Forecast sales units of product Q for the year = 18,135 units

2   Closing stocks of finished units of product Q at the end of next year will be increased by 15% from their opening level of 1,200 units.

3   All units are subject to a quality control check. The budget plans are to allow for 1% of all units checked to be rejected and scrapped at the end of the process. All closing stocks will have passed this quality control check.

4   Five direct labour hours are to be worked for each unit of product Q processed, including those which are scrapped after the quality control check. Of the total hours to be paid for, 7.5% are budgeted to be idle time.

5   The standard hourly rate of pay for direct employees is £6 per hour.

6   Material M is used in the manufacture of product Q. One finished unit of product Q contains 9 kg of M but there is a wastage of 10% of input of material M due to evaporation and spillage during the process.

7   By the end of next year, stocks of material M are to be increased by 12% from their opening level of 8,000 kg. During the year, a loss of 1,000 kg is expected due to deterioration of the material in store.

Required

(a)   Prepare the following budgets for the forthcoming year.

   (i)   Production budget for product Q, in units.

   (ii)   Direct labour budget for product Q, in hours and in £.

   (iii)   Material usage budget for material M, in kg.

   (iv)   Material purchases budget for material M, in kg.

(b)   The supplier of material M has warned that available supplies will be below the amount indicated in your budget for part (a) (iv) above.

   Explain the implications of this shortage and suggest *four* possible actions which could be taken to overcome the problem. For each suggestion, identify any problems which may arise.

Summary

This chapter contains the detail of how budgets are administered and prepared.

The budget must be prepared in a logical and orderly manner, ensuring co-ordination and co-operation between departments and different levels of management. Final proposals must be fully understood and accepted by all involved via a clear set of instructions and detailed discussions where necessary.

You should be prepared to discuss the types of budgets that may be required for a particular business and how they might be prepared, probably with numerical illustrations.

CHAPTER 5

Budgetary Control and Responsibility Accounting

Objectives

This chapter explains how to prepare a flexed budget and how to use budgets to control costs and motivate the workforce. It covers the following performance criteria.

8.1.2 Relevant individuals are given the opportunity to raise queries and clarify forecasts.

8.1.4 The validity of forecasts is reviewed in the light of any significant anticipated changes.

8.2.4 Discussions with budget holders are conducted in a manner which maintains goodwill.

8.3.1 Budget figures are checked and reconciled on an ongoing basis.

8.3.2 Actual cost and revenue data are correctly coded and allocated to responsibility centres.

When you have completed this chapter, you should be able to:

◆ prepare a flexed budget

◆ understand the technique of zero based budgeting

◆ understand the importance of staff participation in budget setting

◆ understand how budgets can be used to motivate staff

◆ prepare performance reports for responsibility centres, showing awareness of the ways in which staff react to targets

◆ understand how computers can be used in budget preparation.

Control against budgets

So that managers can exercise control, the **actual results** of the business will be reported period by period to the managers responsible and will be **compared with the budgeted allowance**. Any discrepancies will be investigated and action will be taken either to modify the budget in line with current conditions or (in most cases more desirable) to adjust future performance so that the discrepancies will be eliminated in the longer run.

These deviations, in money value, between an item and the corresponding budget are **variances**, the computation of which will be covered in Chapter 7.

Feedback

The reporting of actual results and of variances from plan is sometimes referred to as the feedback arising from the budgetary control system.

Feedback is the process of continuous self-adjustment of a system. It requires some predetermined standards against which to compare actual results. Any differences between the actual results and standard targets which are outside **tolerance limits** will indicate the need for action to be taken in an attempt to bring about consistency between actual and target.

Feedback is therefore a fundamental part of any system of control including financial control systems such as **budgetary control**.

Timing of feedback

Ideally feedback should take place with **as little delay as possible** from the occurrence of the event it reports. If there is undue delay then, in the intervening period, the underlying position itself may alter; there is then the danger that action correctly taken, given the information contained in the feedback report, will not be the action required by the position then existing.

It is possible that delay in feedback may **increase**, rather than reduce, deviations from target.

Analysis of variances

The identification of variance from budget is only the first step in exercising control. So that effective action can be taken it will be necessary to identify:

♦ *who* was responsible for its occurrence – **analysis by responsibility**

♦ *why* the variance has arisen – **analysis by cause**.

Analysis of variances by responsibility

With a well-designed budgetary control system the analysis of variances by responsibility is simple because the organisation will have been subdivided into budget centres which represent areas of responsibility (hence also known as *responsibility centres*) and separate operating statements will be prepared for each. For this to operate effectively, an integral part of the budgeting process will be to ensure that actual cost and revenue data are correctly coded and allocated to responsibility centres.

The general title for such a system is *responsibility accounting*; that is, a system which recognises various decision centres within a business and traces the results of those decisions to the individual managers who are primarily responsible for making them.

Analysis of variances by cause

In dealing with the analysis of variances by cause (whether sales variances or cost variances) one will be dealing always with two aspects:

♦   a **physical aspect** – quantities of products sold, or material used or hours worked, for example

♦   a **pricing aspect** – the selling price per unit in the case of sales; the cost price per unit in the case of materials, labour and other expenses. (The cost of labour is, of course, the rate of pay.)

In some cases, it may not be possible to identify quantity changes without more effort than would be justified by any improvement in control, but in these cases it must be recognised that this weakness does exist in the control being exercised.

Flexible budgetary control

In connection with expense budgeting, the budget working sheets should include some indication of the **'basis of variability'** of each item of cost.

The most common general bases of variability of costs are **sales** or the **volume of productive output**. In some systems of budgetary control, therefore, costs are divided between those which tend to **vary** with the output or sales achieved, and those which tend to remain **fixed** regardless of sales or the volume of output over an expected range of volumes.

This distinction having been established then, for variable costs, it is possible to establish in any period an allowable level of cost appropriate to the output actually achieved. This new level is known as the *budget allowance* for that volume of output. The total variance from the original budget figure will then be divided into two parts:

♦   The difference between the *original budget* and the *budget allowance*, assumed to arise from the nature of the business. This is sometimes referred to as an **'activity variance'** and may be excluded from sectional control reports.

♦   The difference between the *budget allowance* and the *actual cost incurred*. This, by definition, should not have occurred and might be thought of the **'controllable variance'** of the manager concerned.

A system incorporating budget allowances is referred to as *flexible budgetary control*.

This idea has been seized on by writers of textbooks and setters of assessment questions and converted into the concept of **'flexible budgets'**; in other words, at the beginning of the year there should be a schedule showing what the various cost allowances would be at various levels of output. With spreadsheet packages being used to assist budgeting, it is now becoming more common in practice.

Example: flexible budgetary control

You are the budget officer of Majestic Limited, which produces a single product. The following forecasts have been prepared from the best information available for the production costs to be incurred at the highest and lowest production levels likely to be encountered in any particular period.

	Production level	
	10,000 units £	20,000 units £
Direct materials	2,000	4,000
Direct labour	15,000	30,000
Warehouse rental	8,000	13,000
Machine maintenance	2,400	3,000
Factory rent, rates, etc	4,000	4,000
Factory power	4,500	6,300

Machine maintenance is under contract with the machine supplier. The period cost is based upon the production level and is charged at £15 per 100 units, with a minimum charge payable of £2,400 per period.

Warehouse rent is fixed per warehouse per period. One warehouse is sufficient to cope with the storage demands up to 12,500 units. Should production exceed this level, a further warehouse will need to be rented for the period, at an additional cost of £5,000. This will give sufficient space to cover the highest production level.

All other variable costs and the variable part of semi-variable costs follow constant linear patterns.

Required

Prepare a set of flexible budgets which show the budget allowance for the period for the following activity levels: 10,000 units; 12,500 units; 15,000 units; 17,500 units; 20,000 units.

Solution

The following steps illustrate a good approach to such a question. You may like to try preparing your own answer as we go through before looking at our solution at the end.

1   **Draw up a proforma statement**.

This will have the cost headings listed down the left-hand side and columns headed up with each production level; in this case, five columns will be needed. It is also a good idea to have an additional column next to the cost headings in which to insert references to workings (eg 'Note 2' etc).

The statement should also have a heading.

2   **Insert known figures**

You have already been given the costs for the lowest and highest production levels, so put these in.

3   **Deal with the particular costs you have further information about** (in this case, machine maintenance and warehouse rental).

Machine maintenance

This cost will be fixed up to a certain production level (to cover the minimum charge) and will then rise linearly (at £15 per 100 units or £0.15 per unit).

The level up to which the minimum charge is applicable is £2,400/£0.15 = 16,000 units. So the charge for the 12,500 and 15,000 unit levels will also be £2,400.

For 17,500 units the charge will be 17,500 × £0.15 = £2,625 and for 20,000 units it will reach 20,000 × £0.15 = £3,000 (as given)

These can now be inserted in your statement.

Warehouse rental

This is an example of a 'stepped' fixed cost. It will remain at £8,000 for all levels up to (and including) 12,500 units, and will rise to £13,000 for all levels above this.

These can now be inserted in your statement.

4   **Deal with remaining costs**

These will be strictly fixed, strictly variable or semi-variable.

Strictly fixed costs

These will be obvious – here, factory rent and rates must be fixed within the range, as the costs for the lowest and highest production levels are the same.

Insert this fixed cost across all levels on your statement.

Strictly variable costs

Invariably, direct materials and direct labour costs will be strictly variable. You can see here that, as the production level doubles, so does the cost. Use either level to determine the cost per unit.

Direct materials: £2,000/10,000   =   £0.20 per unit

Direct labour: £15,000/10,000   =   £1.50 per unit

Use these to calculate the appropriate cost for the other levels and insert them on the statement.

Semi-variable costs

These costs will not be the same for the two extreme levels, but they will not increase proportionately from one to the other either. If you are not sure, calculate a cost per unit at the two levels; these will not be the same, as they would be if the cost were strictly variable.

In this example, the power cost is semi-variable. It can be split between the fixed and variable elements by the 'high-low' method which we saw in Chapter 3.

	Production level (units)	Cost (£)
Highest	20,000	6,300
Lowest	10,000	4,500
Change	+10,000	+1,800

Variable cost = £1,800/10,000 = £0.18 per unit

Using the lowest level to determine the fixed cost element.

	£
Total cost	4,500
Less: variable element (10,000 × £0.18)	(1,800)
Fixed element	2,700

So for each level, the total power cost can be calculated as follows.

£2,700 + £0.18 × Production level

For example, the cost for 15,000 units will be as follows.

£2,700 + £0.18 × 15,000 = £5,400

The remaining costs can be calculated in this way and the statement completed, as below.

	Production level				
	10,000 units	12,500 units	15,000 units	17,500 units	20,000 units
	£	£	£	£	£
Direct materials	2,000	2,500	3,000	3,500	4,000
Direct labour	15,000	18,750	22,500	26,250	30,000
Warehouse rental	8,000	8,000	13,000	13,000	13,000
Machine maintenance	2,400	2,400	2,400	2,625	3,000
Factory rent, rates	4,000	4,000	4,000	4,000	4,000
Factory power	4,500	4,950	5,400	5,850	6,300
Total	35,900	40,600	50,300	55,225	60,300

Budgetary control statement

A typical continuation to the above example would be the requirement to produce a budgetary control statement (or **budget report**) given some actual data for the period.

Example: budgetary control statement

In period 3 Majestic Limited produced 17,500 units and incurred the following costs.

	£
Direct materials	3,200
Direct labour	29,750
Warehouse rental	13,000
Machine maintenance	3,150
Factory rent, rates, etc	3,800
Factory power	4,720

The budgetary control statement will compare these costs with the relevant budget allowances from the flexible budget to highlight variances. In this case, the relevant budget is that for 17,500 units.

	Budget £	Actual £	Variance £
Direct materials	3,500	3,200	300 F
Direct labour	26,250	29,750	3,500 A
Warehouse rental	13,000	13,000	–
Machine maintenance	2,625	3,150	525 A
Factory rent, rates, etc	4,000	3,800	200 F
Factory power	5,850	4,720	1,130 F
	55,225	57,620	2,395 A

You may then be asked to comment on the variances, suggesting any further investigations or action that might be required.

Zero-based budgeting (ZBB)

ZBB (or priority-based budgeting) is a **cost justification technique** first developed by Texas Instruments, which is of particular use in controlling the costs of **service departments and overheads**. It does not simply look at last year's budget and add or subtract a little, but starts 'from scratch' each time a budget is prepared. It is particularly applicable for service cost centres, for non-product costs.

ZBB involves the following:

♦ developing **decision packages** for each company activity

♦ **evaluating and ranking** theses packages

♦ **allocating resources** to the various activities accordingly.

Decision packages include the following information:

♦ The **function of the activity** or department. This sets out the minimum goals that it must achieve.

♦ The **goal** of the department. This details the aim of the department – what it would like to achieve.

♦ The **measure of the performance** of the department.

♦ The costs and benefits associated with **different ways of organising the department** (at different levels of funding).

♦ The **consequence of non-performance** of the activity or department.

Advantages of ZBB

♦ It establishes minimum requirements for service departments; ranks departments; and allocates resources.

♦ It produces a plan to work to when more resources are available.

♦ It makes managers think about what they are doing.

♦ It can be done annually, quarterly, or when crises are envisaged.

Disadvantages of ZBB

♦ It takes up a good deal of management time and so may not be used every year.

♦ It generates a great deal of paper, requires education and training, and results may be initially disappointing.

♦ It is costly.

Most budgets are prepared on an **incremental basis**. In other words, based on last time's figures plus/minus an incremental amount to cover inflation, etc. However, this technique has the obvious disadvantage of perpetuating poor spending control. As an alternative ZBB may be employed.

Use of budget information to control and motivate

In addition to asking you to analyse and explain variances, assessments frequently require a discussion on whether the budgeting procedures used within an organisation are **likely to achieve their aims**.

These aims, and the methods used to achieve them, can be broadly categorised as follows.

♦   Efficient management – **management by exception**

♦   Motivation of workforce – **responsibility accounting**

Management by exception

The features of this method of reporting are that:

(a)   attention is drawn only to areas where operations are seen to be **'out of control'**

(b)   this may be achieved by identifying those variances that are deemed to be **'exceptional'**

(c)   only these variances will be **investigated** and (where possible) **corrected**

(d)   **management time and expertise** are utilised where it can be most effective in improving the efficiency of future operations.

For it to be effective, it is important that:

♦   exceptional variances are **correctly isolated**

♦   only such variances owing to **factors capable of correction** be considered for investigation

♦   **costs and benefits of investigation** are assessed.

Chapter 7 will cover the investigation of variances in greater depth.

Responsibility accounting

The aim of a responsibility accounting system is to **motivate management** at all levels to work towards the company's objectives with the minimum of direction.

What is involved?

(a)   The use of budgets as **'targets'** against which management performance may be measured and (often) rewarded.

(b)   The presentation of 'performance reports' relating to particular responsibility centres. These centres fall into three categories as follows.

   (i)   **Cost centre** or expense centre where a manager is held responsible for control of expenditure.

   (ii)   **Profit centre** where a manager is held responsible for control of sales revenue and expenditure.

   (iii) **Investment centre** where a manager is held responsible for investment decisions as well as the control of sales revenue and expenditure.

(c)   The requirement that the person deemed responsible for that area give **explanations of significant variances** shown therein.

Assessments on this subject tend to concentrate on a practical application of the principles necessary for a system of responsibility accounting to work effectively, and often require the preparation of a **draft performance report**, or the criticism of such a report. An in-depth theoretical knowledge of the work carried out in this field is not needed; a commonsense approach to a practical problem suffices.

Three main areas need to be examined in relation to the use of budgets in responsibility accounting:

(a)   **participation** in budget setting

(b)   budgets as **motivational targets**

(c)   **performance evaluation and reward**.

The conclusions under each of these headings are largely common sense – you should try to think up practical examples in relation to your own position in study or at work to help you remember them.

Participation

Conventional wisdom suggests that managers should be encouraged to **participate in the budget setting process** and that the budget should be built up from the lower rungs of management (**'bottom up' budgeting**) rather than imposed from above ('top down' budgeting). These are the **advantages**:

♦   managers will then feel that **they 'own' the budget** and will therefore be more committed to the targets and motivated to achieve them

♦   operating managers are often the only people with **sufficient detailed knowledge** to develop a meaningful budget.

However, there are **disadvantages to participation**.

♦   The objectives of the managers and the objectives of the organisation may not be the same. **'Goal congruence'** does not automatically result from empowering managers to develop their own budgets.

♦   Operating management may use their knowledge to **manipulate the budget**. They may deliberately set targets that they cannot fail to achieve, particularly if bonuses are awarded for meeting the budget.

♦   **Managers may not wish to participate** in the budget setting process. This may be because:

(i)   they simply want to know what their targets are

(ii)   they do not have the technical expertise to participate in budget setting

(iii)   they do not have the necessary commitment to the organisation

(iv)   they feel that the budget will be 'used against them'.

Budgets as motivational targets

In general, it is accepted that corporate objectives are more likely to be met if they are expressed as **quantified targets**, often in the form of budgets.

If a target is to have any influence on performance:

◆   the recipient must be aware of its existence and feel committed to achieving it

◆   it must be set at the right level of difficulty to act as a motivator; both unrealistic and over-generous targets will be demotivational

In theory, there may be a need for two budgets to be prepared for the same area.

◆   One should be a **challenging (aspirations) budget** to motivate the manager

◆   The second should be a lower, and more realistic, **expectations budget** for planning and decision purposes.

Care should be taken to **reward success** as well as penalising failure, in order that a benefit is perceived in bettering rather than just achieving the target.

Budgets become stronger motivators as they become tighter up to a point, but thereafter motivation declines. The **optimal degree of tightness** depends on both the situation and the personality of the individuals concerned.

Performance evaluation and reward

Managers should only be held accountable for **items over which they have control**, and measures of performance should be devised that promote decisions in line with corporate objectives.

Thus a manager of a **profit centre** may be judged by variances affecting sales and direct costs (before allocated fixed costs); the performance of the centre itself will be measured by direct controllable contribution (having accounted for costs that are directly attributable to that centre, but not necessarily all controlled by the manager).

There are three main styles of management in the use of budget performance reports:

(a)   the *budget-constrained* style, which lays particular emphasis on results being closely in accordance with the budget plan

(b)   the *profit-conscious* style, which is less concerned with current deviations from budget than with a manager's ability to achieve a trend of results which is acceptable in relation to changing conditions

(c)   the *non-accounting* style, which tends to disregard accounting reports as a means of measuring management performance and instead looks at factors such as:

♦   the number of customer complaints or substandard items produced

♦   staff turnover

♦   morale in the department

♦   other qualitative measures

Of the three styles, the middle is probably the most successful in achieving the company's long-term goals. The first creates good cost consciousness but also a great deal of tension between a manager and his subordinates, and manipulation of accounting information. The last promotes general good morale, but managers have a low involvement with costs.

Performance-related pay

Many managers feel the full effect of responsibility accounting by having some, or even all, of their remuneration in the form of **performance-related pay,** such as bonuses. They are therefore not only measured against budget but are paid in relation to it as well. In many cases performance-related pay has been motivational but it can result in a great deal of hard feeling and resentment if not implemented sensitively and consistently.

♦   Managers need to be aware of the **organisation's objectives**; these must be achieveable and they must feel that the budget is consistent with them.

♦   Managers must have **goal congruence** with the organisation to the extent that they want to achieve the objectives and are challenged by them.

♦   Managers must have the **information, resources and skills** required to achieve the expected performance; they must feel they can influence achievement of the objectives.

♦   The **level of performance-related pay** should be high enough to motivate managers, and keep motivating them (there should be no caps).

Example: responsibility accounting

A conference centre has a newly appointed management accountant who has sent the following report to the supervisor of the restaurant. Prior to the receipt of this report, the restaurant supervisor has been congratulating herself on a good start to the year, with a substantial increase in the use of the restaurant.

To: Restaurant supervisor   Date: 5 April

From: Management accountant

Subject: Performance report

As part of the campaign to improve efficiency within the conference centre, quarterly budgets have been prepared for each department.

I attach a performance report for your department for the three months to the end of March, showing all discrepancies between budgeted and actual expenditure.

'A' indicates an adverse variance and 'F' a favourable variance.

	Budget £	Actual £	Discrepancy £	
Food and other consumables	97,500	111,540	14,040	A
Labour - hourly paid	15,000	16,500	1,500	A
– supervisor	3,750	3,700	50	F
Power	8,500	9,250	750	A
Breakages	1,000	800	200	F
Allocated overheads	21,000	24,000	3,000	A
	146,750	165,790	19,040	A
Number of meals served	32,500	39,000	6,500	F

You have apparently incurred costs which exceed the budget by £19,040. Please explain this to me at the meeting of the management committee on 15 April.

Required

(a)   Discuss the various possible effects on the restaurant supervisor's behaviour caused by receipt of this report.

(b)   Redraft the performance report and supporting memorandum in a way which, in your opinion, would make them more effective management tools.

Solution

Before looking at the answer, have a go for yourself. Jot down the different aspects that need to be considered (headings) and the points that can be made under these headings, including relevant research findings where these are known.

The possible effects on motivation

♦ **The way in which the targets were communicated to, and understood by, the supervisor**

If a target is to have any influence on performance, the recipient must be aware of its existence and feel committed to achieving it. From the wording of the memo, it would seem likely that until she received the performance report the restaurant supervisor was unaware of the budget.

Furthermore, the reaction of the supervisor to the memo comparing the department's performance to a previously unheard-of budget is likely to be defensive and rebellious. With no knowledge of how the budget was calculated, the supervisor is very likely to devote time and energy to attacking the 'unfair budget'. How can management hope to obtain commitment by issuing budgets 'from on high', with no scope for consultation or explanation with those responsible for fulfilling the budget?

♦ **Does the supervisor feel able to achieve the target? Is she being held responsible for costs which she is unable to control? Has the budget been properly prepared?**

If a target is to act as a motivator the recipients must feel that they are able to reach the target by their own efforts. Clearly the supervisor is not in a position to influence the level of allocated overheads, which is presumably determined by the amount paid for such things as: rent; rates and administrative salaries; and the chosen method of allocation to the departments. Thus the inclusion of such costs in the performance report will demotivate the supervisor.

Also, she can hardly be held responsible for the fact that her own salary differs from the budget. Indeed, becoming aware that she has been paid less than anticipated is likely to alienate her from the senior management.

Finally, the variances have been calculated by comparing the original budget with actual costs. The original budget is based on an anticipated usage of the restaurant of 32,500 meals; in fact, 39,000 meals have been served. If the explanation of variances is to be meaningful it should have been based on a comparison of actual costs with flexed budget. (This has been done in the suggested redraft of the performance report.)

♦ **Is the supervisor being offered rewards for achieving the target?**

The memo with the report is very brief, concentrating on the fact that costs have been above budget, with no mention of the fact that the restaurant has served more meals than was anticipated. There is no indication that the supervisor is to be rewarded in any way for her efforts to increase the use of the restaurant, and the summons to explain the 'excessive' costs at a formal meeting seems threatening. This is likely to demotivate the supervisor. She will feel that the successful aspects of the restaurant's operation are being ignored while any less successful aspects that there might be are being unfairly highlighted.

♦ **Is the target of the right degree of difficulty?**

As discussed above, the target costs communicated to the supervisor in the performance report are unrealistic because they have been left at the level of the original budget and have not been flexed to take account of the greater use made of the restaurant. Unrealistic budgets are bound to demotivate. Indeed, rather than working to reach the target, management is likely to expend time and effort criticising the target as unfair.

♦ **Is the supervisor the sort of person who reacts well to targets?**

As a final consideration it is important to remember that even the most perfect responsibility accounting system will fail if the managers of the responsibility centres are the sort of people who find any target frightening and thus demotivating. Although there are such people, evidence supports the view that most managers are motivated by well-designed, clearly understood targets.

Revised performance report

With all these considerations in mind we can now redraft the performance report and memo in a form which is more likely to have a positive effect on the performance of the restaurant supervisor.

To: Restaurant supervisor   Date: 5 April

From: Management accountant

Subject: Performance report

I enclose a performance report for your department for the three months to the end of March. The aim of this report is to assist in the efficient use of resources by providing information about which costs differ from their expected level (the original budget figures), and why.

The original budget figures were based on last year's costs; I would like to meet you next Tuesday to discuss whether these figures are sensible targets for this year. I have tried to make the budget more realistic by adjusting the costs upward to reflect the increased use of the restaurant (the flexed budget figures). I have assumed that all controllable costs are entirely variable and have increased the original budget by a factor of 1.2 (39,000 ÷ 32,500). It may be that some of these costs have a fixed element, in which case I have been unduly generous. I would welcome any ideas you have as to:

♦ other adjustments that are necessary to the figures in this report; and

♦ how the budgets should be established for future periods.

Page 1/ 2

	Original budget	Flexed budget	Actual	Variance flexed budget to actual
Number of meals served	32,500	39,000	39,000	
Controllable costs	£	£	£	
Food and other consumables	97,500	117,000	111,540	5,460 F
Labour: hourly paid	15,000	18,000	16,500	1,500 F
Power	8,500	10,200	9,250	950 F
Breakages	1,000	1,200	800	400 F
	122,000	146,400	138,090	8,310 F
Allocated costs				
Overheads	21,000	21,000	24,000	3,000 A
	143,000	167,400	162,090	5,310 F

F = favourable variance
A = adverse variance

The restaurant is evidently being well-managed, with many more meals served than in the same period last year, whilst costs have risen by a small proportion. Following our discussion on Tuesday, the performance report, with any agreed amendments, will be reviewed at the meeting of the management committee on 15 April; please ensure you attend to participate in the discussion and explain the reasons for the variances.

Page 2/2

Budgets and budgetary control using a PC

General principles

Budget preparation requires a good deal of data analysis. For example **sales** have to be analysed by product groups, **direct costs** need to be analysed by areas of responsibility, **indirect costs** must be apportioned on some basis between cost centres, and finally **costs and revenues** are generally analysed over control periods. This type of analysis would be laborious by manual methods. However the advent of PCs has meant that tools for computation and analysis are readily available in **spreadsheet software**.

The user of a typical spreadsheet package can generally call upon the following features:

(a) *formulation* – the contents of a cell can be specified in a formula and the inputs of variables in the formula will produce the desired result on the spreadsheet

(b) *arithmetical operations* – the spreadsheet will sum the contents of cells and store the result in specified locations

(c)   *deletion* – the contents of a cell can be deleted if fresh data is to be input

(d)   *manipulation* – the contents of a cell can be copied or moved to another part of the spreadsheet.

Spreadsheets are particularly useful for analyses of **variances**, multi-period **cash budgets** and multi-period forecast profit and loss accounts and balance sheets (master budgets).

Being able to change variables and thus bring about an automatic change in all the cells affected by the calculation lets the cost accountant easily prepare complex analyses which are arithmetically correct.

Budgetary control using a PC

The essence of a system of budgetary control lies in its ability to produce various comparisons with the budget and to report the deviations or variations – **exception reporting**.

Flexible budgets have already been discussed. In this section we will turn our attention to ways in which computer systems can be used to aid the process of exception reporting.

(a)   **Sales reports**

A sales report generally makes its greatest impact if it contains the following details by product type:

(i)   sales for the control period

(ii)   budget for the control period

(iii)   variance for the control period

(iv)   sales year to date

(v)   budget year to date

(vi)   variance year to date ($\pm$);

(vii)   totals of the above.

A **budget file** is created showing the individual budgetary amounts for each product group month by month and in total. Summarised transactions are analysed by product group and accumulated, and variances for the control period are computed. Totals for the control period are then added to the corresponding brought forward figures in order to provide cumulative year to date totals. When the processing is complete the updated budget file is then printed out in order to provide a sales report that might look like Figure 5.1.

(b)   **Reporting on overhead costs**

A similar principle may be adopted in processing overhead costs. Costs are allocated to cost centres by coding all source documents with **both** expense type and cost centre identity. A record for each cost centre can be developed forming the 'expenses' ledger. When costs are extracted from the purchase invoice process, petty cash process and cash payments routines they are accumulated by type and by cost centre. These accumulated costs are then compared with the month's budgetary allowance and a variance extracted.

The current month totals are added to the year to date totals and the individual costs and variances are summed to provide a total cost variance for the month. The details are provided to the manager on a report that is shown in Figure 5.2.

Page 01

		Month			Year to date	
Product code	*Budget*	*Actual*	*Variance*	*Budget*	*Actual*	*Variance*
Shirts	XXX	XXX	XXX	XXX	XXX	XXX
Blousons	XXX	XXX	XXX	XXX	XXX	XXX
Jackets	XXX	XXX	XXX	XXX	XXX	XXX
Trousers	XXX	XXX	XXX	XXX	XXX	XXX
Knitwear	XXX	XXX	XXX	XXX	XXX	XXX
Tracksuit	XXX	XXX	XXX	XXX	XXX	XXX
Flying suit	XXX	XXX	XXX	XXX	XXX	XXX
	XXX	XXX	XXX	XXX	XXX	XXX

Figure 5.1:   Report – Monthly sales budget comparison

Expense			Month			Year to date	
		Budget	*Actual*	*Variance*	*Budget*	*Actual*	*Variance*
021	Salaries	XXX	XXX	XXX	XXX	XXX	XXX
022	Payroll costs	XXX	XXX	XXX	XXX	XXX	XXX
043	Travel	XXX	XXX	XXX	XXX	XXX	XXX
046	Entertainment	XXX	XXX	XXX	XXX	XXX	XXX
047	Recruitment	XXX	XXX	XXX	XXX	XXX	XXX
049	Training	XXX	XXX	XXX	XXX	XXX	XXX
067	Dep'n – car	XXX	XXX	XXX	XXX	XXX	XXX
068	Motor expenses	XXX	XXX	XXX	XXX	XXX	XXX
074	Leasing charges	XXX	XXX	XXX	XXX	XXX	XXX
094	Misc. expenses	XXX	XXX	XXX	XXX	XXX	XXX

Figure 5.2:   Monthly budgetary comparison

Questions

1   Excelsior Manufacturing Company

Excelsior Manufacturing Company produces a single product on an assembly line. As budget officer you have prepared the following production budgets from the best information available, to represent the extremes of high and low volume of production likely to be encountered by the company over a three-month period.

	Production of 4,000 units £	Production of 8,000 units £
Direct materials	80,000	160,000
Indirect materials	12,000	20,000
Direct labour	50,000	100,000
Power	18,000	24,000
Repairs	20,000	30,000
Supervision	20,000	36,000
Rent, insurance and rates	9,000	9,000

Supervision is a 'step function'. One supervisor is employed for all production levels up to and including 5,000 units. For higher levels of production, an assistant supervisor (£16,000) is also required. For power, a minimum charge is payable on all production up to and including 6,000 units. For production above this level, there is an additional variable charge based on the power consumed.

Other variable and semi-variable costs are incurred evenly over the production range.

Required

(a)   Prepare a set of flexible budgets for presentation to the production manager to cover the following levels of production over a period of three months:

(i)   4,000 units

(ii)   5,000 units

(iii)   6,000 units

(iv)   7,000 units

(v)   8,000 units

(b)   During the three months July to September (covering most of the summer holiday period) 5,000 units were produced. Costs incurred during the three-month period were as follows:

	£
Direct materials	110,000
Indirect materials	14,000
Direct labour	70,000
Power	18,000
Repairs	30,000
Supervision	20,000
Rent, insurance and rates	8,000

Note that *price variances* have been deducted from the figures for direct and indirect materials and *rate variances* have been deducted from the labour and supervision costs.

Prepare a budget report for presentation to the production manager. For each variance, suggest any further investigations which might be required and any action which might be taken by the production manager.

2   World History Museum (AAT CA J94)

The World History Museum has an Education Department which specialises in running courses in various subjects. The courses are run on premises which the museum rents for the purpose and they are presented by freelance expert speakers. Each course is of standard type and format and can therefore be treated alike for budgetary control purposes.

The museum currently uses fixed budgets to control expenditure. The following data shows the actual costs of the Education Department for the month of April compared with the budgeted figures.

Education Department – April

	Actual	Budget	Variance
Number of courses run	5	6	(1)
	£	£	£
Expenditure			
Speakers' fees	2,500	3,180	680
Hire of premises	1,500	1,500	–
Depreciation of equipment	200	180	(20)
Stationery	530	600	70
Catering	1,500	1,750	250
Insurance	700	820	120
Administration	1,650	1,620	(30)
	8,580	9,650	1,070

You have recently started work as the assistant management accountant for the museum. During a discussion with Chris Brooks, the general manager, she expresses to you some doubt about the usefulness of the above statement in providing control information for the Education Department manager.

Chris is interested in the possibility of using flexible budgets to control the activities of the Education Department. You therefore spend some time analysing the behaviour patterns of the costs incurred in the Education Department. Your findings can be summarised as follows:

1   Depreciation of equipment is a fixed cost.

2   Administration is a fixed cost.

3   The budget figures for the catering costs and insurance costs include a fixed element as follows.

   Catering   £250

   Insurance   £100

   The remaining elements of the catering and insurance costs follow linear variable patterns.

4   All other costs follow linear variable patterns.

Required

(a)   Use the above information to produce a budgetary control statement for April, based on a flexible budget for the actual number of courses run.

(b)   Calculate the revised variances based on your flexible budget.

(c)   Chris Brooks's interest in the control aspects of budgeting has been sparked by her attendance on a course entitled *Budgetary control for managers*. She has shown you the following extract from the course notes she was given:

   'A system of participative budgeting involves managers in the process of setting their own budgets. Participative systems are likely to be more successful in planning and controlling the activities of an organisation.'

   Write a brief memo to Chris Brooks which explains the advantages and disadvantages of participative budgeting as a part of the budgetary planning and control process.

3   Responsibility accounting

A company manufactures a range of products by passing materials through a number of processes. A number of service departments provide support to the production processes.

(a)   Define *responsibility accounting* and comment on the application of responsibility accounting in the context of the above situation.

(b)   Explain how responsibility may be shared in respect of the cost of the maintenance department and suggest ways in which the management accounting system may assist in recognising such shared responsibility.

(c)   Explain ways in which the provision of more information need not lead to more effective management of a cost centre.

4   Henry Limited (AAT J95)

Data

You work as the assistant to the management accountant for Henry Limited, a medium-sized manufacturing company. One of their products, product P, has been very successful in recent years showing a steadily increasing trend in sales volumes.

Sales volumes for the four quarters of last year were as follows.

	Quarter 1	Quarter 2	Quarter 3	Quarter 4
Actual sales volume (units)	420,000	450,000	475,000	475,000

A new assistant has recently joined the marketing department and she has asked you for help in understanding the terminology which is used in preparing sales forecasts and analysing sales trends.

She has said: 'My main problem is that I do not see why my boss is so enthusiastic about the growth in product P's sales volume. It looks to me as though the rate of growth is really slowing down and actually stopped in Quarter 4. I am told that I should be looking at the deseasonalised or seasonally adjusted sales data but I do not understand what is meant by this'.

You have found that product P's sales are subject to the following seasonal variations:

	Quarter 1	Quarter 2	Quarter 3	Quarter 4
Seasonal variation (units)	+25,000	+15,000	0	−40,000

Required

(a)   Adjust for the seasonal variations to calculate deseasonalised or seasonally adjusted sales volumes (ie the trend figures) for each quarter of last year.

(b)   Assuming that the trend and seasonal variations will continue, forecast the sales volumes for each of the four quarters of next year.

(c)   Prepare a memorandum to the marketing assistant which explains the following.

(i)   What is meant by seasonal variations and deseasonalised or seasonally adjusted data.

(ii)   How they can be useful in analysing a time series and preparing forecasts.

Use the figures for product P's sales to illustrate your explanations.

Further data

The marketing assistant has now approached you for more help in understanding the company's planning and control systems. She has been talking with the distribution manager who has tried to explain how flexible budgets are used to control distribution costs within Henry Limited. She makes the following comment:

'I thought that budgets were supposed to provide a target to plan our activities and against which to monitor our costs. How can we possibly plan and control our costs if we simply change the budgets when activity levels alter?'

Required

(d)   Prepare a further memorandum to the marketing assistant which explains the following.

(i)   Why fixed budgets are useful for planning but flexible budgets may be more useful to enable management to exercise effective control over distribution costs.

(ii)   *Two* possible activity indicators which could be used as a basis for flexing the budget for distribution costs.

(iii)   How a flexible budget cost allowance is calculated and used for control purposes. Use your own examples and figures where appropriate to illustrate your explanations.

5   Trygon Limited

Six months ago, Parmod plc established a new subsidiary, Trygon Limited. Trygon was formed to assemble and sell computers direct to the public. Its annual budget was drawn up by Mike Barratt, Parmod's Finance Director. Trygon's plant was capable of producing 150,000 computers per year although the budget for the first year was only 80% of this amount. Factory overheads – defined as all factory fixed costs other than labour – were to be charged to finished stocks **at all times** on the basis of this 80% activity, irrespective of actual activity.

Trygon had entered into an agreement with the employees whereby their wages were guaranteed provided the employees made themselves available to produce 120,000 computers per year. Because of this agreement, the labour element in finished stocks was always to be based on the production level of 120,000 computers. If output exceeded the 120,000 units, additional overtime equivalent to £70 per computer would be paid. Managers were also to be given a bonus of £15 per computer produced in excess of 120,000 units in the year.

At the beginning of the year, Mike had given all the managers a financial statement showing the annual budget (based on 80% activity) and the effect of operating at only half the planned activity. This is reproduced below.

Trygon Limited budgeted profit for the year to 31 December 19X6

Activity	Annual budget £	40% £
Direct materials	24,000,000	12,000,000
Direct labour	7,200,000	7,200,000
Light, heat and power	4,000,000	2,200,000
Production management salaries	1,500,000	1,500,000
Factory rent, rates and insurance	9,400,000	9,400,000
Depreciation of factory machinery	5,500,000	5,500,000
National advertising	20,000,000	20,000,000
Marketing and administration	2,300,000	2,300,000
Delivery costs	2,400,000	1,200,000
Total costs	76,300,000	61,300,000
Sales revenue	84,000,000	42,000,000
Operating profit/(loss)	7,700,000	(19,300,000)

In preparing the financial statement, Mike Barratt had made the following assumptions:

(a) (i) unit selling prices were the same over the different activity levels

(ii) no quantity discounts or other similar efficiencies had been assumed for purchases.

(b) production fixed overheads comprised the depreciation of the machinery, the rent, rates and insurance, the production management salaries (other than any possible bonus) and part of the cost of light, heat and power.

Six months after Mike Barratt had issued the statement, you are called to a meeting of the directors of Trygon Limited. Anne Darcy, the managing director, tells you that production and sales for the year are likely to be 112,500 computers.

Required

(a) You are the Management Accountant to Trygon. Anne Darcy asks you to prepare a flexible budget for the year using the data given by Mike Barratt and assuming 112,500 computers are produced and sold. She also asks you to identity the budgeted profit.

Further data

On receiving your flexible budget, Anne Darcy reminds her fellow directors that Trygon plans a major marketing campaign at the beginning of the next financial year and this will require a building up of stocks in preparation for the campaign. The production director, Alan Williams believes it is feasible to increase production close to capacity without increasing any of the fixed costs. As a result, the Board agrees to budget for sales of 112,500 units by the year end but to produce at 95% capacity.

A discussion then followed about the role of budgeting in Trygon Limited "I do not know why we should take up all this time discussing budgets" said Anne Darcy. "They are not my figures. I had no say in their preparation. Let Mike Barratt take responsibility for them – after all, it was his budget – and let us get on with the job of building up a business."

"I agree," Alan Williams said. "I wish Mike would make up his mind what we are supposed to be doing. Are we just concerned with making short-term profits or are we supposed to be building up a quality product? Just what are our objectives when budgeting? Besides, you can prove anything with figures. Just look at the budget prepared by the Management Accountant compared with the annual budget prepared by Mike Barratt."

Anne Darcy then turns to you. "We need to resolve these issues. Will you please write a short report to the Board members giving us your advice."

Required

(b)   In response to Anne Darcy's request, you are asked to write a short report drawing on the information given above. The report should:

    (i)   recalculate the flexible budget based on production at 95% capacity assuming fixed overheads in finished stock are based on 80% activity.

    (ii)   explain why the revised flexible budget may differ from the one prepared in (a).

    (iii)   answer the issues raised by Alan Williams regarding the two different budget statements, the uncertainty about budgetary objectives and the manipulation of budget data.

    (iv)   briefly discuss whether or not Anne Darcy should have been responsible for preparing the original budget.

Summary

Variance analysis will be studied in detail in a later chapter; from this chapter you should be aware of how it relates to the following:

♦   management by exception

♦   responsibility accounting.

The main topics are as follows:

♦   the form and content of a performance report

♦   how people react to targets and how a system of responsibility accounting should be developed to get the best reaction from managers

---

CHAPTER 6

Standard Costing

Objectives

This chapter explains the various methods of setting cost standards, which are then used as the basis for budgets. It covers the following performance criterion.

7.1.3 Standard costs are compared with actual costs and any variances are analysed.

When you have completed this chapter, you should be able to:

♦   understand how cost standards are developed and set

♦   calculate standard costs.

Introduction

We have seen that a budget can be prepared for the period in question, actual costs can be accumulated and analysed after they have been incurred, and a comparison of budget and actual cost can subsequently be made. That is the basis of traditional cost accounting.

But waiting for actual cost information and analysing it against budget suffers from two basic problems:

(a)   any information obtained from the comparison may be **too late to be effective**

(b)   the cost headings are frequently too **general** to enable management to pinpoint reasons for the deviations from budget.

Standard costing provides us with a system that provides more immediate and detailed information to management as to **why** budgeted performance differs from actual performance.

Standard costing systems are widely used because they provide cost data which can be used for many different **purposes**, including the following.

(a)   To assist in budget setting and **evaluating performance.**

(b)   To act as a **control device** by highlighting those activities that do not conform to plan and thus alerting managers to those situations which may be 'out of control' and hence in need of corrective action.

(c)   To provide a **prediction of future costs** to be used in decision-making.

(d)   To **simplify** the task of tracing costs to products for **stock valuation**.

(e)   To provide a challenging **target** that individuals are motivated to achieve.

An effective standard costing system relies on **standard cost reports**, with variances clearly identified, to be presented in an intelligible form to management as part of the overall cost reporting cycle.

Definition: standard cost

A **standard cost** is a predetermined cost which is calculated from management's standards of efficient operation and the relevant necessary expenditure. It may be used as a basis for fixing selling prices, for valuing stock and work in progress, and to provide control over actual costs through the process of variance analysis.

Definition: standard costing

Standard costing is the preparation and use of standard costs, their comparison with actual costs, and the analysis of variances to their causes and points of incidence.

Methods of developing standards

The nature of standards

Whenever identical operations are performed or identical products are manufactured time and time again, it should be possible to decide in advance not only what they are likely to cost but also **what they** *ought* **to cost**. In other words, it is possible to set a standard cost for each operation or product unit, taking account of:

(a) **technical standards for the quantities of material** to be used and the working time required

(b) **cost standards for the material prices and hourly rates** that should be paid.

Standards from past records

Past data can be used to predict future costs if operating conditions are fairly constant between past and future time periods. This method may not be appropriate for newly introduced operations due to learning curve effects (see later).

The main disadvantage with this method is that past data may contain **inefficiencies** which would then be built into the standards.

Engineering standards

This involves engineers developing standards for materials, direct labour and variable overheads by studying the product and the production process, possibly with the help of time and motion studies. This method is particularly useful when managers are **evaluating new products** as the historical records are only of value where they can be related to operations needed to make the new product.

The main disadvantage is that engineering standards may be **too tight** as they may not allow for the behaviour of the workers.

Setting technical (usage) standards

Standard material usage

In setting material usage standards, the first stage is to define what **quantity of material** input is theoretically required to achieve one unit of measured output.

In most manufacturing operations the quantity or volume of product emerging will be less than the quantity of materials introduced. This type of **waste** is normal to the type of operation and the usage figure would be increased by an allowance for this normal waste.

Standard time allowed

The standard or allowed time for an operation is a **realistic estimate** of the amount of productive time required to perform that operation based on work study methods. It is normally expressed in standard hours.

Various allowances may be added to the theoretical operating time, to take account of **operator fatigue** and **personal needs** and periodical activities such as **machine setting, clearing up, regrinding tools and on-line quality inspection.** An allowance may also be made for **spoilt work** as indicated under material usage above, or for rectification of defects appearing in the course of processing.

Setting cost standards

Basic approach to prices

When **setting cost standards**, there are two basic approaches.

(a)   To use the **prices or rates which are** *current* **at the time the standards are set**.

This has the advantage that each standard is clearly identifiable with a known fact. On the other hand, if prices are likely to change then the standards based on them will have a limited value for planning purposes.

The standards would have to be revised in detail from time to time to ensure that they are up to date. If this is not done, then any differences between standard and actual costs are likely to be largely due to invalid standards.

(b)   To use a *forecast* **of average prices or rates over the period** for which the standard is to be used.

This can postpone the need for revision, but has the disadvantages that the standard may never correspond with observed fact (so there will be a price variance on all transactions) and that the forecast may be subject to significant error.

Neither method, therefore, will be ideal for all purposes and in deciding between them it will be necessary to consider whether the cost standards are being set principally to put a **consistent value on technical variances**, or as a **help in budgeting**, or as a **means of exercising cost control**, or merely to **simplify bookkeeping**.

Material price standards

In setting material price standards, a particular item of material may be purchased from several suppliers at slightly different prices; which price shall be adopted as standard? There are three possible approaches.

(a) *To identify the major supplier and to use his price as the standard*

This is particularly appropriate where there is no intention of buying large quantities from the alternative suppliers, but merely to use them as a means of ensuring continuity of supply should there be any delay or failure by the principal supplier.

(b) *To use the lower quoted price as the standard*

This method can be used if it is desirable to put pressure on the buyer to obtain price reductions from other suppliers.

(c) *To forecast the proportion of supplies to be bought from each supplier and to calculate a weighted average price as the costing standard*

This is the most satisfactory method for control purposes if the required forecast can be made with reasonable accuracy.

Another question in relation to material price standards is whether to include the cost of **carriage inwards** and other costs such as non-returnable packing and transit insurance. The object always will be to price incoming goods at their total delivered cost, so the costs such as those instanced above should be included in the standards.

Standard labour rates

When setting standard labour rates, one can either use basic pay rates only, or incorporate overtime premiums as well. The nature of the overtime work and the approach to cost control adopted by management will decide this issue.

(a) If a **normal level of overtime** work can be identified and is accepted as necessary, or if overtime is planned for the company's convenience, then the relative overtime premium payments will normally be included in the standard labour rate.

(b) If it is a management objective to **reduce or eliminate overtime working,** the standard rate may be restricted to basic pay.

(c) Where overtime is worked at the **request of particular customers,** then the related premium payments are a direct cost of the work done and would not be included in a standard rate which was applied generally to other work.

(d) Where part of employee remuneration takes the form of **incentive bonuses,** then it will be necessary to forecast the level of efficiency to be achieved and the bonus payments appropriate to that performance. These bonuses will then be included in the calculation of the standard rate.

Learning curves

The concept

There are certain types of industry where the unit of production changes **at regular intervals** rather than **the same** unit of production being manufactured for a very long period of time. Examples of such industries are clothing manufacture, where patterns change with the season and current fashion, and light engineering where many production runs are to a customer's particular specification.

In such industries it is known that the time taken to produce a unit in the early stages of a new product is significantly longer than the time per unit once the item has been manufactured for some time. The successive reduction in the time taken for each unit is caused by a **learning process affecting the labour force**.

Wright's law

When an operator is given a new task to carry out, it will initially take a long time, but as the operator becomes familiar with the routine, the time will diminish progressively until a **steady state** is reached.

The first observations of this phenomenon were made by TP Wright in the US aircraft industry and his findings were formalised as **Wright's law** which states:

'For any operation which is repeated, the overall average time for the operation will decrease by a fixed percentage as the number of repetitions is doubled'.

Wright found that the reduction percentage for aircraft manufacture was 20%, so that there was an 80% learning curve or a learning factor of 0.8.

Example: learning curve

The distinction between overall average time per unit and time to produce the latest unit is demonstrated in the following example of a firm experiencing a learning factor of 0.8.

A trial batch of 100 units of a new product is produced in an average time of 20 minutes per unit. Production times based on continually doubling the batch size would be as follows:

Batch quantity (units)	Cumulative quantity (units)	Overall average time per unit (minutes)	Total time (minutes)	Batch time (minutes)
100	100	20.00	2,000	2,000
100	200	$20 \times 0.8 = 16.00$	3,200	1,200
200	400	$16 \times 0.8 = 12.80$	5,120	1,920
400	800	$12.8 \times 0.8 = 10.24$	8,192	3,072

If the planned production of this item for the coming month was, say, 300 (over and above the initial 100 and making cumulative production 400), the total time and average time per unit for this 300 would be:

Total time for 300 units = 5,120 – 2,000 = 3,120 minutes

Average time for these units = 3,120 ÷ 300 = 10.4 minutes

From this example, it can be seen that the total estimated time to complete the total of 800 units is 8,192 minutes. This is considerably less than we would expect if there were no learning effect and each unit required 20 minutes, as in the first batch. In this case the total time required would be $800 \times 20 = 16,000$ minutes.

Effect of learning curve on budgeting

If it is known that a learning effect is likely to occur, it should be taken into account when **preparing budgets**.

When preparing cost budgets it must be remembered that costs other than the direct labour cost will be affected by the learning process. **Variable overhead costs** (typically machine power) are normally dependent on direct labour hours. A saving in labour hours will therefore result in cost savings on both labour and variable overhead.

Effect of learning curve on standard setting

When **setting a standard for labour time**, particularly at the onset of a new product's life, we must take into account the possibility of any learning curve.

Why not, then, set a standard at the steady state level? The drawback here is that this will initially cause **very high adverse variances**, and so may lead to **demotivation** of the workforce as a consequence.

Perhaps we may try to eliminate both of the preceding problems by continuously **resetting the standard** period on period to reflect the reduction in anticipated time that the learning effect causes. But this has two effects.

(a)   We lose the benefits that predetermined standards give.

(b)   The workforce may become disillusioned if they feel the standard is following the actual result and not vice versa.

In the real world the practical solution may well be as follows.

(a)   Set standards that management are aware of to compare to actual performance.

(b)   Ensure that workers do achieve maximum efficiency by **linking actual performance to rewards** – perhaps by some form of piece-rate working.

Types of standard

The way in which control is exercised and the interpretation and use of variances from standards will depend on which type of standard is used.

Ideal standards

In some cases standards are established on the assumption that machines and employees will work with **optimal efficiency** at all times, and that there will be no stoppages and no losses of material or services. Such standards would represent an ideal state of affairs and therefore the objectives they set are never achieved.

Managers who are responsible for the costs can hardly approve of targets which they can never reach and which, therefore, result in large adverse variances from the standards. This is demotivating for managers, particularly if there is an element of performance-related pay in their remuneration.

Attainable (expected) standards

In other cases the standards set will be those which are **reasonably attainable**, consideration being given to the state of efficiency which can be achieved from the existing facilities. There is no question of assuming, as for ideal standard costs, that production resources will be used at maximum efficiency.

A positive effort is still made to achieve a high level of efficiency, but there is no question of going beyond what is attainable.

Basic standards

A basic standard is one which, having been fixed, is not generally revised with changing conditions, but **remains in force for a long period of time**. It may be set originally having regard to either ideal or expected conditions. Under circumstances of rapid technological change or of significant price changes, basic standards are of limited value in relation to the achievement of the benefits outlined above.

There may be variations on these methods, but the aim should be to **select the standard cost which is likely to be the most realistic for the business concerned**. It should be remembered that standards are the yardstick against which efficiency is measured and therefore, if they are unrealistic then the variances will be of little meaning.

Advantages and disadvantages of standard costing

Advantages

The advantages of standard costing fall into two broad categories: **planning** and **control**.

Planning

Predetermined standards make the **preparation of forecasts and budgets** much easier. If the standards are to be used for these operational decisions then they must obviously be as accurate as possible. This again means that standards should be revised on a frequent basis.

Control

Control is primarily exercised through the comparison of standard and actual results, and the **isolation of variances**. This will highlight areas of apparent efficiency and inefficiency, and as necessary investigations as to the causes of the variance can be made. If these investigations discover the causes of the variances, then corrective action can be taken to improve efficiency in the future.

In addition to the above, there are subsidiary advantages such as:

(a)   If the standards are perceived to be attainable, then they will serve to **motivate the employees** concerned.

(b)   A **standard costing bookkeeping system** can be set up that will fulfil all requirements, for both internal and external reporting.

(c)   **Recording of stock issues is simplified,** as it is done at the standard price.

Disadvantages

A standard costing system is **costly** to set up and maintain, and standards must be **revised on a regular basis** to retain effectiveness. It is for this reason that standard costing is most effective for **well-established and repetitive processes**, so that the revisions of standards are kept to a minimum.

Valuing stocks of finished goods

Not all of the production in any period may be sold; some will be left in **closing stock**.

The stock can be valued at two different amounts: **actual cost** or **standard cost**.

Example: stock valuation

Let us assume that, for a particular business, only 7,500 of 8,000 units produced were sold in a particular period. The standard cost is £4 per unit. Total costs incurred were £37,000 which were £5,000 more than the flexed budget.

We could simply carry forward the balance of 500 units at the **standard cost** of £4 each (total £2,000), whilst transferring the 7,500 produced and sold to cost of sales.

Under this method, the £5,000 overspend would be written off in full against profits for the period.

If closing stock is to be carried forward at actual cost, then we must convert the stock value back to actual cost. This is done by transferring a proportion of the overspend back to finished goods stock, rather than writing it all off against profits.

The proportion would be $^{500}/_{8,000}$ since of 8,000 units produced, 500 are in stock and 7,500 have been sold.

Actual cost incurred in total to produce 8,000 items = £37,000.

Finished goods stock: $^{500}/_{8,000} \times £37,000 = £2,312.50$.

This is £312.50 higher than when valued at standard, representing the closing stock's share of the total overspend: $^{500}/_{8,000} \times £5,000 = £312.50$.

We have seen that valuing stock at standard or at actual cost will give two different results. The impact of this is that, since closing stock is valued differently, then under the two methods cost of sales would be different and so reported profit would also be different.

Thus:

	£	£
Stock at standard cost		
Actual cost of production	37,000.00	
Less closing stock	(2,000.00)	
Cost of sales		35,000.00
Stock at actual cost		
Actual cost of production	37,000.00	
Less closing stock	(2,312.50)	
Cost of sales		(34,687.50)
Net effect on profit		312.50

In this case, because of the overspend, stock at actual cost has a higher value than stock at standard cost. Consequently, valuing stock at actual rather than standard cost gives the following:

♦ a higher closing stock figure, so

♦ a lower cost of sales figure, and therefore

♦ a higher profit figure.

Points to note from the above:

♦ The result will only be a **timing difference** – after all, this period's closing stock will form next period's opening stock.

♦ **Both alternatives are used in practice.**

♦ What we are effectively doing is deciding whether or not to **capitalise part of the overspend** and carry it forward. There is an argument that says, if cost variances arise from factors peculiar to a particular period, then they should be written off in full in that period, since the profit figure will be distorted if this is not done. Thus we are really considering whether the cause of the variances is a normal business occurrence and, if it is, then we may well decide to pro-rate them over the cost of goods sold and closing stock.

♦ If the net production variance were favourable, then **actual cost would be lower than standard cost.** Thus valuing stocks at standard cost could lead to a higher reported profit figure.

In the absence of instructions to the contrary, always value stocks at standard cost in the assessment, since this avoids the need to pro-rate the variances.

Other issues when valuing finished goods stock

The point to note about valuing finished goods stock is that there **is no entirely objective way of doing it**. We have seen above that using standard or actual costs will nearly always give a different result. We also saw in Chapter 3 that using a marginal costing approach (ignoring fixed overheads) would give a different result from a total absorption costing approach. Remember too that standard costs can be on the basis of either TAC or MC.

The point to bear in mind in an assessment on finished goods stock is that the cost itself will always be borne by the business; the different bases for valuing the stock simply allows the business to defer some of the costs to a later period in finished goods stock. Applying the same policy to opening stock however will even out what is essentially a **timing difference**.

Questions

1   Standard revision

A company operates a system of 'rolling budgets' with quarterly reviews. What guidelines would you lay down for the revision of technical and cost standards?

2   Standards come unstuck?

A company manufactures a standard range of petroleum-based adhesives which are packaged to meet the requirements of particular distributors or industrial users. There are no catalogue prices, each batch being made for a particular customer and being priced by negotiation. Would a standard costing system be helpful to this company?

3   WH Limited I (AAT CA D94)

WH Limited uses a standard costing system which produces monthly control statements to monitor and control costs. One of their products is product M.

To manufacture product M, a perishable, high quality raw material is carefully weighed by direct employees. Some wastage and quality control rejects occur at this stage. The employees then compress the material to change its shape and create product M.

All direct employees are paid a basic hourly rate appropriate to their individual skill level and a bonus scheme is in operation. Bonuses are paid according to the daily rate of output achieved by each individual.

A standard allowance for all of the above operational factors is included in the standard cost of product M. Standard cost data for one unit of product M is as follows.

	Standard cost £ per unit
Direct material X: 4.5kg x £4.90 per kg	22.05
Direct labour: 10.3 hours x £3.50 per hour	36.05
Standard direct cost	58.10

The production manager has approached you for further explanations concerning the standard costing control system. He is particularly interested in understanding how the standard price is set per kg of material used.

Required

Write a memo to the production manager, explaining the following:

(a)   what information would be needed to determine the standard price per kg of material X;

(b)   the possible sources from which this information might be obtained.

4   Attainable and ideal standard

(a)   Explain the terms *attainable standard* and *ideal standard*, and explain briefly why attainable standards tend to be used in preference to ideal standards.

(b)   The budget for product A for a period is as follows:

Production	2,000 units
Sales	2,000 units: £15 per unit
Direct material cost	6,000 kg of XYZ: £2 per kg
Direct labour cost	4,000 hours: £2 per hour

Actual results for the period were:

Production	2,500 units
Sales	2,250 units: £15 per unit
Direct materials	5,000 kg purchased and consumed at a total cost of £12,000
Direct labour	6,000 hours at a total cost of £9,000

There were no opening stocks. It is company policy to value stocks at standard cost.

(i)   Prepare a statement of actual profit for the period.

(ii)   Calculate the following:

♦   material price variance

♦   material usage variance

♦   labour rate variance

♦   labour efficiency variance.

Summary

In this chapter, we have looked at the various ways of establishing standard costs within a standard cost reporting system.

The important differences between possible stock valuations and their impacts on profit have also been examined.

CHAPTER 7

Variance Analysis

Objectives

This chapter explains how the differences (variances) between standard costs and actual costs incurred are calculated and analysed in order to determine how the variance arose. We then see how variance analysis can be used to control costs. It covers the following performance criteria.

7.1.3 Standard costs are compared with actual costs and any variances are analysed.

7.2.1 Routine cost reports are analysed, compared with other sources of information and the implications of findings are identified.

7.2.4 Exception reports to follow up matters which require further investigation are prepared.

8.3.3 Variances are clearly identified and reported to management in routine reports.

8.3.4 Significant variances are discussed with managers and assistance is given to managers to take remedial action.

When you have completed this chapter you should be able to:

♦ calculate the following variances:

   – sales volume and price

   – materials price and usage

   – labour rate and efficiency

   – variable overhead price and efficiency

   – fixed overhead price, volume, efficiency and capacity

♦ understand what these variances measure

♦ interpret a report comparing actual costs with budgeted costs

♦ identify the possible causes of variances

♦ understand the ways in which variances may be interdependent

♦ understand and discuss the problem of identifying the person responsible for a particular variance.

Introduction

We have seen that standard costs are developed in advance of the period under review. During the course of that period, actual costs are compared with standard costs. Any variances are isolated for investigation as to their cause, enabling corrective action to be taken as soon as possible.

Management will wish to see a **clear and succinct summary** of the results for the period and in particular will want any unusual or unexpected items to be brought to their attention **(exception reporting)**. In general, this will take the form of a **reconciliation** between budgeted and actual profits which highlights the variances between them. To be useful as a management tool, the reconciliation should be part of an overall **report to management**.

Traditional variance analysis: a review example

You will have already covered as part of your Intermediate level studies the calculation of basic or 'traditional' cost variances.

The following budgeted and actual data for TJB Limited for 19X1 will be used to revise the principles and computations.

TJB Limited – budgeted profit for the year ending 31 December 19X1

Produce and sell 10,000 units

	Produce and sell 10,000 units		
		£	£
Budgeted sales	10,000 units		100,000
Production cost	£/unit		
Direct materials – 10,000 tons @ £1 per ton (1 ton per unit)	1.00	10,000	
Direct labour – 20,000 hours @ 50p per hour (2 hours per unit)	1.00	10,000	
Variable production overhead – 20,000 hours @ 25p per hour	0.50	5,000	
Fixed production overhead – 20,000 hours @ 75p per hour	1.50	15,000	
Total budgeted production cost	4.00		40,000
Budgeted profit for the period			60,000

During the year to 31 December 19X1, the following actual results were obtained.

TJB Limited – actual profit for the year ending 31 December 19X1

Production and sales	8,000 units
	15,500 hours worked on actual production

	£	£
Sales		96,000
Production cost		
Direct materials – 7,750 tons purchased and used (£1.0968)	8,500	
Direct labour – 16,500 hours paid (£0.4545 per hour)	7,500	
Variable production overhead incurred (15,500 hours @ £0.3548)	5,500	
Fixed production overhead incurred	15,500	
Total actual production cost		37,000
Total profit		59,000

The purpose of the analysis is to reconcile the budgeted profit of £60,000 to the actual profit of £59,000.

Such a reconciliation is a **budgetary control statement** or **budgetary control report**.

Cost variances

	Flexed budget cost of producing 8,000 units £	*Actual cost of producing 8,000 units* £	*Difference (variance)* £	
Direct materials	8,000	8,500	500	A
Direct labour	8,000	7,500	500	F
Variable production overhead	4,000	5,500	1,500	A
Fixed production overhead	12,000	15,500	3,500	A
Total	32,000	37,000	5,000	A

All these total variances can be analysed into at least two further types of variance:

(a)   a price variance

(b)   a usage or utilisation variance, when in some cases can be broken down further.

Total direct material cost variance

		£
(a)	The actual amount of material used at the actual price	8,500
(b)	The standard amount of material that should have been used for the actual production at the standard price – 8,000kg x £1	8,000
		500 A

To analyse this further we need first to get the **actual amount of material used** at the **standard price**: the direct materials price variance.

Direct materials price variance

	Tons	£
Actual materials purchased, at actual price	7,750	8,500
Actual materials purchased, at standard price per ton (£1)	7,750	7,750
Materials price variance	–	750 A

We next need to compare this with the standard materials that *should have been used* for that level of production: the direct materials usage variance.

Direct materials usage variance

	Tons	£
Actual materials used at standard price	7,750	7,750
Standard materials allowed for production achieved at standard price	8,000	8,000
Materials usage variance (@ £1 per ton)	250	250 F

Total direct material cost variance = £750 A + £250 F

= £500A

Total direct labour cost variance

		£
(a)	The actual hours paid at the actual rate per hour	7,500
(b)	The standard time allowed to produce the output, priced at the standard rate per hour (16,000 x £0.50)	8,000
		500 F

The total variance can be analysed into *price* and *usage* variances as with materials, but the usage variance is itself sub-analysed further into an *idle time* and a *utilisation or efficiency variance*, if idle time is present.

(a) *Labour usage: idle time*

The labour may be idle for part of the time it is being paid. There may be many reasons for this (eg machine breakdown, shortage of materials, power failure etc).

(b) *Labour usage: utilisation or efficiency*

When the labour is actually working it may actually produce more (or less) than the standard number of units per hour.

Rate of pay (price) variance

	Hours	£
Actual hours paid at actual rate per hour	16,500	7,500
Actual hours paid at standard rate per hour	16,500	8,250
Direct labour rate variance	–	750 F

Total labour usage variance

	Hours	£
Actual hours paid at standard rate per hour	16,500	8,250
Standard hours allowed for production achieved at standard rate per hour (50p)	16,000	8,000
Direct labour usage variance		250 A

This is then broken down into **idle time** and **efficiency**.

Idle time variance

The part of the total variance that is caused by labour not working for all the hours paid (16,500 hours paid – 15,500 hours worked).

	Hours	£
Actual hours paid at standard rate per hour	16,500	8,250
Actual hours worked at standard rate per hour (50p)	15,500	7,750
Direct labour idle time variance	1,000	500 A

Utilisation or efficiency variance

	Hours	£
Actual hours worked at standard rate	15,500	7,750
Standard hours allowed for production achieved	16,000	8,000
Direct labour efficiency variance	500	250 F

Make sure that you understand the labour cost variances.

The rate of **pay variance** (price) performs the usual role of accounting for that part of the total variance caused by the actual price being different from the standard price.

The idle time and efficiency variances simply explain (at the standard rate) the total usage variance: why a certain number of hours of labour was paid for and a different amount of output (measured in labour hours) was produced.

Total variable overhead cost variance

	Hours	£
Actual hours worked at actual cost per hour	15,500	5,500
Standard cost of overhead for production achieved (8,000 units x 2 hours x £0.25)	16,000	4,000
Total variable overhead variance	500 A	1,500 A

As with materials and labour, the total variable overhead variance is analysed further into a price variance and a usage variance.

Variable overhead price variance

	Hours	£
Actual hours worked at actual cost per hour	15,500	5,500
Actual hours worked at standard cost (25p/hour)	15,500	3,875
Variable overhead price variance		1,625 A

Variable overhead usage variance

	Hours	£
Actual hours worked at standard cost	15,500	3,875
Standard hours allowed for actual production achieved at standard cost	16,000	4,000
Variable overhead usage variance	500	125 F

Note: In our example, we have recovered variable overheads at the standard rate of 25p per labour hour. This infers that the incurring of variable overheads is related to **labour hours** worked. It is possible that variable overheads might depend on some other activity base, such as machine hours. Another alternative might be to compute a variable overhead rate per unit, in which case there would be no usage variance and the price variance will be equal to the total cost variance.

Total fixed overhead cost variance

	£
Actual fixed overhead cost	15,500
Standard cost absorbed into actual production (8,000 x £1.50 per unit)	12,000
Total fixed overhead cost variance	3,500 A

This is then analysed into price (expenditure) and volume variances. The volume variance is then sub-analysed into usage (efficiency) and capacity variances.

(a)   *Fixed overhead volume: usage (efficiency)*

Were the workforce inefficient, producing each unit in more than the standard number of hours? We already know from previous work on labour variances that in fact the workforce was efficient to the tune of 500 hours. This would, on its own, lead to **extra** production and **over-absorption** of fixed overheads. Thus this will in fact be a **favourable** element of the volume variance.

(b)   *Fixed overhead volume: capacity*

Another reason for producing fewer units would be if, instead of being inefficient, the workforce simply worked shorter hours in total during the period. The capacity variance compares the actual number of hours worked with the number of hours budgeted for the period. Here we have a shortfall of 4,500 hours, which will restrict production and thus absorption of fixed overheads.

Fixed overhead price variance

	£
Actual fixed overhead cost	15,500
Budgeted expenditure	15,000
Fixed overhead price variance	500 A

Fixed overhead volume variance

This is the under-absorption (at standard rates) due to the lower actual production level than that budgeted.

	Units	£
Actual production	8,000	
Budgeted production	10,000	
Fixed overhead volume variance (in units)	2,000	
Valued at standard absorption rate (£1.50 per unit)		3,000 A

The variance is adverse because we have under-absorbed fixed overhead by 2,000 units' worth. We thus require an extra charge to the cost account to compensate for this under-absorption. The £3,000 adverse volume variance can be analysed further.

Fixed overhead usage (efficiency) variance

	Hours
Actual hours worked for actual production	15,500
Standard hours allowed for actual production achieved	16,000
Efficiency variance @ £0.75 per hour	500 = £375 F

Fixed overhead capacity variance

	Hours
Actual hours worked	15,500
Budgeted hours for the period	20,000
Capacity variance @ £0.75 per hour	4,500 = £3,375 A

The two variances add up to the volume variance (£3,375 – £325 = £3,000 adverse), and shows that the principal reason for our under–production was a failure to devote sufficient hours to production (4,500 hours short). The workforce's efficiency could not make up for this.

Sales related variances

So far we have revised what you saw at Intermediate stage, namely cost variances. In order to be able to **reconcile budgeted profit fully to actual profit**, however, we need to look at how to analyse that most important element – **sales**!

The total sales variance compares budgeted sales with actual sales. This can then be sub-analysed into two further variances – **sales price** (the price we sold goods at) and **sales margin volume** (how many we sold).

Example: TJB Limited

TJB planned to sell all of the units that it budgeted to make in 19X1, at £10 per unit. In fact it only sold the 8,000 units made, at £12 per unit. Sales variances are analysed slightly differently to cost variances, as we shall see.

Sales margin volume variance

The sales margin volume variance seeks to analyse only the effect on profit of **selling more or fewer than was budgeted.** To do this it is necessary to ignore the cost of the units oversold or undersold. Profit will decrease as a result of selling 2,000 fewer than was budgeted not by £20,000 (2,000 x the budgeted selling price) but by 2,000 x budgeted selling price *less* the cost of those sales.

So in order to analyse this we need to work out the **standard margin on sales**.

	Standard £
Selling price	10
Cost	4
Standard margin	6

	Units
Budgeted sales	10,000
Actual sales	8,000
Sales volume variance	2,000

Sales volume variance at standard margin (2,000 x £6)	£12,000 A

Sales price variance

The sales price variance compares actual sales at actual selling price to actual sales at budgeted selling price.

	Unit	£
Actual sales at budgeted selling price	8,000	80,000
Actual sales at actual selling price (£12)	8,000	96,000
Sales price variance		16,000 F

We can see therefore that the total favourable sales variance of £4,000 is made up of an adverse volume variance of £12,000 compensated for by the favourable sales price variance of £16,000.

Comparison of budgeted with actual results

Having computed all the variances, we can now reconcile budgeted profit with actual profit. This is a more detailed version of the **budgetary control statement** in a slightly different format.

		£ Adverse	£ Favourable	£
Budgeted profit				60,000
Sales variances	Volume	12,000		
	Price		16,000	
		12,000	16,000	4,000
Cost variances				
Materials	Price	750		
	Usage		250	
Labour	Price		750	
	Idle time	500		
	Utilisation/efficiency		250	
Variable overheads	Price	1,625		
	Usage		125	
Fixed overheads	Price	500		
	Usage		375	
	Capacity	3,375		
Total / net cost variances		6,750	1,750	(5,000)
Actual profit				59,000

Price variances and foreign exchange fluctuations

An added complication you may encounter is where a direct cost is expressed in a foreign currency. If the price does not fluctuate, but the **rate of exchange** between sterling and the foreign currency does, then the price variance will be down to the fact that the exchange rate has made the actual price more or less expensive.

In the context of **responsibility accounting**, the manager in charge of usage and purchasing should only be held accountable for variances caused in this manner if he can control them – which he can only do if he is a position to hedge against foreign currency risk. Usually, therefore, **exchange rate price variances** should not be included in a budgetary control statement for operating managers.

Example: exchange rate price variances

Gulliver Limited sources its copper components from the US, renegotiating its contract every three months. From January 19X6 (when the exchange rate was $1.50 : £) to March 19X6 copper costs $15 per kilo. Over this period the £ : $ exchange rate changed twice – at the beginning of February (to $1.55 : £) and again at the beginning of March (to $1.60 : £). Purchases were as follows:

January	10,000 kilos
February	12,000 kilos
March	13,500 kilos

What is the price variance due to exchange rate fluctuations?

Solution

Since it is a fixed price contract the only price variance is down to exchange rate differences as follows.

Month		*January*	*February*	*March*
Kilos purchased		10,000	12,000	13,500
Agreed price at $15		$225,000	$180,000	$202,500
Exchange rate		$1.50	$1.55	$1.60
		£	£	£
Actual cost in £	Agreed price/ prevailing exchange rate	150,000	116,129	126,562
Standard cost	Agreed price/ $1.50	150,000	120,000	135,000
Exchange rate price variance		0	3,871 F	8,438 F

Measuring the significance of variances

Introduction

As we have seen, the key tool for management control within a standard costing system is some form of *variance analysis report* or *budgetary control statement*. The aim is to prepare a report to management on a routine basis in which variances are clearly identified and can be acted upon as appropriate.

In exercising control, it is generally impracticable to review every variance in detail at each accounting period and attention will usually be concentrated on those variances which have the **greatest impact** on the achievement of the budget plan.

One method of identifying significant variances is to express each variance as a *percentage of the related budget allowance or standard value*. Those showing the highest percentage deviation would then be given the most urgent attention.

This method, however, could result in lack of attention to variances which, although representing a small percentage of the standard value, nevertheless involve **significant sums of money**. Both percentages and money should be looked at in deciding where the priorities for control actually lie

In practice, management will review the variance report presented to them and decide which variances should be investigated on the basis of whether the *costs of investigation are outweighed by the benefits*. Management will often request a more detailed analysis and explanation of specific variances to be produced as the decision as to whether or not a variance merits investigation may need more information than is provided in the original variance report.

Fluctuating variances – looking at trends

The variances of a particular period may not be representative of a general trend. Items like stationery costs can fluctuate widely from month to month, dependent on the amount of stationery that has been invoiced. Sometimes the accountant will make estimated adjustments to either the budget or the actual figures in an attempt to give a better picture of the underlying trend but this is not a completely satisfactory way of dealing with the matter. The simplest way of getting the month's figures into context is to show also the **accumulated cost for the year to date**. High cost and low cost periods will then be revealed but will balance out in the cumulative figures.

A development of the above idea is also to report each period the manager's **latest forecast compared with the annual budget**. It will then be possible to see whether variances from budget currently being reported are likely to continue to accumulate during the remainder of the year, or whether they will be offset by later opposite variances. Although this technique of forecasting is dependent on managers' subjective assessments, it is a good way of ensuring that the correct control action gets taken on the current figures.

Example: forecasts

You might like to spend a few minutes considering what the report below tells you about the business.

Profit and loss account – Seven periods cumulative to … 19…

| | Period 7 | | | Cumulative | | | Whole year | |
	Budget £000	Actual £000	Variances F or (A) £000	Budget £000	Actual £000	Variances F or (A) £000	Budget £000	Latest forecast £000
Sales	500	600	100	3,500	3,420	(80)	6,000	6,200
Direct cost of sales	280	322	(42)	1,960	1,951	9	3,500	3,850
Factory overhead	58	69	(11)	420	400	20	700	750
Administration and selling costs	122	123	(1)	840	800	40	1,320	1,147
Total costs	460	514	(54)	3,220	3,151	69	5,520	5,747
Operating profit	40	86	46	280	269	(11)	480	453
Profit: Sales %	8	14.3	–	8	7.9	–	8	7.3

Solution

(a) Sales, which had obviously been below budget on the first six periods of the year, are significantly in excess of budget on period 7 (reducing the cumulative shortfall to £80,000), and are now expected to exceed the budget for the year as a whole.

(b) Direct costs are naturally higher when sales are higher. The percentage of direct costs to sales value is not consistent, however, as the following calculations show:

	Budget	Actual
Period 7	56.0%	53.6%
Cumulative	56.0%	57.0%
Forecast	58.3%	62.1%

For the seven periods as a whole, direct costs have been in excess of the budgeted percentage and even though the budget for the twelve months provides for an increase in that percentage the forecast actual increase is still higher. Period 7 in isolation shows an anomalous result, perhaps due to some peculiarity in sales mix.

(c)   The variance on factory overhead, which is favourable over the seven periods as a whole, has become adverse in period 7 and is forecast as adverse for the year as a whole (though not at the rate experienced in period 7). Failure to budget adequately for inflationary increases is one possibility.

(d)   Administration and selling costs have a cumulative favourable variance of £40,000 against a budget of £840,000, ie 4.8%. By the end of the year a favourable variance of £173,000 (13.1% on budget) is expected. It would appear that considerable economies are planned, and have already commenced. The fact that period 7 above shows a small adverse variance is obviously not significant. Such results can emerge in administration costs, which can be influenced by random occurrences like a large purchase of stationery or a major visit overseas by the managing director.

Comparing against forecasts

Some large organisations in the UK have taken the idea of comparing against forecasts a step further. Many companies employ the following comparisons.

	Comparison	*Information*
1	Budget v actual	What progress have we made towards achieving objectives?
2	Budget v forecast	Will we continue to progress towards achievement of objectives?
3	Budget v revised forecast	Will suggested corrective actions lead us back to achievement of objectives?
4	Latest forecast v previous	Why are the forecasts different and are circumstances getting better or worse?
5	Actual v past forecast	Why were forecasts incorrect and can they be improved?

It may not be necessary to perform each of these control comparisons every month or quarter. The actual versus past forecast may only be necessary annually or less frequently.

It must be remembered that managers will need to be motivated to produce these forecasts and use them. They must be educated to recognise why and how they can use them to enable them to do a better job and not feel that they are just another means for higher level management to check on them and apply pressure.

Finally, this year's results are sometimes compared with those for the corresponding period last year. In some cases this may be helpful in establishing a trend, but it must never be forgotten that the budget is this year's plan, and it is against that plan that performance must be controlled.

Investigation of variances

Variance analysis, if properly carried out, can be a useful cost-controlling and cost-saving tool. However, the traditional variance analysis seen so far is only a step towards the final goal of **controlling and saving costs**.

Generalised reasons for variances

The causes of variances can be classified under four headings:

♦   planning errors

♦   measurement errors

♦   random factors

♦   operational causes.

Planning errors lead to the setting of inappropriate standards or budgets. This may be due to carelessness on the part of the standard setter (not taking account of known changes in the production process or expected price rises, for example) or due to unexpected external changes (a market shortage of a resource leading to increased price or technological advancements by competitors, leading to loss of sales). These need to be isolated from hindsight information and a revision of the standard considered for future budgets.

Measurement errors include errors caused by inaccurate completion of timesheets or job cards, inaccurate measurement of quantities issued from stores, etc. The rectification of such errors or errors caused by random factors will probably not give rise to any cost savings (though this is a generalisation).

Random factors are by definition uncontrollable, although they need careful monitoring to ensure that they are not, in fact, one of the other types of variance.

We will now look at **specific operational causes of variances** and how they may be rectified.

Specific reasons for variances

Examples of some specific reasons for individual variances are shown below.

Variance		*Possible causes*
Sales	Price	Increased quality
		Fashion
		Competitive pressures
		Marketing campaign
	Volume	Competitive pressure
		Marketing campaign
		Breakdown in production
Materials:	Price	Bulk discounts
		Different suppliers
		Different materials
		Unexpected delivery costs
		Different buying procedures
	Usage	Different quality material
		Theft, obsolescence, deterioration
		Different quality of staff
		Different mix of material
		Different batch sizes and trim loss
Labour:	Price	Different class of labour
		Excessive overtime
		Productivity bonuses
		National wage negotiations
		Union action
	Utilisation	Different levels of skill
		Different working conditions
		The learning effect
		Lack of supervision
		Works to rule
	Idle time	Machine breakdowns
		Lack of material
		Lack of orders
		Strikes (if paid)
		Too long over coffee breaks
Overhead:	Price	Change in nature of overhead
		Incorrect split of semi-variable costs
	Usage	Excessive idle time
		Increase in workforce

It will nearly always be useful to **consult staff working in operational departments** to resolve any queries in the data as they will have 'local' knowledge of the day-to-day operations.

Example: causes of variance

An adverse materials usage variance of £50,000 arose in a month as follows:

Standard cost per kg	£10
Actual cost per kg	£12
Units produced	2,000
Standard quantity per unit	25 kg
Actual quantity used	55,000 kg

	£
Standard cost of actual usage (55,000 kg × £10)	550,000
Standard cost of standard usage (2,000 × 25 kg × £10)	500,000
	_____
Adverse usage variance	50,000
	_____

On further investigation, the following is ascertained.

1   The actual quantity used was based on estimated stock figures. A stocktake showed that 53,000 kg were in fact used.

2   3,000 kg is the best estimate for what might politely be called 'shrinkage' but, in less polite circles, theft.

3   2,000 kg of stock were damaged by hoodlums who broke into the stores through some of the shaky panelling.

4   The foreman feels that existing machinery is outmoded and more efficient machinery could save 1,000 kg a month.

Additional considerations

1   A security guard would cost £9,000 a year to employ and would stop 20% of all theft. Resultant dissatisfaction amongst works staff might cost £20,000 per annum.

2   Given the easy access to stores, vandals might be expected to break in every other month; £10,000 would make the stores vandal-proof.

3   New machinery would cost £720,000.

Required

Analyse the usage variance in the light of this information and comment on your results.

Solution

The original £50,000 usage variance could be analysed as follows.

		Adverse/(favourable) variance £
(a)	Bad measurement (53,000 – 55,000) × £10	20,000
(b)	Theft (3,000 × £10)	30,000
(c)	Damage (2,000 × £10)	20,000
(d)	Obsolete machinery (1,000 × £10)	10,000
(e)	Other operational factors (balance)	(30,000)
		50,000

In each case, the variances should be studied and compared with the cost of rectification.

(a) *Bad measurement* – Assuming no costly decisions were made, or are likely to be made in the future, such as over-stocking, the component is of no consequence.

(b) *Theft* – Annual cost due to theft is 12 × £30,000 or £360,000; 20% of this saved would amount to £72,000 at a cost of £9,000 + £20,000, thus the security guard is worth employing.

(c) *Damage* – Annual cost due to vandalism is 6 × £20,000 or £120,000; this would presumably be avoided by spending £10,000 now; again worthwhile.

(d) *Obsolete machinery* – Annual cost of using old machines is 12 × £10,000 or £120,000; the cost of making this saving (the saving would increase as purchase prices increased or if production increased) is £720,000; the decision over this investment would require further consideration such as discounted cash flow analysis. This technique is considered in a later session.

(e) *Other factors* – We now see a favourable usage variance once all known factors above have been accounted for. This may need further investigation, particularly if it affects the quality of goods produced.

Fixed overhead variances

These are worth a special note, due to the particular nature of the fixed overhead volume variance.

We have seen that the volume variance is a product of the **TAC system**, and represents the adjustment for over-/under-absorption of fixed costs due to actual production being higher or lower than budgeted. Unlike the other variances, it does not actually represent a cost saving or overspend.

If this is the case, is it worth spending any time on the investigation of fixed overhead volume variances? Does it really matter if overheads are under-/over-absorbed, since it will all be adjusted for in the end?

The problem with having an inappropriate absorption rate is that **decisions** may have been taken on a unit cost that is too high or too low – for example, in setting the price of a product. If this is too high, sales may have been unnecessarily lost; if it is too low, profit margins may have been significantly eroded.

To minimise such effects of over-/under-absorption, regular reviews should be conducted of expenditure and activity levels arising throughout the period. The **absorption rate** can then be adjusted if it is felt necessary to reflect more recent estimates of expenditure and activity levels.

The cost of variance analysis

The provision of any information involves the costs of collecting the basic data, processing it, and reporting the results. Variance analysis is no exception and, as with other forms of management information, the **benefits** to which it gives rise must be commensurate with the **costs** incurred.

(a)   Variance analysis allows **'management by exception'** and it is presumably for this purpose that a standard costing system has been introduced.

(b)   When variances are known to exist, failure to make adequate investigations, even on a random basis, will **weaken the control system** and thus the motivation of managers.

(c)   The amount of analysis required can sometimes be reduced by defining **levels of significance** below which detailed investigation is not required.

(d)   The costs of clerical work can be **over-estimated**. In most working days there will be some spare capacity that can be utilised without extra cost.

What has to be considered, therefore, is the amount of detail that can be incorporated usefully in variance analysis. This will fall into two categories.

(a)   Including **more detailed codings** in source documents indicating causes and responsibilities. Such coding is likely to involve people outside the accounts department, who may be unwilling to give time to the task. How useful the analysis will be, will depend on whether or not it is practicable to identify causes and responsibilities at the time the document is initiated.

(b)   **Investigations and re-analysis of variances after the event** (possibly incorporating the distinction between planning and operational variances outlined earlier). This can involve the time of quite senior people, but the process of investigation may well be more useful from the point of view of the management of the business than any quantity of formal variance calculations.

Responsibility accounting and the interdependence of variances

It is part of any system aimed at improving the performance of a business or any part of the business, that actions shall be traced to the person responsible. This may give the impression of **'laying the blame'**, but it is equally possible to award praise (and remunerate accordingly).

We have seen that **responsibility accounting** is a system which recognises various decision centres within a business and traces costs (and possibly revenues) to the individual managers who are primarily responsible for making decisions about the items in question.

Example: who is responsible?

An opportunity arises for a buying department to obtain a consignment of a particular material at an exceptionally low price. The purchase is made; a favourable price variance is recorded and the buying department is duly praised.

Subsequently, when products are being manufactured using this type of material, significant adverse material usage variances and labour efficiency variances are recorded, and are initially regarded as the responsibility of the department where the work is done.

Investigations, however, reveal a number of relevant facts, for example:

♦ The 'cheap' material was of poor quality, and in consequence much of it was wasted in the process of machining. The resultant material usage and labour efficiency variances should presumably be regarded as the responsibility of the buying department, to offset the favourable price variance.

♦ Due to an employee leaving it had been necessary to use an operator who was not familiar with the job. At least part of the excess usage of materials could be attributed to this cause; but whether it should be regarded as the responsibility of the operating department or of the personnel department (for failing to recruit a replacement) is still open to question. If the employee who left had been highly paid, his removal might cause a favourable wage rate variance in the period under review – an offset to the adverse efficiency variance.

♦ The tools used had been badly worn, thus causing excessive time on the job. It would be necessary to consider whether this condition was attributable to the operating department (failing to sharpen tools or to requisition replacements) or to the tools store-keeper or to the buying department (for failing to buy on time or for buying poor quality items again).

The important points to bear in mind are as follows.

♦ Different types of variance can be **inter-linked by a common cause**.

♦ In many cases, the responsibility for variances cannot be identified merely by reference to the cost centre where the variance has been reported. **Responsibility may be shared** by several managers or may lie completely outside the cost centre in which the variance has arisen.

Questions

1 Revamp Furniture Limited

Revamp Furniture Limited manufacture a lounge chair by subjecting plasticised metal to a moulding process, thereby producing the chair in one piece.

(a) From the information provided below, you are required to analyse the cost variances and prepare a reconciliation of budgeted with actual cost incorporating the result of your analysis.

Standard/budget data

Unit variable costs:

Direct material	6lb at 50p per lb
Direct labour	2 hours at 160p per hour
Variable overhead	60p per direct labour hour

Budgeted fixed overhead for the year (240 working days)   £30,000
Budgeted production/sales for the year   60,000 chairs

Actual data for period 1

Number of working days   20
Production/sales   5,200 chairs

Direct material received and used:

Delivery No. 1	12,000 lb	Cost	£5,880
Delivery No. 2	14,000 lb	Cost	£6,790
Delivery No. 3	6,000 lb	Cost	£3,060

Direct labour hours worked	10,080	Cost	£17,540

Variable overhead	£6,150

Fixed overhead	£2,550

(b) 'Cost variances are often found, upon investigation of causes, to be interdependent.'

Briefly explain this statement using as illustrations:

(i)   material price and usage variances

(ii) labour rates and efficiency variances

taken from your answer to (a) above and comment briefly on any possible interdependence between material cost variances and labour cost variances.

2   XYZ Manufacturing Company (AAT CA Pilot)

As the management accountant of the XYZ Manufacturing Company, you have prepared the following variance report for the general manager.

Variance report: July 19X3

	Adverse variance £	*Favourable variance* £	*Total variance* £
Materials			(2,000)
Usage	(5,500)		
Price		3,500	
Labour			(1,500)
Utilisation	(3,000)		
Rate		1,500	
Overheads			(500)
Price		4,500	
Efficiency	(2,000)		
Volume	(3,000)		

Actual costs for July 19X3 were as follows.

	£
Materials	100,000
Labour	80,000
Overheads	75,000
Total	255,000

The general manager tells you he is quite satisfied with this result because the total adverse variance of £4,000 is only 1.57% of total costs.

Required

Write a brief report to the general manager giving your *own* interpretation of the month's results.

3   WH Limited II (AAT CA D94)

Data

WH Limited uses a standard costing system which produces monthly control statements to monitor and control costs. One of their products is product M.

To manufacture product M, a perishable, high quality raw material is carefully weighed by direct employees. Some wastage and quality control rejects occur at this stage. The employees then compress the material to change its shape and create product M.

All direct employees are paid a basic hourly rate appropriate to their individual skill level and a bonus scheme is in operation. Bonuses are paid according to the daily rate of output achieved by each individual.

A standard allowance for all of the above operational factors is included in the standard cost of product M. Standard cost data for one unit of product M is as follows.

		Standard cost £ per unit
Direct material X:	4.5 kg × £4.90 per kg	22.05
Direct labour:	10.3 hours × £3.50 per hour	36.05
Standard direct cost		58.10

During November, the following costs were incurred producing 400 units of product M:

		Actual costs £
Direct material X:	2,100 kg	9,660
Direct labour:	4,000 hrs	16,000
Actual direct cost		25,660

Required

(a)   Calculate the following direct cost variances for product M for November:

    (i)   direct material price

    (ii)   direct material usage

    (iii)   direct labour rate

    (iv)   direct labour utilisation or efficiency.

(b)   Present the variances in a statement which reconciles the total standard direct cost of production with the actual direct cost for product M in November.

Further data

The production manager receives a copy of the standard costing control statement for product M every month. However, he has recently confessed to you that he does not really have a clear understanding of the meaning of the variances.

He has also been baffled by the following statement made by the finance director at a recent meeting of senior managers:

'Assigning responsibility for variances can be complicated if the variances are interdependent, for example if an adverse variance in one part of the organisation is caused by a favourable variance elsewhere.'

Required

As assistant accountant for WH Limited, you are asked to write a memo to the production manager which explains the following.

(c)   The meaning of each of the direct cost variances calculated for product M

(d)   Two possible causes of each of the variances which you have calculated for product M for November

(e)   Two examples of interdependence which may be present in the variances which you have calculated for product M for November. Explain clearly why the variances may be interdependent, so that the manager can better understand the meaning of the finance director's statement.

4 Product XY

The following data relate to actual output, costs and variances for the four-weekly accounting period number four of a company which makes only one product. Opening and closing work-in-progress figures were the same.

Actual production of product XY	18,000 units

Actual costs incurred

	£000
Direct materials purchased and used 150,000 kg	210
Direct wages for 32,000 hours	136
Variable production overhead	38

Variances

	£000
Direct materials price	15 favourable
Direct materials usage	9 adverse
Direct labour rate	8 adverse
Direct labour efficiency	16 favourable
Variable production overhead expenditure	6 adverse
Variable production overhead efficiency	4 favourable

Variable production overhead varies with labour hours worked.

A standard marginal costing system is operated.

Required

Present a standard product cost sheet for one unit of product XY.

5 AB Limited II (AAT CA J94)

Refer back to question 1 in Chapter 3 before attempting this question.

Data

You work as assistant accountant for AB Limited. The company manufactures a single product and uses a standard costing system to monitor and control costs.

Standard and actual cost data for direct costs for the month of June are shown below:

Standard costs		*£ per unit*
Direct material:	4.3 kg × £8 per kg	34.40
Direct labour:	1.5 hours × £4 per hour	6.00
Total direct costs		40.40

Actual results

Direct material purchased and used = 19,500 kg at £8.50 per kg

Direct labour costs incurred = £26,286 paid for 6,740 hours

4,500 units were produced in June.

Required

(a)   Calculate the direct cost variances for June.

(b)   Present the variances in a statement which reconciles the standard direct cost of production with the actual direct cost for June, using the following format.

Reconciliation of standard direct cost of production with actual direct cost for June

	£	£
Standard direct cost of production = 4,500 x £40.40		181,800
Direct cost variances		
Direct material price		
Direct material usage		
	———	
Direct labour rate		
Direct labour utilisation		
	———	
		———
Actual direct cost of production		
		═══

Further data

A colleague at AB Limited has prepared the following statement of fixed production overhead variances for June but is finding it difficult to suggest possible reasons for the variances.

Statement of fixed production overhead variances for June

	£
Overhead price variance	(450)
Overhead efficiency variance	65
Overhead volume variance	208
	——
Total overhead variance	(177)
	——

Note: Variances in brackets are adverse.

Required

(c)   Write a memo to your colleague, explaining for each overhead variance the significance of the adverse or favourable result, and suggesting one possible reason for each of the overhead variances.

Summary

In this chapter, we have examined the causes of variances and outlined techniques which may be used to decide whether to investigate them.

We have revised the computation and interpretations of variances; in particular, fixed overhead variances which are a little more taxing.

Remember that the expenditure variance simply compares the budgeted cost with the actual cost. The volume variance compares budgeted activity level with the standard activity level and can be split further into a capacity and efficiency variance.

We have seen how the sales price and volume variances are calculated and how they allow us to reconcile budgeted profit to actual profit. Remember that the *sales volume variance* is always calculated in terms of *standard margin,* leaving the price variance to take account of the effect of a price rise or fall.

Exchange rate charges can introduce cost variances which are (usually) uncontrollable by the manager responsible for the cost. They should generally be highlighted as such when undertaking responsibility accounting.

We have also considered the possible interaction of variances and the implications for responsibility accounting.

CHAPTER 8

Performance Indicators

Objectives

This chapter explains how to calculate and use performance indicators to interpret management accounting information. It covers the following performance criterion.

7.2.2 Relevant performance indicators are monitored and the results are assessed to identify potential improvements.

When you have completed this chapter you should be able to:

♦ calculate ratios to measure profitability and liquidity

♦ interpret information using ratios

♦ select and calculate appropriate performance indicators for manufacturing industries, service sectors and not for profit organisations.

Introduction

Performance indicators may be categorised in the following ways: **quantitative** or **qualitative**, **monetary** or **non-monetary**.

Quantitative or qualitative

Quantitative measures are expressed in numerical terms which include the following.

(a) Variances

(b) Profit, sales, costs, etc.

(c) Ratios and percentages

(d) Indices

Qualitative indicators are far more subjective and cannot be expressed as an objective, numerical measure. Examples relevant to business and managerial performance would include the following.

(a) level of customer satisfaction: expressed as a subjective level 'very satisfied' ... to ...'not at all satisfied'

(b) staff performance grades: 'excellent', 'average', 'poor', etc.

(c) company performance: 'steady', 'volatile results', 'disappointing', etc.

A lot of these measures may be turned into quantitative measures, by assigning numbers to the various categories (1 = excellent, 4 = poor), etc. but this does not overcome their fundamental subjective nature, as someone has to judge which category is appropriate in the first place.

Monetary or non-monetary

Monetary measures are necessarily quantitative. They are expressed in financial terms (ie for UK businesses, in £) and are often referred to as *financial measures*. These would include profits, revenues, costs, cash flows, share price, variances and average wages.

In order to provide a means of measuring performance, monetary measures must be compared with something else. Such comparatives would include budgets, standard costs, previous periods, other departments of the business, other companies within the business sector and the market as a whole.

Non-monetary measures are those that are not expressed in financial terms and can be quantitative or qualitative (indeed the latter are, by necessity, non-monetary). Examples of non-monetary, quantitative measures would be as follows.

(a)   *Ratios and percentages*: return on capital employed (ROCE), contribution to sales, staff to customers, defective to good output, wastage, market share, labour turnover rates, etc.

(b)   *Indices* – materials price index, retail price index, national wage index

The calculation and use of indices is covered in detail in the next session. They are very often used as a method of expressing a trend.

The above are examples of **relative measures**. Non-monetary, quantitative measures can also be expressed in absolute terms, in anything other than money (eg hours, units, production volumes, numbers of customers, etc.).

Efficiency and effectiveness

Performance indicators are used to measure the efficiency and effectiveness of organisations.

Efficiency can be defined as the relationship between inputs and outputs achieved. The fewer the inputs used by an organisation to achieve any given output, the more efficient is that organisation. In commercial organisations, efficiency is usually measured in terms of profitability, often in relation to assets employed.

Effectiveness is the degree to which an objective or target is met.

Ratio analysis

Ratio analysis is one of the main tools utilised in appraising the performance of a company, the main advantage being that the magnitude of the individual figures is eliminated allowing the appraiser to concentrate on **relative movements.**

Ratio analysis is generally utilised in two ways as follows.

(a)   comparison of performance **year to year**

(b)   comparison **with other companies.**

The techniques covered here occur in many branches of accountancy and it is important that you can calculate and interpret appropriate ratios.

The main types of ratio used are:

(a)   **profitability** ratios

(b)   **liquidity** ratios

(c)   **gearing** ratios

(d)   **investment** ratios.

Of these, **profitability** and **liquidity** ratios are of the greatest significance to the management accountant and it is those we shall examine in more detail.

Ratios are not only used for internal appraisal but also for assessment of **potential targets**. They are therefore often based on published accounts. This also raises some problems.

Example: Knotty plc

In order to illustrate the most common ratios, let's look at some calculations based on the summarised accounts of Knotty plc.

Profit and loss account year ended 31 July 19X9

	19X9 £'000	19X9 £'000	19X8 £'000	19X8 £'000
Turnover		37,589		30,209
Cost of sales		(28,380)		(22,808)
Gross profit		9,209		7,401
Distribution costs	(3,755)		(3,098)	
Administrative expenses	(2,291)		(2,030)	
		(6,046)		(5,128)
		3,163		2,273
Other operating income		108		279
Operating profit		3,271		2,552
Interest receivable		7		28
		3,278		2,580
Interest payable		(442)		(471)
Profit on ordinary activities before taxation		2,836		2,109
Tax on profit on ordinary activities		(1,038)		(650)
Profit on ordinary activities after taxation		1,798		1,459
Preference dividend		(6)		(6)
		1,792		1,453
Ordinary dividends		(606)		(441)
Retained profit for the year		1,186		1,012

Balance sheet as at 31 July 19X9

	Notes	19X9		19X8	
		£000	£000	£000	£000
Fixed assets					
Tangible assets			8,687		5,669
Investments			15		15
			8,702		5,684
Current assets					
Stocks		8,486		6,519	
Debtors	1	8,836		6,261	
Cash at bank and in hand		479		250	
		17,801		13,030	
Creditors: Amounts falling due within one year					
Bank loans and overdrafts		(929)		(511)	
Other amounts falling due within one year		(9,178)		(6,645)	
		(10,107)		(7,156)	
Net current assets			7,694		5,874
Total assets less current liabilities			16,396		11,558
Creditors: Amounts falling due after more than one year					
Debentures			(2,840)		(2,853)
Net assets			13,556		8,705
Capital and reserves					
Called-up share capital					
Ordinary shares of 20p each	2		2,003		1,762
4.2% cumulative preference shares of £1 each			150		150
			2,153		1,912
Share premium account			123		123
Other reserves			2,576		–
Profit and loss account			8,704		6,670
			13,556		8,705

Notes

1   Debtors at 31 July 19X9 include trade debtors of £8,233,000 (19X8 £5,735,000).
2   The number of ordinary shares in issue at 31 July 19X9 was 10,014,514 (19X8 8,808,214).

Profitability

Return on capital employed (ROCE)

Return on capital employed (ROCE) expresses profit as a percentage of the assets in use/capital employed in the business and can be further sub-divided into *profit margin* and *asset turnover* (use of assets):

Profit margin $\times$ Asset turnover $=$ Return on capital employed (ROCE)

$$\frac{\text{Profit}}{\text{Turnover}} \times \frac{\text{Turnover}}{\text{Assets}} = \frac{\text{Profit}}{\text{Assets}}$$

The equation helps to demonstrate how management can influence the rate of return on capital employed:

(a)   By increasing profit margins:

(i)   increase prices

(ii)   reduce costs.

(b)   By increasing asset turnover (use of assets):

(i)   increase sales

(ii)   reduce assets (capital employed).

Year-end or average capital employed

Ideally, the profits for the year ended 31 July 19X9 should be related to the assets in use/capital employed **throughout the year** (average capital employed). In practice, the ratio is usually computed using the assets/capital employed at the year-end (year-end capital employed). Using year-end figures of capital employed can distort trends and inter-company comparison; if new investment has been undertaken near to the year-end and financed (for example) by the issue of new shares, the capital employed will have risen by the total finance raised, whereas the profits will only have a month or two of the new investment's contribution.

A range of different acceptable measures of assets in use/capital employed is available; the matter of principle should be that the profit figure which is related to the capital employed should include **all types of return** on those assets/capital before charging any remuneration for the providers of that capital.

For Knotty plc, a suitable calculation would be as follows.

	19X9 £'000	19X8 £'000
Capital and reserves	13,556	8,705
Add: debentures	2,840	2,853
Year-end capital employed	16,396	11,558

	19X9 £'000	19X8 £'000
Operating profit	3,271	2,552
Interest receivable	7	28
Profit before interest payable and tax	3,278	2,580

Thus the return on capital employed is calculated as:

$$\frac{\text{Profit before interest and tax}}{\text{Capital and reserves and long - term debt}} \times 100$$

19X9 $\quad \dfrac{3,278}{16,396} \times 100 = 20.0\%$

19X8 $\quad \dfrac{2,580}{11,558} \times 100 = 22.3\%$

The rate of return on year-end capital employed has fallen compared with 19X8, and might indicate less effective management. To comment further, we need to sub-analyse the ratio into **profit margin** and **asset turnover**.

Profit margin

If the profitability ratios are to interlock perfectly, the **profit margin** will be calculated expressing the same profit before interest payable and tax as a percentage of turnover:

$$\frac{\text{Profit before interest and tax}}{\text{Turnover}} \times 100$$

A small problem with the approach in this example is that the profit includes interest receivable which is not represented in turnover; however, as the amount is small, this can be ignored.

(In order that the profit can be related more fairly to turnover, profit margin is sometimes calculated using **operating profit**.)

For Knotty plc: 19X9 $\dfrac{3,278}{37,589} \times 100 = 8.7\%$

19X8 $\dfrac{2,580}{30,209} \times 100 = 8.5\%$

Profit margins have improved slightly over the last year, possibly due to better cost control.

Sectors which have traditionally generated relatively **high margins** include publishing, electronics manufacturing, distillers and brewers, whereas food retailing and motor vehicle distribution are examples of low margin businesses.

Low margins within a sector may arise from a policy designed to increase market share by cutting selling prices, or may be due to high development costs associated with new products, both of which may be positive factors for the future. However, low margins are often associated with inefficiency and poor quality management.

Conversely, high margins relative to competitors, or improving margins, are usually taken as indicators of efficiency and good management. High margins achieved by dominating a particular market may, however, attract competitors into that market and imply lower margins in the longer term.

Asset turnover

Another aspect of efficient management is to '**make the assets work**'. This may involve disposing of those 'underperforming' assets which cannot be made to generate sales, as well as developing and marketing the company's products or services.

Once again, the simplest method of computing the ratio is to relate turnover to the same figure of year-end capital employed used in calculating return on capital employed:

$$\frac{\text{Turnover}}{\text{Capital employed}} \times 100$$

19X9 $\dfrac{37,589}{16,396} \times 100 = 2.3$

19X8 $\dfrac{30,209}{11,558} \times 100 = 2.6$

However, as with profit margins, certain assets represented by capital employed have no turnover implications. One method of avoiding this illogicality is to **exclude long and short-term investments** from capital employed. For companies with substantial investments this will make a considerable difference.

Asset turnover will tend to be lower in capital-intensive manufacturing industries, which carry substantial stocks and trade debtors, than in service industries where the principal resource is people rather than plant and machinery, and where stocks are low.

There are often trade-offs between asset turnover and profit margins in different sectors. For example, food retailers have relatively low profit margins compared to electronic equipment manufacturers, but asset turnover is higher.

	Profit margin	×	*Asset turnover*	=	*ROCE*
	%				%
Food retailer	3.7	×	6.7	=	24.8
Electronic equipment manufacturer	10.3	×	2.3	=	23.7

Gross profit margin

The profit margin given above used a profit figure that included non-productive overheads and sundry items of income. The **gross profit margin** looks at the profitability of the pure trading activities of the business:

$$\frac{\text{Gross profit}}{\text{Turnover}} \times 100$$

For Knotty: 19X9 $\dfrac{9,209}{37,589} \times 100 = 24.5\%$

19X8 $\dfrac{7,401}{30,209} \times 100 = 24.5\%$

The company has maintained its gross profit margin; thus the slight rise in net profit margin must be due to overhead costs being better controlled (sundry income has, in fact, gone down).

Liquidity

When analysing a company's balance sheet without access to management information, it is customary to calculate two ratios as indicators of the company's ability to pay its way:

$$\textbf{Current ratio} = \frac{\text{Current assets}}{\text{Creditors due within one year}}$$

$$\textbf{Quick ratio} \text{ (or acid test ratio)} = \frac{\text{Current assets less stocks}}{\text{Creditors due within one year}}$$

For Knotty plc:

		19X9	*19X8*
(a)	current ratio	$\dfrac{17,801}{10,107} = 1.76$	$\dfrac{13,030}{7,156} = 1.82$
(b)	quick ratio	$\dfrac{9,315}{10,107} = 0.92$	$\dfrac{6,511}{7,156} = 0.91$

Distortions in the current ratio

Taking one year as the 'current' period, then the current ratio is a reflection of liquidity as demonstrated at that point in time, unless for example:

(a) the **operating cycle is so long** that part of the stocks or work in progress will not be converted into sales invoicing until after the end of the year, as might be the case with a public works contractor

(b) because **spasmodic customer demand** is linked to a high level of service from stock, it is necessary to hold some stocks which will not be turned over within the year (eg a capital equipment spares supply business)

(c) the figure of debtors includes **contract retention moneys** or items under dispute which will not be collected within the year.

If such features exist, then this should be known from the nature of the business and one would expect to see a higher current ratio than in a business with fast-moving stocks and restricted credit terms. Thus current ratios for a heavy engineering company will be higher than those for a supermarket.

Cash and funds flow analysis

Although current and quick ratios are used to measure liquidity, they are limited insofar as they concentrate on only one area of the balance sheet. If the company needs adequate cash to meet its obligations, there are sources other than the sale of stocks and the collection of amounts owed by debtors.

Analysis of cashflows is a more comprehensive method of assessing liquidity, although significant variations in the liquidity ratios may indicate important changes.

Other working capital ratios

A more detailed analysis of the movement in the elements of working capital can be made with the help of the following ratios.

Stock turnover

Stock turnover ratios can be compared if they relate costs of sales as a measure of activity to stocks which are usually included at cost:

$$\frac{\text{Cost of sales}}{\text{Stocks}}$$

19X9 $\dfrac{28,380}{8,486} = 3.34$

19X8 $\dfrac{22,808}{6,519} = 3.5$

There has been a slight fall in stock turnover, indicating stock is taking longer to sell. A review of stocks may be necessary to determine whether levels of obsolete or damaged stocks are increasing. There may be a deliberate policy to increase stocks.

Average debtors collection period

This calculation is always made using turnover since trade debtors includes the profit element:

$$\frac{\text{Trade debtors}}{\text{Turnover}} \times 365 \text{ days}$$

19X9 $\dfrac{8,233}{37,589} \times 365 = 79.9$ days

19X8 $\dfrac{5,735}{30,209} \times 365 = 69.3$ days

The company is taking approximately 10 days longer, on average, to collect its debts.

As the year-end figures may be unrepresentative (due perhaps to seasonality of sales), an average debtors figure for the year might be used if this were available.

A similar calculation can be made to determine *creditors payment (settlement) period*:

$$\frac{\text{Trade creditors}}{\text{Purchases or Cost of sales}} \times 365$$

Inter-firm and intra-group comparisons

Problems with comparisons using ratio analysis

(a) *Need for comparison*

   (i) over time, to observe trends (time series analysis)

   (ii) with other departments within the company or with other firms (cross-sectional analysis).

(b) *Use of 'norm' or average*

   One should look not only at the average ratio for an industry (or department or division), but also at the ratios for various percentiles, because the norm may be in a 'bad' industry (or department or division).

(c) *Comparison of different entities*

   Not all companies within an industry are of a similar nature, nor are all departments/division within a particular company necessarily similar, so any comparison is meaningless. For example, in a company which diversifies into different areas, comparison of ratios between the areas is invalid and comparison of ratios for the company as a whole with those of an undiversified firm in the same industry has little point.

(d) *Size*

   Within any industry, there will be a wide range of companies in terms of size, which is a further factor to consider when comparing ratios within an industry.

(e)   *Estimated accounting data*

A lot of accounting data is comprised of estimates rather than absolute measures, eg bad debt provision.

(f)   *Accounting conventions*

Companies do not all conform to the same accounting conventions and many will have unstandardised data.

(g)   *Time factors*

Different companies have different financial years and some will be in a seasonal business.

(h)   *Inflation*

Comparisons of one year with the next can be distorted by inflation, particularly over a long period. We will see in a later session how data can be adjusted to put on a comparable basis using appropriate indices but, within a set of accounts, there will be many different rates of inflation affecting the figures and this becomes a complex task.

Example: calculating and interpreting ratios

Work through the following example to ensure that you understand how to calculate and interpret basic ratios.

The outline balance sheets of the Nantred Trading Co Limited were as shown below.

Balance sheets as at 30 September

	19X6		19X5	
	£	£	£	£
Fixed assets (at written-down values)				
Premises	98,000		40,000	
Plant and equipment	162,000		65,000	
		260,000		105,000
Current costs				
Stock	95,300		31,200	
Trade debtors	30,700		19,700	
Bank and cash	26,500		15,600	
	152,500		66,500	
Current liabilities				
Trade creditors	55,800		23,900	
Corporation tax	13,100		11,400	
Proposed dividends	17,000		17,000	
	85,900		52,300	
Working capital		66,600		14,200
Net assets employed		326,600		119,200
Financed by				
Ordinary share capital	200,000		100,000	
Reserves	26,600		19,200	
Shareholders' funds		226,600		119,200
7% debentures		100,000		–
		326,600		119,200

The only other information available is that:

♦ turnover for the years ended 30 September 19X5 and 19X6 was £202,900 and £490,700 respectively

♦ profit before tax and interest (operating profit) for the years 30 September 19X5 and 19X6 was £21,500 and £44,500 respectively.

Required

(a) Calculate, for each of the two years, two suitable ratios to highlight the liquidity and two suitable ratios to highlight the profitability of the company.

(b) Comment on the situation revealed by the figures you have calculated in your answer to (a) above.

Solution

(a)

		19X6		*19X5*	
(i)	$\dfrac{\text{Current assets}}{\text{Current liabilities}}$	$\dfrac{152{,}500}{85{,}900}$	$= 1.78{:}1$	$\dfrac{66{,}500}{52{,}300}$	$= 1.27{:}1$
(ii)	$\dfrac{\text{Quick assets}}{\text{Current liabilities}}$	$\dfrac{57{,}200}{85{,}900}$	$= 0.67{:}1$	$\dfrac{35{,}300}{52{,}300}$	$= 0.67{:}1$
(iii)	$\dfrac{\text{Profit before tax and interest}}{\text{Capital (net assets) employed}}$	$\dfrac{44{,}500}{326{,}600}$	$\times 100 = 13.6\%$	$\dfrac{21{,}500}{119{,}200}$	$\times 100 = 18.0\%$
(iv)	$\dfrac{\text{Profit before tax and interest}}{\text{Sales}}$	$\dfrac{44{,}500}{490{,}700}$	$\times 100 = 9.1\%$	$\dfrac{21{,}500}{202{,}900}$	$\times 100 = 10.6\%$

(b) The situation revealed by the ratios calculated in (a) above may be summarised as follows.

Liquidity ratios (i) and (ii)

The current ratio indicates a substantial surplus of current assets over current liabilities and this has improved over the year. The liquid assets (debtors and bank) to current liabilities ratio shows no change and based on past experience does not signify any liquidity difficulties.

Profitability ratios (iii) and (iv)

The overall return on capital employed has decreased by a substantial amount. This may be because full benefit has not yet been received from the additional investment of £100,000 from the debentures issued during the year. The level of net profit per £ of sales has also decreased and this may be due to the same reasons. Fortunately the overall return is high enough to mean that the 7% paid to the debentureholders is still easily achieved and the surplus return will improve returns to the ordinary shareholders, compensating them for the risk they have undertaken in introducing gearing (the debentures) into the organisation.

Manufacturing industries

The performance of a manufacturing business and its constituent activities will commonly be measured in **quantitative terms,** mainly monetary. However, we shall also consider relevant non-monetary and **qualitative factors** that can be useful.

Productivity

This is a measure of the **efficiency of resource usage** and expresses the rate of output in relation to resource used.

Examples include the following:

(a)   units per labour or machine hour

(b)   productive hours to total hours paid

(c)   actual output to full capacity output

(d)   sales per salesperson

Productivity is closely linked with both **efficiency and resource utilisation** (which is considered later).

Three ratios are often used to measure productivity, as follows.

Activity ratio: $\dfrac{\text{Actual output measured in standard hours}}{\text{Budgeted production hours}}$

Capacity ratio: $\dfrac{\text{Actual hours worked}}{\text{Budgeted hours}}$

Efficiency ratio: $\dfrac{\text{Actual output measured in standard hours}}{\text{Actual production hours}}$

Example: productivity

	Budget	Actual
Output (units)	10,000	9,000
Hours worked	200	190

Activity ratio: $\dfrac{180}{200} = 90\%$

In other words, the production level was only 90% of the budgeted level.

Capacity ratio: $\dfrac{190}{200} = 95\%$

Only 95% of budgeted hours were actually worked and used to produce units.

Efficiency ratio: $\dfrac{180}{190} = 94.74\%$

According to the budget, 50 units should have been produced in an hour and therefore in the 190 hours that were actually worked, 9,500 units should have been produced. Only 94.74% of that quantity (9,000) were actually produced.

Unit costs

Here, traditional variances will play a major part. Each element of unit cost (materials, labour, overheads) will have a standard against which to compare actual costs. This standard cost will incorporate a technical standard (kg per unit, hours per unit) and a price standard (£ per kg, £ per hour).

Technical standards may be used on their own as **non-monetary performance measures**, particularly where a full-scale costing system is not in place, or where prices of resources are essentially fixed by external forces.

Resource utilisation

This is a measure of the extent to which resources were used in relation to **maximum capacity**. Examples of utilisation and related measures for different resources include the following.

Machines	–	utilisation (hours used : potential hours)
	–	down time (machine down hours : total hours)
Materials	–	wastage (normal/abnormal loss percentage)
	–	stock turnover (linked to levels of slow-moving stocks)
Labour	–	utilisation (productive : total hours)
	–	absenteeism, lateness
	–	mix variances (where different grades are used)
	–	idle time variances
	–	labour turnover (leavers replaced : total employed)

Profitability

The most common measures of profitability have been covered (ROCE, profit margins). Many of the factors considered under other headings will also effect profitability, including all cost variances. Sales measures will also be relevant, such as volumes, mix between products and market shares, etc.

Product profitability should be measured in terms of **contribution per unit** or, for a budgeted activity level, contribution less directly attributable fixed costs (ie excluding costs that are shared by other products).

Quality of service

For a manufacturing business, this can be categorised into quality of service **to customers** and quality of service **from service departments**. The latter is covered in the section on the service sector.

Quality of service to customers is essentially a subjective, qualitative measure, although some quantitative measures can be used in connection with it – for example, ratios such as customer returns to total sales and customer complaints per units sold. Speed of service can be measured in retail outlets or numbers waiting per checkout in a supermarket.

The main source of measure of customer satisfaction will generally be through some sort of **questionnaire**.

Other non-monetary measures

Quality is a particular area in which such indicators are required; two others that have been recently been identified as important attributes of world-class manufacturing are *innovation* and *flexibility*.

Innovation is concerned with the business's ability to beat their competitors in developing new products, improvements to existing ones or additional customer services.

Measurement of innovation must concentrate on its effectiveness as well as its existence – counting the number of new products developed is of little help without knowing the extent to which they have been accepted by the market.

Possible measures include the following:

(a) **research and development** expenditure related to new sales (in value and timing, ie payback)

(b) **viable new products** to existing products

(c) **percentage of total profits** relating to new products/ improvements.

Flexibility is concerned with the business's ability to respond to customers' needs, in terms of speed of delivery of existing products, speed of reaction to changes in demand patterns and ability to respond to particular customer requests or specifications.

In a manufacturing context, it is often the case that flexibility is connected with the amounts of products using common parts. If demand for one type of product falls, it is easier to switch stock and processing to another if there is a common base between them.

Service departments

Many of the measures discussed above will be relevant in the assessment of the performance of service departments within a business. Unless an internal charge-out system operates (for example, the charging of user departments per hour of computer department time spent on their work), the **emphasis will be on costs rather than profits.**

As well as the normal cost variances (with activity levels based on the departments own cost unit, eg maintenance hours, meals served, data processing hours) other cost ratios will be appropriate, for example:

(a)   **meal cost per employee per period** (canteen)

(b)   **running costs per van-mile** (deliveries)

(c)   **cost per call-out** (maintenance department).

Example: service department indicators

We shall consider a transport/distribution department in more detail. In a transport organisation, vehicle costs fall into two categories.

(a)   **Standing costs** (ascertained as a rate per day), including:

     (i)   road tax

     (ii)   insurance

     (iii)   garage and administration costs

     (iv)   drivers' wages

     (v)   depreciation.

(b)   **Running costs** (ascertained as a rate per ton/mile), including:

     (i)   fuel and lubricants

     (ii)   tyres

     (iii)   repairs

     (iv)   maintenance.

Standing costs will be incurred for vehicles owned whether or not they are in use and are in the nature of stepped fixed costs. Fixed because, for each vehicle, they do not vary in amount and 'stepped' because for each additional vehicle required, costs, on a graph, will rise by a further step and remain fixed for a further range of activity until another vehicle is required.

In addition to these, there will be **depot administration and establishment costs** to be absorbed. These should be ascertained in total and related to the activity of the depot. Statistical information such as mileage run, loaded and empty, and tonnages carried should also be collected so that a reasonable method of absorption may be derived.

The analysis of expenditure between fixed and variable costs (standing and running costs) gives potential for the use of **marginal costing** and the consequent improvements in management information.

With such information available, management will be **better equipped** to deal with:

(a)   control over costs for each vehicle or group of similar vehicles

(b)   pricing

(c)   choice of most economic vehicle for specific tasks

(d)   acceptability of contracts

(e)   vehicle purchase and replacement decisions

(f)   many other day-to-day decisions.

Service sectors

Service organisations include the following.

(a)   *Professional services*, such as firms of accountants, architects, surveyors, solicitors whose main assets will be their employees and who provide individual, personalised services to their customers.

(b)   *Mass services*, such as transport, which are highly capital asset based and provide a standard range of services to a wide range of customers.

(c)   *Public sector services*, such as health, education and local authorities, which fall under the 'not for profit organisations' section covered later in the session.

Service sector measures can be considered under very similar headings as those for manufacturing organisations, although there will be a different emphasis on their relative importance.

The main difference between the two types of organisation is the nature of their output.

Output from manufacturing businesses comprises **tangible, clearly identifiable** products, usually of a standard design and quality which can be rejected by a customer if not required or unsuitable, and produced in advance of demand and stored until needed.

Think about a service provided to you – can it be said to have any of these characteristics? This leads to a different approach needed for performance measurement where costs per product or units per hour are of little relevance or meaning. However, in earlier sessions, we have seen that cost units do not have to be in terms of products and that measures may be activity rather than product based.

So, using similar headings as before, particular areas to be considered about the performance indicators of service organisations are **productivity, unit costs, resource utilisation, profitability and quality of service.**

Productivity

Productivity can be difficult to measure, because services rarely have a standard unit of output. For example, it would be meaningless to measure a conveyancing solicitor's productivity on the basis of 'property purchase completions per month', as each will have a different degree of complexity and value to the business. Similarly, it would be inappropriate to assess a bus line on the basis of 'journeys per day', as the contribution to the company's profits would depend upon the number of people carried at each stage of the journey and how many buses were operating on the line.

Meaningful measures of productivity or efficiency for a service depend upon a clearly defined measures of activity and resource.

So, for example, the measure of activity for the bus line might be 'passenger miles' and of the resource might be 'driver hours'.

Professional firms, such as accountants and solicitors, will generally use 'chargeable hours' as a measure of activity and employees' productivity will be judged by 'chargeable hours per employee'.

Unit costs

Again, the difficulty here is in defining an appropriate unit for the activity being measured. Once this has been established, appropriate costs need to be attributed to it. So the cost of a professional chargeable hour would mainly consist of employee costs (salaries, NICs, benefits, etc.) but will also include a recovery of general overheads.

The cost of a 'passenger mile' for a transport company will include driver costs, vehicle running costs and overheads.

Resource utilisation

Resource utilisation is the extent to which available resources are used for productive service. Examples of suitable measures for various types of service businesses are as follows.

Professional	Chargeable hours	:	Total hours available
Transport	Passenger miles	:	Train miles available
Hotel	Rooms occupied	:	Rooms available
Car hire	Car-Days hired	:	Car-days available

Profitability

Clearly, for the service business overall, the usual measures can apply – ROCE, profit margins, etc. Unit profitability measures will again depend upon the clear definition of the cost unit or unit of activity. The profit can then determined by comparison of the cost per unit (as discussed above) with the income generated (eg the charge-out rate for a professional chargeable hour or the average fare per mile on a bus/train route).

Quality of service

This has far more significance than in the manufacturing sector, where it was perhaps subsidiary to the quality of the product. Customers will make their buying decisions on the basis of how well the service is provided.

The factors contributing to quality of service will vary according to the nature of the business. As an illustration, consider the service provided to trainee accountancy students by a private college. Possible factors that would influence a potential student in their choice of college and the ways in which these might be measured are as follows.

Factor	*Possible measures*
Technical expertise	Pass rates
Communication	Clarity of lectures, study material and administrative information
Access	Staff/student ratios Availability of tutorial help outside lecture hours Ease of finding department/member of staff required Location of college
Friendliness	Approachability of staff
Flexibility	Ability to tailor service to individual student's needs
Facilities	Availability and standard of canteen, library, phones, etc.
Aesthetics	Appearance of college Staff presentation
Comfort	Roominess of classrooms Heating/air-conditioning Comfort of seats, size of desks

You can no doubt think of some more factors and different ways in which those given could be measured. For example, it is perhaps a little glib to use pass rates as a measure of the college's technical expertise, as theses are also likely to be significantly influenced by the abilities and commitment of the students themselves.

Having identified what needs to be measured, how can this be achieved? Some are a matter of fact or record – like pass rates or the existence of facilities; most of the rest are qualitative judgement, and would need to be measured by the use of assessment forms completed by students.

An overall measure of the quality of service provided by the college could be the trend in the number of students enrolling for courses, although again this can be affected by other factors, such as the location of the college and students, the policy of the students' employers and the size of the market for trainee accountants.

Not-for-profit organisations

Not for profit organisations (NFPOs) are largely operating in the public sector, in areas such as education, policing, housing, health, libraries; perhaps the most common private sector example would be charities. These are also predominantly in the service sector.

For NFPOs, there is no profit objective or similar target. Their services, which represent the output of each organisation, are vague, abstract and very difficult to quantify in financial terms. There is no mathematical relationship between money spent and the value of the service received and ultimately no method of making decisions about where the funds should be allocated, to increase or decrease the level of service.

Why do we need measurements in NFPOs?

♦   To ensure that performance is meeting **the objectives of the organisation,** ie to measure the effectiveness of the policy in fulfilling stated objectives.

♦   To allow **comparisons of performance** between services and other organisations, thus providing an indicator of efficiency, and to discover where improvements may be made.

♦   To provide a **guideline for the decision-maker** to help decide the value of increasing the outlay of resources in one area as opposed to another. To free the decision-maker from making subjective judgements, objective measures need to be sought.

Input

Definition of units of input is easy as resources can be expressed in terms of **money, manpower or a combination of the two.**

Output – general problems of output measurement

It is the characteristics of output in performance measurement which cause NFPOs the most problems. It is a complex and difficult process to assess the level and quality of service provided.

The main problems are as follows.

(a)   It is **difficult to define output** – services are more concerned with long-term social improvement definable only in moral or political terms. For example, improving the quality of life may be an objective but how is it defined?

(b)   There is **no single criterion or objective function** for analysing proposed alternative courses of action. This contrasts with the private sector which has the profit measure to judge performance.

(c)   No accurate way of **estimating the relationship between inputs and outputs** (cause and effect relationship) eg what causes better examination results, is it teachers or equipment?

(d)   Some services contribute to **more than one objective;** for example, a local authority's education service is concerned with all aspects of children's lives.

(e) Difficulties in the **collection of data.**

(f) Difficulty in establishing **national and relevant standards** for public sector NFPOs.

(g) **Cost of collection** may be prohibitive when measured against usefulness of output measures.

(h) Products and services supplied to the community by public sector NFPOs are often **not physical assets.** If they are intangible, then how can they be measured?

Use of output indicators

The **social, economic and community objectives** of most NPFO operations mean that performance cannot be measured directly and must be measured by indicators of **the value of the output being produced** and the relationship of the output to the input in terms of costs involved.

Example: social services

In areas such as social services, it is probably impossible to obtain quantitative measures of the absolute value of the output being achieved but such indicators could be:

(a) *Education*

    (i) Examination results
    (ii) Attendance records of schools
    (iii) Numbers going into higher education
    (iv) Ability to meet requirements of employers

(b) *Housing*

    (i) Age structure of houses in area
    (ii) Occupancy levels
    (iii) Number on housing waiting list
    (iv) Length of time on housing waiting list

(c) *Libraries*

    (i) Range of books offered
    (ii) Total hours open
    (iii) Numbers of mobile libraries
    (iv) Lending patterns of books

(d) *National Health Service*

    (i) Beds per 1,000 population
    (ii) Bed occupancy rate
    (iii) Beds per nurse
    (iv) Operations per annum

Standard budgetary control

Often a method of assessing performance in NFPOs is by the use of such a **standard budgetary control system.** Actual performance is measured against budget for income and expenditure week-by-week or month-by-month, and this will reveal variances. In this way, the performance of a centre can be monitored throughout the year. Indeed, if the figures are split into functions or activities, closer control of each sub-division of the centre is facilitated. Whilst fulfilling this function it can also be used to assess the performance of resource allocation.

Questions

1   Transport company II (AAT CA J94)

A transport company is reviewing the way in which it reports vehicle operating costs to the company management. In particular, it is interested in the use of performance ratios which will help to assess the efficiency and effectiveness of the use of its vehicles.

Information on the following items is available for each vehicle for the period is as follows.

Costs

Variable costs

Fuel   Tyres
Oil   Other parts
Hydraulic fluid   Repairs and maintenance

Fixed costs

Road fund licence   Cleaning
Insurance   Depreciation
Drivers' wages

Activity

Miles driven   Number of days available for use
Tonnes carried   Number of days vehicle actually used
Journeys made

Required

You are asked to indicate *six* suitable performance ratios which could be used to monitor the effectiveness and efficiency of the usage of each vehicle.

Three of your ratios should relate to the efficient control of costs and three should relate to the effective usage of vehicles.

2 Retail ratios (AAT CA Pilot)

In respect of each of the following ratios calculated for a retail store (a), explain how the ratio is calculated and (b) the use of the ratio as a management tool in retail trading.

♦ Rate of stock turnover

♦ Gross profit margin

♦ Creditors average settlement period (assume that all purchases were on credit)

♦ Net profit (before tax) to capital employed

3 WH Limited III (AAT CA D94)

WH Limited is a member of a trade association which operates an inter-company comparison scheme. The scheme is designed to help its member companies to monitor their own performance against that of other companies in the same industry.

At the end of each year, the member companies submit detailed annual accounts to the scheme organisers. The results are processed and a number of accounting ratios are published and circulated to members. The ratios indicate the average results for all member companies.

Your manager has given you the following extract, which shows the average profitability and asset turnover ratios for the latest year. For comparison purposes, WH Limited's accounts analyst has added the ratios for your company.

	Results for year 4	
	Trade association average	*WH Limited*
Return on capital employed	20.5%	18.4%
Net (operating) profit margin	5.4%	6.8%
Asset turnover	3.8 times	2.7 times
Gross margin	14.2%	12.9%

Required

As assistant accountant for WH Limited, your manager has asked you to prepare a report for the senior management committee. The report should cover the following points:

(a) an explanation of what each ratio is designed to show;

(b) an interpretation of WH Limited's profitability and asset turnover compared with the trade association average;

(c) comments on any limitations of these ratios and of comparisons made on this basis.

4   Loamshire County Council II

Refer back to question 4 in Chapter 4 before attempting this question.

A number of councillors have argued that, if the service continues to purchase books at this rate for a number of years, the stock will soon become out of date and worn out. This has led to a general discussion about the total quality of the Library Service. In addition to the information contained in budgets, statistics are available over a number of years on the following items:

♦   number of employees in different categories

♦   number of books issued over a period

♦   total book stock

♦   numbers of books/CDs/cassettes purchased in a year

♦   numbers of members of the public using the Library Service

♦   total population in the county.

You have been asked to suggest performance indicators which might give some guidance to councillors and the public at large on the quality of the service provided.

Required

Suggest:

(a)   one ratio which measures the efficiency of staff in carrying out routine duties

(b)   two ratios which measure the extent of the service provided for the public

(c)   one method of measuring the contribution made by income-generating activities

(d)   two indicators which would provide relevant information about the quality of the stock.

5   Homely Limited

Data

Stately Hotels plc is considering making an offer to buy a small privately owned chain of hotels, Homely Limited. In order to carry out an initial appraisal, you have been provided with an abbreviated set of their accounts for 19X4.

Homely Limited – Profit and loss account for the year ended 31 December 19X4 (extract)

	£000
Turnover	820
Operating costs	754
Operating profit	66
Interest	4
Profit before tax	62
Taxation	18
Profit after tax	44
Dividends	22
Retained profits	22

Homely Limited – Balance sheet as at 31 December 19X4 (extract)

	£000
Fixed assets at net book value	230
Net current assets	70
Total assets	300
Long-term loans	50
Shareholders' funds	250
Number of employees (full-time equivalents)	20
Number of rooms, each available for 365 nights	18
Number of room nights achieved in 19X4	5,900

Stately Hotels plc uses a number of key accounting ratios to monitor the performance of the group of hotels and of individual hotels in the chain. An extract from the target ratios for 19X4 is as follows.

Stately Hotels plc – target ratios for 19X4 (extract)

(i)	Return on capital employed, based on profit before interest and tax	26%
(ii)	Operating profit percentage	13%
(iii)	Asset turnover	2 times
(iv)	Working capital period = $\dfrac{\text{Working capital}}{\text{Operating costs}} \times 365$	20 days
(v)	Percentage room occupancy = $\dfrac{\text{Number of room nights let}}{\text{Number of room nights available}} \times 100\%$	85%
(vi)	Turnover per employee (full-time equivalent)	£30,000

Required

(a) Calculate the six target ratios above based on Homely Limited's accounts and present them in a table which enables easy comparison with Stately Hotels' target ratios for 19X4.

(b) Prepare a memorandum for the management accountant of Stately Hotels plc, giving your initial assessment of Homely Limited based on a comparison of these ratios with Stately Hotels' target ratios. Your memorandum should provide the following information for *each* of the six ratios.

    (i) Comments on the performance of Homely Limited and suggestions about the management action which might be necessary to correct any apparent adverse performance.

    (ii) A discussion of any limitations in the use of the ratio for this performance comparison.

6 Gransden Limited (AAT J96)

Gransden Limited makes and retails a variety of furniture products. One year ago, the directors realised that their traditional financial accounting system was not providing sufficient information for the managers. As a result, they established a management accounting department headed by William Jones. He quickly established standard costing throughout the organisation as well as introducing performance reports for each division in the company. Both techniques have been effective and, as a result, you were recently appointed as the Assistant Management Accountant to the company.

Some managers, however, are still having difficulty understanding the meaning of the standard costing reports prepared each month. One manager, Helen Dale, particularly feels that the report for May was misleading. Her department manufactures high quality wooden display cabinets. She wrote to William Jones about the report, and an extract from the letter is reproduced below.

"In May, my department produced 5,000 cabinets, 500 more than required in my budget. According to your own figures each cabinet requires five metres of wood at a standard price of £100 per metre, a total cost of £2,500,000. For some reason, you show the result of this as being an overall adverse material variance of £200,000, which you then break down into price and usage, despite my department only using 22,500 metres of wood in May.

Also, only yesterday, I read that the Retail Price Index stood at 168 compared with an index of 160 when the standards were agreed. This shows inflation at 3% and so the £200,000 overspend on standard cost is entirely due to price inflation, which is out of my control. Your standard costing information is not therefore particularly helpful to me as a manager."

Required

William Jones plans to discuss with Helen the issues raised in her letter. Before doing so, however has asked you to:

(a)   (i)   determine the material price and usage variances within the overall adverse variance

      (ii)   check the accuracy of the index of inflation calculated by Helen Dale.

(b)   Prepare a diagram or graph showing the standard cost, the variances and the extent of inflation within the price variance which may help Helen understand the overall variance.

(c)   Identify **three** difficulties which might be experienced in interpreting the price variance, including the inflation element.

Further data

Another problem faced by William Jones has arisen from the splitting of the company into separate divisions. This restructuring had the full agreement of the Board of Directors, who viewed it as a way of giving responsibility to operating managers. Two functions, however, were deliberately retained at the centre: capital investment decisions and cash management.

Gransden's cash management system operates through a central accounting unit within the head office finance department. Divisions inform the unit when a creditor is to be paid. The unit then makes the necessary arrangements for the payment to be made. Similarly, although the divisions retain overall responsibility for credit control, all remittances from debtors are handled directly by the central accounting unit. As a result of this, each division's capital employed is defined as fixed assets plus current assets (other than cash) less current liabilities.

Two divisions, the Northern Division and the Southern Division, are entirely retailing operations. Over the last year, anxieties have been expressed about the Southern Division not adequately contributing to overall company profitability. Details of their results for the year to 31 May 19X6 and the relevant management ratios for the North division are reproduced below.

Operating results for the year ending 31 May 19X6

| | North | | South | |
	£000	£000	£000	£000
Turnover		135,000		191,000
Opening stocks	25,000		55,000	
Purchases	75,000		105,000	
Closing stocks	20,000		40,000	
Cost of sales		80,000		120,000
Gross profit		55,000		71,000
Wages and salaries	10,000		12,000	
Depreciation	10,000		16,000	
Other costs	9,688		8,620	
		29,688		36,620
Operating profit for the year		25,312		34,380
Net assets				
Fixed assets		100,000		160,000
Depreciation		40,000		48,000
Net book value		60,000		112,000
Finished stocks		20,000		40,000
Debtors		16,875		47,750
Creditors		(12,500)		(8,750)
Capital employed		84,375		191,000

Management ratios for the North Division

Return on capital employed	30.00%	Average age of debtors	1.5 months
Gross profit margin	40.75%	Average age of stock	3 months
Sales margin (operating profit/turnover)	18.75%	Average age of creditors	2 months
Asset turnover	1.6 times		

Required

You are informed by the Management Accountant that the Board plans to investigate ways of improving the efficiency of the Southern Division and a meeting has been called for this purpose in one week's time. William Jones has asked you to:

(d)   Calculate the relevant management ratios for the Southern Division.

(e)   Estimate what the return on capital employed would have been for the Southern Division if:

       (i)   it has achieved the same asset turnover as the Northern Division;

       (ii)   it had the same average age of debtors, stock and creditors as the Northern Division.

      Note: For the purpose of Task (b)(i) only, you should assume that the wages and salaries, the depreciation and the other costs are all fixed costs and that stock, debtors and creditors remain unaltered.

(f)   Identify **two** limitations to your analysis in parts (a) and (b).

Summary

As you have seen, there are numerous possible performance indicators and their relevance will depend upon the type of organisation and the aspect of performance being assessed.

The five categories of indicators used initially (productivity, unit cost, etc.) can be used as a framework for the assessment of most types of organisation, but you need to be able to adapt them as necessary.

The important ratios for you to be able to compute (and interpret) are as follows:

Profitability:	Return on capital employed (ROCE)
	Gross and net profit margins
Liquidity:	Current ratio
	Quick (acid test) ratio
	Stock turnover
	Debtors' collection period
	Creditors' payment (settlement) period

Remember that a ratio on its own is not useful information; it needs to be **compared**, internally or externally. This gives rise to problems of comparability, which you should be able to discuss.

Many of the ideas covered in earlier chapters will have relevance here (eg variance analysis and the use of indices).

Make sure you are quite clear about the necessary attributes of a cost unit (or unit of activity) in order for it to provide a useful basis for measurement. This is particularly important for service activities. Try to think of services you have had experience of yourself and how the various aspects may be measured.

There will rarely be a right or wrong answer, so do not be afraid to use your imagination!

CHAPTER 9

Presentation of Reports

Objectives

This chapter explains how to prepare reports and examines the various ways in which information can be presented, such as tables and diagrams. It covers the following performance criteria.

7.1.6 **Reports highlighting significant trends are presented to management in an appropriate form.**

7.2.4 **Exception reports to follow up matters which require further investigation are prepared.**

7.2.5 **Specific recommendations are made to management and are explained in a clear and appropriate form.**

When you have completed this chapter, you should be able to:

♦ plan, structure and write a report

♦ understand the different ways in which information can be presented

♦ interpret information presented in tables and diagrams.

Introduction

A report could be defined as an orderly and objective *communication* of factual *information* which serves some business aim. Its purpose is to convey information to particular readers or to answer a question.

Report is a general term. A letter containing specific information or a memo drawing someone's attention to certain details could be classified as a report.

Reports do not even have to be written; people are often requested to, or offer to, make oral reports.

Its object is **communication**, not to show how much knowledge the writer possesses. Reports vary in length and status from simple printed forms (such as *accident reports*) to the major investigative reports commissioned by governments.

Planning the report

Once you have gathered all the facts and data that may be relevant to the report, there are two further steps to be carried out before you start actually writing it:

♦ select what is needed

♦ plan how to set it out.

Select what is needed

Resist the temptation to put all you know into the report. Knowing what to leave out is as important as knowing what to put in. Ask yourself the following questions.

♦ What is the purpose of this report?

♦ What do I want to tell my readers?

♦ What do they need to know?

♦ Who is going to read it?

♦ What do they know already?

♦ When are they going to read it?

The answers to these questions will determine such matters as:

♦ how much information is included

♦ how technical or simple the report should be

♦ how much background material is required

♦ whether some of the material will be irrelevant when the report is read.

Plan how to set it out

The aim at this stage is to get a **logical sequence** of what you are going to write.

The report should be clearly structured into sections under relevant headings, so that the main topic of the report is clearly set out, developed and explained, and the subsequent conclusions fully supported.

Check that your **main headings** are in the right order and that sections most closely connected in ideas stand next to each other physically (as far as possible) and that they follow in logical sequence. Within these sections, you might want to write in **subheadings**; if so, make sure that these too are in a logical order. All headings, and sub–headings if you like, should be included in the table of contents.

Paragraphs should be more than one sentence long and each should revolve around a common theme or sub-topic. Paragraphs usually consist of a key sentence making a point, with examples or evidence in support of the point.

The **conclusions should not come as a surprise,** due to inadequate preparation of the reader in the main body of the report. You should be clear what your conclusions are before you write the report.

The structure of the report

Reports can take many forms and can vary in length and status. They:

♦ inform

♦ analyse

♦ evaluate

♦ recommend

♦ describe.

The structure of any report should reflect its function. The questions that need to be answered are as follows.

♦ Is there a specific aim?

♦ Is it just a presentation of facts?

♦ Does it need a demonstration of analysis used?

All reports, whether short or long, formal or informal, need the basic structure of beginning, middle and end.

The **beginning** should determine:

♦ what the document is about

♦ the relevance for the reader.

The **middle** should contain:

♦ the main analysis

♦ the detailed argument supporting your conclusions, recommendations or proposed action.

The **end** should tell the reader:

♦ what will happen or what you want them to do

♦ conclusions and recommendations.

The short informal report

This is generally only a two or three section report. The main areas are as follows:

♦ the name of the person requesting the report

♦ the date of the report

♦ the title

♦ an introduction, which may also give the background

♦ the procedure, findings and 'overview' of the problem

♦ the conclusion

♦ the name and position within the company of the writer.

Example: short informal report

The following example shows the basic structure but may be adapted to suit different requirements.

REPORT

To: D Fagen   Date: 29 May 19X4

From: J Ely, Office Junior, Accounts Department

Subject: Accounts Department reaction to proposed hot drinks vending machine installation

Introduction

This report describes the reaction of staff in the Accounts Department of the Kenilworth branch office of Teck Bros. to a proposal to replace existing tea and coffee-making arrangements with a hot drinks vending machine. The report was prepared on the instructions of D Fagen, Branch Manager and written by J Ely, Office Junior, Accounts Department. Instructions to prepare the report were received on 24 July 19X6 and it was submitted on 29 July 19X6.

Procedure

It was decided to interview personally all twelve members of staff in the Accounts Department. All staff were notified in advance. Questions were devised, three to establish staff reactions and a fourth inviting comments. All staff were then interviewed and the results noted. (A copy is appended to this report.)

Findings

(a)   In response to the question 'Would you be happy to see a vending machine installed?' EIGHT people said Yes, THREE said No and ONE was uncertain.

(b)   In response to the question 'Are you happy with the present arrangements?' THREE people said Yes, EIGHT people said No and ONE appeared unconcerned.

(c)   In response to the question 'Would you like to have a wider range of hot drinks available to you?' EIGHT people said Yes, THREE people said No and ONE was uncertain.

(d)   Amongst the comments made when staff were invited to comment on the proposal were 'Will fixed times for coffee and tea breaks disappear?' 'What about the tea ladies?' and 'I would prefer to obtain drinks at my own convenience'.

Conclusion

A clear majority of the staff (two-thirds) are in favour of this proposal.

The letter report

As the name implies this is a report written in letter form. Primarily it is used to present information to someone outside the company. For example, an outside consultant may write his analysis and recommendations in the form of a letter, signing the letter as normal.

Memorandum reports

Memorandum reports are used primarily for routine reporting within an organisation, although some companies use them for external communicating. Because they are internal communications, often they are informally written on standardised inter-office memorandum stationery.

Following the company's identification, if there is one, the words From, To and Subject appear at the page top. Sometimes the date is also part of the heading. Like letters the memorandum may carry a signature or the writer may merely initial the heading.

Example: memorandum report

The business supplies buyer of Datewise has asked one of his clerks to investigate the costs and supply of 108mm × 219mm white envelopes, with a view to finding a cheaper source.

MEMORANDUM

To: Mr Hopkins   Date: 4 January 19X7

From: A Clerk

Subject: Supply of envelopes

As requested I have investigated the local suppliers of the 108mm × 219mm white envelopes and compared the costs.

There are three main office suppliers to choose from: Paper Products, Office Treasures and Bestbuy.

Our current supplier, Bestbuy, has free delivery and offers us a 25% discount on orders over £100.

Paper Products offer boxes of 1,000 envelopes £3 cheaper than Bestbuy on orders of six or more boxes. They offer the same discount and have a free delivery once a fortnight in this area. Special deliveries carry a charge of £20.

Office Treasures are the same price as Paper Products but, as we would be new customers, they will not discuss discounts.

Paper Products would be most suitable for us as we always order more than six boxes and rarely need special delivery. I would recommend them for future supplies of envelopes.

The short formal report

This type of report is suitable for more complex and important investigations that are to be reported to senior management.

The most common plan begins with a quick **summary** of the report, including and emphasising conclusions and recommendations. There usually follows a single paragraph covering the facts of **authorisation** and a brief statement of the **problem and its scope**. After the **introductory words** come the findings of the investigation. From all this comes a final **conclusion** and, if needed, a **recommendation**.

Where detailed tables of figures or computations are to be supplied to support the findings of the report, these will often be included at the end of the main text, as **appendices**.

Tables

The purposes of tabulation

Any method of data collection will often result in **large amounts of data** being available. This is the case when an organisation's own internal sources are used or when the data collection is by either a survey, abstraction from secondary sources or other sampling methods. These large amounts of data will need to be examined to obtain relevant information. This means we must discard any irrelevant details, usually leaving us with a number of categories and sub-categories from which we wish to obtain some overall impression. The data remaining from the elimination of irrelevant details can be summarised using either **narrative** or by **use of tables.**

The narrative approach

As will be seen in the example below, a major drawback of the narrative approach is that the information required is **not clearly presented** and only a **limited amount of data** can be presented. A properly constructed tabular presentation, however, gives the required information immediately and clearly.

Example: bank account

A major bank is interested in the types of accounts held by its customers. The information below has recently been collected:

A sample of 5,000 accounts was taken, each account belonging to a different customer. 729 accounts were held by customers aged under 25 of whom 522 held current accounts, the remainder holding ordinary deposit accounts. 1,383 of the accounts were held by customers aged between 25 and 44, 1,020 being current accounts, 271 were ordinary deposit accounts and the remainder were high-interest deposit accounts. There were 1,621 accounts belonging to customers aged between 45 and 59, of these 61% were current accounts, 29% were ordinary deposit accounts and 10% high interest deposit accounts. Of customers aged 60 and over, 628 held current accounts, 410 held ordinary deposit accounts and the remainder held high interest deposit accounts.

Here the data on the 5,000 accounts has already been examined and irrelevant details on, for example, sex of customer or length of time the account has been held for have been eliminated. We are thus left with a reasonable amount of data and, by reading the narrative a few times, we are able to gain some useful information.

The main drawbacks, however, in using this approach to present the data are as follows:

(i) What if the two eliminated variables, sex of customer and age of account, are considered relevant? This would make the narrative much longer and more cumbersome.

(ii) What if other categories were included (for example, an investment account)? This would have a similar effect to (i).

(iii) Perhaps we might like to make comparisons with another major bank or a similar sample of customers. We would then have two pieces of narrative to consider.

These points highlight the problems of using solely a narrative approach and hence point us to the benefits of tabulation.

Using tables

Reconsidering the above example we will work through the process of constructing a single table to summarise all the information contained in the narrative.

A simple one-way table

A major point of interest in the given data is obviously the age breakdown of account holders. Working through the narrative, this could be presented as follows.

	Ages of customers
Age	*Number of customers*
Under 25	729
25–44	1,383
45–59	1,621
60 and over	1,267
	————
Total	5,000
	————

The figure for the 60 and over group is given by 5,000 – (729 + 1,383 + 1,621) since there are a total of 5,000 accounts each held by different customers.

Note that for clarity, you should label both columns clearly and tell the reader what the subject of the table is. It is also useful to show relevant totals (ie in this case the total number of accounts).

A two-way table

Another major point of interest in the data is the number of accounts held of each type. A table of this information is more difficult to extract from the narrative and some steps of working may be helpful. Once this information has been extracted, we can combine it with the previous table to show both ages and types of account held.

There are three types of account: current accounts, ordinary deposit accounts and high interest deposit accounts.

(i)   *Current accounts*

522 (age under 25)

1,020 (aged 25 – 44)

989 (aged 45 – 59; 61% of 1,621 accounts = 0.61 × 1,621 = 988.81 or 989 accounts by rounding to nearest whole number of accounts)

628 (aged 60 and over).

(ii)   *Ordinary deposit accounts*

207 (aged under 25; ie 729 minus the number of current accounts = 729 – 522)

271 (aged 25 – 44)

470 (aged 45 – 59; 29% of 1,621 accounts = 0.29 × 1,621 = 470)

410 (aged 60 and over).

(iii)   *High interest deposit account*

0 (aged under 25; we must assume this since no other detail is given)

92 (aged 25 – 44; 1,383 minus the number of current and ordinary deposit accounts = 1,383 – (1,020 + 271) = 1,383 – 1,291)

162 (aged 45 – 59; 10% of 1,621 accounts = 0.10 × 1,621 = 162.1 or 162)

229 (aged 60 and over; total aged 60 and over minus number of current and ordinary deposit accounts = 1,267 (from (a)) – (628 + 410) = 229).

To summarise all the information contained in the narrative is now easily done by employing a two-way table (sometimes called a **cross-tabulation**). In this example, the two 'variables' are obviously age of customers and type of account held. These become the headings for the following required two-way table:

Ages and types of account held by sample of 5,000 customers

Type of account	under 25	Age 25–44	45–59	60 and over	Total
Current	522	1,020	989	628	3,159
Ordinary deposit	207	271	470	410	1,358
High interest deposit	0	92	162	229	483
Total	729	1,383	1,621	1,267	5,000

Guidelines for constructing tables

There are no set rules for constructing tables since tables often vary markedly in content and format. The following guidelines should however be adhered to.

(a)   Always give the table a title and suitable headings.

(b)   If the data contains a number of categories or sub-categories, use a two-way table.

(c)   Give column and row sub-totals where appropriate.

(d)   If the draft table contains too much detail, it will fail in its objective of summarising the data. Further simplified tables should then be constructed, each dealing with different aspects of the data.

(e)   It is important to state the source of the data. This may be included in the title or given beneath the table.

(f)   The units in the table should be 'manageable'. This can be accomplished by, for example, dividing particular column entries by 1,000 and including this fact in the column heading.

(g)   It is sometimes useful to show *percentages* in the table in addition to the actual figures.

Charts and diagrams

Charts and diagrams are frequently used to present data in a clear and eye-catching way. Large masses of complicated data can be presented in such a way as to be readily understood. There are many different charts and diagrams which can be used. The choice depends on the following:

(a)   the type of data

(b)   the amount of data

(c)   what factors should be emphasised, if any.

You should always ensure that the end result is a chart or diagram which is **clear** and **intelligible**. Also, remember that charts and diagrams give visual information for comparing relative size. As such, they are unsuitable for conveying precise numerical information. Where precision is required, tables of data should be used.

Drawing charts and diagrams

When drawing diagrams and charts, there are several common-sense rules to follow.

(a)   Try to make the diagrams neat and uncluttered. Use a ruler.

(b)   If graph paper is available, use it.

(c)   The diagram should have a title.

(d)   The variables and scales should be shown on each *axis*.

(e)   Set the scale so that you use as much of the paper as you can for the diagram; this will keep the diagram neater and assist accuracy.

(f)   Units must be indicated on both axes.

(g)   Where diagrams are combined or superimposed ensure that each is recognisable separately and suitably labelled.

(h)   Too much detail on a diagram makes it confusing rather than enlightening.

(i)   Remember the key where appropriate.

(j)   Remember to start scales at zero on bar charts.

(k)   Remember that component and compound bar charts become less and less effective the more sub-divisions you use. It is often worth considering a pie chart as an alternative.

Pie charts

A pie chart consists of a circle split into *segments*. The circle represents a total and the segments represent the parts which go to make up the total. The 360° of the circle is divided in *proportion* to the figures making the total. Suppose a family's income in 19X5 is £1,000 per month.

There now follows the split of their expenditure, along with the proportion each category represents of the whole and the angle this will represent on a pie chart.

	Amount £	*Proportion* %	*Angle* (degrees) – see note
Mortgage and insurance	300	30	108
Electricity and gas	50	5	18
Food and drink	200	20	72
Clothes	40	4	14
Car and petrol	150	15	54
Telephone	10	1	4
Savings	70	7	25
Fares	60	6	22
Miscellaneous	120	12	43
	1,000	100	360

Note: The degrees are calculated as the percentage proportion 360° (eg the first category will be represented by 30% × 360 = 108°).

The corresponding pie chart is shown in Figure 9.1.

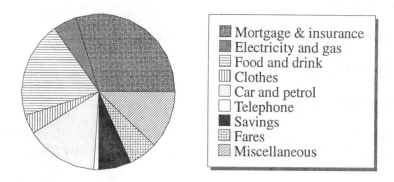

Figure 9.1   Pie chart

You can replace the names in the segments with different colours or shadings provided a key is given. Again, we do not obtain a precise idea of expenditure on certain items or services, just an idea of their relative proportions.

Simple bar charts

In a simple bar chart the figures we wish to compare are represented by bars. These can either be drawn vertically or horizontally. The height or length of a bar is proportional to the size of the figure being illustrated. Suppose we know that production figures of different car companies are as follows:

Firm	Number of cars produced
Ausota	180,000
Vauxsun	145,000
Moruar	165,000
Trihall	160,000
Fortin	170,000

The vertical bar chart for these figures is shown in Figure 9.2.

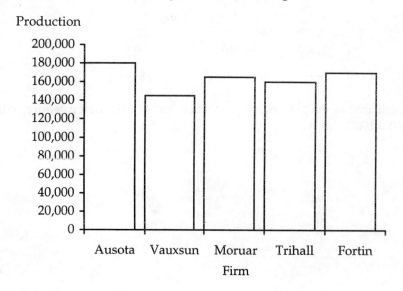

Figure 9.2   Vertical bar chart

Figure 9.3 is the horizontal bar chart for the same figures.

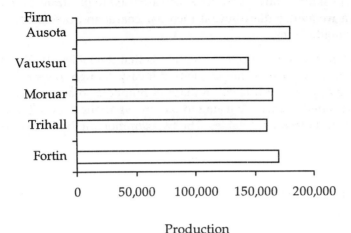

Production

Figure 9.2 Horizontal bar chart

We can put the appropriate identification either in the bar itself, immediately adjacent to the bar, or use a key for shadings or colours. There is no need to draw 3-dimensional bars, 2-dimensional are perfectly adequate and often less confusing. When drawing these charts it is very important to start the scale from zero. A very misleading picture may be shown otherwise. This is, in fact, a very common way in which readers are misled. Look out for the trick in your newspaper!

Component bar charts

When we draw bar charts the totals we wish to illustrate can often be broken down into sub-divisions or components. Suppose we have the following table of wine consumption by type and year:

	Consumption figures (10,000 litres)			
	White	*Red*	*Rosé*	*Total*
19X2	59.3	46.5	14.2	120.0
19X3	63.6	47.0	14.4	125.0
19X4	72.3	48.2	14.5	135.0

We start by drawing a simple bar chart of the total figures. The columns or bars are then split up into the component parts. Remember to put the key on the diagram otherwise it is useless. This chart can still be drawn either vertically or horizontally.

Litres ('0,000)

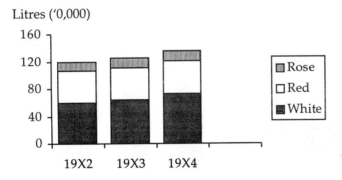

Figure 9.3 Component bar chart (wine consumption)

Here different colours for the different components would be especially effective.

Charts showing frequency distributions

Up to now in this chapter we have considered various charts which are used to illustrate data. If, however, the data is contained in a **frequency distribution** then bar charts and pie charts are limited in the amount of data they can illustrate.

When frequency tables or distributions are drawn up the intention is that the tables should tell us what sort of data and spread of data we have. Some people find it easy enough to spot these characteristics from a table but for many people it is still a mass of numbers so an alternative simpler method of presentation is required. As we are trying to picture what our data is like we use pictures or pictorial representations of frequency tables. The two common methods used are as follows.

(a)   Histograms

(b)   Frequency polygons (and frequency curves)

Histograms

The usual diagram used to illustrate a frequency distribution is a histogram. The horizontal scale is used for the variable or measurement of importance and the vertical scale to indicate frequency.

Consider the following data for the weights of sweets in a particular box of assorted sweets.

Weight of package (grams)			*Frequency* (number of sweet boxes)
≥ 485	but	< 490	1
≥ 490	but	< 495	3
≥ 495	but	< 500	12
≥ 500	but	< 505	22
≥ 505	but	< 510	8
≥ 510	but	< 515	2
			—
			48
			—

The histogram for this frequency distribution would be drawn as shown in Figure 9.4.

Number of sweet boxes

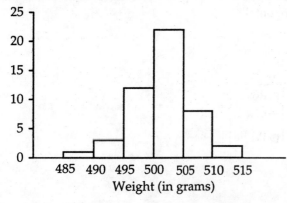

Figure 9.4   Histogram

The columns are drawn up from the horizontal axis and, because the intervals we have are of equal width, are drawn to a height on the vertical scale representing frequency. Because the horizontal scale represents a (continuous) variable, the bars touch each other.

Difficulties with discrete data

If our data is discrete, then there are difficulties in specifying the values on the horizontal axis since it is a continuous scale. The way round the problem is to treat each integer as if it represented all values which would round to it. In other words, 6 would be treated as 5.5 to 6.5 and so on.

Alternatively, discrete intervals of 0–4, 5–9 could be re-expressed as 0 to <5, ≥ 5 to < 10, etc.

Frequency polygons

As an alternative to histograms, we may use **frequency polygons**. The diagram that follows attempts to emphasise the 'shape' of our data. The easiest way to illustrate the frequency polygon is to assume we have already drawn a histogram. To obtain the frequency polygon mark the mid-point of the top of each histogram column, then join them up. (This could be said to treat each interval as if all its frequency were at the mid-point of the interval.)

The polygon is usually neatened up at the ends of the distribution by bringing it down to meet the horizontal axis at what would have been the mid-point of the adjacent class interval if it had existed. If you do not have a histogram to work from then follow the same rules as were used in the construction of the histogram as regards treatment of unequal class intervals and open-ended class intervals.

A histogram is shown in Figure 9.5, together with a frequency polygon superimposed.

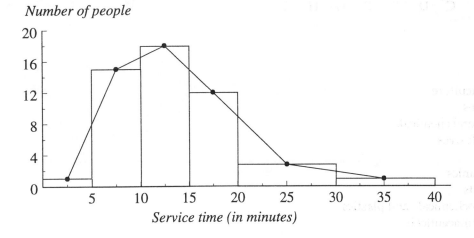

Figure 9.5   Frequency polygon

Frequency curves

The frequency polygons we have obtained were rather jagged figures. If we had a histogram with very small *class intervals*, and therefore with very many columns, then points of the frequency polygon would be close together. This has a smoothing effect on the polygon and, if we continued the process, we should eventually arrive at a smooth curve (a **frequency curve**).

Questions

1   ICI profits

Interpret the following diagram.

ICI trading profits by division (£)

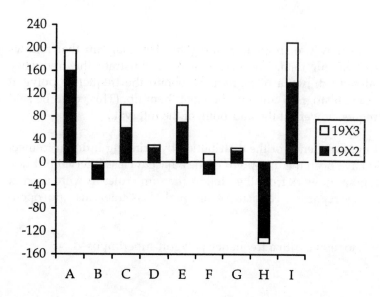

Key

A	=	Agriculture
B	=	Fibres
C	=	General chemicals
D	=	Explosives
E	=	Oil
F	=	Organics
G	=	Paints
H	=	Petrochemicals and plastics
I	=	Pharmaceuticals

2 Pydec

Pydec Limited is a British company manufacturing television sets and audio equipment. The attached is a section from their company report for 19X1/X2.

REPORT

Pydec Limited – Difficult times ahead?

As you all know this has been a very difficult year for the company. The following diagrams illustrate this all too clearly.

Profits tumble

From the following graph, you can see just how badly we have done in respect of profits. There are two main reasons for this fall in profits (down by almost 20%). Firstly, and most importantly, we have had sold fewer of our products. Secondly, we have to contend with inflation which has greatly increased both our overheads and our costs of production (not least of which has been the increase in wages – see later).

Total profits

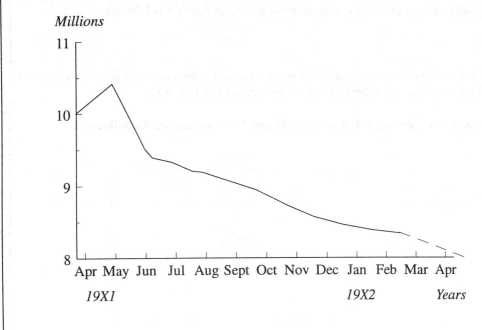

Page 1/3

Production falls

As you know, we have three factories, at Dundee, London and here at Leicester (Head office). The following bar chart gives a breakdown of the production of TV sets at the three factories.

Number of TV sets produced (thousands)

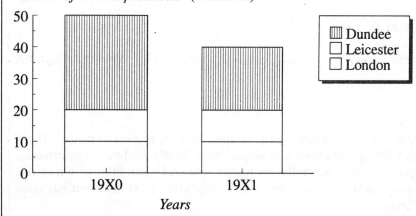

From this one can clearly see that production has fallen significantly over the last year. This is disturbing, especially since some of our competitors have been doing much better.

Wages up

In the past we have always rewarded our employees well; last year was no different. In fact, the average wage of all employees rose by £7.23 per week from 19X0 to 19X1.

In fact, if we compare average wages between 19W5 and 19X0 we can see the following.

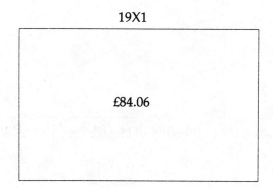

Prospects for the future are not good and any wage increases must be earned by increasing our efficiency.

Page 2/3

The future

The above diagrams give a gloomy forecast for the coming years. To remain competitive we may have to reduce our workforce significantly. However, in some respects we can help ourselves quite a lot.

Our main cost is employees' wages. If wage increases are kept to a minimum this can only do us good and may help us retain staff.

Our aim for the coming year must be to try and become more competitive.

I look forward to your support.

James Telly
Chairman

Page 3/3

Required

You have been asked by the co-ordinating committee of a trade union at the Leicester factory of Pydec to comment critically on this report.

3   Not at all obvious

Look at the following extract from a written report.

Ten newsagent shops in the Bristol area were selected to test the effectiveness of two different display stands in generating sales. For the purposes of the survey the shops were designated with the letters A–J (see Appendix for the address of each shop).

During the period 15 March to 20 March, the total sales for the three items were recorded. Two different stands were used to display those items for sale. Five of the stands were the traditional sloping top 5 ft wide stand made of formica with perspex divisions while the other five were the metal revolving type, 2 ft in diameter. Shops A, C, D, G, I, used the traditional stand and shops B, E, F, H, J, used the revolving stand.

Total sales of the items during the six day test period (Monday to Saturday inclusive) were as follows: Shops E, F, G, H showed sales of 435, 475, 286 and 575 cards and Shop I 275 with Shop J at 525.

There is an obvious correlation between sales and type of display stand. This correlation is reflected in similar studies carried out in Manchester and Aberdeen.

This material is taken from a survey report. How well have you been able to assimilate the information? Was the correlation between the sales and the type of display stand quite as 'obvious' as the author suggests?

Required

(a)   Your immediate superior, Mrs Jenkins, has asked you to rewrite this report in the short report format, presenting the facts in a more understandable manner.

(b)   Write a memo to the author, Jo Bloggs, raising any further queries you may have about the survey report.

Summary

This chapter has revised the main principles to be followed in preparing a report and the various ways in which data may be presented – by tabulation or diagrammatically.

Many of the questions in your assessment will either require you to present the answer in report format or to interpret information presented in a table or diagrammatic form.

CHAPTER 10

Cost Reduction, Quality and Value Enhancement

Objectives

This chapter describes the ways in which organisations can reduce costs and enhance the value of the goods and services that they provide. It covers the following performance criterion.

7.2.3 **Relevant specialists are consulted to assist in the identification of ways to reduce costs and enhance value.**

When you have completed this chapter, you should:

♦ understand and be able to discuss ways of reducing costs in specific situations

♦ understand the technique of value analysis

♦ understand the concept of total quality management.

Cost reduction

Most companies are in business to make profit; non-profit organisations, such as charities and local authorities, are equally expected to keep expenses and costs down to a minimum. In times of inflation, costs are continually rising and it is not always possible to balance this with a rise in sales revenue. Thus improvements to profit may rely heavily upon a cost reduction programme.

Cost reduction has been defined as a process which leads to 'the achievement of real and permanent reductions in the unit costs of goods manufactured or services rendered without impairing their suitability for the use intended'.

Note the importance of maintaining the characteristics and quality of the product.

It is not to be confused with **cost control**, which is based upon the acceptance of target costs and which aims to achieve those costs by preventing or eliminating the causes of variances or excess costs. Cost control accepts the standards which have been set and endeavours to enforce them; cost reduction actively challenges the agreed standards to find ways of achieving savings of one kind or another. The definition also suggests that there is scope for the use of cost reduction techniques throughout an organisation's activities, from design to production and from distribution and marketing to finance and administration.

Planning cost reduction

The successful application of cost reduction techniques requires the commitment and involvement of **senior management**. If they are seen to be interested and to have a real conviction of the need for cost reduction, it will be easier to secure the co-operation of other managers, supervisors, employees and their representatives. However committed and enthusiastic the top management is, experiments show that the **gradual introduction** and development of cost reduction techniques is more likely to succeed than a hasty movement. The whole exercise must be thought out first and all stages carefully planned, preferably on a participative basis.

Obviously it is important to determine the **overall objective** towards which cost reduction should lead. For a manufacturing business, this may be a reduction in the costs of materials or overheads; a service activity will perhaps look at manpower.

It is also important to consider whether cost reduction is being thought of as **economic necessity** – 'if we do not start doing this, we shall go out of business' – or as a matter of **setting realistic targets** under a comparison of the firm's prices and margins, against those of competitors. Clearly, a plan for survival will be very different from one aimed at maintaining a relative market position.

Applications of cost reduction – manufacturing

Virtually all areas of both manufacturing and service businesses are open to the use of cost reduction techniques.

To illustrate the principles and techniques, we shall initially look at the particular functions of a manufacturing business. Later we shall consider how these may be applied, in more general form, to activities in the service sector.

The functions to be considered are as follows:

- design

- production and purchasing

- marketing and distribution

- finance

- labour.

Design

Design often offers the greatest scope for cost reduction initiatives. Management training increasingly emphasises the importance of introducing cost reduction techniques at the earliest possible stage, **when the product is still on the drawing board.**

The introduction of cost reduction in design activity, however, is fraught with difficulty because design activity has traditionally emphasised the following:

- low cost and functional efficiency

- widest possible application

- quality and durability (or obsolescence threshold)

- appearance.

Not all these factors lend themselves to cost reduction considerations.

The potential for cost reduction needs to be investigated throughout the design stage in the following ways.

♦ Materials specification: use or otherwise of standard parts; suitability of metal in handling and working; yield factor; storage and stock investment

♦ Labour: effect of design on manufacturing processes – tolerance, performance standards

♦ Cost of tooling

♦ Standardisation and simplification

♦ Compactness: the impact of size and shape on storage and transportation

♦ Time control: gearing product to possible changes in fashion and to seasonal demands, thus reducing stock obsolescence rates; or developing products that transcend fashion

Production and purchasing

♦ **Factory organisation and production methods**

The production function is rich with potential for cost reduction. It is also one that has already been thoroughly explored and as a result many cost savings have been incorporated into standard procedures. It would also be true to say that cost reduction in this area has pervaded the whole of manufacturing business.

Cost reduction effort in the factory begins by checking the allocation and distribution of authority and responsibility, for it is surprising how costs can be increased through **inefficiencies in organisational arrangements.** Channels of communication are not always properly aligned to the authority structure, leading to waste and increased operating costs.

The effective **arrangement of plant and equipment** is a key feature of successful production planning. Good plant layout will:

(i) achieve the optimal use of space

(ii) allow for the most efficient flow of work

(iii) facilitate effective control

(iv) reduce materials handling to a minimum

(v) minimise waste

(vi) promote employee satisfaction and motivation

(vii) allow for change and development

(viii) maximise productivity.

♦ **Purchasing**

Material cost may be controlled and reduced in two ways:

(a) by **price,** through purchasing policy – this is easy to follow and can lead to immediate gains

(b) by **quality organisation** through stock control and material handling, usage and yield. This is more difficult and more long-term, although the gains can be considerable.

Purchasing makes full use of **value analysis** (which we shall see later) to identify materials that match specification cost. Purchasing also employs **equipment analysis** to establish levels of relative cost-effectiveness for investing in new, as compared to reconditioning old equipment.

Any firm should attempt to obtain from existing suppliers either a **price reduction** or a **discount** of some kind. If negotiations do not succeed, then it is always possible to investigate the likelihood of achieving better deals with other suppliers. It is one of the functions of the purchasing department to keep prices under constant review in these ways.

Obtaining a **quantity discount** in order to obtain a lower price is a common method of achieving reductions in cost. Firms have to be careful, however, not to increase storage cost and interest charges to the point at which the advantages of the quantity discount are lost.

It is essential to evaluate the effect of discounts on the **economic order quantity.** Purchasing should also ensure that the delivery of materials is geared to production needs and a defined level of short-term capital investment in stocks.

♦ **Stock control**

Materials can be handled more efficiently by improving stock control, including:

(a) storage location and its associated costs

(b) indirect services to stock control, such as stores administration, and their costs

(c) amount and causes of stock losses and write-offs – pilfering, deterioration, obsolescence

(d) arrangements for inspections and stocktaking

(e) insurance of stock.

♦ **Materials handling**

Reductions may be made in the costs of **materials handling, usage and yield.** Developments in technology have reduced considerably the costs of handling material through computerised information systems and more advanced material handling techniques.

♦ **Economies in usage**

Finding ways of using less material to obtain existing or improved output can result in spectacular cost reductions. In some industries the yield of saleable product from raw materials is high, but in others the waste may be at 10 to 50% of the materials purchased. It is therefore important for firms to know what their existing yield is and to see if it can be improved. Analysis may reveal **waste** through the use of too much material or through the loss of material – unusable off-cuts etc.; it may also reveal opportunities for reworking scrap.

♦ **Overhead control**

Overheads can be effectively controlled and monitored through **budgetary control** and by the use of **standard costing.**

Close inspection of works services often reveal room for further reductions; the cost of maintenance and the canteen have been shown on many occasions to be open to reduction.

Marketing and distribution

Marketing covers selling and distribution: the former entails representatives, advertising, market research, sales, office support and administration and after-sales servicing, while the latter takes in packing, transportation and merchandising. It has been said that marketing does not lend itself so readily to cost reduction as the other business functions. However, experience shows that there is scope for cost reduction in each of the functions of marketing.

♦ **Representatives**

When looking at the costs of representatives it is worthwhile asking: is the organisation of territories and consequential arrangement of routes and calls, the most cost-effective way of achieving representation? Some reorganisation and replanning aimed at reduction in travelling time and associated costs may be possible. It may also be found that it is more economical to use agents, rather than representatives, especially in remote areas.

♦ **Advertising**

The tendency in recent times has been to place more emphasis on analysing the effectiveness of advertising and to exercise more control over it. For example, an examination of expenditure on advertising as a percentage of sales and, if possible, a comparison of the figure with that of competitors may reveal that particular advertisements are ineffective and produce significant on costs.

♦ **Market research**

The usefulness of market research is obvious. It leads to the provision of information about market size, the source of business, customer preferences and much else that aids management in policy formation, planning, strategy determination and decision making.

Market research can, however, be used directly to investigate opportunities for cost reduction in the analysis of customer and proportion of market and sales, the analysis of order size, particularly in relation to the unit cost of selling per order and so forth. In these effects, the technique of value analysis is especially helpful.

♦   **Sales office**

The setting of sales targets makes possible the analysis and assessment of individual performance on either a personal or group basis or both. The advantage of this type of investigation is that it throws light on the inefficiencies and deficiencies that lie behind a substandard performance.

A salesman may perform poorly, not because he is inherently a bad salesman, or lacks interest and commitment, but because he has not received adequate **training** in sales techniques or does not have sufficient **knowledge** about his products or competing products. It may be that the sales force lacks **leadership, incentive and motivation** but this too can be exposed by analysing actual performance against sales targets.

Something useful may come out of an examination of the type of **support** that is given to the sales force. The effectiveness of the sales office staff and the procedures that they use may be well below the standards attained in other areas and improvements could mean significant reduction in the sales element of unit costs.

♦   **After-sales service**

There are essentially three ways of reducing costs here:

(a)   by minimising the amount of after-sales service needed

(b)   by employing local agents to service faulty products

(c)   by offering maintenance deals.

♦   **Packing**

The question of packing must be considered at the design stage – it is necessary for safe distribution and to avoid pilferage, but its cost should not be out of proportion to its usefulness.

♦   **Transport**

Carriage charges are usually a variable in overhead costs, moving up and down with changes in the volume of business. Cost reductions may be achieved by securing lower haulage costs by, for example, switching from road to rail, minimising premium charges for urgent deliveries and so forth. They may also be reduced by, for example, dispensing with company transport and using someone else's transport by leasing, contract hire, casual hire or by whatever arrangement is calculated to be most cost-beneficial. Furthermore, reductions can flow from **bulk despatch** which gives lower costs per unit despatched. Some caution is necessary in this area, however, since savings in carriage charges may have to be set against the increased costs of improved packing and storage.

In general, three points must always be looked at in cost reduction exercises affecting transport.

(i)   Is the existing method of transport entirely suitable and can it be adapted for higher volumes if required?

(ii)   Is the type of transport cost-effective, best suited to distances covered, satisfactory to the customer and sufficiently protective?

(iii)   Is the matter of transportation currently employed efficient and effective from the standpoint of distribution and sales?

Finance

Every company should seek to achieve the most effective use of its capital. Capital should be employed in ways that produce the maximum possible return. Capital is frequently tied up unproductively in stocks, idle fixed assets and uncooperative debtors.

One way of releasing this unproductive capital is to introduce more effective control systems. In the case of debtors, it may be beneficial for a company to make a contract with a factoring company, rather than introduce an improved system of credit control of its own. Idle fixed assets may be capable of redeployment in a proposed extension of production, or they may be adopted for new products. If no use can be found for them within the organisation, there is the alternative of selling them or, for some types of plant, leasing them.

New capital investment and capital expenditure must always be carefully appraised beforehand. It is important also to consider the additional working capital requirements when contemplating any new capital investment.

Capital investment in improved or new equipment can lead to substantial cost savings by reducing manpower costs per unit of output, or increasing material yield.

Capital replacement and refurbishment programmes should be devised with an eye on both profit forecasts and likely changes in price levels. They should be implemented systematically according to some order of need. The cost-effectiveness of the different methods of funding capital expenditure should be examined to enable the selection of the best method of funding.

Labour

Although rising unemployment and recession have led in the UK to the resuscitation of ideas that were long thought to be dead – such as the notion of reducing labour costs by cutting wage rates or the idea that wages ought to be determined by market forces – the best hope for reduction in labour costs would still seem to be with increased efficiency and productivity. Indeed, many businessmen believe that improved productivity is the only practical way of reducing labour costs.

Productivity is the ratio of output to input and improvements in this ratio can be achieved by reducing the average time required to make a product or provide a service. Such a reduction may be sought in many ways:

(a)   by controlling withdrawal (eg absenteeism, labour turnover) and the incidence of accidents and industrial diseases

(b)   through the use of appropriate financial and non-financial incentives, like bonus payments for regular attendance or offering opportunities for advancement

(c)   by improving the working environment, operating conditions and general facilities

(d)   by the use of piecework or bonus schemes

(e)   productivity agreements and perks of various kinds

(f)   by the careful selection and training of employees.

The most dramatic improvements in productivity, however, usually follow the introduction of either better and faster machines or improved methods of working, or both. These developments often provide additional bonuses by reducing indirect labour costs on maintenance and repairs and by making possible savings in the costs of other items, such as materials (better usage and yield) and fuel.

Applications of cost reductions – the service sector

The above detailed analysis concentrated upon the functions of a product-based business. Such a business will also inevitably incorporate service departments to which cost reduction programmes can be applied and, of course, some businesses will be entirely service-based, including those in the public sector.

Due to the wide divergence in the nature of the services provided by such departments or businesses, it is not possible to be very specific about the techniques to be used. Many of the ideas discussed for the manufacturing business will apply, with perhaps a little modification, to the service sector, in particular those regarding marketing, finance and labour. Thus we shall consider the general approach to cost reduction programmes that can be applied in a wide context.

The starting point will often be the examination of existing activities, to determine whether the use of resources by those activities is excessive. Over-consumption of resources may arise from one or a combination of:

◆ over-resourced activities

◆ inefficiently managed activities

◆ unnecessary activities

Over-resourced activities

An activity is over-resourced when the same objective could be achieved with the use of less resource. For example, in a library, the number of counter staff employed may have remained relatively constant for a number of years, despite increasing sophistication of computerised check-out systems.

Individual offices of a firm of accountants may each employ a computer audit specialist, when the same level of service could be achieved at lower cost by employing one specialist per region and requiring him/her to travel to offices as required.

Inefficiently managed activities

Activities are inefficiently managed when current standards of achievement are not being attained. For example, excessive overtime may be incurred by staff in the accounts department at the accounting year-end, which could have been avoided by better planning of schedules and other information-gathering exercises that could be partially completed in advance of the year-end.

Excessive travel time may be incurred by maintenance engineers where their activities have not been properly co-ordinated.

Such deficiencies will usually be highlighted in normal variance reports.

Unnecessary activities

These will normally be activities of service or overhead departments within a business, or activities that are supplementary to the main service activity of the business.

To control the resources consumed by overhead departments effectively, it is necessary to understand:

♦ why such departments exist

♦ the services they provide

♦ their relationship to other areas of the business.

It may be decided that costs can best be reduced by curtailing the activities of the department, or, in extreme cases, closing it down altogether. For example, it may be that some or all of the routine computer processing currently carried out by the DP department could be cost-effectively sub-contracted out to an agency, without affecting the level or quality of the service provided to the other areas of the business.

Activities that are offered to the customer of a business as an addition to the main service provided should be assessed from a 'value-added' perspective – that is whether the cost spent on the activity is perceived to result in something of extra value to the customer, for which they are willing to pay. If not, the activity should be eliminated.

For example, a college may offer an out-of-hours student help service, for which it has to employ staff on overtime. If, however, this does not influence the students in their choice of college and thus the level of funding (private or public) attracted, it is a non-value added activity and should be stopped.

The techniques of **value analysis** are important in their own right, not just as part of a cost reduction exercise, and are now discussed further.

Value analysis

Value analysis (VA) was developed by HL Erlichter at General Electric of America in 1947 and has been adopted worldwide. Major British companies who have used VA extensively include Vickers, Ford (UK) and Rolls Royce.

VA is a technique that seeks to find an alternative way to provide a function at a lower cost. Its greatest application occurs in high-volume industries where fractional savings on product costs can be multiplied many times and so produce substantial savings. VA has been of great importance in emphasising the importance of the cost factor in the design function.

Application

Value analysis is not planned obsolescence nor is it cost-cutting. The purpose of VA is to provide the same value at a lower price – the essential element is the safeguarding of the quality involved.

In practice, a team, drawn from various disciplines or a trained quality control team, takes a product, breaks it into its component parts and systematically studies each part in turn.

In analysing each part, the team will initially decide the use value and esteem value of that part.

(a)   *Use value* is the term given to the properties and qualities that accomplish a particular use, purpose or service.

(b)   *Esteem value* is the term given to the properties and qualities needed to be added to protect sales appeal. For example, a pen top for a ballpoint might have a use value since it:

    (i)   protects owner's pocket/clothes

    (ii)   protects ink application

    (iii)   provides clip for storage

    (iv)   denotes colour of ink

and an esteem value since it:

    (i)   promotes manufacturer's name

    (ii)   could bestow sense of luxury/pride.

The group would analyse each part by asking the following sequence of questions:

(a)   What is it? Detailed statement of size, material, etc.

(b)   What does it cost?

(c)   What does it do? (Use and esteem value.)

(d)   How many do we use?

(e)   What is its primary function?

(f)   What else will do?

(g)   What would these alternatives cost?

(h)   Can we identify a cheaper alternative whilst maintaining use and esteem values?

An example of VA

One of the most frequently quoted examples is Bic biro for which a fractional saving in design is multiplied many thousands of times per day during manufacture. Similarly, the substitution of plastic for metal in ball points has maintained the same use value, not damaged esteem value and greatly reduced costs.

Quality control

Quality control function

Quality control is concerned with maintaining quality standards. There are usually procedures to check quality of bought-in materials, work in progress and finished goods. Sometimes one or all of these functions is the responsibility of the research and development department on the premise that production should not self-regulate its own quality.

Statistical quality control through sampling techniques is commonly used to reduce costs and production interruptions. On some occasions, customers have the contractual right to visit a manufacturer unannounced and carry out quality checks. This is normal practice with Sainsbury's and Tesco's contracts with manufacturers producing 'own label' goods (eg Tesco Baked Beans).

In the past, failure to screen quality successfully has resulted in rejections, re-work and scrap, all of which add to manufacturing costs. Modern trends in industry of competition, mass production and increasing standards of quality requirements have resulted in a thorough reappraisal of the problem and two important points have emerged.

(a)   It is necessary to single out and remove the causes for poor quality goods *before* production instead of waiting for the end result. This is cost-effective since customer complaints, etc. reduce dramatically.

(b)   The co-ordination of all activities from the preparation of the specification, through the purchasing and inspection functions, right up to the function of delivery of the finished product is essential.

It is accepted that it is not possible to achieve perfection in products because of the variations in raw material quality, operating skills, different types of machines used, wear and tear, etc. but quality control attempts to ascertain the amount of variation from perfect that can be expected in any operation. If this variation is acceptable according to engineering requirements, then production must be established within controlled limits and, if the variation is more than the acceptable one, then corrective action must be taken to bring the variation within acceptable limits.

Overall quality control may be looked at under the following five headings.

(a)   *Setting standards* – Sometimes called 'new design control' this function involves the preparatory work necessary before production commences. It includes the location of possible sources of manufacturing troubles from trial runs, preparing inspection specifications after sampling, and planning the production and inspection functions, based on the results of these preliminary activities.

(b)   *Incoming material control* – This ensures the availability of the necessary material of the required quality standards during production. Close quality contacts must be made with the supplier to establish quality control at the source. The first deliveries received are subjected to 100% inspection to establish the supplier's level of quality. Information is given to the supplier to allow him to take remedial action if necessary. When the required quality level has been reached, other deliveries are subjected to sampling tests only.

(c) *Product control* – This involves the control of processed parts at the production sources so that most differences from quality specifications that may have arisen are put right before any defective parts are produced. The three aspects of product control are as follows.

    (i) Quality mindedness of the operatives and, to this end, extensive training programmes in quality control are arranged.

    (ii) Inspectors and testers with good training and experience help foremen to pinpoint potential causes of defects by showing them how to apply control techniques.

    (iii) Applying sampling checks to the finished product before delivery.

(d) *Special purpose studies* – This is the investigation of the causes of defective products and looking for ways of improving elements of production quality.

(e) *Appraisal* – This is critical appraisal of the overall results obtained from the programme and consideration of ways to deal with changing conditions.

Quality itself must be regarded as relative to other factors such as price, consistency and utility. The market for a product or service will accommodate itself to various degrees of quality.

A concept you may encounter is that of a **quality and reliability system**, including the following elements.

♦ A study of customer requirements, particularly as they relate to performance and price.

♦ The design of the product or service.

♦ Full specification of the requirements of the design, clearly understood by everybody concerned with production.

♦ Assurance that operational processes can meet the requirements of the design.

♦ Acceptance by everybody of responsibility for meeting standards. Many people share in this responsibility. The manager plays a part by declaring what quality standards are to be. Design engineers must work within the parameters which give satisfaction to the customer. Production controllers make sure that output of the right quality is produced on time. Purchasing officers must find reliable suppliers. Operatives must be trained to achieve standards.

♦ Checking that the product or service conforms to the specification.

♦ Instructions on the use, application and limitation of the product or service.

♦ Study of consumer experience of the product, feedback to the departments concerned and immediate remedial action, if necessary, otherwise praise all round.

The **quality control function** looks at the process as a continuous operation, a series of trends and rejection rates. Reports from the quality control department to management include the following:

(a)   analysis of defects by cause

(b)   comparisons between processes and departments

(c)   comparison of defect levels with previous levels and standard levels

(d)   longer-term trends in quality

(e)   reports on customers' complaints

(f)   developments in quality control practice

(g)   special reports.

Advantages of quality control

The responsibility for quality control cannot be isolated as we have seen and can only be effective when it is the result of joint effort. The advantages lie in the fact that quality control points out why faulty work is being produced and the extent of it. Action taken as a result can reduce scrap and the amount of necessary re-work. It shows where a design modification could raise efficiency in manufacture. It minimises the chances of poor materials being processed.

The most effective areas where control can be usefully applied in most enterprises are:

(a)   goods inwards

(b)   inspection at the supplier's business to see the type of plant and the methods used;

(c)   inspection of all new tools and plant

(d)   inspection of the first part completed at each stage

(e)   inspection between processes

(f)   a final check at the end of the production line with any minor adjustments being made.

It is as much a fault to produce goods of too high a quality as goods of poor quality.

The requirements of the customers must be borne in mind and the sales department and market research can advise on this. They will be aware of competitors' prices and qualities and a decision must be taken whether or not to increase quality. To increase quality means increasing costs and establishing the point at which the customer will decide that the quality is more than he can afford.

One definition of quality is **'a degree of excellence'**. It is the correct degree of excellence compatible with costs that management must agree on. If they can arrive at this and maintain it, they will have overcome one of the most difficult factors of production.

Total quality management (TQM)

Total quality management (TQM) can be defined as **'a continuous improvement in quality, efficiency and effectiveness'**.

♦ It aims towards an environment of **zero defects at a minimum cost.**

♦ It requires an **awareness by all personnel** of the quality requirements with supplying the customer with products of the agreed design specification.

♦ It aims towards the **elimination of waste** where waste is defined as anything other than the minimum essential amount of equipment, materials, space and workers' time.

♦ It must embrace **all aspects of operations** from pre-production to post-production stages in the business cycle.

Total quality management will, therefore, seek method changes which will help in achieving such objectives. Examples include the use of **Just-in-time (JIT) production procedures** whereby each component or product is produced or purchased only when needed by production or by a customer, rather than for stock.

The cost of quality

Traditionally failure rates, scrap and reworking were subsumed within the costs of production while other aspects of poor quality were accounted for in either production or marketing overheads. TQM does not accept the cost of poor quality as inevitable and requires that the cost of quality is highlighted in management reports. This enables alternative approaches (such as built-in quality at the design stage) to be developed.

Quality-related costs are the expenditure incurred in defect prevention and appraisal activities and the losses due to internal and external failure of a product or service through failure to meet agreed specifications.

Quality-related costs may be classified as follows.

(a) **Failure costs** are the costs required to evaluate, dispose of, and either correct or replace a defective or deficient product.

    (i) *Internal failure costs* are costs discovered before the product is delivered to the customer. Examples include the following.

        ♦ Rework costs

        ♦ Net cost of scrap

        ♦ Disposal of defective products

        ♦ Downtime due to quality problems

(ii) *External failure costs* are costs discovered after the product is delivered to customers. Examples include the following.

- Complaint investigation and processing

- Warranty claims

- Cost of lost sales

- Product recalls

(b) **Appraisal costs** are costs of monitoring and inspecting products in terms of specified standards before the products are released to the customer. Examples include the following.

- Measurement equipment

- Inspection and tests

- Product quality audits

- Process control monitoring

- Test equipment expense

(c) **Prevention costs** include investments in machinery, technology, and education programs designed to reduce the number of defective products during production. Examples include the following.

- Customer surveys

- Research of customer needs

- Field trials

- Quality education and training programs

- Supplier reviews

- Investment in improved production equipment

- Quality engineering

- Quality circles

Example: Total quality management

Calton Limited make and sell a single product.

The following information affects its costs and revenues.

1   5% of income material from suppliers is scrapped owing to poor receipt and storage organisation.

2   4% of material X input to the machine process is wasted owing to processing problems.

3   Inspection and storage of material X costs 10 pence per square metre purchased.

4   Inspection during the production cycle, calibration checks on inspection equipment, ventor rating and other checks cost £25,000 per period.

5   Production quantity is increased to allow for the downgrading of 12.5% of product units at the final inspection stage. Downgraded units are sold as 'second quality' units at a discount of 30% on the standard selling price.

6   Production quantity is increased to allow for returns from customers which are replaced free of charge. Returns are due to specification failure and account for five per cent of units initially delivered to customers. Replacement units incur a delivery cost of £8 per unit. 80% of the returns from customers are rectified using 0.2 hours of machine running time per unit and are re-sold as 'third quality' products at a discount of 50% on the standard selling price. The remaining returned units are sold as scrap for £5 per unit.

7   Product liability and other claims by customers are estimated at 3% of sales revenue from standard product sales.

8   Machine idle time is 20% of gross machine hours used (ie running hours = 80% of gross hours).

9   Sundry costs of administration, selling and distribution total £60,000 per period.

10   Calton Limited is aware of the problem of excess costs and currently spends £20,000 per period on training staff in efforts to prevent a number of such problems from occurring.

Required

Give examples of internal failure costs, external failure costs, appraisal costs and prevention costs borne by Calton Limited.

Solution

Internal failure costs. The machine processing losses, downgrading of products, and materials which are scrapped due to poor receipt and storage.

External failure costs. Product liability claims and the costs of making free replacements, including delivery costs.

Appraisal costs. Inspection during the production process, inspection of materials in storage, calibration checks, and vendor rating.

Prevention costs. Training costs.

Quality circles

A **quality circle** (QC) usually consists of five to eight employees who meet on a regular basis to discuss any problems related to quality in their area and to make suggestions for improvement. There is a leader who is usually appointed by the organisation initially but can be elected by the group when established.

All members of the circle are voluntary and receive no extra pay for their involvement. The success of quality circles in Japan has been an important contributing factor towards raising standards of quality in Japanese industries. In Japan, there are instances of joint quality circles between manufacturer and supplier seeking to improve the quality of the bought-in components.

Normally, the QC comprises a supervisor and workers who meet within a single area of an organisation. Everyone is trained in identifying quality problems and in problem-solving techniques. Once established, the circle either looks at problems sent down by management or identifies the problem needing consideration for itself. Either way, it will have established financial targets to meet, thus justifying its existence. One important aspect of the QC is that both the financing and the eventual meetings happen in company time, although this often develops into a voluntary meeting in the employees' time.

During the discussions within the group, all members are encouraged to contribute, the subject matter is thoroughly aired, all possible solutions are considered and a written report submitted to management. After agreement, the implementation of the chosen solution often involves the members of the QC.

Wherever it is employed, QC requires both the individual and the organisation to be motivated to improve quality by error reduction, material utilisation, machine operation, productivity etc. The procedure is designed to supplement the conventional quality control procedures.

The decision to install a QC must come from top management, who will allocate finance to it, consider the cost of installing the system, train people to make an adequate contribution, launch the scheme and appoint leaders, etc.

The objectives of QC extend beyond the essential problems of quality. General productivity is considered as well as methods to reduce frustration and grievances, reduce labour turnover and push power down the echelons of the organisation (albeit within the parameters of Japanese traditions of responsibility).

The **benefits** arising from the use of quality circles are substantial:

♦ improved quality leading to greater customer satisfaction

♦ greater motivation of employees

♦ improved productivity

♦ shop floor understand and share management/customers problems

♦ a spirit of seeking improvements is generated

♦ staff become more aware of opportunities for improvement because of training, in areas outside quality circles.

Questions

1 Product design

How does product design create opportunities for reducing costs?

2 Control v reduction

Distinguish between *cost control* and *cost reduction*.

3 Value analysis

What is value analysis and how does it relate to cost reduction?

4 Quality circles

Write brief notes on quality circles.

Summary

In this chapter we have seen that there are many ways of reducing costs at every stage of an organisation's activities. Enhancing the quality of the organisation's products and services is important for its own sake and may indirectly help to reduce costs.

For the purposes of your assessment, total quality management (TQM) is the most important concept used in enhancing value.

CHAPTER 11

Answers to Chapter Questions

Chapter 1

Attributes of management accounting information

(a)   Criteria for management accounting information.

(i)   *Verifiability*

Management information to be used in the planning and control of operations should be capable of verification to some reputable source. For example, estimates of future sales figures may be based on past trends which are verifiable.

(ii)   *Objectivity*

The information should be objective rather than subjective as far as possible. Estimates of the material cost per unit should be based on a study of procedures and actual experience to measure the quantity required. However, the future price charged by suppliers may not be capable of such objective measurement.

(iii)   *Timeliness*

For information to be useful, it must be produced in time for actions to be taken if necessary. For example, cost data must be assembled in time for a decision as to the price to offer to a customer.

(iv)   *Comparability*

When comparing performance against a budget or against previous performance, the results must have been produced in such a way as to facilitate comparability. For example, a change in the method of valuing work in progress from one period to the next would have to be allowed for in any profit statement comparison.

(v)   *Reliability*

Unreliable information should not be used for the planning, control or decision-making of activities. Other actions taken may themselves be unreliable. For example, the amount of raw material used on a job must not be guessed at but rather, taken from a reliable source such as stores requisitions.

(vi)   *Understandability*

The information presented must be understandable to the user if he is to act upon it. A variances report where there is no indication of adverse or favourable would make it very difficult for the manager to answer.

(vii)   *Relevance*

Management's time should not be wasted with information which is not relevant to them. They should be allowed to focus on their own specific areas of responsibility. Variance reports should restrict themselves to those variances for which the manager is responsible.

(b)   The need to produce timely information may create pressure which causes some of the other criteria such as reliability or understandability to be compromised. For example, reports may be issued in 'jargon' form to speed things up but people outside a certain department may not fully understand the terms used.

Chapter 2

1 Time series example

The quarterly sales of alcoholic drinks in off-licences and supermarkets in the UK is an example of a time series.

The trend would probably be a gradual but steady increase due to increased standards of living.

Seasonal variations would appear as a dramatic increase in sales just before Christmas.

Cyclical variations would not be apparent over a short period of time but if the figures could be scrutinised over many years there should be some evidence that the sales of alcohol were linked with the economic situation. In a period of economic depression people do not have as much money to spend on luxuries such as alcohol.

Random variations could occur because of a budget decision to raise the duty on alcoholic drinks sharply.

2 Your organisation I

(a) (i) *Seasonal variations* are regular patterns of fluctuations which occur over the year. For example, the seasonal variation for quarter 1 is minus 50 units. This indicates that the sales volume for quarter 1 is on average 50 units below the general trend in sales. Similarly, the sales volume for quarter 2 is generally 22 units above the general trend.

(ii) A *trend line* is the underlying direction in which a time series of data is moving. The trend is determined by removing the effect of seasonal variations, usually by using the technique of moving averages.

In the data provided, the monthly sales volume appears to be increasing by an average of 45 units in each quarter, after eliminating the seasonal variations. This is the underlying trend in the data, which the analyst suggests should be used to project the sales data into the future. This is known as *extrapolating the trend* (ie continuing its general direction as a basis for the sales forecast).

(b) *Sales volume forecasts*

Working: calculating the average quarterly increase in the trend

Year	Quarter	Trend (units)	Increase in trend (units)
3	4	3,407	
4	1	3,452	45
	2	3,496	44
	3	3,541	45
	4	3,587	46
			180 Average = 180/4 = 45 units

Sales volume forecast for year 5

	Quarter 1 units	Quarter 2 units	Quarter 3 units	Quarter 4 units
Trend	3,632	3,677	3,722	3,767
Seasonal adjustment	–50	+22	+60	–32
Forecast	3,582	3,699	3,782	3,735

Quarter 1 trend = Year 4 Quarter 4 trend + average quarterly trend

 = 3,587 + 45

 = 3,632

3 Transport company I

Fuel costs expressed in terms of year 4 prices

Year	Expenditure £	Adjust for movement in fuel price index £	Expenditure at year 4 prices £
1	18,000	× 128/100	23,040
2	19,292	× 128/106	23,296
3	21,468	× 128/120	22,899
4	23,010		23,010

The increases in expenditure on fuel are mainly the result of increases in fuel prices. When expenditure is adjusted to year 4 prices, it is possible to see that expenditure has not varied significantly in real terms.

Chapter 3

1   AB Limited I

(a)

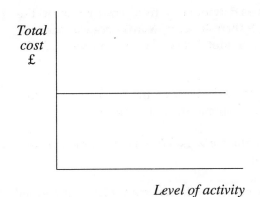

Level of activity

(i)   *Fixed costs*

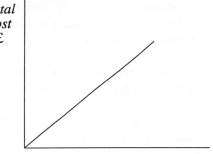

Level of activity

(ii)   *Variable costs*

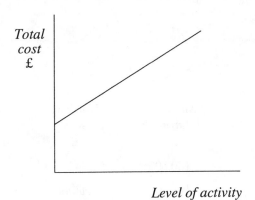

Level of activity

(iii)   *Semi-variable costs*

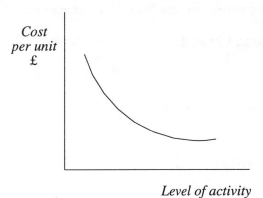

Level of activity

(iv)   *Fixed cost per unit*

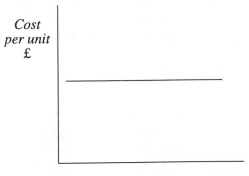

Level of activity

(v)   *Variable cost per unit*

(b) (i) *Fixed costs* – The graph is a straight horizontal line because the cost remains constant for all levels of activity. Two examples could be office rent and administrative salaries.

(ii) *Variable costs* – The graph slopes upwards because each unit adds a constant amount to the total cost. Two examples could be direct materials and direct labour.

(iii) *Semi-variable costs* – The cost includes a basic amount of fixed cost, therefore the graph starts part-way up the vertical axis. It then slopes upwards because each unit adds a constant amount of variable cost to the total cost. Two examples could be telephone costs and electricity costs.

(iv) *Fixed cost per unit* – The graph slopes downwards because the fixed cost per unit reduces as the constant amount of fixed cost is spread over more units.

(v) *Variable cost per unit* – The graph is a straight horizontal line because the cost per unit remains constant for all levels of activity.

(c) An understanding of cost behaviour patterns is necessary for effective planning so that managers can predict the effect on cost of proposed changes in activity levels.

It is also necessary for effective control so that realistic targets can be set for the purposes of comparison with the actual cost incurred.

2 Luda Limited

(a)

Fixed overhead absorption rates			*Machine area* £	*Finishing shop* £
Fixed overhead			100,800	94,500
			Hours	*Hours*
(i)	Labour hours	P 6,000 units × 2, 1.5	12,000	9,000
		Q 8,000 units × 1, 1	8,000	8,000
		R 2,000 units × 2, 2	4,000	4,000
			24,000	21,000
	Overhead absorption rate per labour hour		£4.20	£4.50
(ii)	Machine hours	P 6,000 × 4, 0.5	24,000	3,000
		Q 8,000 × 1.5, 0.5	12,000	4,000
		R 2,000 × 3, 1	6,000	2,000
			42,000	9,000
	Overhead absorption rate per machine hour		£2.40	£10.50

(b)   *Product costs*

	P £	Q £	R £
Materials	18.50	15.00	22.50
Wages	16.00	9.00	18.00
Prime cost	34.50	24.00	40.50

(i)   *Labour hour rate absorption*

	P £	Q £	R £
Prime costs as above	34.50	24.00	40.50
Fixed overheads			
Machine area £4.20 x 2, 1, 2	8.40	4.20	8.40
Finishing shop £4.50 x 1.5, 1, 2	6.75	4.50	9.00
	49.65	32.70	57.90

(ii)   *Machine hour rate absorption*

	P £	Q £	R £
Prime costs as above	34.50	24.00	40.50
Fixed overheads			
Machine area £2.40 x 4, 1.5, 3	9.60	3.60	7.20
Finishing shop £10.50 x 0.5, 0.5, 1	5.25	5.25	10.50
	49.35	32.85	58.20

(c)   The alternatives shown in (b) above produce very similar results. If a labour hour rate were used in total, the rate to be applied would be (£195,300/45,000) – £4.34 per hour – not greatly different from either of the two rates calculated separately. However the same cannot be said of the machine hour rate which in total would be £195,300/51,000) £3.83 per hour, compared with rates of £2.40 and £10.50 calculated separately.

3   Lorus Limited

(a)   Memorandum re overheads

MEMORANDUM

To: Managing Director   Date:

Copy: Production heads – sawing, assembly, finishing, materials handling, maintenance

From: Management Accountant

Subject: Statement to show allotment of overhead

(a)

	Sawing £	*Assembly* £	*Finishing* £	*MH* £	*Maintenance* £
Overhead	75,000	50,000	20,000	9,000	20,000
Apportion service department overhead					
Maintenance	6,000	8,000	4,000	2,000	(20,000)
MH	5,500	2,200	3,300	(11,000)	–
Total allotted	86,500	60,200	27,300	–	–

Note: Service department overhead has been apportioned to production departments on the basis of percentage estimates of relative benefit, as specified.

(b)   4,000 cupboards produced with the following costs incurred.

	Sawing £	*Assembly* £	*Finishing* £	*Total* £	*Unit cost* £
Materials	120,000	80,000	20,000	220,000	55.00
Wages	50,000	25,000	40,000	115,000	28.75
Overheads	86,500	60,200	27,300	174,000	43.50
	256,500	165,200	87,300	509,000	127.25

(b)   The unit cost of a cupboard is £127.25.

4   Costing methods

Cost allocation, cost apportionment and **cost absorption** are methods used in management accounting to charge overhead costs to the units of product passing through the production process. First the business must identify the cost unit to be used; this is a quantitative unit of product or service in relation to which costs are ascertained (for example a ton of coal or a man-hour of service provided). Next the business must identify its cost centres; these are locations, functions or items of equipment in respect of which costs may be ascertained and related to cost units for control purposes.

Cost allocation is defined as the charging of discrete identifiable items of cost to cost centres or cost units. For example if a business has identified factory A as being a cost centre, then the electricity bill for the factory is wholly attributable to that cost centre; the cost of that bill is allocated to factory A. No other cost centres are involved.

Cost apportionment is defined as the division of costs amongst two or more cost centres in proportion to the estimated benefit received. For example, a canteen might serve meals to the employees of two production centres A and B. When the canteen costs for a period come to be attributed to the cost centres, they can be apportioned between centres A and B, perhaps on the basis of the number of employees in each centre. The basis of apportionment has to be chosen in each situation as best reflecting the amount of benefit received by each cost centre.

The costs of the business have now been allocated and apportioned to the production cost centres. The final task is to charge these tasks to the units of product themselves. This is achieved by the process of cost absorption.

Absorption is the process of charging overheads into the costs of specific products or saleable services by means of a predetermined absorption rate. This rate will depend on production volume. It is common to calculate absorption rates as an amount per labour hour, but alternative rates could be per machine hour or per unit of output.

The above has explained the traditional method of attributing costs to products, by a process of allocation, apportionment and then absorption. However, in recent years the traditional method has been subject to heavy attack from detractors who query the relevance, in particular, of fixed overhead absorption. The last 20 years have seen businesses switching from labour-intensive activities to capital-intensive activities, so the absolute amount of fixed overheads has increased while the number of labour hours worked in the business has fallen. In such circumstances the absorption rate for fixed overhead per labour hour has increased very sharply, to a level where its relevance is now being seriously questioned.

Attention has now turned to the method of **activity-based costing** (ABC) rather than the traditional method. Proponents of ABC point out that it is not labour hours that result in overhead cost, but the incidence of so-called cost-drivers, those activities performed in the manufacturing process which lead to costs being incurred. An example cost-driver is the number of production set-ups carried out in a particular period. ABC uses an absorption rate calculated from the number of cost-drivers in the period rather than the number of labour hours worked and in this form ABC can be seen as a refinement of the traditional method of charging costs to product units.

Chapter 4

1 Your organisation II

MEMORANDUM

To: Marketing Manager   Date: 12 December 19X4

From: Assistant Management Accountant

Subject: Budgetary planning process

As requested, I provide below answers to your queries about the budgetary planning process.

(a)   *The key factor*

Otherwise known as the principal budget factor or limiting factor, the key factor is the factor which limits the activity of an organisation. In our organisation it is sales volume, since there is a limit to how much we can sell. However, it is possible for other factors to be key factors, especially in the short term. Examples could be cash, machine capacity or skilled labour.

The determination of the key factor is important in the budgetary process because this is the budget which must be prepared first. Then all other budgets can be co-ordinated to this budget.

For example, once the sales budget has been determined, this will provide the basis for the production budget and for other budgets such as the purchasing budget and the cash budget.

(b)   A number of steps can be taken to achieve co-ordination in the budgetary planning process, including the following.

(i)   Set up a budget committee which consists of representatives from all parts of the organisation. Regular meetings of this committee should ensure that each part of the organisation is aware of what all other parts are doing.

(ii)   Give one person the overall responsibility for ensuring that budgets are prepared on time and that they take into account all relevant factors. This person is often called the budget officer and will usually chair the budget committee.

(iii)   Provide a timetable to all those involved in the budgetary process, detailing who is responsible for preparing each budget and when it must be prepared. This should reduce the risk of bottlenecks in the budgetary process and will co-ordinate the order of budget preparation.

(iv)   Provide a budget manual to all those involved in the budgetary process. The contents of the budget manual would include the budget timetable mentioned above, instructions on completing the budget planning forms, details on key assumptions to be made in the planning process (such as the inflation rate and exchange rate), and so on.

(v)   Provide regular feedback on the progress of budget preparation.

The key to co-ordinated budget preparation is communication.

---

2 Master budget

(a) The necessary preliminary steps before commencing to prepare budgets would include the following:

    (i) Consideration of the longer-term plans for the business and setting goals for such aspects as market share, profit and capital investment.

    (ii) Confirmation of the organisation structure of the business, including profit, cost and investment centres.

    (iii) Issue of budget instructions.

    (iv) Preparation of forecasts of the relevant exogeneous conditions for the budget period (and possibly for some additional period). This might be regarded either as preliminary work or as the first step in budget development.

(b) The main budgets to be found in a manufacturing business are likely to be:

    (i) Sales budget, by areas of responsibility, consistent with assumptions and forecasts above and within production and inventory capacity (subject to policy on buying-in), and based on estimates of demand schedules.

    (ii) Production budget, based on sales budget, allowing for controlled inventory policy and incorporating specific plans for resource acquisition and disposition (materials, labour, energy, overheads).

    (iii) Resource budgets within production centres, by area and level of responsibility.

    (iv) Budgets of marketing, selling and distribution expense.

    (v) Budgets of general administrative expense.

    (vi) Budgets for R&D, including product development.

    (vii) Profit budgets by areas of profit responsibility (product group, geographical area, etc.).

    (viii) Capital expenditure budget.

    (ix) Working capital budgets, including inventory, debt management, cash management, borrowing capacity.

    (x) Master budget, with suitably analysed profit and loss account and balance sheet.

(c) Managers may be reluctant to participate in setting budgets, because 'participation' may not be on an acceptable basis. According to the management style of a business the term may cover almost any degree or lack of consultation.

At one extreme minimal discussion may be used as the basis for an authoritarian, imposed budget. At the other extreme a laissez-faire management style may lead to a lack of interest by or incentive for managers to set budgets which provide real targets for improvement. For participation in budgeting to be successful it must stem from full and frank discussion between managers at all levels. It must be based on accepted areas of responsibility and full knowledge of the objectives to be achieved and of the interaction of one department's activities with those of others. Managers must also be capable of understanding the financial and accounting implications of their actions, and may need to be given training in these subjects.

Finally any budget will be based on forecasts of future circumstances, and these will often be imperfect. In exercising control against budgets, therefore, it is necessary to judge whether managers' achievement has been satisfactory in relation to the actual circumstances then prevailing. This is not to say that the ultimate profit objective should be abandoned, but that 'participation' should be a continuous activity in modifying detailed targets where necessary in order to approach the achievement of the required profit in a different way.

3   Tiger plc

(a)   Although it is not specifically required by the question, a production budget is essential for material and labour budgets.

Information relating to production levels is therefore the first thing you must look for.

In this question, you are not given this information directly. You are, however, given information about sales quantities and stock levels, which can be used to derive production levels as follows:

Production   =   Sales   +   Closing stock   –   Opening stock
                              (finished goods)   (finished goods)

The monthly sales need a little computation, so this will be your first working. Note that you only need units for the production budget, but part (b) requires a profit and loss, so you will also need revenue, which you may as well incorporate into this working.

Your second working will then be the production budget, using the results from your sales working and the stock level requirements given in the question.

These and other workings should be done on a separate sheet of paper, to be included at the end of your answer, cross-referenced as appropriate.

These first two workings should enable you to complete the three parts of part (a).

Note that, although it is not a necessary requirement of (a), it will be useful to calculate total production quantity and total costs for materials purchases and labour for (b).

(i)   *Material usage*

	Jan	Feb	Mar	Apr	May	Jun	Total
Production quantity (W2) @ 10kg/unit	5,000	7,500	10,000	10,000	7,500	5,000	45,000
	50,000	75,000	100,000	100,000	75,000	50,000	450,000

(ii)   *Material purchases*

Remember the link between materials usage and purchases quantities:

Purchases   =   Usage   +   Closing stock   –   Opening stock
                                (raw materials)   (raw materials)

Usage is taken from your answer to (i) and stock information from the question – 'stocks to meet 80% of the following month's production quota' simply means 80% of the following month's usage.

	Jan	Feb	Mar	Apr	May	June	Total
Materials used (i)	50,000	75,000	100,000	100,000	75,000	50,000	450,000
Less: Opening stock	(40,000)	(60,000)	(80,000)	(80,000)	(60,000)	(40,000)	(40,000)
	10,000	15,000	20,000	20,000	15,000	10,000	410,000
Add: Closing stock	60,000	80,000	80,000	60,000	40,000	40,000	40,000
Purchases (kg)	70,000	95,000	100,000	80,000	55,000	50,000	450,000
@	60p	60p	60p	60p	75p	75p	
Purchases	£42,000	£57,000	£60,000	£48,000	£41,250	£37,500	£285,750

(iii) *Skilled labour utilisation*

	Jan	Feb	Mar	Apr	May	June	Total
Units produced (W2)	5,000	7,500	10,000	10,000	7,500	5,000	45,000
Skilled labour cost (£5 per unit)	£25,000	£37,500	£50,000	£50,000	£37,500	£25,000	£225,000

Unskilled labour utilisation

	Jan	Feb	Mar	Apr	May	June	Total
Units produced (W2)	5,000	7,500	10,000	10,000	7,500	5,000	45,000
Unskilled labour cost (£6 per unit)	£30,000	£45,000	£60,000	£60,000	£45,000	£30,000	£270,000

(b)   Most of the figures for the profit and loss can be taken from the answers/workings to part (a). Additional workings will be required for valuation of stocks of raw materials and finished goods.

The former can be easily calculated by multiplying the opening/closing stock quantities (in your purchases budget) by the opening/closing prices (60p/75p); this can be indicated on the face of the profit and loss itself.

The valuation of stocks of finished goods involves the calculation of unit costs – not forgetting the change of materials cost over the period. This is shown in working 3 at the end of the answer.

Finally, do not forget overheads – easy to calculate (£5 × total production) but also easy to miss!

Budgeted profit and loss account for six months to 30 June 19X5

		£	£
Sales (W1)			1,250,000
Cost of sales			
Opening stock:	Raw materials (60p)	24,000	
	Finished goods (W3)	55,000	
		79,000	
Materials purchased		285,750	
Skilled labour		225,000	
Unskilled labour		270,000	
Production overheads (45,000 x £5)		225,000	
		1,084,750	
Closing stock:	Raw materials (75p)	(30,000)	
	Finished goods (W3)	(58,750)	
			(996,000)
Gross profit			254,000

(c)   *Reason for introducing a budgetary system*

The objectives of budgets are:

(i)   to plan and control income and expenditure in order to achieve maximum profitability

(ii)   to ensure that sufficient working capital is available for the efficient operation of the company

(iii)   to direct capital expenditure in the most profitable direction

(iv)   to centralise control

(v)   to decentralise responsibility

(vi)   to provide a yardstick against which actual results may be compared

(vii)   to show management when action is needed to remedy a situation

(viii) to aid management in decision-making when unforeseen conditions affect the budget.

Workings

1   *Sales by month*

The easiest way to calculate these is to assign weights to each month – an 'ordinary' month having a weighting of 1, with the 'seasonal' months having twice this weighting. Thus, over the six-month period, there will be the equivalent of (3 × 1) plus (3 × 2) = 9 'ordinary' months worth of sales. As total sales are expected to be 45,000, this implies an 'ordinary' month's sales of 45,000/9 = 5,000 units.

	Jan	Feb	Mar	Apr	May	June	Total
Weighting	1	1	2	2	2	1	9
Sales quantity	5,000	5,000	10,000	10,000	10,000	5,000	45,000
Selling price	£25	£25	£25	£30	£30	£30	
Sales revenue	£125,000	£125,000	£250,000	£300,000	£300,000	£150,000	£1,250,000

2   *Production budget (units)*

The opening and closing stocks for the period are given in the question (2,500 units). In between, the closing stock for each month (and the opening stock for the following month) represents 50% of the following month's sales units.

	Jan	Feb	Mar	Apr	May	June
Sales	5,000	5,000	10,000	10,000	10,000	5,000
Less: Opening stock	(2,500)	(2,500)	(5,000)	(5,000)	(5,000)	(2,500)
	2,500	2,500	5,000	5,000	5,000	2,500
Add: Closing stock	2,500	5,000	5,000	5,000	2,500	2,500
Production	5,000	7,500	10,000	10,000	7,500	5,000

Total production = 45,000 units

3   *Cost per unit*

		To April £	From May £
Raw materials (10 kg)		6.00	7.50
Labour:	Skilled	5.00	5.00
	Semi-skilled	6.00	6.00
Production overheads		5.00	5.00
		22.00	23.50

Stocks of finished goods – opening 2,500 units @ £22   £55,000

– closing 2,500 units @ £23.50   £58,750

4 Loamshire County Council I

(a)

	A	B	C	D	E
		Policy		Inflation	
	Budget	variations	A+B	allowance	Budget
	19X2/X3	19X3/X4		19X3/X4	19X3/X4
	£000	£000	£000	£000	£000
Employees					
Professional	1,200	24	1,224	24	1,248
Clerical	2,100	42	2,142	43	2,185
Other	305	6	311	6	317
Premises	550	–	550	16	566
Supplies and services					
Book fund	1,700	–150	1,550	62	1,612
Cassettes and CDs	160	–20	140	6	146
Other	70	–	70	2	72
Transport	120	–10	110	3	113
Establishment expenses	210	–	210	6	216
Debt charges	550	20	570	–	570
	6,965	–88	6,877	168	7,045
Income from fees, charges and trading	400	80	480	–	480
Cash allocated to the Library Service	6,565	–168	6,397	168	6,565

(b) Book fund reduced by £150,000 at 19X2/X3 price.

$$\% \text{ reduction} = \frac{150}{1,700} \times 100 = 8.8\%$$

5 Product Q

(a) (i) *Production budget for product Q*

		Units
Forecast sales for year		18,135
Increase in stock (15% × 1,200)		180
Finished units required		18,315
Quality control loss (1/99)		185
Total units input to production		18,500

(ii) *Direct labour budget for product Q*

	Hours
Active labour hours required (18,500 × 5)	92,500
Idle time allowance (7.5/92.5)	7,500
Total hours to be paid for	100,000
Standard hourly rate	£6
Budgeted labour cost	£600,000

(iii) *Material usage budget for material M*

	kg
Material required for processing (18,500 × 9 kg)	166,500
Wastage (10/90)	18,500
Material usage for year	185,000

(iv) *Material purchases budget for material M*

	kg
Material required for production input	185,000
Increase in material stocks	960
Expected loss in stores	1,000
Material purchases required	186,960

(b)   The implications of this shortage are that the budget plans cannot be achieved and the availability of material is a limiting factor. If the limiting factor cannot be alleviated, then the budgetary plans will need to be altered and raw material M will in fact become the principal budget factor. The material purchases budget would be prepared first and all other budgets would be co-ordinated to this one.

Four possible actions to overcome the problem could be as follows.

1   *Reduce the budgeted sales of product Q*

The problem with this course of action is that valued customers may be lost forever to competitors, who may be able to obtain the necessary material to take over Henry's customers permanently. Profits are likely to be reduced next year and possibly also in subsequent years.

2   *Reduce the rate of scrap due to quality control rejections of product Q at the end of the process*

This course of action should not cause problems if quality standards are not compromised and the reduction in scrapped units is achieved as part of a programme of total quality throughout the organisation.

A problem could arise, however, if there is not a genuine reduction in poor quality work, but instead a relaxation in the quality control standards used. Customer dissatisfaction could have a permanent detrimental effect on sales, with consequent reductions in profit.

3   *Reduce the closing stock required of product Q and material M*

This could cause a problem of stock-outs, ie not having enough stock available when it is required, leading to disruptions in production and lost sales.

4   *Seek alternative suppliers for material M*

Possible problems that could arise are control over quality and reliability of supply. Any potential suppliers should be carefully vetted to ensure that their standards are acceptable.

Chapter 5

1 Excelsior Manufacturing Company

(a)

	4,000 £	5,000 £	6,000 £	7,000 £	8,000 £
Direct materials	80,000	100,000	120,000	140,000	160,000
Indirect materials	12,000	14,000	16,000	18,000	20,000
Direct labour	50,000	62,500	75,000	87,500	100,000
Power	18,000	18,000	18,000	21,000	24,000
Repairs	20,000	22,500	25,000	27,500	30,000
Supervision	20,000	20,000	36,000	36,000	36,000
Rent, insurance and rates	9,000	9,000	9,000	9,000	9,000
	209,000	246,000	299,000	339,000	379,000

(b)

	Budget (5,000) £	Actual (5,000) £	Variance £
Direct materials	100,000	110,000	10,000 (A)
Indirect materials	14,000	14,000	–
Direct labour	62,500	70,000	7,500 (A)
Power	18,000	18,000	–
Repairs	22,500	30,000	7,500 (A)
Supervision	20,000	20,000	–
Rent, insurance and rates	9,000	8,000	1,000 (F)
	246,000	270,000	24,000 (A)

Comments on variances

- Direct materials: Waste in production, poor quality materials, operatives need more training. Is a particular department or machine at fault?

- Direct labour: Supervision? Excessive overtime (should not be needed at a low level of production)?

- Repairs: Needs investigation. Possible exceptional item. Do some pieces of capital equipment need replacing?

- Rent, insurance and rates: This is probably a price variance. Is this an exceptional item or does the budget need to be altered in future?

2   World History Museum

(a) and (b) **Analysis of budgeted costs:**

	Fixed cost	Variable cost	Variable cost per course
	£	£	£
Speakers' fees	–	3,180	530
Hire of premises	–	1,500	250
Depreciation of equipment	180	–	–
Stationery	–	600	100
Catering	250	1,500	250
Insurance	100	720	120
Administration	1,620	–	–

Flexible budget control statement for April

Expenditure	Fixed cost allowance	Variable cost allowance	Total cost allowance	Actual cost	Variance
	£	£	£	£	£
Speakers' fees	–	2,650	2,650	2,500	150
Hire of premises	–	1,250	1,250	1,500	(250)
Depreciation of equipment	180	–	180	200	(20)
Stationery	–	500	500	530	(30)
Catering	250	1,250	1,500	1,500	–
Insurance	100	600	700	700	–
Administration	1,620	–	1,620	1,650	(30)
	2,150	6,250	8,400	8,580	(180)

(c)

MEMORANDUM

To: Chris Brooks   Date: 13 June 19X4

From: Assistant Management Accountant

Subject: Participative budgeting

As requested, I enclose brief explanations of the advantages and disadvantages of participative budgeting.

Advantages

(i)   Managers are likely to be demotivated if budgets are imposed on them without any prior consultation. If they are consulted, they are more likely to accept the budgets as realistic targets.

(ii)   If managers are consulted, then the budgets are more likely to take account of their own aspiration levels. Aspiration levels are personal targets which individuals or departments set for themselves. If budget targets exceed aspiration levels, then the budgets can have a negative motivational impact because they will be perceived as unachievable. However, if the targets fall too far below aspiration levels, then the performance of the individuals or departments may be lower than might otherwise have been achieved.

(iii)   Managers who are consulted may be motivated by the feeling that their views are valuable to senior management.

(iv)   Managers who are closely involved with the day to day running of operations may be able to give very valuable input to the forecasting and planning process.

Disadvantages

(i)   If too many people are involved in budgetary planning, it can make the process very slow and difficult to manage.

(ii)   Senior managers may need to overrule decisions made by local managers. This can be demotivating if it is not dealt with correctly.

(iii)   The participative process may not be genuine. Managers must feel that their participation is really valued by senior management. A false attempt to appear to be interested in their views can be even more demotivating than a system of imposed budgets.

(iv)   Managers may attempt to include excess expenditure in their budgets, due to 'empire-building' or to a desire to guard against unforeseen circumstances.

---

3   Responsibility accounting

(a)   *Responsibility accounting* has been defined as 'a system of accounting that segregates revenues and costs into areas of personal responsibility in order to assess the performance attained by persons to whom authority has been assigned'.

The idea derives from the need simultaneously to motivate divisional managers whilst at the same time evaluating their financial performance. For example, if a manager is held responsible for a decision over which he had only partial control then he will be demotivated. Similarly he should be rewarded personally for excellent results arising from areas for which he was responsible.

One main problem in practice arises from the need to define the scope of each manager's responsibility (ie the boundaries of the division to be controlled and the nature of the responsibility). The situation given in the question tells of a range of products, a number of processes and a number of service departments.

Each separate process may already have a manager responsible for the process. If each process is given the status of a cost centre, then the costs for each process will be separately recorded and monitored, and management will be held responsible for the reporting of costs and explanation of variances from budgeted figures. Production costs which are incurred by several processes and which are apportioned among those processes for reporting purposes may be excluded from the costs for which process managers are responsible, since no individual process manager will feel responsible for the apportioned cost; a more senior manager responsible for the suite of processes may instead be held responsible for the apportioned costs.

The costs of the service departments should be charged to the production departments on the basis of service used in the period. It will be helpful if predetermined rates can be set for each service activity as part of the budgeting process before the start of each year. That way, if a service department is inefficient in providing its service, an adverse variance arises in the service department for which the service manager is answerable, rather than the production manager feeling aggrieved that he is going to have to pay for someone else's inefficiency. The converse is also the case, so that the service manager is not aggrieved when his team has to stand idle for a period of time before they are allowed to start supplying their service, the delay arising from incompetence in the production department; in such a situation, the production manager should be held responsible for the adverse variance arising.

(b)   The maintenance department is likely to carry out work throughout the business operations, ranging from repairing broken down machines to carrying out regular preventative maintenance on the process plant and working for other service departments. The departmental staff should be trained to keep detailed documentation concerning their activities, including timesheets and material requisitions and returns.

Once it is clear what work has been carried out, the next step is to ensure that the responsible manager is charged for the cost of operations under his ambit. Cost incurred in mending a broken down machine, for example, could have arisen because the purchasing department had bought inappropriate raw materials, or the training department had wrongly advised the operator on proper procedures, or the machine had been improperly installed in the first place. The chief engineer should ensure that the responsibility accounting principle is applied to charge the manager for costs for which he is responsible.

The management accounting system can assist in recognising the managers responsible for costs incurred by insisting on the detailed record-keeping described above, by anticipating problems at the time of the budgetary process, and by analysing variances according to their causes. In particular a system of planning and operational variances will help to identify the manager responsible for each variance arising.

(c)   The provision of more information need not automatically lead to more effective management of a cost centre for the following reasons.

    (i)   *Information overload* – If a manager is faced with more information than he thinks he can cope with, then he will just give up and apply 'seat of the pants' management rather than try to take any sort of rigorous approach to his decision-making responsibilities.

    (ii)   *Good quality information* – Quality is more important than quantity in the area of information provision. Modern information technology has enabled vast volumes of information to be produced quickly, but management needs the important points to be highlighted, so that for example information should be provided on an exception basis, clearly pointing out major deviations from standard to be investigated.

    (iii)   *Lack of goal congruence* – A manager may be given all the information that he needs to carry out his objective, but that objective might not be in the best interests of the company as a whole. For example, the manager might be seeking to build up a personal empire or to maximise sales revenue or to maximise his own departmental profits rather than thinking of optimising overall company performance.

4   Henry Limited

(a)

	Quarter 1 units	Quarter 2 units	Quarter 3 units	Quarter 4 units
Actual sales volume	420,000	450,000	475,000	475,000
Seasonal variation	+25,000	+15,000	–	–40,000
Deseasonalised sales volumes	395,000	435,000	475,000	515,000

(b)   The trend is for sales volume to increase by 40,000 units each quarter.

Forecast for next year:	Quarter 1 units	Quarter 2 units	Quarter 3 units	Quarter 4 units
Trend projection	555,000	595,000	635,000	675,000
Seasonal variation	+25,000	+15,000	–	–40,000
Forecast sales volumes	580,000	610,000	635,000	635,000

(c)

MEMORANDUM

To: Marketing assistant   Date: 21 June X5

From: Assistant to the management accountant

Subject: Deseasonalised sales data

I am writing in response to your request for an explanation of deseasonalised or seasonally adjusted data.

What is meant by deseasonalised data and seasonal variations?

Seasonal variations are consistent patterns in sales volumes which arise during each year. For example, for Product P, the seasonal variation for quarter 1 is +25,000 units. This means that sales volumes in quarter 1 tend to be 25,000 units higher than the underlying trend in sales. In contrast, the seasonal variation for quarter 4 is minus 40,000 units. This means that sales volumes in quarter 4 are generally 40,000 units below the underlying trend.

Deseasonalised data is data from which these seasonal variations have been removed. Apart from any random variations, the remaining figures show the trend in the data. It is then possible to see the general direction of movement of the time series.

In the case of product P, the underlying trend is upwards, at a rate of increase of 40,000 units each quarter. This upward trend was masked in the actual data because of the distorting effect of the seasonal variations. These variations meant that, when one year's actual sales volumes were viewed in isolation, the rate of increase in sales appeared to be slowing.

How can deseasonalised data and seasonal variations be used in preparing forecasts?

If the trend revealed by deseasonalised data can be assumed to continue, then it can be projected to forecast the trend for future quarters. These trend values can then be adjusted, ie increased or decreased, to allow for the seasonal variations in each quarter. The resulting figure represents the forecast for each quarter's sales volumes.

If I can help with providing any further information or explanations, please let me know.

(d)

MEMORANDUM

To: Marketing assistant Date: 21 June X5

From: Assistant to the management accountant

Subject: Fixed and flexible budgets

In response to your query, I hope that the following explanations will help you to understand the use of fixed and flexible budgets.

(i) *Fixed budgets and flexible budgets*

A fixed budget is one which is designed to remain unaltered regardless of changes in activity levels. It is useful for planning because it provides a single activity level for planning and co-ordinating the activities of all parts of the organisation. An expected activity level has to be determined initially in order to ensure that all departments plan to provide the appropriate capacity.

However, if activity levels alter, then a fixed budget may not be very useful for exercising control over distribution costs. For example, if activity increases, then certain costs (such as petrol and wages costs) may increase above the level planned in the original budget. A comparison with a fixed budget would reveal adverse cost variances and it would not be possible to tell whether these variances were a result of overspending, or whether they were due to the increased activity.

A flexible budget identifies the fixed and variable costs. It is designed to increase to provide a higher expenditure allowance for variable costs if activity levels increase. The budget cost allowance can correspondingly be decreased if activity levels fall. The resulting variances are more meaningful for cost control because the effect of the change in activity levels has been eliminated.

(ii) *Possible activity indicators*

Possible activity indicators for flexing the budget for distribution costs include the following.

♦ Miles travelled

♦ Journeys made

♦ Tonnes carried

♦ Tonne-miles achieved

♦ Deliveries made

Page 1 of 2

(iii)   *How a flexible budget cost allowance is calculated and used*

A flexible budget cost allowance is calculated by giving a fixed allowance for the budgeted fixed costs and then adding an amount for variable costs based on the actual activity level achieved:

Flexible budget cost allowance = Budgeted fixed costs + (Standard variable cost per unit × Number of units activity)

For example if 'miles travelled' is to be used as the activity indicator, the budgeted fixed cost is £10,000, the standard variable cost per mile is £5 and 3,000 miles are travelled:

Flexible budget cost allowance = £10,000 + (£5 × 3,000) = £25,000

This allowance would then be compared with the actual cost and the resulting variance would indicate whether management attention was needed.

Page 2 of 2

5   Trygon Limited

(a)   *Trygon Limited: Flexible budget at 75% activity*

Activity	80%	50%		75%
Sales and production (units)	120,000	60,000		112,500
			Variable cost	
	£	£	£	£
Direct materials	24,000,000	12,000,000	200	22,500,000
Direct labour	7,200,000	7,200,000		7,200,000
Light, heat and power*	4,000,000	2,200,000	30	3,775,000
Production management salaries	1,500,000	1,500,000		1,500,000
Factory rent, rates and insurance	9,400,000	9,400,000		9,400,000
Depreciation of factory machinery	5,500,000	5,500,000		5,500,000
National advertising	20,000,000	20,000,000		20,000,000
Marketing and administration	2,300,000	2,300,000		2,300,000
Delivery costs	2,400,000	1,200,000	20	2,250,000
Total costs	76,300,000	61,300,000		74,425,000
Sales revenue	84,000,000	42,000,000		78,750,000
Operating profit				4,325,000

*Variable cost for 120,000 units = £3,600,000 to give fixed costs of £400,000.

(b)

REPORT

To: The Board of Directors   Date: June 19X6

From: The Management Accountant

Subject: Budgeting within Trygon Limited

Following the instructions from the Group Finance Director, finished stocks are to be valued as material and labour plus an appropriate proportion of factory overheads based on normal activity. Each unsold computer will therefore be valued at £430 and comprise the following costs:

Valuation of closing stock

	£
Fixed overheads	
Production management salaries	1,500,000
Factory rent, rates and insurance	9,400,000
Depreciation of factory machinery	5,500,000
Fixed element of light heat and power	400,000
	————
Total fixed overheads	16,800,000
	————
	£
Unit fixed cost based on normal activity – £16,800,000/120,000	140
Unit direct costs	
Light, heat and power	30
Direct material	200
Direct labour £7,200,000/120,000	60
	——
Unit cost for stock valuation	430
	——

With each unit of closing stock valued at £430, the total closing stock will be valued at £12,900,000 to give an operating profit of £8.4 million. The revised budget is reproduced below.

(i)   *Trygon Limited: Flexible budget at 75% sales activity but 95% production activity*

	£
Direct material – 142,500 × £200	28,500,000
Direct labour – £7,200,000 + (£70 × 22,500)	8,775,000
Light, heat and power – £400,000 + (£30 × 142,500)	4,675,000
Production management salaries – £1,500,000 + (£15 × 22,500)	1,837,500
Factory rent, rates and insurance	9,400,000
Depreciation of factory machinery	5,500,000
Factory cost of production	58,687,500
Less closing stock – 30,000 × £430	12,900,000
Factory cost of sales	45,787,500
Marketing, administration and distribution expenses	
National advertising	20,000,000
Marketing and administration	2,300,000
Delivery costs – 112,500 × £20	2,250,000
Total expenses	70,337,500
Sales turnover – 112,500 × £700	78,750,000
Operating profit	8,412,500

The reason for this increase in budgeted profit from £4,325,000 to £8,412,500 despite the additional costs of overtime and bonus payments is mainly due to the treatment of overheads. Fixed costs are essentially time-based but by using absorption costing some of these are carried forward in the value of unsold stocks. With no opening stocks and production equalling sales, all overheads are charged to the current period, even under an absorption costing system. With production being greater than sales volume and with overheads being based on normal activity, the difference in profit can be explained in terms of the treatment of fixed costs and the additional payments resulting from production being greater than the budgeted activity.

(ii)   *Fixed and flexible budgets*

The original budget prepared by the Group Director was a fixed budget. Fixed budgets are designed to remain unaltered. Their primary uses are for planning and co-ordinating. Prior to commencing sales and production activity, the enterprise needs to know what is possible and what is achievable. The co-ordination role of budgeting helps to identify possible bottlenecks and to resolve them before production and selling commences. The planning role is concerned with where the enterprise wants to be at the end of the budget period and provides a target and a commitment to that target.

The flexible budgets I prepared serve two purposes. First, they help to show likely outcomes as conditions change. Secondly, they help managers to control the business by identifying what expenses and turnover should be at different levels of activity. The flexible budget can then be compared with the actual results which enables meaningful variances to be produced. This a flexible budget does by recognising (i) that fixed costs are unlikely to change as a matter of course over a range of activity levels and (ii) that variable costs, by their nature, will increase in proportion to increases in volume.

(iii) *Budgetary objectives*

For a budget to have meaning, there has to be a clear, unambiguous objective. Traditionally, this has involved the key or principal budget factor being identified, that is the factor which will limit the possible achievements for the period. Normally, this is sales although it could be production if there is a shortage of inputs or limited capacity. Being asked to both maximise sales and develop a long-term market position may not be compatible.

Confusion about the company's objectives or how those objectives can be achieved can lead to difficulties for the managers of Trygon. This might lead you to attempt to achieve the budget – but not in the way anticipated. For Trygon, it is clear that we are unlikely to achieve the budget target set at the beginning of the year. However, if Parmod plc is only concerned with profits, the directors of Trygon are more than able to meet the original profit target, not by actually selling more but by manipulating the results. This we can do by simply producing more. As a consequence, some of the fixed costs are carried forward to another period. The outcome is that we will have appeared to have achieved the target. The reality is we will have caused an increase in costs such as storekeeping costs which do not directly appear in the budget or the actual results.

(iv) *Participation in budgets*

Turning to the issue raised by Anne Darcy, conventional wisdom suggests that managers should be encouraged to participate in the budget process and that the budget should be built up from the lower rungs of management rather than imposed from the top. The belief is that managers will then feel they have ownership of the budget and this will encourage commitment and motivation. More than that it is argued that the operating managers are the only ones with sufficient detailed knowledge to develop a meaningful budget.

Unfortunately, the budget process is not always as simple as that. First, the objectives of the managers and the objectives of the organisation may not be the same. There is a need for a similarity of goals – goal congruence – and this does not automatically result from empowering managers to develop their own budgets. Secondly, the operating management may have detailed knowledge but they might use this to their own benefits – as with the current plan to build up stocks and so manipulate the budget. Thirdly the managers may not wish to participate in the budget setting process. This may be because of some psychological fear resulting in managers simply wanting to be told what their targets are; it might be because they do not have the technical knowledge to participate in budget setting; or it might be that they either do not have the necessary degree of commitment to the organisation or they feel that the budgetary control system will be used against them. Because of this, it is not self-evident that participation will always help managers and the organisation.

Chapter 6

1   Standard revision

The revision of technical standards (material quantities and specification and labour hours and grades) is quite divorced from questions of budget revision. Technical standards are there to be complied with. They must therefore be revised every time there are changes in method, specification or product design. Does this mean that every revision of technical standards must be reflected immediately in the standard costing system? In general the answer is 'no'. Standard costs should be revised when accumulations of changes result in variances becoming excessive in relation to existing standards. Within this context, the revision of cost standards (wage rates and material prices) is conveniently undertaken at the time new budgets are set.

Under a system of rolling budgets this opportunity will occur at each review period. Note, however, that whilst all cost standards may be reviewed, it may not be necessary to revise all of them. Revision may be confined to selected major items. It may be desirable to update all standards once a year.

2   Standards come unstuck?

It cannot be repeated too often that, subject to statutory controls, selling prices should be related to the level of costs which will be experienced during the manufacture (or purchase) of what is to be sold; in order words, selling prices are based on forecast costs, even though it may not be possible due to market pressures to cover those costs completely. A standard costing system can help price-fixing in three ways:

(a)   Once technical standards have been fixed, it is relatively easy to apply alternative cost figures to them. The existence of technical standards thus helps price fixing.

(b)   If forecast cost standards are used they will represent the sort of forecast that is needed for price fixing over the period during which they remain in force.

(c)   Whatever type of cost standards are used, the trend of variances from these standards will often assist the estimator in forecasting future cost trends.

3   WH Limited I

WH Limited

MEMORANDUM

To: Production Manager   Date: 12 December 19X4

From: Assistant Accountant

Subject: Determining the standard price per kg of material

As requested I detail below the information which would be needed to determine the standard price of material and possible sources of the information.

(a)   *The information which is needed*   (b)   *Possible sources*

- ◆   Type and quality of material   Technical specification

- ◆   Quantity and timing of   Production and purchasing schedules
       purchases, for determining any
       bulk discounts

- ◆   Past trend in prices   Historical records in company
                                                             Supplier records
                                                             Government statistics
                                                             Trade association statistics
                                                             Movements in price indexes

- ◆   Future trend in prices   Discussions/negotiations with suppliers
                                                             Trade association forecasts
                                                             Financial press forecasts
                                                             Government forecasts of key indexes

- ◆   Carriage costs to be added   Historical records in company
                                                             Supplier records

- ◆   Type of standard to be set, eg   Company policy on standard setting
       average for year, or increasing
       with inflation

---

4   Attainable and ideal standard

(a)   An **attainable standard** is a standard which can be attained if a standard unit of work is carried out efficiently, a machine properly operated or material properly used.   The standard makes allowances for normal shrinkage, waste and machine breakdowns.   It is intended to have a motivational impact on employees.

An **ideal standard** is a standard which can be attained under the most favourable conditions.   The standard makes no provision for shrinkage, spoilage or machine breakdowns.

Ideal standards are not widely used in practice because of their adverse effect on employee motivation. Unfavourable variances usually result, making them less useful for planning purposes.

(b)

(i)	*Actual profit for the period*	£	£
	Sales (2,250 units x £15)		33,750
	Production costs (2,500 units)		
	Direct materials	12,000	
	Direct labour	9,000	
		21,000	
	Less: closing stock (250 units at £10 per unit) (W1)	2,500	
	Cost of sales		18,500
	Actual profit		15,250

Working

Standard cost data per unit

	£
Direct materials ($\dfrac{6,000\,\text{kg}}{2,000\,\text{units}}$ @ £2/kg)	6.00
Direct labour ($\dfrac{4,000\,\text{hours}}{2,000\,\text{units}}$ @ £2/hour)	4.00
	10.00

(ii)	*Material price variance*	£
	Actual usage (5,000 kg) at actual cost	12,000
	Actual usage (5,000 kg) at standard cost (£2/kg)	10,000
	Material price variance	2,000 (A)

	Material usage variance	£
	Actual usage (5,000 kg) at standard cost (£2/kg)	10,000
	Standard usage (for actual production (7,500 kg)) at standard cost £2/kg	15,000
	Material usage variance	5,000 (F)

Labour rate variance	£
Actual hours (6,000 hours) at actual rate (£1.50/hour)	9,000
Actual hours (6,000 hours) at standard rate (£2/hour)	12,000
Labour rate variance	3,000 (F)

Labour efficiency variance	£
Actual hours (6,000 hours) at standard rate (£2/hour)	12,000
Standard hours for actual production (5,000 hours) at standard rate (£2/hour)	10,000
Labour efficiency variance	2,000 (A)

Chapter 7

1   Revamp Furniture Limited

(a)   *Reconciliation for Period 1 (see workings)*

		Favourable £	Adverse £	£
1	Flexed budgeted cost			41,080
	Cost variances			
2	Materials			
	Price	270		
	Usage		400	
3	Labour			
	Rate of pay		1,412	
	Efficiency	512		
4	Variable overhead			
	Expenditure		102	
	Efficiency	192		
5	Fixed overhead			
	Expenditure		50	
	Efficiency	80		
	Capacity	20		
		1,074	1,964	890
6	Actual cost			41,970

(b)   (i)   Although standard costing has, as one of its purposes, the allocation of responsibility for cost variances, it is often found in practice that the analysis of variances is merely the beginning of a further task of investigation before ultimate responsibility can be equitably assigned.

On the operating statement submitted for part (a) of this question there is disclosed a favourable material price variance and an adverse usage variance. Theoretically this should indicate that the buyer is operating efficiently and the production manager inefficiently. This need not necessarily be true, however. The buyer could have taken advantage of a special offer of material at less than standard price, not appreciating that the material was slightly below standard quality. It is very likely that the inferior material would give rise to production problems of machining, handling and possibly others which could well result in excess usage; hence the adverse usage variance.

(ii)   As regards labour, the payment of higher than standard rates (suggested by the adverse rate of pay variance in the operating statement) may well have had the effect of providing greater motivation, and hence speedier work, which is reflected in the favourable efficiency variance.

There may well be interdependence between the material and labour cost variances; for instance, the speedier work suggested by the favourable labour efficiency variance may have been accomplished by disregarding material usage standards.

From the foregoing it will be seen that not only is there possible interdependence between the variances of each element of cost, but also cross-interdependence between the elements of cost.

Workings

1   *Standard cost per unit*

		£
Materials		3.00
Labour		3.20
Variable overhead		1.20
Fixed overhead $\dfrac{£30,000}{120,000}$ = 25p per hr × 2 hrs		0.50
		‾‾‾‾
		7.90
		‾‾‾‾
Flexed budgeted cost 5,200 × £7.90		£41,080

2   *Materials*

(i)   *Price variance*

	£
Actual cost of 32,000 lb	15,730
Standard cost	16,000
	‾‾‾‾‾
	270 (F)
	‾‾‾‾‾

(ii)   *Usage variance*

	lb
Expected usage for 5,200 chairs	31,200
Actual usage	32,000
	‾‾‾‾‾
Excessive usage	800
	‾‾‾‾‾
@ 50p per lb	£400 (A)
	‾‾‾‾‾

3   *Labour*

   (i)   *Rate of pay*

	£
Actual cost of 10,080 hrs	17,540
Standard cost	16,128
	1,412 (A)

   (ii)   *Efficiency*

	Hrs
Standard time for 5,200 chairs	10,400
Actual time taken	10,080
Hours gained through efficiency	320
@ 160p per hour	512 (F)

4   *Variable overhead*

   (i)   *Expenditure variance*

	£
Actual cost of 10,080 hours	6,150
Standard cost	6,048
	102 (A)

   (ii)   *Efficiency variance*
          320 hours @ 60p   192 (F)

5   *Fixed overhead*

   (i)   *Expenditure variance*

	£
Budgeted cost	2,500
Actual cost	2,550
	50 (A)

    (ii)   *Efficiency variance*

           320 hours @ 25p   80 (F)

(The absorption rate is calculated by dividing the budgeted cost by the budgeted number of hours to be worked: £30,000 / (60,000 × 2 hrs) = 25p)

    (iii)   *Volume variance*

	£
Actual hours worked	10,080
Budgeted 20/240 × 120,000	10,000
	80
@ 25p per hour	20 (F)

6   *Actual cost statement*

	£
Materials	15,730
Labour	17,540
Variable overhead	6,150
Fixed overhead	2,550
	41,970

2   XYZ Manufacturing Company

Key points in the report

♦   Although the total variance is only 1.57% of the total, this disguises significant individual variances which require investigation.

♦   The favourable variances are entirely price variances and therefore largely outside management control. The controllable variances are all adverse.

♦   Investigation of materials wastage, labour utilisation and usage of overhead facilities required. The relevant adverse valances are 5.5%, 3.75% and 2.6% of actual cost.

♦   Adverse volume variance due to operating below planned capacity. Not substantial but efforts should be made to increase capacity.

3   WH Limited II

(a)   (i)   Direct material price variance   = $(£4.90 - £4.60) \times 2,100$

                =   £630 favourable

      (ii)   Direct material usage variance   = $[(400 \times 4.5) - 2,100] \times £4.90$

                =   £1,470 adverse

      (iii)   Direct labour rate variance   = $(£3.50 - £4) \times 4,000$

                =   £2,000 adverse

      (iv)   Direct labour utilisation variance   = $[(400 \times 10.3) - 4,000] \times £3.50$

                =   £420 favourable

(b)   *Reconciliation of standard direct cost of production with actual direct cost for November*

			£	£
Standard direct cost of production (400 x £58.10)				23,240
Direct cost variances:				
Direct material	– price		630 (F)	
	– usage		1,470 (A)	
				840 (A)
Direct labour	– rate		2,000 (A)	
	– utilisation		420 (F)	
				1,580 (A)
Actual direct cost of production				25,660

Note: A = adverse variance; F = favourable variance

(c) – (e)

WH Limited

MEMORANDUM

To: Production Manager   Date: 12 December 19X4

From: Assistant Accountant

Subject: Direct cost variances for November

As you requested, I detail below explanations of the direct cost variances and possible suggestions as to their cause in November.

(c)   *The meaning of the variances*

    Direct material price variance

    This variance shows the saving or over-spending which resulted from paying a lower or higher price than standard for the direct material used in the period. The favourable variance indicates that a lower than standard price was paid.

    Direct material usage variance

    This variance shows the saving or over-spending, at standard prices, which resulted from using less or more material than standard to manufacture the production for the period. The adverse variance indicates that more material was used than standard.

    Direct labour rate variance

    This variance shows the saving or over-spending which resulted from paying a lower or higher hourly rate than standard for the hours worked in the period. The adverse variance indicates that a higher than standard hourly rate was paid.

    Direct labour utilisation variance

    This variance shows the saving or overspending, at standard rates, which resulted from working less or more hours than standard to manufacture the production for the period. The favourable variance indicates that less hours were worked than standard.

(d)   *Possible causes of the variances*

    Favourable direct material price variance

    Bulk discounts were received which were not allowed for in the standard.
    The standard price of material was set too high.
    A lower quality material was purchased, at a lower price than standard.
    Effective negotiations by the buyer secured a price lower than the standard.

    Adverse direct material usage variance

    Material wastage was higher than allowed in the standard.
    The standard usage was set too low.
    There was a higher than standard level of rejects.
    Theft of material.

Adverse direct labour rate variance

High levels of overtime were paid for compared with the standard allowance.
The standard wage rate was set too low.
A higher grade of labour was used.
Bonus payments were higher than standard.

Favourable direct labour utilisation variance

Employees were working faster than standard.
More skilled employees were used.
There were savings through the learning effect.
The standard labour time was set too high.
The material was easy to process, leading to savings against the standard time.

(e) Two examples of interdependence, where one variance can be related to others, could include the following.

The savings made on material price (favourable material price variance) may indicate that poor quality material was purchased, leading to high wastage, rejects and an adverse usage variance.

Bulk discounts may have resulted in the saving on material price. However, the consequent excessive stocks may have led to deterioration and write-offs, hence the adverse usage variance.

Direct workers may have been of a higher grade than standard, resulting in higher hourly rates and the adverse rate variance. However, the higher skill level may have led to time savings and the favourable utilisation variance.

Higher than standard bonus payments may have caused the adverse labour rate variance, but the bonuses may have resulted from faster working and hence the favourable utilisation variance.

Faster working resulted in the favourable utilisation variance, but less care may have been taken over weighing and handling the material, hence the adverse material usage variance.

Page 2/ 2

4   Product XY

Standard product cost sheet for one unit of product XY

	£
Materials – 8 kg at £1.50 per kg	12.00
Labour – 2 hours at £4 per hour	8.00
Variable overhead – 2 hours at £1 per hour	2.00
	22.00

Workings

1   *Materials*

	Kg	£
Actual materials used at actual cost	150,000	210,000
Price variance	–	15,000 (F)
Actual materials used at standard cost, ie £1.50/kg	150,000	225,000
Usage variance (@ £1.50/kg)	6,000	9,000 (A)
Standard materials at standard cost	144,000	216,000

With a production level of 18,000 units:

Standard material usage $\dfrac{144,000\,\text{kg}}{18,000\,\text{units}} = 8$ kg per unit

Standard material price $\dfrac{£216,000}{144,000\,\text{kg}} = £1.50$ per kg

2   *Labour*

	Hours	£
Actual hours worked at actual rate	32,000	136,000
Rate variance	–	8,000 (A)
Actual hours worked at standard rate, ie £4/hour	32,000	128,000
Efficiency variance (@ £4/hour)	4,000	16,000 (F)
Standard hours at standard rate	36,000	144,000

With a production level of 18,000 units:

Standard labour efficiency $\dfrac{36,000\,\text{hours}}{18,000\,\text{units}} = 2$ hours per unit

Standard labour rate $\dfrac{£144,000}{36,000\,\text{hours}} = £4$ per hour

3   *Variable production overhead*

	Hours	£
Actual hours worked at actual rate	32,000	38,000
Expenditure variance	–	6,000 (A)
Actual hours worked at standard rate, ie £1/hour	32,000	32,000
Efficiency variance (@ £1/hour)	4,000	4,000 (F)
Standard hours at standard rate	36,000	36,000

With a production level of 18,000 units:

Standard variable overhead efficiency $\dfrac{36,000 \text{ hours}}{18,000 \text{ units}} = 2$ hours per unit

Standard variable overhead expenditure $\dfrac{£36,000}{36,000 \text{ hours}} = £1$ per hour

Notes

1   There are a number of ways of approaching the answer to this question. The suggestion here is just one of those methods.

2   Common sense and a thorough understanding of the meaning of variances as well as methods of calculation are essential.

3   The resulting standards will usually be fairly 'round number' figures. If they are not, it is worth an extra check.

5   AB Limited II

(a)

Direct material price variance	=	$(£8 – £8.50) \times 19,500$
	=	£9,750 adverse
Direct material usage variance	=	$[(4,500 \times 4.3\text{kg}) – 19,500] \times £8$
	=	£1,200 adverse
Direct labour rate variance	=	$(£4 – £3.90) \times 6,740$
	=	£674 favourable
Direct labour utilisation variance	=	$[(4,500 \times 1.5 \text{ hours}) – 6,740] \times £4$
	=	£40 favourable

(b)   *Reconciliation of standard direct cost of production with actual direct cost for June*

Actual production = 4,500 units

	£	£
Standard direct cost of production = 4,500 x £40.40		181,800
Direct cost variances		
Direct material price	9,750 (A)	
Direct material usage	1,200 (A)	
		10,950 (A)
Direct labour rate	674 (F)	
Direct labour utilisation	40 (F)	
		714 (F)
Actual direct cost of production		192,036

(c)

MEMORANDUM

To: A N Other   Date: June 19X4

From: Assistant Accountant

Subject: Explanations for overhead variances

As you requested, I outline below possible explanations for each of the overhead variances which you have calculated.

Overhead price variance

The adverse variance would have been caused by production overhead expenditure being higher than budgeted. This could have resulted from the expenditure on any item of fixed production overhead being higher than budgeted. One possible reason was that the factory rent was higher than had been budgeted.

Overhead efficiency variance

The efficiency variance is favourable and this is directly related to the favourable labour utilisation variance. We know from the calculation of the direct labour utilisation variance that the labour force took less time than the standard hours expected for 4,500 units. Therefore the overhead efficiency variance could have been caused by any factor which enabled time to be saved against the standard allowance. One possible reason could be that the standard time allowance was set too high.

Overhead volume variance

The volume variance is favourable, indicating that more use was made of available capacity than was originally budgeted (ie more hours were worked in total). One possible reason for this could be that there were more employees than had been budgeted.

Chapter 8

1   Transport company II

Cost control performance ratios

Cost per mile

Cost per tonne carried

Cost per journey

Cost per tonne/mile

} each of these ratios could be calculated for fixed and variable costs separately

Fixed cost per available day

Fixed cost per working day

Usage performance ratios

Tonne/miles per period

Days available as a percentage of total working days

Days used as a percentage of available days

Tonnes carried per available day

Journeys made per available day

Tonnes/miles per journey

2   Retail ratios

◆   Rate of stock turnover = Total sales/Average stock

The higher the better. Reduces the risk of obsolescence. Makes best use of working capital.

◆   Gross profit margin = (Sales – Cost of sales) as % of sales (or as % of purchases). Trading profitability. Preferably as high as possible but the company might have a policy of low margins with high turnover.

◆   Creditors average settlement period = 12 divided by (Annual purchases/Average creditors) months. Could also be expressed in weeks or days. How quickly is the company settling its debts?. The higher the period, the better use being made of working capital but, if too high it could lead to lack of goodwill with creditors.

◆   Net profit before tax to capital employed: overall profitability of the company's investment in the business.

3　WH Limited III

WH Limited

REPORT

To:　　Senior Management Committee　　　　Date:　　12 December 19X4

From:　　Assistant Accountant

Subject:　Profitability and asset turnover ratios

We have received the Trade Association results for year 4 and this report looks in detail at the profitability and asset turnover ratios.

(a)　*What each ratio is designed to show*

　　(i)　*Return on capital employed (ROCE)*

　　　　This ratio shows the percentage rate of profit which has been earned on the capital invested in the business, (ie the return on the resources controlled by management). The expected return would vary depending on the type of business and it is usually calculated as follows:

$$\text{Return on capital employed} = \frac{\text{Profit before interest and tax}}{\text{Capital employed}} \times 100\%$$

　　　　Other profit figures can be used, as well as various definitions of capital employed.

　　(ii)　*Net operating profit margin*

　　　　This ratio shows the operating profit as a percentage of sales. The operating profit is calculated before interest and tax and it is the profit over which operational managers can exercise day to day control. It is the amount left out of sales value after all direct costs and overheads have been deducted.

$$\text{Net operating profit margin} = \frac{\text{Operating profit}}{\text{Sales value}} \times 100\%$$

　　(iii)　*Asset turnover*

　　　　This ratio shows how effectively the assets of a business are being used to generate sales:

$$\text{Asset turnover} = \frac{\text{Sales}}{\text{Capital employed}}$$

　　　　If the same figure for capital employed is used as in ROCE, then ratios (i) to (iii) can be related together as follows.

　　　　(i)　ROCE = (ii) Net operating profit margin × (iii) Asset turnover

Page 1/2

(iv) *Gross margin*

This ratio measures the profitability of sales:

$$\text{Gross margin} = \frac{\text{Gross profit}}{\text{Sales value}} \times 100\%$$

The gross profit is calculated as the sales value less the cost of goods sold and this ratio therefore focuses on the company's manufacturing and trading activities.

(b) *WH Limited's profitability and asset turnover*

WH Limited's ROCE is lower than the trade association average, possibly indicating that the assets are not being used as profitably in this company as the average for the industry.

WH Limited's operating profit margin is higher than the trade association average, despite a lower than average gross profit margin. This suggests that overheads are lower relative to sales value in WH Limited.

WH Limited's asset turnover ratio is lower than the trade association average. This may mean that assets are not being used as effectively in our company and it is the cause of the lower than average ROCE.

WH Limited's gross profit margin is lower than the trade association average. This suggests either that WH's direct costs are higher than average, or that selling prices are lower.

(c) *Limitations of the ratios and of inter-company comparisons*

There are a number of limitations of which management should be aware before drawing any firm conclusions from a comparison of these ratios:

(i) The ratios are merely averages, based on year-end balance sheet data, which may not be representative.

(ii) One particular factor which could affect these ratios is if there has been any new investment towards the end of the financial year. This investment would increase the value of the assets or capital employed, but the profits from the investment would not yet have accumulated in the profit and loss account. Generally, newer assets tend to depress the asset turnover and hence the ROCE in the short term. It is possible that this is the cause of our company's lower asset turnover and ROCE.

(iii) Although the trade association probably makes some attempt to standardise the data, different member companies may be using different accounting policies, for example in calculating depreciation and valuing stock.

(iv) Our company's analyst may have used a different formula for calculating any of the ratios. For example, as noted above, there is a variety of ways of calculating capital employed. However, it is likely that the trade association would provide information on the basis of calculation of the ratios.

(v) The member companies will have some activities in common, hence their membership of the trade association. However, some may have a diversified range of activities, which will distort the ratios and make direct comparison difficult.

Page 2/2

4 Loamshire County Council II

(a) Measures of efficiency in routine tasks: issues per clerical employee or accessions per clerical employee.

(b) Level of service measures: library users as percentage of county population. Issues per user.

(c) Measure of income generation: income as percentage of total budget.

(d) Quality of the stock: average cost per item (books, cassettes, CDs). Stock analysed by age of accession. Number of accessions in the current year (or other period) as percentage of total stock.

5 Homely Limited

(a) *Target ratios*

$$\text{Return on capital employed} = \frac{66}{300} \times 100\% = 22\%$$

$$\text{Operating profit percentage} = \frac{66}{820} \times 100\% = 8\%$$

$$\text{Asset turnover} = \frac{820}{300} = 2.7 \text{ times}$$

$$\text{Working capital period} = \frac{70}{754} \times 365 = 34 \text{ days}$$

$$\text{Percentage room occupancy} = \frac{5,900}{18 \times 365} \times 100\% = 90\%$$

$$\text{Turnover per employee} = \frac{820,000}{20} = \pounds41,000$$

Key ratios for 19X4

	Stately Hotels plc target	*Homely Limited actual*
Return on capital employed	26%	22%
Operating profit percentage	13%	8%
Asset turnover	2.0 times	2.7 times
Working capital period	20 days	34 days
Percentage room occupancy	85%	90%
Turnover per employee	£30,000	£41,000

(b)

MEMORANDUM

To: Management accountant, Stately Hotels plc   Date: 21 June X5

From: Assistant to the management accountant

Subject: Initial assessment of the performance of Homely Limited

I have carried out an initial assessment of Homely Limited, based on an extract from their accounts for 1994. I have calculated their key accounting ratios and compared them with our company's target ratios and my conclusions and recommendations are as follows.

Return on capital employed (ROCE)

At 22% this is below the target which we set for the hotels in our chain. Management action will be necessary to improve the return on capital employed, through improved profitability of operations, increased asset turnover, or both.

The main limitations in the use of this ratio is that the valuation of the capital employed can have a considerable effect on the apparent ROCE. For example, if the capital employed is undervalued, this will artificially inflate the ROCE.

Operating profit percentage

This is considerably below the target ratio set by Stately Hotels plc and it is the cause of the depressed ROCE. Management action will be necessary to improve this, either by increasing prices or by controlling operating costs relative to sales revenue. Since the former action may depress demand in Homely Limited's market, it is likely that management will need to focus on the control of operating costs.

A limitation in the use of this ratio is that Homely's operations may not be comparable to the average hotel in the Stately group. For example, they may not have conference facilities, which would affect the profile of their costs.

Asset turnover

At 2.7 times this is higher than the target ratio, indicating that, although Homely's operations are not as profitable, they generate more turnover per £ of capital employed. It may be that Homely has a different basis of operating, ie charging lower prices, and thus reducing the profitability of sales, but in the process generating a higher turnover for the level of capital employed.

The main limitation of this ratio stems from the limitation of the ROCE, ie its accuracy relies on the correct valuation of capital employed.

Working capital period

This is 34 days of operating costs, almost double the level which we require in our target performance ratios. Working capital levels are probably unacceptably high and need to be reduced. This will require more attention to debtor control, reduction in stocks of, for example, consumable materials and foodstuffs, and an investigation into whether full use is being made of available credit facilities.

Page 1/2

A limitation of this ratio is that it relies on the accurate valuation of working capital. For example, although stocks should not account for a high proportion of working capital in a hotel, their valuation can be very subjective.

Another major limitation is that the ratio is based on balance sheet data, which depicts the working capital level on a single day. This may not be representative of the year as a whole and therefore incorrect conclusions may be drawn from the analysis.

Percentage room occupancy

Homely Limited is achieving a room occupancy rate which is above the level expected in our organisation's target ratios. This is a healthy sign which is encouraging.

Turnover per employee

Homely Limited's turnover per employee is also healthy. However, we must ensure that customer service and quality are not suffering as a result of operating with a lower level of staffing.

Overall, Homely Limited seems to have some strengths which would be worth exploiting. However, their control of operating costs and of working capital needs some attention.

Page 2/2

6   Gransden Limited

(a)   (i)   *Material price and usage variances*

Standard cost	£2,500,000	*Material price variance*		
Total variance	£200,000 (A	(£120 – £100) × 22,500 metres =	£450,000 (A)	
Actual cost	£2,700,000	*Material usage variance*		
		Standard metres: £2,500,000/£100	25,000	
Actual usage (metres)	22,500	Actual metres	22,500	
Actual cost per metre	£120			
		Physical variance (metres)	2,500 (F)	
		2,500 metres × £100 =	£250,000 (F)	

(ii)   *Increase in RPI*

Current index	168
Index at beginning of period	160
Price inflation ((168/160 – 1) × 100	5%

(b)   The difference between the standard and actual price per metre is £20. With an original standard cost of £100 and inflation of 5%, £5 must represent the inflation element, leaving £15 of the difference due to other factors. The total effect of this is shown graphically below along with the price and usage variances.

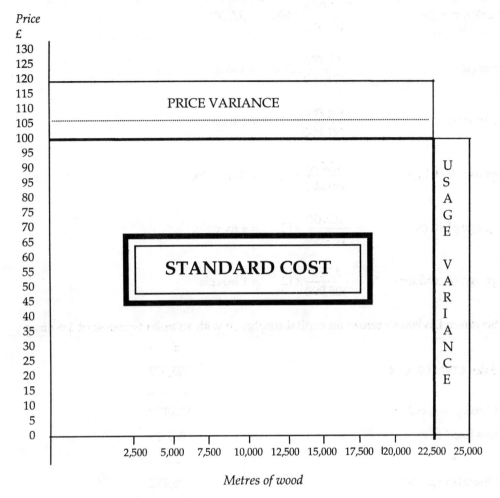

Metres of wood

Key to diagram

The area bounded by darker lines represents the standard cost of producing 5,000 tables.

The area representing the price variance is subdivided by a dotted line. The lower portion represents the effect of inflation as measured by the RPI.

(c)   *Difficulties in interpreting the price variance*

(i)   The original standard may not have been appropriate.

(ii)   There might be a link between the adverse price variance and the favourable usage variance. This might occur if a superior, but more expensive, material has been used.

(iii) The Retail Price Index is a measure of the cost of living for the average household in the UK. It may not be an appropriate index for measuring prices rises in manufacturing generally nor prices rises for wood in particular.

(d) Return on capital employed $\dfrac{34,380}{191,000} \times 100$ = 18.00%

Gross profit margin $\dfrac{71,000}{191,000} \times 100$ = 37.17%

Sales margin $\dfrac{34,380}{191,000} \times 100$ = 18.00%

Asset turnover $\dfrac{191,000}{191,000}$ = 1 time

Average age of debtors $\dfrac{47,750}{191,000} \times 12$ = 3 months

Average age of stock $\dfrac{40,000}{120,000} \times 12$ = 4 months

Average age of creditors $\dfrac{8,750}{105,000} \times 12$ = 1 month

(e) (i) Southern Division's return on capital employed with an asset turnover of 1.6 times

	£
Sales £191,000 × 1.6	305,600
Gross profit @ 37%	113,072
less fixed costs =	36,620
Operating profit	76,452
Capital employed	£191,000
Return on capital employed	40%

(ii) Southern Division's return on capital employed with Northern's working capital ratios

	£
Fixed assets	112,000
Stock £120,000 × 3/12 =	30,000
Debtors £191,000 × 1.5/12 =	23,875
Creditors £105,000 × 2/12 =	(17,500)
Capital employed	148,375
Operating profit	£34,380
Return on capital employed	23%

(f)   (i)   Both divisions appear to be charging straight-line depreciation at 10% per annum. On that basis, the average age of Northern's fixed assets is four years old (£40,000/£10,000) while the comparable figure for the Southern Division is only three years (£48,000/£16,000). Because of this, Southern will have lower accumulated depreciation and hence a higher capital employed.

       (ii)   Although the average age of creditors and debtors result from past activity – buying and selling respectively – the average age of stock has a different perspective. Although the cost of sales is backward looking in the same way as purchases and sales, the stock level at the year end may not be a direct consequence of this activity. Stock could be being built up in anticipation of higher sales next year.

      (iii)   Southern Division may be paying its creditors more quickly to obtain cash discounts.

Chapter 9

1   ICI profits

The diagram shown is a component bar chart with a slight difference from those already seen. Each bar shows the trading profit for a different division. For example, the Agriculture division had a trading profit of just under £200 million in 19X3 and approximately £160 million in 19X2. The total height of the bar thus represents the 19X3 figure and the 19X2 figure is included within this. Previous examples would have represented these figures with a bar of height £360 million (200 + 160).

From the diagram the following points can be noted.

(a)   The future for ICI looks rosy since a major recovery in profits has taken place.

(b)   In 19X3 only the Fibres, Organics and Petrochemicals & Plastics divisions made losses. These were very small and in two of these divisions the losses were significantly lower than the 19X2 losses.

(c)   The Organics division is the only one which made a profit in 19X2 but then a loss in 19X3.

(d)   All other divisions made increased profits in 19X3 (compared with 19X2).

(e)   Total profit made by ICI (approximately):

19X2   £350m

19X3   £630m

This represents an 80% increase in profits, although it is important to remember that these figures are only approximate.

2   Pydec

The following points in the extract from the company report would give the trade union cause for concern.

Profits

(a)   The vertical axis of the graph starts at eight thus distorting the actual change in profits. Profits have in fact fallen from £10 million to just below 8.5 million, ie approximately 15%. (The report, on the other hand, refers to 'almost 20%'.)

(b)   The vertical scale is presumably profit (labelled 'millions') rather than £ millions.

(c)   Is the picture as bad as that painted? The rate of decrease in profits seems to be getting smaller; perhaps levelling out.

(d)   What does the dotted line mean? Presumably it is a projection but what evidence is it based upon?

(e)   The graph gives only a general indication of the behaviour of profits. More definite conclusions could be drawn if more detailed figures were available.

Production

(a)   The scale of the bar chart is correct this time.

(b)   Production has fallen as stated (by 10,000 sets or 20% overall) but this is confined to the Dundee factory.

(c)   A 20% fall in production that only gives rise to a 15% fall in profits shows strong evidence of successful cost control.

(d)   Are production figures for audio equipment available?

(e)   Report states 'some of our competitors have been doing much better'. Where is the evidence for this?

(f)   Since production probably follows demand, the split between factories is irrelevant; more important are sales by region.

Wages

(a)   The report states 'the average wage of all employees rose by £7.23 per week' and claims this is good. What percentage increase is this? What was the rate of inflation and have *real* wages increased?

(b)   Commentary and data are inconsistent: 'If we compare average wages between 19W5 and 19X0...' but diagrams are for 19W6 and 19X1.

(c)   The pictogram is misleading. In terms of the figures, wages have almost doubled, yet the diagram looks like a four-fold increase took place (twice the height and twice the width).

3   Not at all obvious

(a)

To: Mrs Jenkins

Survey report comparing the ability of two types of display stand to generate sales of cards

Introduction

The object of this report is to compare two types of display stand by analysing their ability to generate sales of cards in newsagents.

The first type of card stand is the traditional one. This is five feet wide, made from formica with sloping perspex divisions.

The second type is the revolving metal card stand. This is two feet in diameter.

For the purpose of this report we will call them Traditional and Revolving.

Procedure

The survey was carried out in three cities, Bristol, Aberdeen and Manchester. The results shown in this report are those from Bristol.

Ten newsagents from Bristol were studied over a period of six working days, the 15th to 20th March. Half of these newsagents have the traditional stand to display cards and the other half have the revolving card stand. Details of the names and addresses of all ten shops are in the Appendix. For easier comparison the shops have been allocated letters from A to E.

Findings

The following table shows the number of cards sold over the six days in Bristol:

Traditional Shop	Card sales	Revolving Shop	Card sales
A		B	
C		E	435
D		F	475
G	286	H	575
I	275	J	525

The findings were similar in the other two cities chosen for the survey.

Conclusion

The higher numbers of cards sold are all in shops which use the revolving card stands.

(b)

MEMORANDUM

To: Jo Bloggs   Date:

From: A Clerk

Report on comparison of display stands and their ability to generate sales

Having read your survey report there are a number of questions that I would like you to answer.

1   How and why were the three cities chosen?

2   How and why were the ten newsagents in Bristol chosen?

3   Only six results are shown out of the ten shops studied. Where are the results from the others?

4   Are the figures for Aberdeen and Manchester available?

5   Have you considered exchanging Traditional for Revolving stands to determine whether the higher level of sales is a function of the type of stand or the size and location of the shop.

Chapter 10

1   Product design

Product design is a fertile source of cost reduction opportunities. Simply by evaluating existing designs against the findings of market research, the designer may find prospects for cost reduction in improved design or in a reduction of the product range and the number of variants from basic models.

Improved design when coupled with improved production methods, may result in considerable cost savings. Improvements of this kind may:

(a)   reduce wastage of material and scrapped work in progress or finished products;

(b)   reduce total production time for increased productivity – this will reduce labour costs and overheads giving reduced costs per unit of output.

Product range and variety has to be examined in relation to:

(a)   the scope of simplification and standardisation of both products and their component parts;

(b)   knowledge of the products market and the customer and/or consumer opinion; the simplification and standardisation of products and their component parts, which may result in a smaller number of products containing fewer components, can bring savings of many kinds: lower production set up costs; reduced material and labour costs; lower overheads of all kinds – including servicing and repair costs.

The market for products may be so complex and competitive that variety of product and relatively broad product range is justified by the additional value of sales that they generate. Motor car manufacturers used to believe this to be the case for their industry, but since the late sixties and early seventies they have aimed for a small number of basic models with largely external variations.

Good or improved design should, of course, affect the behaviour and attitudes of the people who make the products and those who manage both these people and the processes in which they are employed. Good design addresses the question of quality control and should tend to reduce inspection time; increasingly it leads to ways of improving motivation and increasing the interest of those who produce to the design specification; in both of these tendencies lie prospects for further cost reduction.

2   Control v reduction

The purpose of cost control is to contain the cost of a product or service, with some predetermined target or budget, or according to some preset standard. By contrast, the aim of cost reduction is to reduce the cost of a product or service without affecting its function, quality or saleable value, and implies a challenging of existing cost standards. Both activities are concerned with the efficient and effective use of resources and both employ the same techniques of cost analysis. However, clearly, the one is different from the other as a more detailed consideration will show.

(a)   Cost control is a general term used to define all methods of controlling the cost of manufacturing or processing products or services through all the various stages. The main methods used by management accountants are as follows:

(i)   standard costing

(ii)   budgetary control.

These both entail targets or standards together with feedback on performance against standards and the correction of deviations or variances. The application of these methods relates to some predetermined time period at the end of which targets or standards are reviewed and set for a subsequent period.

(b)   Cost reduction actively seeks to make real reductions in the cost of a product or a service by lowering the cost of any item that contributes to the total cost, without impairing the suitability of the products for their intended use.

Broad methods of reducing costs are:

(i)   unit cost reduction by expenditure reduction or greater volume of output

(ii)   unit cost reduction by an increase in productivity, ie an increase in output yield or rate of output for a given amount of expenditure. Unlike cost control which is a relatively stable activity, cost reduction activity is dynamic because it includes a continuous search for opportunities to change the current standards or targets.

3   Value analysis

Value analysis has been defined as: 'the analysis of the utilitarian or marketing function of a product or procedure in an organised way with the aim of identifying any alternative ways of achieving the required end and in choosing the least cost method of doing this from the alternatives found'.

Briefly, value analysis is a means of eliminating costs by a systematic search for ways of achieving the same, or a better, performance for an existing manufactured product at a lower cost without reducing the quality. Quite obviously, value analysis is a technique of cost reduction.

Value analysis proceeds by an analysis of the function of a product or of its component parts. Function is the criterion for determining the value of an item; one with a high value is one that satisfies exactly the function which makes the item work or sell at the lowest cost. Value analysis may result in the substitution of materials, or modifications to the design in order to make the best use of materials, or cheaper marketing methods and so forth.

4   Quality circles

Quality circles were invented by the American IBM Company, during the late 1950s, but are associated more with the operation of Japanese organisations. Quality circles comprise small groups of either staff or operatives who meet regularly to discuss problems of quality control in their work area. They advance possible solutions and ideas to resolve the problems, and possibly on how to improve the quality of output.

Supervisors obviously play a big role in operating the circles since they do the training and lead the groups. In the Western world this creates a problem, since the responsibility for operational planning and the essential tooling standards and control is the province of a staff technician, rather than the operatives. Consequently, for effective implementation in the Western world, attitudes need to change about the employment of operatives in a consultative session. Worse still, the functional experts may resent their potential loss of status if they are not put in charge of the circles, or if they are made to relate with the operatives. As a result of this, quality circles have been less than successful in traditional Western industrial environment of computer engineering.

A further failing in the West has been that the participants were expected to give of their own time to attend the meetings, rather than go in the firm's time. By contrast, in Japan, where the success has been considerable, the employees attend in the company time, encouraged to volunteer to serve on the quality circles which are often seen as a means of being noticed for promotion.

CHAPTER 12

Practice Central Assessments (Questions)

Objectives

In this chapter you will find two Practice Central Assessments, one for Unit 7 and one for Unit 8. They are in the style of the real thing, and are at the same level of difficulty as the real thing. Doing these Practice Central Assessments as trial runs for the real thing will really help your chances of success on the day.

We recommend that you only attempt these Practice Central Assessments once you have completely finished your work on this Study Pack. It is particularly important that you complete all, or as many as you can, of the questions at the end of each chapter. Whilst these are generally not of full assessment standard, they help you to build up your skills and confidence to the level of the full central assessment represented in these Practice Central Assessments.

Try these Practice Central Assessments under assessment conditions unless guided otherwise. And if you look at the answers before you have tried the Practice Central Assessment properly, you are cheating no–one but yourself!

Unit 7: Practice Central Assessment

Time Allowed – 3 hours plus 15 minutes reading time
This central assessment is in two sections.
You are reminded that competence must be achieved in EACH section. You should therefore complete EVERY task in EACH section.
You are advised to spend approximately 105 minutes on Section 1 and 75 minutes on Section 2.
All essential workings should be included within your answers, where appropriate.

SECTION 1   *(Suggested time allocation: 105 minutes)*

Data

You are employed as an accounting technician by Original Holidays Limited. Original Holidays commenced business one year ago as a tour operator specialising in arranging holidays to the small island of Zed. Recent newspaper reports have stated that the cost of hotel bedrooms per night in Zed has been increasing over the last twelve months due to its government refusing to allow further hotels to be built despite increasing demand from tourists.

The managing director of Original Holidays, Jane Armstrong, is concerned that this will affect the profitability of the company's operations to the island. She asked Colin Ware, the financial accountant, to provide data showing the nightly cost of a bedroom charged to Original Holidays over the last four quarters. Colin's response is reproduced below.

MEMORANDUM

To: Jane Armstrong   Date: 5 January 19X8

From: Colin Ware

Subject: Nightly cost per bedroom

Thank you for your recent enquiry concerning the cost per night of a bedroom in Zed. I have analysed the amounts paid per quarter over the last twelve months and divided that amount by the number of bedrooms hired per night. The nightly cost per bedroom is as follows:

	Quarter 1	Quarter 2	Quarter 3	Quarter 4
Cost per night	£102.400	£137.760	£134.480	£68.921

(*Note*. all figures in pounds to 3 decimal places.)

On receiving the memo, Jane noticed that the cost to Original Holidays per bedroom per night had actually been falling over the last three quarters and has asked for your help in reconciling this with the newspaper reports. You obtain the following information.

Over several years, there has been a consistent seasonal variation in the cost of bedrooms per night. According to the marketing manager, these are:

Seasonal variations	Quarter 1	Quarter 2	Quarter 3	Quarter 4
as percentage of trend	−20%	+5%	+40%	−25%

A financial newspaper provides you with the following exchange rates between the UK pound and the Zed franc:

Quarter 1	Quarter 2	Quarter 3	Quarter 4
2,000 francs	2,000 francs	2,800 francs	3,000 francs

Task 1.1

(a) Using the quarterly exchange rates given, identify the actual nightly cost per bedroom in Zed francs for each quarter.

(b) Using the information provided by the marketing manager, identify the trend in costs in Zed francs for each quarter.

(c) Identify the quarterly percentage increase in the cost of a bedroom per night in Zed francs and express this as an annual percentage to 2 decimal places.

(d) Forecast the cost in British pounds of a bedroom per night for the first quarter of 19X8 using the exchange rate for the fourth quarter.

Data

On receiving your analysis of the cost per bedroom per night, Jane Armstrong expresses concern that the company's existing reporting system does not provide sufficient information to monitor operations. She shows you a copy of the operating statement for the third quarter prepared using the existing system. The statement excludes marketing, administrative and other head-office overheads and is reproduced below.

Original Holidays Operating Statement for the 3rd Quarter – 19X7

	Budget	Actual
Number of holidays	6,000	7,800
	£	£
Turnover	1,800,000	2,262,000
Accommodation	840,000	1,048,944
Air transport	720,000	792,000
Operating profit	240,000	421,056

Jane has shared her concerns with Colin Ware, the financial accountant. He has suggested that a standard costing report, reconciling standard cost to actual cost, would provide more meaningful information for management. To demonstrate to Jane Armstrong the improved quality of a standard costing system of reporting, Colin asks you to reanalyse the operating statement for the third quarter. To help you, he provides you with the following information:

The accommodation is a variable cost. Its usage variance is nil.

Air transport is a fixed cost and relates to the company's own 105-seat aircraft.

The budget provided for 80 return flights in the quarter with each flight carrying 75 tourists. This volume was used to calculate the fixed overhead absorption rate when costing individual holidays.

Due to operational difficulties, the aircraft only undertook 78 return flights, carrying a total of 7,800 passengers in quarter 3.

Task 1.2

(a)   Using the budgeted data, calculate the standard absorption cost per holiday.

(b)   Using your answer to part a), calculate the standard absorption cost of 7,800 holidays.

(c)   Calculate the following variances:

    (i)   material price variance for the accommodation;

    (ii)   fixed overhead expenditure variance for the air transport;

    (iii)   fixed overhead capacity variance for the air transport;

    (iv)   fixed overhead efficiency variance for the air transport;

    (v)   sales price variance;

    (vi)   sales margin volume variance (using the unit standard absorption cost to determine profit).

(d)   Prepare a statement reconciling the budgeted (or standard) absorption cost to the actual cost.

(e)   Identify the single most important reason for the increase in the actual profit.

Task 1.3

Write a memo to Jane Armstrong *briefly* explaining what the following variances attempt to measure and giving **one** possible reason why each variance might have occurred:

♦   the fixed overhead expenditure variance;

♦   the fixed overhead capacity variance;

♦   the fixed overhead efficiency variance.

SECTION 2   *(Suggested time allocation: 75 minutes)*

Data

Diamond Limited is a retail jeweller operating 30 branches in similar localities. Common accounting policies operate throughout all branches, including a policy of using straight-line depreciation for fixed assets.

All branches use rented premises. These are accounted for under 'other costs' in the operating statement. Fixed assets are predominantly fixtures and fittings.

Each branch is individually responsible for ordering stock, the authorising of payments to creditors and the control of debtors. Cash management, however, is managed by Diamond's head office with any cash received by a branch being paid into a head office bank account twice daily.

You are employed in the head office of Diamond Limited as a financial analyst monitoring the performance of all 30 branches. This involves calculating performance indicators for each branch and comparing each branch's performance with company standards. Financial data relating to Branch 24 is reproduced below.

Diamond Limited – Branch 24 – Year ended 31 December 19X7

Operating statement	£000	£000	*Operating net assets at year end*	£000	£000
Turnover		720.0	Fixed assets		
Opening stock	80.0		Cost		225.0
Purchases	340.0		Accumulated depreciation		(90.0)
Closing stock	(60.0)				———
		360.0	Net book value		135.0
		———	*Working capital*		
Gross profit		360.0	Stocks	60.0	
Wages and salaries	220.6		Debtors	96.0	
Depreciation	45.0		Creditors	(51.0)	
Other costs	36.8			———	105.0
	———				———
		302.4	*Net assets*		240.0
		———			═══
Operating profit		57.6			
		═══			

Task 2.1

Prepare a statement showing the following performance indicators for Branch 24:

(a)   the return on capital employed;

(b)   the gross profit margin as a percentage;

(c)   the asset turnover;

(d)   the sales (or net profit) margin as a percentage;

(e)   the average age of debtors in months;

(f)   the average age of creditors in months;

(g)   the average age of the closing stock in months.

Data

The financial director of Diamond Limited is Charles Warden. He is concerned that Branch 24 is not performing as well as the other branches. All other branches are able to meet or exceed most of the performance standards laid down by the company.

Charles is particularly concerned the branches should achieve the standards for return on capital employed and for asset turnover. He also feels that managers should try to achieve the standards laid down for working capital management. The relevant standards are:

return on capital employed	40%
asset turnover	4 times per annum
average age of debtors	0.5 months
average age of creditors	3 months
average age of closing stock	1 month

Charles Walden has recently attended a course on financial modelling and scenario planning. Charles explains that scenario planning shows the likely performance of a business under different assumed circumstances. It requires an understanding of the relationship between the different elements within the financial statements and how these change as the circumstances being modelled change. As an example, he tells you that if the volume of branch turnover was to increase then the cost of sales would also increase but that all other expenses would remain the same as they are fixed costs.

He believes scenario planning would be particularly helpful to the manager of Branch 24, Angela Newton. Charles had previously discussed the performance of the branch with Angela and emphasised the importance of improving the asset turnover and maintaining control of working capital. However, Angela raised the following objections:

◆   turning over assets is not important, making profit should be the main objective;

◆   Branch 24 has been in existence for two years less than all the other branches.

Task 2.2

Charles Walden asks you to write a memo to Angela Newton. Your memo should:

(a)   show the return on capital employed that Branch 24 would have achieved had it been able to achieve the company's asset turnover during the year to 31 December 19X7 while maintaining prices and the existing capital employed;

(b)   show the return on capital employed and the asset turnover for the year if Branch 24 had been able to achieve the company's standards for the average age of debtors, the average age of creditors and the average age of finished stock while maintaining its existing sales volume;

(c)   *using the data in task 2.1 and your solution to task 2.2 a)*, address the issues raised by Angela Newton.

Unit 8: Practice Central Assessment

Time Allowed – 3 hours plus 15 minutes reading time
This central assessment is in two sections.
You are reminded that competence must be achieved in EACH section. You should therefore complete EVERY task in EACH section.
You are advised to spend approximately 75 minutes on Section 1 and 105 minutes on Section 2.
All essential workings should be included within your answers, where appropriate.

SECTION 1   *(Suggested time allocation: 75 minutes)*

Data

Star Fuels is a multinational oil company selling oil for industrial and domestic purposes through a network of distributors. Distributors purchase fuel oil from Star Fuels and then sell it on to their own customers.

A regular complaint of the distributors is that they either have to pay for fuel on delivery to their storage tanks or be charged interest on a daily basis on the amount owed. This problem could be reduced if the distributors were able to forecast their demands more accurately.

You are employed as the Assistant Management Accountant to Northern Fuel Distributors Ltd, a major distributor of Star Fuel's fuel oils. You recently attended a meeting with Mary Lamberton, a member of Star Fuel's central staff. At the meeting, she demonstrated a statistical software package used for estimating the demand for fuel oil. The user enters sales volumes per period and the package then calculates the least-squares regression equation for the data. This is in the form $y = a + bx$ where x is the time period, y is the forecast and a and b are terms derived from the original data. Following further inputs by the user the package can also estimate seasonal variations. Two forms of seasonal variation are calculated: the first calculates the seasonal variance as an absolute amount, the second as a percentage.

One week after the meeting, your copy of the software arrives at the head office of Northern Fuel Distributors Limited and you immediately set about testing its capability. Purely for the purpose of testing, you assume seasonal variations occur quarterly. You enter this assumption along with the sales turnover figures for fuel oil for the last 20 quarters. Within moments, the software outputs the following information.

Regression line $y = £2,000,000 + £40,000x$

Seasonal variations

Quarter	A	B	C	D
Amount	+£350,000	+£250,000	–£400,000	–£200,000
Percentage	+15%	+10%	–15%	–10%

Quarter A refers to the first quarter of annual data, B to the second Quarter, C to the third and D to the fourth. The pattern then repeats itself. In terms of the specific data you input, seasonal variation A refers to Quarter 17, B to Quarter 18, C to Quarter 19 and D to Quarter 20.

Quarter	17	18	19	20
Sales turnover	£3,079,500	£3,002,400	£2,346,500	£2,490,200

Task 1.1

Making use of the formula derived by the software package, calculate the forecast sales turnover for quarters 17 to 20 using:

(a)   the absolute seasonal variations;

(b)   the percentage seasonal variations.

Task 1.2

(a)   From your answers to Task 1.1, determine which method of calculating seasonal variations gives the best estimate of actual sales turnover.

(b)   Having identified the preferred method, use that method to forecast the sales turnover for quarters 21 to 24.

Task 1.3

Write a memorandum to your Managing Director. The memorandum should:

(a)   explain what is meant by seasonal variations and seasonally adjusted data. Illustrate your explanation with examples relevant to Northern Fuel Distributors;

(b)   suggest why your chosen method of seasonal adjustment might be more accurate;

(c)   show how an understanding of seasonal variations and seasonally adjusted data can help Northern Fuel Distributors to be more efficient;

(d)   identify **two** weaknesses within your approach to forecasting undertaken in Tasks 1.1 and 1.2.

SECTION 2   *(Suggested time allocation: 105 minutes)*

Data

It is 1 March and Professor Pauline Heath has just taken up her new appointment as the head of the postgraduate business studies department in a new university. Due to unfilled vacancies throughout the current academic year, the department has had to rely on part-time academic staff. The cost of part-time staff who are self-employed is coded to account number 321, while part–time staff who are taxed under the pay-as-you-earn system are charged to account code 002. Both types of staff enter their claims within ten days of each month-end and these then appear in the management reports of the subsequent month. There are also unfilled clerical and administrative staff vacancies.

The university has a residential conference centre, which the department makes use of from time to time. Sometimes this is because the department's allocated rooms are all in use and sometimes because the department teaches at weekends. The charge for the use of the centre is coded to account 673. An alternative to using the conference centre is to hire outside facilities at local hotels, in which case the expenditure is coded 341.

The main forms of income are tuition fees and a higher education grant from the government. The extent of this grant is known before the commencement of the academic year and is payable in two parts, one-third at the end of December and the balance at the end of April.

One of Professor Heath's first tasks was to check the enrolments for the current year. The financial and academic year commenced on 1 September and is subdivided into three terms, each lasting four months. The Autumn term commenced on 1 September and the Spring term on 1 January. All courses commence at the beginning of the Autumn term, the MBA and MSc courses lasting three terms and the diploma course two terms.

The departmental administrator has presented Professor Heath with the enrolment data for the current academic year. Whilst absorbing this information, she has also received the latest management accounts for the department. Both sets of information are reproduced below.

Professor Heath is experiencing difficulties understanding the latest management report. She has written a memo to the university's finance director expressing her anxieties about the presentation of the report and its detailed contents.

Enrolment data - current academic year	*Fee*	*Enrolment*	*Income*
	£		£
MBA - three terms	3,500	160	560,000
MSc - three terms	3,200	80	256,000
Diploma Course - two terms	1,200	100	120,000
			936,000

DEPARTMENT OF POSTGRADUATE BUSINESS STUDIES

Monthly Management Report--February

Code	Account heading	Annual	6 months to 28 February			Budget
	EXPENSES	budget	Actual	Budget	Variance	remaining
001	Full-time academic	600,000	230,000	300,000	70,000	370,000
002	Part-time academic	84,000	48,000	42,000	(6,000)	36,000
003	Clerical and administration	84,000	36,000	42,000	6,000	48,000
218	Teaching and learning material	30,000	0	15,000	15,000	30,000
321	Teaching and research fees	20,000	19,000	10,000	(9,000)	1,000
331	Agency staff (clerical and administrative)	300	2,400	150	(2,250)	(2,100)
341	External room hire	1,000	400	500	100	600
434	Course advertising (press)	26,000	600	13,000	12,400	25,400
455	Postage and telephone recharge	8,000	1,200	4,000	2,800	6,800
673	Internal room hire	24,000	14,000	12,000	(2,000)	10,000
679	Central services recharge	340,000	170,000	170,000	0	170,000
680	Rental light and heat recharge	260,000	130,000	130,000	0	130,000
		1,477,300	651,600	738,650	87,050	825,700
	INCOME					
802	Tuition fees	900,000	936,000	900,000	(36,000)	(36,000)
890	Higher education grant	750,000	250,000	250,000	0	500,000
		1,650,000	1,186,000	1,150,000	(36,000)	464,000
	Net surplus/deficit	172,700	534,400	411,350	(123,050)	(361,700)

Task 2.1

(a) Rearrange the account headings into a more meaningful form for managers. This should include columnar headings for any financial data you feel is appropriate but you DO NOT need to include any figures.

(b) Briefly justify your proposals.

Task 2.2

In her memo, Professor Heath states that the current form of report does not help her manage her department. Identify the strengths and weaknesses apparent in the current system, other than the presentational ones covered in Task 2.1, and make and justify outline proposals that will help her manage the department.

Task 2.3

Referring to the detailed financial data under the heading of INCOME above, reproduce the actual income to data in a form consistent with accounting principles.

All workings should be shown.

CHAPTER 12

Practice Central Assessments (Answers)

Unit 7: Practice Central Assessment

SECTION 1

Task 1

		Quarter 1	Quarter 2	Quarter 3	Quarter 4
	UK cost (£)	£102,400	£137,760	£134,480	£69,921
	Exchange rate	2,000	2,000	2,800	3,000
(a)	Zed cost (ZF)	ZF 204,800	ZF 275,520	ZF 376,544	ZF 206,763
	Seasonal variations*	−20%	5%	40%	−25%
(b)	Trend unit cost (ZF)	ZF 256,000	ZF 262,400	ZF 268,960	ZF 275,684
	Increase (ZF)		ZF 6,400	ZF 6,560	ZF 6,724
(c)	Increase (%)		2.5%	2.5%	2.5%

$$\text{Annual rate} = (1,025)^4 - 1$$
$$= 10.38\%$$

*Seasonal variations are expressed as a percentage of the trend. If the trend is 100% and the seasonal variation 20% then the forecast actual is 80%. Deriving the trend from the actual, therefore, involves a 25% adjustment (20%/80%) and not a 20% adjustment.

		ZF
(d)	Trend cost, quarter 4	275,684
	Add 2 ½ %	6,892
	Trend forecast	282,576
	Seasonal adjustment (−20%)	(56,515)
	Forecast cost	226,061
	Exchange rate	ZF 3,000: £
	Forecast cost	£75.35

Task 2

				£
(a)	Accommodation (variable cost)	£840,000/6,000		140
	Air transport (fixed cost)	£720,000/6,000		120
	Standard absorption cost per holiday			260
(b)	Standard absorption cost for 7,800 holidays	£260 x 7,800		£2,028,000

(c)   Cost variances

(i)	Material price variance	£(140 – 134.48) x 7,800	£43,056 (F)
(ii)	Fixed overhead expenditure variance	£720,000 – £792,000	£72,000 (A)
(iii)	Fixed overhead volume variance	(7,800 – 6,000) x £120	£216,000 (F)
(iv)	Fixed overhead capacity variance	(78 – 80) x 75 x £120	£18,000 (A)
(v)	Fixed overhead efficiency variance	£(100 – 75) x 78 x £120	£234,000 (F)

(d)

Original holidays cost reconciliation statement 3rd quarter 19X7

	£
Standard absorption cost for 7,800 holidays	2,028,000
Material price variance	43,056 (F)
Fixed overhead expenditure variance	72,000 (A)
Fixed overhead capacity variance	18,000 (A)
Fixed overhead efficiency variance	234,000 (F)
Actual absorption cost	1,840,944

(e)   The single most important reason for the increased profit is the more intensive use of the aircraft. This is represented by the favourable fixed overhead efficiency variance of £234,000.

Task 3

MEMORANDUM

To: Jane Armstrong   Date: 5 January 19X8

From: Accounting Technician

Subject:

Fixed overheads behave differently from variable costs such as accommodation. Over the relevant range, fixed costs remain the same irrespective of activity. The only way they can change is if the price paid for those overheads changes. This is what the fixed overhead expenditure variance measures. For quarter 3, this was an adverse variance of £72,000. This might have been due to increased costs of parking the aircraft when not being used.

This fixed overhead capacity variance is a measure of asset usage. If it is favourable, the aircraft would have been used more than budgeted, if adverse, less than budgeted. The adverse variance in the case of Original Holidays has been identified as operational difficulties. It represents the loss of the two flights compared with budget. This would have arisen if the aircraft had to be taken out of service to await spare parts which were not readily available.

Finally, the fixed overhead efficiency variance is a measure of productivity. It measures how intensively the aircraft was being used while it was operating rather than standing idle. For each of the 78 return flights actually operated, 100 passengers (7,800 passengers divided by 78 flights) were carried compared with the budget of 75. This explains the favourable variance.

SECTION 2

Task 1

Diamond Ltd
Performance report – Branch 24
Year ended 31 December 19X7

(a)	Return on capital employed	57.6/240.0	24%
(b)	Gross profit margin	360.0/720.0	50%
(c)	Asset turnover	720.0/240.0	3 times
(d)	Sales margin	57.6/720.0	8%
(e)	Average age of debtors	(96.0/720.0) x 12	1.6 months
(f)	Average age of creditors	(51.0/340.0) x 12	1.8 months
(g)	Average age of stock	(60.0/360.0) x 12	2.0 months

Task 2

Workings

			£
(a)	Revised turnover	£240,000 x 4	960,000
	Cost of sales = 50%		480,000
	Gross profit		480,000
	Fixed costs		302,400
	Operating profit		177,600
	Revised return on capital employed	£177,600/£240,000	74%

			£
(b)	*Revised working capital*		
	Revised debtors	(0.5 x £720,000)/12	30,000
	Revised stock	(1 x £360,000)/12	30,000
	Revised creditors	(3 x £340,000)/12	(85,000)
	Revised working capital		(25,000)
	Add fixed assets		135,000
	Revised capital employed		110,000
	Return on capital employed	£57,600/£110,000	52%
	Asset turnover	£720,000/£110,000	6.5 times

(c)

MEMORANDUM

To: Angela Newton   Date: 5 January 19X8

From: Financial analyst

Subject: Branch 24 performance indicators

Charles Walden has asked me to write to you concerning the performance indicators of Branch 24 and the extent of improvement possible if the branch was able to achieve the performance standards established by the company.

Had Branch 24 been able to achieve the same asset turnover as other branches, the return on capital employed would have been 74%, comfortably in excess of the standard return on capital employed.

Likewise, had the branch controlled its working capital at standard levels, not only would the return on capital employed have been 52% but it would also have achieved an asset turnover of 6.5 times.

You are quite correct to emphasise the need for profitability. If the asset turnover can be improved while maintaining the existing level of net assets, then turnover will increase. If the cost of this increased turnover is less than its value, then this will lead to both increased profits and an increase in the return on capital employed.

The suggestion that your performance might be less than other branches because your branch has been established for less time may be valid. From the financial data related to your branch, it would appear that Branch 24 was only opened two years ago. (The annual depreciation is £45,000 and the accumulated depreciation is £90,000). If other branches have been established longer, then the accumulated depreciation will be greater, leading to a lower net book value and a lower capital employed. It is also possible that the older fixtures and fittings would have been purchased at a lower price, resulting in the annual depreciation charge also being less and hence increasing operating profit.

Unit 8: Practice Central Assessment

SECTION 1

Task 1

Quarter	Season	Trend	Absolute variance	Forecast (absolute)	Percentage variance	Forecast (percentage)
17	A	2,680,000	350,000	3,030,000	115	3,082,000
18	B	2,720,000	250,000	2,970,000	110	2,992,000
19	C	2,760,000	–400,000	2,360,000	85	2,346,000
20	D	2,800,000	–200,000	2,600,000	90	2,520,000

Task 2

Quarter	Actual	Forecast (absolute)	Error forecast	Forecast (percentage)	Error forecast
17	3,079,500	3,030,000	49,500	3,082,000	–2,500
18	3,002,400	2,970,000	32,400	2,992,000	10,400
19	2,346,500	2,360,000	–13,500	2,346,000	500
20	2,490,200	2,600,000	–109,800	2,520,000	–29,800

(a) Examining the residual errors from using the two different methods of measuring seasonal variations, the percentage seasonal variation always results in a lower error than the absolute variance. On the basis of the sample of four quarters, the percentage seasonal variation thus appears to be the more accurate method for calculating seasonal variations.

(b)

Quarter	Season	Trend	Seasonal variation	Forecast
21	A	2,840,000	115	3,266,000
22	B	2,880,000	110	3,168,000
23	C	2,920,000	85	2,482,000
24	D	2,960,000	90	2,664,000

Task 3

MEMORANDUM

To: The Managing Director   Date: June 19X7

From: The Assistant Management Accountant

Subject: Seasonal variations and seasonally adjusted data

Seasonal variations are regular, predictable and consistent changes in activity that occur over a period of time, normally one year. For oil distribution, the demand will be higher in winter months than summer months, and this is reflected in the seasonal variations for Northern Fuel Distributors. Quarter A is likely to include the winter months, with demand being 115% above the average quarter. Quarter C, with demand only being 85% of the average quarterly, is likely to include mainly summer months.

Seasonally adjusted data is the actual data from which the seasonal variations have been removed. It comprises two elements; the trend, or general direction in which the data is moving, plus any random variations. For example, the forecast seasonal variation for quarter 17 was $15/115 \times £3,082,000$ or $+£402,000$. Deducting this from the actual demand of £3,079,500 leaves an underlying figure of £2,667,500. As the trend was forecast as £2,680,000, the random error is − £2,500. Possible reasons for this error might be an unusually mild winter or insufficient stock of fuel to meet customers' needs. Provided that these random variations are small, the seasonally adjusted data allows the general direction of the demand for fuel oil over time to be seen.

Seasonal variations can be viewed in two ways: as an absolute amount or as a percentage. Doubling the activity being considered is likely to double the seasonal variation. Therefore, when the trend is either an increasing or decreasing one, measuring seasonal variations as a percentage is likely to be more accurate. As the demand for Northern Fuel Distributors' fuel oil is increasing through time, the percentage method has been used to forecast demand.

An awareness of seasonal variations and seasonally adjusted data enables future trends to be determined, along with variations about that trend. Not only does this help Northern Fuel Distributors to forecast future profits, but it also helps in stock control. By accurate forecasting of demand, excessive stocks are minimised. This helps cash flow in two ways: it reduces cash tied up in stocks and minimises the interest charged on amounts owing to Star Fuels.

There are, however, limitations to the forecasting technique demonstrated. First, the assumption implicit in linear regression is that demand is a linear function of time. Secondly, it assumes that demand is based only on time, whereas there might be other variables influencing demand (such as other competitors and the prices they charge for their energy). Thirdly, the data used is measured in monetary terms. Part of any increased demand may be due to rising prices rather than increased volume. It might, therefore, be better to measure demand in litres rather than value. Fourthly, quarterly measurement may hide peaks and troughs of demand; forecasting by the week is likely to reduce this problem.

SECTION 2

Task 1

(a)   Rearrangement of account headings

	Actual this month	Budget this month	Variance this month	Actual to date	Budget to date	Variance to date	Annual budget	Budget remaining
Tuition fees								
Higher education grant								
TOTAL REVENUE								
Full–time academic								
Part–time academic								
Teaching and research fees								
DIRECT LABOUR COST								
Teaching and learning material								
OTHER DIRECT COURSE COSTS								
Clerical and administration								
Agency staff (clerical)								
SUPPORT COSTS								
Rental light and heat recharge								
External room hire								
Internal room hire								
ACCOMMODATION COSTS								
Course advertising (press)								
Postage and telephone recharge								
OTHER OVERHEADS								
DEPARTMENTAL CONTRIBUTION								
Central services recharge								
DEPARTMENTAL SURPLUS/DEFICIT								

(b)   Justification

Budgets serve a variety of purposes, including planning, controlling and acting as authority to incur expenditure. In the original format, the monthly management report produced accounting information in the order of the financial accounting codes. This may be the appropriate order for the user. For example, Professor Heath is unlikely to be interested in whether part-time staff are on the payroll or invoice the university for their services. Within the constraints of the existing system, accounts have been brought together by function. This makes clear the total expenditure on lecturing, other direct course costs, the cost of support services and the cost of accommodation. Again, it is only likely to be a detail for an operating manager whether room hire is an internal or an external charge. Rearranging the account headings in this format begins to show Professor Heath where expenses are being incurred and should help her control expenditure. It will also highlight the net effect of favourable variances – such as the saving in staff costs resulting from the vacancies – being balanced by the adverse variances on similar functional expense headings such as part-time academic staff.

The revised management report has introduced monthly data. In the original format, the only way monthly information could be derived was by comparing this month's year-to-date figures with those of the previous month. If control is to be effective, the extent of any variance should be clear, unambiguous and timely. Introducing monthly budget, actual and variance columns helps in this task.

The 'budget remaining' figure has been retained. This represents the difference between the annual budget and expenditure to date and shows how much further authorised expenditure is possible under the various account headings. Finally, in the variance columns, the direction of the variance should be made clearer. If actual expenditure was different from budgeted, the absolute variance should be shown, followed by (A) where expenditure was in excess of the budget and (F) where it was below budget. The reverse should apply to revenues, with (F) representing revenues greater than budget and (A) revenues less than budget.

Task 2

The main strength of the current system is that it identifies the amount of the budget yet to be consumed under the various account headings. In that sense, it is fulfilling its authorisation role. However, to begin to manage the department effectively, Professor Heath needs to know the sources of income and why expenses are being incurred, and this is not being provided by the current system.

At the moment, the university is viewing the department as one activity, whereas the department comprises several activities in the form of different courses. In the private sector, these would probably be called products. Currently, the department supports three products, the two degree courses and the diploma course. Although these all bring in revenue, they also consume expenses, and so it is important to know what contribution each product makes to the overall departmental surplus. The first priority is therefore to extend the coding and account-heading system to enable expenditure by course to be recorded. Some costs such as the teaching materials can be directly attributable to individual courses, while other costs – such as lecturers – may have to be apportioned.

Consideration should also be given to introducing some form of flexible budgeting as a control mechanism – although this will be of only limited use because of the high proportion of fixed costs within any teaching department. Nevertheless, it would explain whether the increased revenue has arisen because fees have been greater than budgeted or the number of students is higher than planned. In addition, the introduction of flexible budgeting would emphasise the effect of contribution on the well-being of the department.

Two further weaknesses of the current system appear to be the arbitrary way that the budget is divided into calendar months and the failure to accrue expenses. For many expenses, it appears that the budget is merely divided by twelve to derive the monthly figure. Some form of profiling is called for. For example, course advertising is likely to be greatest towards the end of the academic year as courses are marketed for the subsequent year. There is also a need to accrue expenses – in particular, the current report fails to accrue for part-time staff salaries. Yet a further weakness is the lack of information about the number of students and other non-financial but relevant management information.

Task 3

Course	Revenue	Number terms	Number months	Six months' revenue £
MBA	£560,000	3	12	280,000
MSc	£256,000	3	12	128,000
Diploma	£120,000	2	8	90,000
				498,000
Government grant (£750,000 pa)				375,000
Revenue for six months				873,000

CHAPTER 1

Management Accounting and Information (Questions)

1.1 Non-monetary management information

(a) Give *four* reasons why it might be appropriate to express some management accounting information in non-monetary terms and give a specific example to illustrate each.

(b) Explain how inaccuracy may exist in each of the following management accounting information situations and how such inaccuracy may be minimised:

   (i) analysis of costs into fixed and variable components

   (ii) calculation of fixed overhead absorption rate

   (iii) calculation of material cost per product unit for inclusion in a product price quotation.

1.2 Department of postgraduate business studies (AAT D95)

Data

It is 1 March and Professor Jean Turner has just taken up her new appointment as the head of the postgraduate business department in a new university. Due to unfilled vacancies throughout the current academic year, the department has had to rely on part-time academic staff. The cost of part-time staff who are self-employed is coded to account number 321, while those who are taxed under the pay-as-you-earn system are charged to account code 002. Both types of staff enter their claims within ten days of each month-end and these then appear in the management reports of the subsequent month. There are also unfilled clerical and administrative staff vacancies.

The university has a residential conference centre which the department makes use of from time to time. Sometimes this is because the department's allocated rooms are all in use and sometimes because the department teaches at weekends. The charge for the use of the centre is coded to account 673. An alternative to using the conference centre is to hire outside facilities at local hotels in which case the expenditure is coded to account 341.

The main forms of income are tuition fees and a higher education grant from the Government. The extent of this grant is known before the commencement of the academic year and is payable in two parts, one third at the end of December and the balance at the end of April.

One of Professor Turner's first tasks was to check the enrolments for the current year. The financial and academic year commenced 1 September and is subdivided into three terms, each lasting four months. The Autumn term commenced 1 September and the Spring term 1 January. All courses commence at the beginning of the Autumn term, the degree courses lasting three terms and the diploma course two terms.

The departmental administrator has presented Professor Turner with the enrolment data for the current academic year. Whilst absorbing this information, she also receives the latest management accounts for the department. Both sets of information are reproduced below.

Professor Turner is experiencing difficulties in understanding the latest management report. She has written a memo to the university's finance director expressing her anxieties about the presentation of the report and its detailed contents.

Enrolment data – current academic year	Fee (£)	Enrolments	Income (£)
MBA – three terms	3,500	160	560,000
MSc – three terms	3,200	80	256,000
Diploma Course – two terms	1,200	100	120,000
			936,000

DEPARTMENT OF POSTGRADUATE BUSINESS STUDIES
MONTHLY MANAGEMENT REPORT – FEBRUARY

Code	Account heading	Annual budget	Actual	Budget	Variance	Budget remaining
			6 months to 28 February			
	Expenses					
001	Full–time academic	600,000	230,000	300,000	70,000	370,000
002	Part–time academic	84,000	48,000	42,000	–6,000	36,000
003	Clerical and administrative	84,000	36,000	42,000	6,000	48,000
218	Teaching and learning material	30,000	0	15,000	15,000	30,000
321	Teaching and research fees	20,000	19,000	10,000	–9,000	1,000
331	Agency staff (Clerical and administrative)	300	2,400	150	–2,250	–2,100
341	External room hire	1,000	400	500	100	600
434	Course advertising (Press)	26,000	600	13,000	12,400	25,400
455	Postage and telephone recharge	8,000	1,200	4,000	2,800	6,800
673	Internal room hire	24,000	14,000	12,000	–2,000	10,000
679	Central services recharge	340,000	170,000	170,000	0	170,000
680	Rental light and heat recharge	260,000	130,000	130,000	0	130,000
		1,477,300	651,600	738,650	87,050	825,700
	Income					
802	Tuition fees	900,000	936,000	900,000	–36,000	–36,000
890	Higher education grant	750,000	250,000	250,000	0	500,000
		1,650,000	1,186,000	1,150,000	–36,000	464,000
	Net surplus/deficit	172,700	534,400	411,350	–123,050	–361,700

Task 1

(a) Rearrange the account headings in a more meaningful form for managers. This should include any existing and extra columnar headings for any financial data you feel is appropriate but *exclude* any figures.

(NB: Restrict your changes to *presentational* matters.)

(b) Briefly justify your proposals.

Task 2

In her memo, Professor Turner states that the current form of report does not help her manage her department. Identify the strengths and weaknesses apparent in the current system, other than the presentational ones covered in Task 1, and make and justify outline proposals which will help her manage the department.

Task 3

Referring to the detailed financial data under the heading of income, reproduce the actual income to date in a form consistent with accounting principles.

1.3 Viking Smelting Company (AAT J97)

Data

The Viking Smelting Company established a division, called the reclamation division, in April 19X5, to extract silver from jewellers' waste materials. The waste materials are processed in a furnace, enabling silver to be recovered. The silver is then further processed into finished products by three other divisions within the company.

A performance report is prepared each month for the reclamation division which is then discussed by the management team. Sharon Houghton, the newly appointed financial controller of the reclamation division, has recently prepared her first report for the four weeks to 31 May 19X7. This is shown below.

Performance Report – Reclamation Division – 4 weeks to 31 May 19X7

	Actual	Budget	Variance		Comments
Production (tonnes)	200	250	50	(F)	
	£	£	£		
Wages and social security costs	46,133	45,586	547	(A)	Overspend
Fuel	15,500	18,750	3,250	(F)	
Consumables	2,100	2,500	400	(F)	
Power	1,590	1,750	160	(F)	
Divisional overheads	21,000	20,000	1,000	(A)	Overspend
Plant maintenance	6,900	5,950	950	(A)	Overspend
Central services	7,300	6,850	450	(A)	Overspend
Total	100,523	101,386	863	(F)	

(A) = adverse, (F) = favourable

In preparing the budgeted figures, the following assumptions were made for May:

♦   the reclamation division was to employ four teams of six production employees

♦   each employee was to work a basic 42 hour week and be paid £7.50 per hour for the four weeks of May

♦   social security and other employment costs were estimated at 40% of basic wages

♦   a bonus, shared amongst the production employees, was payable if production exceeded 150 tonnes. This varied depending on the output achieved:

(i)   if output was between 150 and 199 tonnes, the bonus was £3 per tonne produced
(ii)   if output was between 200 and 249 tonnes, the bonus was £8 per tonne produced
(iii)   if output exceeded 249 tonnes, the bonus was £13 per tonne produced

♦   the cost of fuel was £75 per tonne

♦   consumables were £10 per tonne

♦   power comprised a fixed charge of £500 per four weeks plus £5 per tonne for every tonne produced

♦   overheads directly attributable to the division were £20,000

♦   plant maintenance was to be apportioned to divisions on the basis of the capital values of each division

♦   the cost of Viking's central services was to be shared equally by all four divisions.

You are the deputy financial controller of the reclamation division. After attending her first monthly meeting with the board of the reclamation division, Sharon Houghton arranges a meeting with you. She is concerned about a number of issues, one of them being that the current report does not clearly identify those expenses and variances which are the direct responsibility of the reclamation division.

Task 1

Sharon Houghton asks you to prepare a flexible budget report for the reclamation division for May 19X7 in a form consistent with responsibility accounting.

Further data

On receiving your revised report, Sharon tells you about the other questions raised at the management meeting when the original report was presented. These are summarised below:

♦   why are the budget figures based on 2-year-old data taken from the proposal recommending the establishment of the reclamation division?

♦   should the budget data be based on what we were proposing to do or what we actually did do?

♦   is it true that the less we produce the more favourable our variances will be?

♦   why is there so much maintenance in a new division with modern equipment and why should we be charged with the actual costs of the maintenance department even when they overspend?

♦   could the comments, explaining the variances, be improved?

♦   should all the variances be investigated?

♦   does showing the cost of central services on the divisional performance report help control these costs and motivate the Divisional managers?

Task 2

Prepare a memo for the management of the reclamation division. Your memo should:

(a)   answer their queries and justify your comments

(b)   highlight the main objective of your revised performance report developed in Task 1 and give two advantages of it over the original report.

CHAPTER 1

Management Accounting and Information (Answers)

1.1 Non-monetary management information

(a) *Reasons for non-monetary terms*

'Non-monetary terms' encompasses various measures such as physical volume or weight, quantity, time and percentages. There are several reasons why it may be appropriate to express management information in non-monetary terms, some of which are as follows:

(i) Comparisons of figures over long periods of time may be distorted as financial measurements are affected by inflation. An example would be comparison of labour efficiency in terms of hours rather than wages.

(ii) Comparison of performance between two divisions or business segments of different sizes where economies of scale make financial comparisons unfair. An example would be to measure output in physical rather than financial terms.

(iii) Non-monetary information may have a greater impact for the user. An example would be to measure material usage in quantity rather than sterling.

(iv) Non-monetary information may be more meaningful. An example would be the reporting of the fixed overhead volume, capacity and efficiency variances without their £ values since the latter implies that fixed overhead costs are dependent on these factors.

(b) *Sources of inaccuracy*

(i) Analysis of fixed and variable costs

Mixed (semi-variable) costs can be analysed using either:

–   the high-low method

–   a scatter graph

–   linear regression analysis.

In all cases the split will be an approximation only. The second and third methods both use the principle of the line of best fit which is, by definition, the line which most closely fits the data. Method one is far more arbitrary and estimates the variable costs by considering two extreme levels of output and their related costs.

The degree of inaccuracy can be minimised by ensuring that the data collected is itself both representative and accurate. Statistical measures of reliability such as correlation and determination can be used to assess the degree of accuracy.

(ii) Calculation of fixed overhead absorption rate

The calculation of a fixed overhead absorption rate requires estimates of budgeted expenditure and the level of activity measured in units, hours or some other agreed basis.

Both of these estimates could be subject to inaccuracy through unanticipated changes in the level of overheads such as rent and rates or changes in productivity or efficiency levels affecting the activity base.

Minimising inaccuracies here depends on establishing a budgeting system where management carefully appraises each resource. The choice of the activity level should always be 'normal' to reduce any over or under absorption.

(iii) Calculation of material cost

The material cost of a product will require estimates of both quantity and price. Establishing a standard per product could be inaccurate if the material quality affects the skill level of the workforce. Changes in production techniques may cause the standard to become inaccurate over time. In addition, price of materials will be fixed externally and sudden changes will affect the product cost.

Accuracy could be improved by regular revision and updating of usage estimates and by monitoring of purchasing policies.

1.2 Department of postgraduate business studies

Task 1

(a) *Rearrangement of account headings*

	Actual this month	Budget this month	Variance this month	Actual to date	Budget to date	Variance to date	Annual budget	Budget remaining
Tuition fees								
Higher education grant								
TOTAL REVENUE								
Full–time academic								
Part–time academic								
Teaching and research fees								
DIRECT LABOUR COST								
Teaching and learning material								
OTHER DIRECT COURSE COSTS								
Clerical and administrative								
Agency staff (clerical)								
SUPPORT COSTS								
Rental light and heat recharge								
External room hire								
Internal room hire								
ACCOMMODATION COSTS								
Course advertising (Press)								
Postage and telephone recharge								
OTHER OVERHEADS								
DEPARTMENTAL CONTRIBUTION								
Central services recharge								
DEPARTMENTAL SURPLUS/DEFICIT								

(b)   *Justification*

Budgets serve a variety of purposes including planning, controlling and acting as authority to incur expenditure. In the original format, the monthly management report produced accounting information in the order of the financial accounting codes. This may not be the appropriate order for the user. For example, Professor Turner is unlikely to be interested in whether part-time staff are on the payroll or invoice the university for their services. Within the constraints of the existing system, accounts have been brought together by function. This makes clear the total expenditure on lecturing, other direct course costs, the cost of support services and the cost of accommodation. Again, it is only likely to be a detail for an operating manager whether room hire is an internal or an external charge. Rearranging the account headings in this format begins to show Professor Turner where expenses are being incurred and should help her control expenditure. It will also highlight the net effect of favourable variances – such as the saving in staff costs resulting from the vacancies – being balanced by the adverse variances on similar functional expense headings such as part time academic staff.

The revised management report has introduced monthly data. In the original format, the only way monthly information could be derived was by comparing this month's year-to-date figures with those of the previous month. If control is to be effective, the extent of any variance should be clear and unambiguous and timely. Introducing monthly budget, actual and variance columns helps in this task. The budget remaining figure has been retained. This represents the difference between the annual budget and expenditure to date and shows how much further authorised expenditure is possible under the various account headings. Finally, in the variance columns, the direction of the variance should be made clearer. If actual expenditure was different from budgeted, the absolute variance should be shown, followed by (A) where expenditure was in excess of the budget and (F) where it was below budget. The reverse should apply to revenues, with (F) representing revenues greater than budget and (A) revenues less than budget.

Task 2

The main strength of the current system is that it identifies the amount of the budget yet to be consumed under the various account headings. In that sense, it is fulfilling its authorisation role. However, to begin to effectively manage the department, Professor Turner needs to know the sources of income and why expenses are being incurred and this is not being provided by the current system.

At the moment, the university is viewing the department as the activity whereas the department comprises several activities in the form of different courses. In the private sector, these would probably be called products. Currently, the department supports three products, the two degree courses and the diploma course. Although these all bring in revenue, they also consume expenses and so it is important to know what contribution each product makes to the overall departmental surplus. The first priority is therefore to extend the coding and account heading system to enable expenditure by course to be recorded. Some costs such as the teaching materials can be directly attributable to individual courses while other costs – such as lecturers – may have to be apportioned.

Consideration should also be given to introducing some form of flexible budgeting as a control mechanism – although this will be of only limited use because of the high proportion of fixed costs within any teaching department. Nevertheless it would explain whether the increased revenue has arisen because fees have been greater than budgeted or the number of students is higher than planned. In addition, the introduction of flexible budgeting would emphasise the effect of contribution on the well-being of the department.

Two further weaknesses of the current system appear to be the arbitrary way the budget is divided into calendar months and the failure to accrue expenses. For many expenses, it appears that the budget is merely divided by twelve to derive the monthly figure. Some form of profiling is called for. For example, course advertising is likely to be greatest towards the end of the academic year as courses are marketed for the subsequent year. There is also a need to accrue expenses. In particular, the current report fails to accrue for part-time staff salaries. Yet a further weakness is the lack of information about the number of students and other non-financial but relevant management information.

Task 3

Course	Revenue	Number of terms	Number of months	Six months' revenue
MBA	£560,000	3	12	£280,000
MSc	£256,000	3	12	£128,000
Diploma	£120,000	2	8	£90,000
				£498,000
Government grant (£750,000 per annum)				£375,000
Revenue for six months				£873,000

1.3 Viking Smelting Company

Task 1

There are many ways of presenting this report but the format should be guided by responsibility accounting, i.e. in responsibility accounting, costs and revenues are traced to the person (manager) responsible for their incurrence, so that each manager is both responsible and accountable for the costs under their control. Concurrent with responsibility accounting is the classification into controllable and non-controllable, therefore a classification along these lines is expected. The layout could also be further classified into variable and fixed or direct and indirect but the optimum presentation would require a controllable/non-controllable classification. Additionally, cost per tonne figures could be added to highlight efficiency.

Reclamation Division Performance Report – 4 weeks to 31 May 19X7

	Actual	Budget		Variance		Comments*
Production tonnage	200	200		–		
	£	£		£		
Controllable						
Wages	46,133	43,936	(i)	2,197	(A)	Overtime payments, one off event
Fuel	15,500	15,000	(ii)	500	(A)	Poor energy efficiency – investigate
Consumables	2,100	2,000	(iii)	100	(A)	
Power	1,590	1,500	(iv)	90	(A)	
Divisional overheads	21,000	20,000		1,000	(A)	Additional employee, no action
Sub–total	86,323	82,436		3,887	(A)	

	Actual £	Budget £	Variance £	
Non–controllable				
Plant maintenance	6,900	5,950	950	(A)
Central services	7,300	6,850	450	(A)
Sub–total	14,200	12,800	1,400	(A)
Grand total	100,523	95,236	5,287	(A)

* These are examples of comments.

Workings

(i)   6 employees x 4 teams x 42 hours/week x £7.50/hour x 4 weeks = £30,240 x 140% = £42,336 + (200 tonnes x £8/tonne) = £42,336 + £1,600 = £43,936

(ii)   200 tonnes x £75/tonne

(iii)   200 tonnes x £10/tonne

(iv)   £500 + (200 tonnes x £5/tonne)

Task 2

MEMO

To: Management Board   **Date:** 18 June 19X7

From: Deputy Financial Controller

Subject: **Budgeting**

The following report covers the questions raised at the recent management meeting. The report format is in the same sequence as that of the questions raised.

(a)   (i)   The use of two year old figures can only be justified on the basis that the company is operating in an environment which has remained unchanged and this is unlikely. Budgeting is concerned with planning and therefore any plan should be prepared from current knowledge of the company's environment. Past knowledge in the form of the original budget may be a guide to the future but it will not be a substitute for using up to date information.

A reconciliation of both budgets (original and revised) may serve a purpose in assessing the accuracy of the original proposal, but it would have limited use in planning.

(ii)   For planning purposes the budget data should be based on what we are proposing to do in a future period. This will act as a target for the managers and it might motivate them to achieve the overall plan. The budget would also serve to co-ordinate the various activities of the company.

For control purposes the budgeted figures should be focused on what we actually produced and the expenses which should have been incurred in producing it to enable a meaningful comparison.

Page 1/2

(iii)   Using fixed budgets, the variable costs also appear fixed, and any changes in volume actually achieved are ignored. Had the division produced nothing then savings would have been shown for the variable costs which would render the information meaningless. The same would apply if the original tonnage was exceeded; in this case an overspend on the variable costs would be reported which would be another meaningless figure when higher actual tonnage had been achieved. As regards the fixed costs these will tend to be unaffected. Using flexible budgeting, the variable costs reflect the changes in the volume of activity. A more balanced assessment, of the division's performance, would result from the inclusion of sales revenue.

(iv)   The basis for charging plant maintenance to the division is flawed since the method of apportionment is not related to the likely use of maintenance resources nor is it a reasonable approximation. A new division will have significant capital costs but it will require less maintenance. As regards the charging of any overspend on the maintenance department to a user department this procedure is likely to mask any inefficiencies in that department.

(v)   The comments explaining the variances are very negative in tone with every adverse variance being reinforced and no praise being given for favourable variances. This may affect the motivation of the managers. The comments do not identify the reasons for the variances arising nor the actions which might be taken to resolve them.

(vi)   The decision to investigate variances will depend on a number of factors; their absolute or relative size (cost/benefit of investigation), whether they are one-off or continuing, whether they have been resolved or whether they are just commencing.

(vii)   The inclusion of central service charges in a divisional report will not help control these costs as they are not being reported to the managers who control them. However, the reporting of these charges to the divisional managers ensures that they are aware of the other cost incurred in running a business. A degree of control may also be exercised by the divisional managers on these costs when the level of divisional charges is perceived to be excessive.

One of the objectives of budgeting is to motivate managers to achieve the goals of the organisation, and the inclusion of central expenses over which the manager has no control in a divisional performance report may be demotivating.

(b)   The main objective of my revised report is to provide meaningful feedback. By providing feedback it should be possible to establish whether the plan is being achieved or whether the plan should be changed because it cannot be achieved as circumstances have changed.

My report has the following advantages over the original report:

(i)   it follows the technique of responsibility accounting by classifying costs into controllable and non-controllable

(ii)   it is prepared on a flexible budget basis, thus comparing like with like

(iii)   the non-controllable expenses are included so that the manager is aware of the other costs which may be incurred in the running of the total organisation

(iv)   the comments column contains the underlying reasons for the variance from plan and the actions necessary to return to the plan.

Page 2/2

CHAPTER 2

Forecasts and Trends (Questions)

2.1 Market v sales forecast

'Market forecasts and sales forecasts are different but complementary.'

(a) In what essential ways does a market forecast differ from a sales forecast?

(b) Briefly describe the key components of a market forecast.

(c) Define and explain three types of change in the environment of a firm which may influence both market and sales forecasting.

2.2 Pan World Petroleum (AAT J96)

Data

Pan World Petroleum is a multinational oil company selling oil for industrial and domestic purposes through a network of distributors. Distributors purchase fuel oil from Pan World and then sell it on to their own customers.

A regular complaint of the distributors is that they either have to pay for the fuel on delivery to their storage tanks or be charged interest on a daily basis on the amount owed. This problem could be reduced if the distributors were able to forecast their demands more accurately.

You are employed as the assistant management accountant to Eastern Fuel Distributors Ltd, a major distributor of Pan World Petroleum's fuel oils. You recently attended a meeting with Elizabeth Armstrong, a member of Pan World's central staff. At the meeting she demonstrated a statistical software package used for estimating demand for fuel oil. The user enters sales volumes per period and the package then calculates the least squares regression equation for the data. This is in the form $y = a + bx$ where x is the time period, y is the forecast and a and b are terms derived from the original data. Following further inputs by the user, the package can also estimate seasonal variations. Two forms of seasonal variations are calculated; the first calculates the seasonal variance as an absolute amount, the second as a percentage.

One week later, your copy of the software arrives at the head office of Eastern Fuel Distributors Ltd and you immediately set about testing its capability. Purely for the purpose of testing, you assume seasonal variations occur quarterly. You enter this assumption along with the sales turnover figures for fuel oil for the last 20 quarters. Within moments, the software outputs the following information.

Regression line

$y = £2,000,000 + £40,000x$

Seasonal variations

Quarter	A	B	C	D
Amount	+£350,000	+£250,000	−£400,000	−£200,000
Percentage	+15%	+10%	−15%	−10%

Quarter A refers to the first quarter of annual data, B to the second quarter, C to the third and D to the fourth. The pattern then repeats itself. In terms of the specific data you input, seasonal variation A refers to quarter 17, B to quarter 18, C to quarter 19 and D to quarter 20.

Actual sales turnover for quarters 17 to 20 was as follows:

Quarter	17	18	19	20
Amount	£3,079,500	£3,002,400	£2,346,500	£2,490,200

Task 1

Making use of the formula derived by the software package, calculate the forecast sales turnover for quarters 17 to 20 using:

(a)   the absolute seasonal variations

(b)   the percentage seasonal variations.

Task 2

(a)   From your answers to Task 1, determine which method of calculating seasonal variations gives the best estimate of actual sales turnover.

(b)   Having identified the preferred method, use that method to forecast the sales turnover for quarters 21 to 24.

Task 3

Write a memorandum to your Managing Director. The memorandum should:

(a)   explain what is meant by seasonal variations and seasonally adjusted data. Illustrate your explanation with examples relevant to Eastern Fuel Distributors

(b)   suggest why your chosen method of seasonal adjustment might be more accurate

(c)   show how an understanding of seasonal variations and seasonally adjusted data can help Eastern Fuel Distributors be more efficient

(d)   identify *two* weaknesses within your approach to forecasting undertaken in Tasks 1 and 2.

2.3   Albion Ltd 1 (AAT D96)

Data

You are employed as the assistant management accountant to Albion Ltd. Albion Ltd manufactures a single product, the Xtra, an ingredient used in food processing. The basis raw material in Xtra production is material X.

The average unit prices for material X in each quarter last year, and the seasonal variations based on several years' observations, are reproduced below.

	Quarter 1	*Quarter 2*	*Quarter 3*	*Quarter 4*
Average unit price of X	£10	£11	£16	£19
Seasonal variations	–£1	–£2	+£1	+£2

Task

(a)   Calculate the seasonally adjusted unit price of material X for each of the four quarters of last year.

(b)   Assuming a similar pattern of price movements in the future, forecast the likely purchase price for the four quarters of the current year.

CHAPTER 2

Forecasts and Trends (Answers)

2.1 Market v sales forecast

(a)   The essential difference between a market forecast and a sales forecast is that the market forecast is a longer-term strategic forecast whereas the sales forecast is a short-term tactical one. The market forecast will therefore precede the sales forecast.

Following from this basic difference, the matters covered by the two forecasts will differ.

The market forecast is likely to cover:

(i)   external economic and social factors, ie. the environment

(ii)   future technological change by the company and its competitors

(iii)   estimates of present and future market size and possible market shares to be obtained.

The sales forecast is likely to cover:

(i)   monthly or quarterly sales targets for divisions or individual members of the sales team

(ii)   effect on sales of the use of different marketing techniques

(iii)   research among existing or potential customers.

(b)   The key components of a market forecast as follows.

(i)   *Review of economic factors*

A large company might have its own expert staff to carry out such a review. A smaller one would have to rely on reports from government agencies, universities and other commentators on the economic position of the UK and other countries to which the company exported or planned to export. The review would cover the medium-term future for the economy as a whole and of the industry in which the company operates.

(ii)   *Review of markets*

This would include study of the extent of the target market, means of expanding that market, existing and planned future market shares. This could include, when appropriate, the study of demographic trends.

(iii)   *Review of products*

The study of the suitability of the existing product range for the market, possible alternative outlets for the product.

(iv)   *Review of price*

The projected effect of alternative price structures on the sales and market share of the company, projected technological change.

(v)   *Review of promotion methods*

Consideration of the best promotion strategy to adopt in each market.

At the conclusion of these reviews, it would be possible to develop a market forecast or possibly a series of alternative forecasts based on varying assumptions as to the marketing mix.

(c)   Factors in the environment of a firm which may influence market and sales forecasts may be derived from the points described in (b) above.

(i)   *Economic factors, UK and abroad*

Changes in the prosperity of the UK or important overseas markets could influence a company's sales and hence need to be allowed for in market and sales forecasts. For example, a company selling into a South American market might encounter difficulties resulting from the heavy borrowings of many countries in this area and the reluctance of banks to continue lending to them. Pressure on their economies from this source could lead to a severe cutback in their imports and hence to a reduction of sales from the UK. (Consider the European Single Market of 1992.)

(ii)   *Technological change*

A possible change in the nature of the product or of other competing products could have a serious effect on the market. For example, the development of more and more applications for computer technology, and advances in computer technology, means that companies operating in this field must allow in their market and sales forecasts for the effect of expected new products. This means that the company must be active in its own research and development and aware of the research and development activities of its competitors. Failure to maintain parity at least in technological advance could lead rapidly to decline and indeed liquidation of the company.

(iii)   *Demographic change*

Changes in the level of the population and in the relative sizes of age groups in the population can have an important effect on sales and hence must be allowed for in the market and sales forecasts. Information of this kind is reasonably easily obtained from official sources like government census details. For example, an increase in the population over retirement age, nationally or locally, may lead to a greater demand for small housing units or protected retirement estates. A builder of residential accommodation must obviously make himself aware of such trends and build accordingly.

2.2   Pan World Petroleum

Task 1

Quarter	Season	Trend	Absolute variance	Absolute forecast	Percentage variance	Percentage forecast
17	A	2,680,000	+350,000	3,030,000	+15	3,082,000
18	B	2,720,000	+250,000	2,970,000	+10	2,992,000
19	C	2,760,000	−400,000	2,360,000	−15	2,346,000
20	D	2,800,000	−200,000	2,600,000	−10	2,520,000

Task 2

Part (a)

Quarter	Actual	Absolute forecast	Error	Percentage forecast	Error
17	3,079,500	3,030,000	+49,500	3,082,000	−2,500
18	3,002,400	2,970,000	+32,400	2,992,000	+10,400
19	2,346,500	2,360,000	−13,500	2,346,000	+500
20	2,490,200	2,600,000	−109,800	2,520,000	−29,800

Examining the residual errors from using the two different methods of measuring seasonal variations, the percentage seasonal variation always results in a lower error than the absolute variation. On the basis of the sample of four quarters, the percentage seasonal variation appears to be the more accurate method for calculating seasonal variations.

Part (b)

Quarter	Season	Trend	Seasonal variation	Forecast
21	A	2,840,000	+15	3,266,000
22	B	2,880,000	+10	3,168,000
23	C	2,920,000	−15	2,482,000
24	D	2,960,000	−10	2,664,000

Task 3

MEMO

To: The Managing Director **From:** The Assistant Management Accountant

Date: June 19X6

Subject: Seasonal variations and seasonally adjusted data

(a) Seasonal variations are regular, predictable and consistent changes in activity which occur over a period of time, normally one year. For oil distribution, the demand will be higher in winter months than summer months and this is reflected in the seasonal variations for Eastern Fuel Distributors. Quarter A is likely to include the winter months with demand being 115% above the average quarter. Quarter C, with demand only being 85% of the average quarterly demand, is likely to include mainly summer months.

Seasonally adjusted data is the actual data from which the seasonal variations have been removed. It comprises two elements; the trend or general direction in which the data is moving plus any random variations. For example, the forecast seasonal variation for quarter 17 was (15/115 × £3,082,000) or +£402,000. Deducting this from the actual demand of £3,079,000 leaves an underlying figure of £2,677,500. As the trend was forecast as £2,680,000, the random error is –£2,500. Possible reasons for this error might be an unusually mild winter or insufficient stock of fuel to meet customers' needs. Providing these random variations are small, the seasonally adjusted data allows the general direction of the demand for fuel oil over time to be seen.

(b) Seasonal variations can be viewed in two ways; as an absolute amount or as a percentage. Doubling the activity being considered is likely to double the seasonal variation. Therefore, when the trend is either an increasing or decreasing one, measuring seasonal variations as a percentage is likely to be more accurate. As the demand for Eastern Fuel Distributors' fuel oil is increasing through time, the percentage method has been used to forecast demand.

(c) An awareness of seasonal variations and seasonally adjusted data enables future trends to be determined along with variations about that trend. Not only does this help Eastern Fuel Distributors forecast future profits, it also helps in stock control. By accurately forecasting demand, excessive stocks are minimised. This helps cashflow in two ways. It reduces cash tied up in stocks and minimises the interest charged on amounts owing to Pan World Petroleum.

(d) There are, however, limitations to the forecasting technique demonstrated. First, the assumption implicit in linear regression is that demand is a linear function of time. Secondly it assumes that demand is based only on time. There might be other variables influencing demand such as other competitors and the prices they charge for their energy. Thirdly, the data used was measured in monetary terms. Part of any increased demand may be due to rising prices rather than increased volume. It might, therefore, be better to measure demand in litres rather than value. Fourthly, quarterly measurement may hide peaks and troughs of demand. Forecasting by the week is likely to reduce this problem.

2.3 Albion Ltd I

(a)

	Quarter 1 £	Quarter 2 £	Quarter 3 £	Quarter 4 £
Actual price	10	11	16	19
Seasonal variation	–1	–2	+1	+2
Trend	11	13	15	17

(b)

	Quarter 1	Quarter 2	Quarter 3	Quarter 4
Trend	19	21	23	25
Seasonal variation	–1	–2	+1	+2
Forecast price	18	19	24	27

CHAPTER 3

The Principles and Techniques of Cost Accounting (Questions)

3.1 Overheads

Departments	Assembly	Finishing	Stores	QC
Floor area (sq metres)	3,000	4,000	1,000	200
Number of employees	24	36	4	2
NBV of assets (£'000)	100	50	5	10

The two service departments, Stores and QC, work for the other departments, as follows.

	Assembly	Finishing	Stores	QC
QC	33%	67%	–	–
Stores	40%	40%	–	20%

Budgeted overheads to be allocated and apportioned

	£
Rent and rates	92,250
Electricity	18,450
Canteen costs	2,640
Equipment repairs	4,290
Insurance (note 1)	1,685
Supervisor's salary (note 2)	7,680

Notes

(1) The cost of insurance includes a £200 special risk premium for one specific piece of equipment held in QC.

(2) From the supervisor's timesheet it can be noted that he spent 540 hours in the Assembly department and 1,380 hours in the Finishing department.

(3) Two products are made; the Alpha and Beta. Both products take three hours in the Assembly department; the Alpha spends four hours in the finishing department, whilst the Beta spends two hours in finishing. 1% of Alphas are rejected after the Assembly stage. Budgeted production is to complete 2,277 Alphas and 737 Betas.

Required

Calculate the budgeted hourly overhead rate for both production departments.

3.2 Total absorption costing and marginal costing

Production data for 1 gizmo

Materials   3kg   @   £5 per kg

Direct labour   2 hours   @   £4 per hour

The variable overhead absorption rate is £2 per direct labour hour.

Total fixed overheads are £120,000.

Budget production is 10,000 gizmos.

Required

(a)   What is the fixed overhead absorption rate per direct labour hour for the period?

(b)   What is the marginal cost of a gizmo?

(c)   What is the total absorption cost of a gizmo?

(d)   If budgeted sales are 9,000 gizmos at £50 each what is the budgeted profit for the period using:

     (i)   marginal costing

     (ii)   absorption costing.

(e)   Reconcile the two profit figures for part (d).

(f)   If actual production *and* sales were *both*:

     (i)   9,500 units

     (ii)   10,500 units

     what would the TAC and MC profits be?

3.3 Anita

Anita is preparing her budget for the next four-week period but is uncertain of her level of activity. She has provided you with the following information:

Materials

She obtains her materials for the period, at the beginning of the four-week period. If she purchases over 6,000 kg, she obtains a discount of 10% on the normal price of £5 per kg.

Labour

She currently employs 10 operators and two supervisors, who are paid at the rate of £4 per hour and £6 per hour respectively. All 12 employees are guaranteed a 30 hour week, and receive overtime of time and a half if required to work more than 35 hours.

Machine time

Anita produces a single product on two machines, both of which are capable of making the one product. Each machine requires five operators and one supervisor. Each machine costs £14 per hour to run.

Overheads

Factory overheads are fixed at £3,000 per week up to 75 units after which they rise by £1,500 per week.

Each unit requires one machine hour and 20 kg of materials.

Required

Calculate the cost per unit (using absorption costing) for each of the following weekly levels of production, 40 units, 50 units, 60 units, 70 units, 80 units and 90 units.

3.4 Oberon Ltd

As cost accountant of Oberon Ltd you have produced budgets for sales quantity, production, materials and labour utilisation and a variable overhead budget for the year ended 31.12.X2. Information from the labour utilisation budget is shown below:

Department	Workforce	Labour hours	Hourly rate
North	20	35,000	£2.80
East	25	45,000	£2.60
West	30	55,000	£2.50

You have produced various estimates for the year's fixed costs some of which can be easily allocated direct to the three departments and some of which need to be apportioned between the three departments. The work so far is shown below:

Fixed cost	£		Allocation or proposed basis of apportionment		
			North	East	West
Factory rent, rates and insurance	70,000	Floor area			
Plant depreciation	40,000		20,000	15,000	5,000
Repairs and maintenance	20,000	Net book value of assets weighted according to average age			
Works canteen	22,500	Number of employees			
Departmental office staff	59,000		15,000	18,000	26,000
Light and heat	10,500	Floor area			
Warehousing costs	21,000	Materials consumed			
Selling and administration	145,000		50,000	40,000	55,000

Your apportionment of fixed costs will be based on the following information:

(1) Floor area (sq. ft) North – 12,000; East – 10,000; West – 6,000

(2) Assets NBV North – £100,000; East – £50,000; West – £20,000

(3) Assets average age North – 3 years; East – 2 years; West – 5 years

(4) Materials consumed North – £260,000; East – £120,000; West – £40,000

Required

(a) Produce a schedule showing the allocation or apportionment of the £388,000 of fixed costs to the three production departments.

(b) Calculate hourly fixed overhead absorption rates for the three departments.

(c) Produce a standard cost card showing how the selling price of a Weber PM2 is arrived at if the following variable costs are incurred:

Materials			£28.50
Labour: Department	North	2 hours	
	East	4 hours	
	West	3 hours	
Variable overheads			£19.85

Oberon Ltd aims for a profit of 35% on sales.

3.5 Overhead apportionment and absorption

A company makes several products which pass through the two production departments in its factory. These two departments are concerned with filling and sealing operations. There are two service departments, maintenance and canteen, in the factory.

Predetermined overhead absorption rates, based on direct labour hours, are established for the two production departments. The budgeted expenditure for these departments for the period just ended, including the apportionment of service department overheads, was £110,040 for filling and £53,300 for sealing. Budgeted direct labour hours were 13,100 for filling and 10,250 for sealing.

Service department overheads are apportioned as follows:

Maintenance	–	Filling	70%
	–	Sealing	27%
	–	Canteen	3%
Canteen	–	Filling	60%
	–	Sealing	32%
	–	Maintenance	8%

During the period just ended, actual overhead costs and activity were as follows:

	Costs £	Direct labour Hours
Filling	74,260	12,820
Sealing	38,115	10,075
Maintenance	25,050	
Canteen	24,375	

Required

(a)   Calculate the overheads absorbed in the period and the extent of the under/over-absorption in each of the two production departments.

(b)   State, and critically assess, the objectives of overhead apportionment and absorption.

3.6   Costing systems

(a)   Discuss the arguments put forward for the use of absorption and marginal costing systems respectively.

(b)   The following information is available for a firm producing and selling a single product.

Budgeted costs (at normal activity)

	£000
Direct materials and labour	264
Variable production overhead	48
Fixed production overhead	144
Variable selling and administration overhead	24
Fixed selling and administration overhead	96

The overhead absorption rates are based upon normal activity of 240,000 units per period.

During the period just ended 260,000 units of product were produced and 230,000 units were sold at £3 per unit.

At the beginning of the period 40,000 units were in stock. These were valued at the budgeted costs shown above.

Actual costs incurred were as per budget.

Required

(i)   Calculate the fixed production overhead absorbed during the period, and the extent of any under/over absorption. For both of these calculations you should use absorption costing.

(ii)   Calculate profits for the period using absorption costing and marginal costing respectively.

(iii)   Reconcile the profit figures which you calculated in (ii) above.

(iv)   State the situations in which the profit figures calculated under both absorption costing and marginal costing would be the same.

CHAPTER 3

The Principles and Techniques of Cost Accounting (Answers)

3.1 Overheads

Overhead	Basis	Total £	Assembly £	Finishing £	Stores £	QC £
Rent and rates	Floor area	92,250	33,750	45,000	11,250	2,250
Electricity	Floor area	18,450	6,750	9,000	2,250	450
Canteen costs	Employees	2,640	960	1,440	160	80
Equipment repairs	WDV	4,290	2,600	1,300	130	260
Insurance	WDV	1,685	900	450	45	290
Supervisor	Timesheet	7,680	2,160	5,520	–	–
		126,995	47,120	62,710	13,835	3,330
Stores	(40:40:20)		5,534	5,534	(13,835)	2,767
QC	(33:67)		2,012	4,085	–	(6,097)
			54,666	72,329		

Budgeted hours for each production department

			Hours
Assembly:	Alpha	(2,277 ÷ 0.99) x 3	6,900
	Beta	737 x 3	2,211
			9,111
Finishing:	Alpha	2,277 x 4	9,108
	Beta	737 x 2	1,474
			10,582

Hourly rate: Assembly 54,666 ÷ 9,111 = £6.00
Finishing 72,329 ÷ 10,582 = £6.84

3.2 Total absorption costing and marginal costing

(a) *Fixed overhead absorption rate*

Fixed overheads = £120,000

Direct labour = 10,000 × 2

  = 20,000 hrs

Absorption rate per direct labour hour = $\dfrac{120,000}{20,000}$

  = £6

(b) *Marginal cost of gizmo*

	£
Materials (3kg at £5)	15
Labour (2 hours at £4)	8
Variable overhead (2 hours at £2)	4
	27

(c) *Total absorption cost of gizmo*

	£
Marginal cost (as part (b))	27
Fixed overheads (2 hours at £6)	12
	39

(d) *Budgeted profit*

    (i) *Marginal costing*

	£
Sales (9,000 at £50)	450,000
Less: Cost of sales (9,000 at £27)	(243,000)
Contribution (9,000 at £23)	207,000
Less: Total fixed overheads	(120,000)
Profit	87,000

(ii) *Total absorption costing*

	£
Sales (9,000 at £50)	450,000
Less: Cost of sales (9,000 at £39)	(351,000)
Profit (9,000 at £11)	99,000

(e) *Reconciliation*

	£
TAC profit	99,000
Fixed overheads in closing stock (1,000 at £12)	(12,000)
MC profit	87,000

(f) *Production below budget*

(i) 9,500 units produced and sold

Total absorption costing:

	£
Sales (9,500 at £50)	475,000
Less: Cost of sales (9,500 at £39)	(370,500)
Standard profit on actual sales (9,500 at £11)	104,500
Less: Under absorption of fixed overheads (500 at £12)	(6,000)
Profit	98,500

Marginal costing:

	£
Sales (9,500 at £50)	475,000
Less: Cost of sales (9,500 at £27)	(256,500)
Contribution (9,500 at £23)	218,500
Less: Total fixed overheads	(120,000)
Profit	98,500

(ii) 10,500 units produced and sold

Total absorption costing:

		£
Sales (10,500 at £50)		525,000
Less: Cost of sales (10,500 at £39)		(409,500)
Standard profit on actual sales (10,500 x £11)		115,500
Add: Over–absorption of fixed overheads (500 at £12)		6,000
Profit		121,500

Marginal costing:

		£
Sales (10,500 at £50)		525,000
Less: Cost of sales (10,500 at £27)		(283,500)
Contribution (10,500 x £27)		241,500
Less: Total fixed overheads		(120,000)
Profit		121,500

3.3 Anita

Cost per unit of production

Units	40	50	60	70	80	90
	£	£	£	£	£	£
Materials (W1)	4,000	5,000	6,000	6,750	7,200	8,100
Labour (W2)	1,560	1,560	1,560	1,820	2,210	2,600
Machine time	560	700	840	980	1,120	1,260
Overhead	3,000	3,000	3,000	3,000	4,500	4,500
	9,120	10,260	11,400	12,550	15,030	16,460
Cost per unit	228.00	205.20	190.00	179.29	187.88	182.89

Workings

(1)   *Materials*

Discount obtained once weekly production exceeds $\dfrac{6,000}{(20\times4)}$ = 75 units

Therefore up to   70 units, cost is 20 x £5 = £100 per unit

80 units, cost is 20 x £5 x 0.9 = £90 per unit

Note however that at 70 units it is cheaper to buy 6,000 kg (rather than the 5,600 kg actually needed) and get the discount. This produces a total cost for materials of £6,750 (compared with a non-discount cost of £7,000).

(2)   *Labour*

Minimum cost for 30-hour week (10 x £4 x 30) + (2 x £6 x 30) = £1,560

60 units can be produced in this time (£26 per unit)

70 units can be produced in a normal 35 hour week at a cost of (10 x £4 x 35) + (2 x £6 x 35) = £1,820 (£26 per unit)

Each unit produced in overtime costs (5 x £ 4 x 1.5) + (1 x £6 x 1.5) = £39

Therefore 80 units cost £1,820 + (10 x £39) = £2,210

Therefore 90 units cost £1,820 + (20 x £39) = £2,600

3.4   Oberon Ltd

(a)   Allocation and apportionment schedule

	Total	North	East	West
	£000	£000	£000	£000
Rent, rates and insurance	70.0	30.0	25.00	15.00
Plant depreciation	40.0	20.0	15.00	5.00
Repairs and maintenance*	20.0	12.0	4.00	4.00
Works canteen	22.5	6.0	7.50	9.00
Departmental office staff	59.0	15.0	18.00	26.00
Light and heat	10.5	4.5	3.75	2.25
Warehousing costs	21.0	13.0	6.00	2.00
Selling and administration	145.0	50.0	40.00	55.00
	388.0	150.5	119.25	118.25

* 'NBV of assets weighted according to average' means that the average ages are weightings to be applied to the NBVs. Weighting simply means multiplication as in the case of the weighted average valuation of stocks.

(b)   Absorption rates

Department	North	East	West
Fixed overheads	£150,500	£119,250	£118,250
Labour hours	35,000	45,000	55,000
Absorption rate (per hour)	£4.30	£2.65	£2.15

(c)   Standard cost card

Weber PM2

		£	£
Materials			28.50
Labour:	North (2 hrs at £2.80)	5.60	
	East (4 hrs at £2.60)	10.40	
	West (3 hrs at £2.50)	7.50	
			23.50
Variable overheads			19.85
			71.85
Fixed overheads:	North (2 x £4.30)	8.60	
	East (4 x £2.65)	10.60	
	West (3 x £2.15)	6.45	
			25.65
			97.50
Profit ($^{35}/_{65}$)			52.50
Selling price			150.00

3.5 Overhead apportionment and absorption

(a) First we could work out the apportionment of actual overheads (since the degree of over- / under-absorption is required for each department – otherwise it is unnecessary).

	Filling £	Sealing £	Maintenance £	Canteen £
Incurred	74,260	38,115	25,050	24,375
Apportioned				
Maintenance	17,535	6,763	(25,050)	752
Canteen	15,076	8,041	2,010	(25,127)
Maintenance	1,407	543	(2,010)	60
Canteen (approx)	39	21		(60)
	108,317	53,483	–	–

The predetermined overhead absorption rates will have been as follows.

	Filling	Sealing
Budgeted expenditure	£110,040	£53,300
÷ Budgeted direct labour hours	13,100	10,250
= Absorption rate/hour	£8.40	£5.20

The actual overhead absorbed in the period will have been as follows.

Filling department: 12,820 hrs × £8.40 per hour = £107,688

Sealing department: 10,075 hrs × £5.20 per hour = £52,390

We can now assess the under-/over-absorption in each production department.

	Filling £	Sealing £
Total overhead apportioned	108,317	53,483
Overhead absorbed	107,688	52,390
Under–absorption	629	1,093

(b) The process of allocation, apportionment and absorption of overheads is designed to charge each product with the full cost of its manufacture. There are three main objectives for such a process.

(i) *Decision-making* – Before making a decision such as the correct price to charge for a product, it is vital to ensure that the product has been charged with the full cost of its manufacture. Otherwise management might be misled into charging an unrealistically low price which may be popular in the market but does not recover the costs of production.

(ii) *External reporting* – Financial accounting requires that stock should be valued at the cost of getting the items to their current condition and location. Such cost includes direct costs plus any attributable production overheads. Such overheads must therefore be shared between the stock items produced in order that a proper valuation can be given to the year-end closing stock.

(iii)   *Performance evaluation* – A proper comparison can only be made between products or departments, or between actual and expected results, if a full charging of costs has first been made to the cost units involved.

However, in practice, a number of objections to the process arise.

(i)   *Lack of precision* – It is tempting to become carried away by the mathematics of overhead absorption while not thinking about whether the result is meaningful. By their very nature overheads are indirect costs, meaning that they do not vary directly with the manufacture of the product, so great care should be taken in charging indirect costs to products.

(ii)   *Lack of responsibilities* – Employees should only be held responsible for costs over which they have control. It is important that all cost categories have a manager with ultimate responsibility, so that he is accountable when the cost runs out of control.

(iii)   *Short-term versus long-term* – In the short-term, fixed costs will be fixed and so irrelevant to any decision-making process. They can be ignored as any decision made would not impact upon them. However it can be argued that no cost is fixed in the long-term and so consideration must be given to the recovery of fixed costs in the long-term so that an acceptable profit level can be attained.

3.6   Costing systems

(a)   Merits of absorption and marginal costing

The major difference between the operation of absorption and marginal costing systems is in the treatment of fixed production overhead. This, in turn, has an effect on the valuation of stock and the determination of profit. In absorption costing, the fixed production overhead is treated as a product cost and is absorbed into the cost of production and included in the valuation of stock according to the normal level of activity. In marginal costing, all fixed overheads are treated as a period cost and charged against profits in the period in which they are incurred.

In order to arrive at a fixed production overhead absorption rate, production overhead costs must first be apportioned to the products or departments to which they relate, and finally absorbed into production. The process of apportionment and absorption is not necessary in marginal costing, and this system is therefore administratively more simple.

The information presented by the marginal costing system is useful for decisions concerning variations in output levels, as it shows the contribution from any level of sales and separately identifies variable costs and fixed costs. However, this system does require the cost information to be collected in a way which is different from the requirements of financial reporting, and is likely to be more costly for that reason.

Over a period of time, both systems will report similar total profits. However, there is likely to be a difference in the way in which the two systems report profits of an individual period, depending on whether stock levels are increasing or decreasing.

(b)   *Profit statements*

(i)   *Fixed production overhead*

Fixed production overhead absorption rate:

$$= \frac{\text{Budgeted fixed production overhead costs}}{\text{Normal activity level}}$$

=   £144,000 ÷ 240,000 = £0.60 per unit

Over-/under-absorption

	£
Fixed production overhead absorbed = 260,000 x £0.60	156,000
Actual fixed production overhead	144,000
Over–absorption	12,000

(ii)   *Absorption costing statement*

	£	£
Sales revenue (230,000 units x £3)		690,000
Production costs (260,000 units)		
Direct materials and labour (£1.10)	286,000	
Variable production overhead (£0.20)	52,000	
Fixed production overhead	144,000	
	482,000	
Add: Opening stock (40,000 units x £1.90)	76,000	
	558,000	
Less: Closing stock (70,000 units x £1.90)	(133,000)	
Cost of sales		(425,000)
Gross profit		265,000
Selling and administration overhead		
Variable (230,000 x £0.10 per unit)	23,000	
Fixed	96,000	
		(119,000)
Net profit		146,000

Marginal costing statement

		£	£
Sales revenue (230,000 units x £3)			690,000

	Per unit £	£	£
Variable costs (260,000 units)			
Production (260,000 units)			
Direct materials and labour	1.10	286,000	
Variable production overhead	0.20	52,000	
	1.30	338,000	
Add Opening stock			
(40,000 units x £1.30)		52,000	
		390,000	
Less Closing stock			
(70,000 units x £1.30)		(91,000)	
		299,000	
Variable selling and administration costs			
(230,000 x £0.10 per unit)		23,000	
Variable cost of sales			(322,000)
			368,000
Contribution			
Less *Fixed costs*			
Production		144,000	
Selling and administration		96,000	
			(240,000)
			128,000

Notes

(1) In absorption costing the stock is valued at the absorption cost of £1.90 per unit. In marginal costing, the stock is valued at the marginal production cost of £1.30 per unit.

(2) Do not forget to calculate the units of closing stock.

(3) There is no need to absorb selling and administration overhead costs as these are not included in the valuation of stock.

(iii)   *Reconciliation of profit figures*

	£
Net profit per absorption costing statement	146,000
Less: Difference in stock valuations	
(30,000 units increase at £0.60 per unit)	(18,000)
Profit per marginal costing statement	128,000

(iv)   *Situations with the same profit figures*

In order for both statements to have the same profit figures, there must be no change in stock levels (ie. sales must equal production).

CHAPTER 4

Budget Preparation (Questions)

4.1 Annie

Annie manufactures exclusive office equipment and is attempting to prepare budgets for March 19X9. The following information is relevant:

	Opening stock in units	Budgeted sales in units – March	Selling price
			£
Chairs	63	290	120
Desks	36	120	208
Stools	90	230	51

Annie requires her closing stock to be 30% of that month's sales.

All three products are made using wood, plastic, unskilled labour, skilled labour and other overheads. The quantities are as follows:

	Wood Cu ft	Plastic Cu ft	Unskilled labour Hrs	Skilled labour Hrs
Chairs	4	2	3	2
Desks	5	3	5	8
Stools	2	1	2	–
Cost	£12/cu ft	£7/cu ft	£4/hr	£6/hr

Annie's opening stocks of raw materials are 142 cu ft of wood and 81 cu ft of plastic. However she intends to increase this during March so that she always has sufficient raw materials to produce 50 units of each item of equipment.

Required

(a) Prepare budgets for sales, production, materials' usage, labour usage and materials' purchases for March.

(b) Prepare a detailed budgeted trading account for the month ended 31 March 19X9.

4.2 Tibby Ltd

Tibby Ltd buys goods, packs them and sells them.

(1) Sales for November and December were £10,000 each month and are forecast to increase by 20% each month from 1 January onwards.

(2) All sales are on credit and debtors settle as follows:

- 30% in month of sale

- 50% in month following sale

- 20% in month two months after sale

(3) Tibby Ltd has a constant gross profit of 40%.

(4) Unpacked units are bought in the month they are sold. Tibby Ltd also has a policy of maintaining a finished goods stock level at the end of each month equal to 20% (in volume terms) of the following month's sales. Suppliers allow one month's credit.

(5) Pre-contracted fixed packaging costs are constant at £2,000 per month and are paid in the month incurred.

(6) Sundry expenses are £500 per month.

(7) At 1 January fixed assets had a net book value of £80,000. Depreciation for the three months to March will be £2,000.

(8) At 1 January, Tibby Ltd had issued share capital of £50,000 and an accumulated profit and loss account of £24,200.

(9) At 31 December, Tibby Ltd has a bank balance of £10,000 overdrawn.

Required

(a) Prepare a budgeted profit and loss account for the period from January to March.

(b) Prepare a budgeted balance sheet as at 31 March.

4.3 Budgetary control

In relation to budgetary control and standard costing you are required to explain, and provide your own examples to illustrate, each of the following:

(a) standard hour

(b) efficiency (productivity) ratio

(c) capacity usage ratio

(d) production/volume ratio.

4.4 Master budget

A master budget is created by the integration of many individual budgets.

(a) Outline what preliminary steps are necessary before the preparation of budgets is commenced.

(b) Detail the main budgets you would normally expect to find in a manufacturing business.

(c) Give reasons why managers may be reluctant to participate in setting budgets.

CHAPTER 4

Budget Preparation (Answers)

4.1 Annie

(a) Functional budgets

Sales budget

	Chairs	Desks	Stools	Total
March				
Quantity	290	120	230	
Value (£)	34,800	24,960	11,730	71,490

Production budget in units

	Chairs	Desks	Stools
March			
Sales	290	120	230
Closing stock	87	36	69
	377	156	299
Opening stock	(63)	(36)	(90)
Production	314	120	209

Materials' usage

		Wood cu ft		Plastic cu ft
March				
Chairs	314 x 4 =	1,256	314 x 2 =	628
Desks	120 x 5 =	600	120 x 3 =	360
Stools	209 x 2 =	418	209 x 1 =	209
		2,274		1,197

Labour usage

		Unskilled Hrs		Skilled Hrs
March				
Chairs	314 x 3	942	314 x 2	628
Desks	120 x 5	600	120 x 8	960
Stools	209 x 2	418		–
		1,960 x 4 = £7,840		1,588 x 6 = £9,528

Materials' purchases

	Wood cu ft		Plastic cu ft
March			
Usage	2,274		1,197
Closing stock 50 x (4 + 5 + 2)	550	50 x (2 + 3 + 1)	300
	2,824		1,497
Opening stock	(142)		(81)
Purchases	2,682 x 12 = £32,184		1,416 x 7 = £9,912

(b)   *Budgeted trading account for the month ended 31 March 19X9*

	£	£
Sales		71,490
Less: Wood (2,274 x £12)	27,288	
Plastic (1,197 x £7)	8,379	
Unskilled labour	7,840	
Skilled labour	9,528	
	53,035	
Opening stock of finished goods (W)	14,292	
	67,327	
Closing stock of finished goods (W)	(15,537)	
		(51,790)
Gross profit		19,700

Working

		Chairs £		Desks £		Stools £	Total £
Wood	12 x 4	48	12 x 5	60	12 x 2	24	
Plastic	7 x 2	14	7 x 3	21	7 x 1	7	
Unskilled labour	4 x 3	12	4 x 5	20	4 x 2	8	
Skilled labour	6 x 2	12	6 x 8	48		–	
		86		149		39	
Opening stock		5,418		5,364		3,510	14,292
Closing stock		7,482		5,364		2,691	15,537

Note. Gross profit

		£
C:	290 x (£120 – £86)	9,860
D:	120 x (£208 – £149)	7,080
S:	230 x (£51 – £39)	2,760
		19,700

4.2   Tibby Ltd

(a)   *Budgeted profit and loss account for the three months ended 31 March*

	£	£
Sales (see Working)		43,680
Less: Cost of sales		
Opening stock	1,440	
Purchases (see Working)	27,256	
	28,696	
Less: Closing stock	(2,488)	
		(26,208)
Gross profit		17,472
Less: Overheads		
Packaging	6,000	
Sundry expenses	1,500	
Depreciation	2,000	
		(9,500)
Net profit		7,972

(b)   *Budgeted balance sheet as at 31 March*

	£	£	£
Fixed assets (NBV)			78,000
Current assets			
Stock		2,488	
Debtors [(0.7 x 17,280) + (0.2 x 14,400)]		14,976	
		17,464	
Current liabilities			
Bank overdraft (balancing figure)	2,510		
Creditors (re. March purchases)	10,782		
		(13,292)	
			4,172
			82,172
Share capital			50,000
Profit and loss account (24,200 + 7,972)			32,172
			82,172

Working

	Nov £	Dec £	Jan £	Feb £	Mar £
Sales	10,000	10,000	12,000	14,400	17,280
Cost of sales		6,000	7,200	8,640	10,368
Opening stock		(1,200)	(1,440)	(1,728)	(2,074)
Closing stock		1,440	1,728	2,074	2,488
Purchases		6,240	7,488	8,986	10,782

4.3   Budgetary control

(a)   *The standard hour*

This can be defined as 'the quantity of work achievable at standard performance, expressed in terms of a standard unit of work in a standard unit of time'.

The standard hour provides a common measure of output where there are varying products. This eliminates difficulties when some products are liquids and others solids. All the products made in a period can be reduced to a number of standard hours. The total standard hours thus computed become the produced hours when calculating the labour efficiency variance. Thus, if product A takes five standard hours to produce and eight units of A are produced, this means that (8 × 5) standard hours have been produced.

From a simple variance analysis standpoint, if the 40 hours worth of work took 42 hours to complete at a standard rate of £5/per worked hour, then the labour efficiency variance can be calculated as follows:

(Standard hours produced – actual hours worked) x rate $\quad = \quad (40 - 42) \times 5$

$$= \quad £(10) \text{ adverse}$$

(b) *The efficiency or productivity ratio*

$$\frac{\text{Standard hours of production achieved}}{\text{Actual number of direct worked hours}} \times 100$$

Thus using the simple example above: $\dfrac{40 \times 100}{42} = 95.2\%$

(c) *The capacity usage ratio*

$$\frac{\text{Actual hours worked}}{\text{Budgeted hours}} \times 100$$

This ratio does not reflect the full level of capacity an organisation could work at, but rather assumes that it has budgeted to work at a certain level, and then measures performance against that predetermined level (practical capacity). In the illustration above, let us assume that the budgeted hours were 48.

Thus: $\dfrac{42 \times 100}{48} = 87.5\%$

(d) *The production volume ratio*

$$\frac{\text{The actual standard hours produced}}{\text{Budgeted standard hours produced *}} \times 100$$

*The official definition by CIMA makes allowances for any rest periods, normal down time, etc., and suggests that this figure may be below the budgeted worked hours. This will depend on how the actual standard hour is computed. Thus, because of legitimate built-in allowances, our budgeted worked hours and produced hours is the same.

Thus using the same source data:

$$\frac{40 \times 100}{48} = 83.33\%$$

4.4 Master budget

(a)   The necessary preliminary steps before commencing to prepare budgets would include the following:

   (i)   Considering the longer-term plans for the business, and setting goals for such aspects as market share, profit and capital investment.

   (ii)   Confirming the organisation structure of the business, including profit, cost and investment centres. Where necessary this will be linked with a statement of policy on transfer pricing.

   (iii)   Issuing budget instructions.

   (iv)   Preparing forecasts of the relevant external conditions for the budget period (and possibly for some additional period). This might be regarded either as preliminary work or as the first step in budget development.

(b)   The main budgets to be found in a manufacturing business are likely to be:

   (i)   Sales budget, by areas of responsibility, consistent with assumptions and forecasts above and within production and inventory capacity (subject to policy on buying-in), and based on estimates of demand schedules.

   (ii)   Production budget, based on sales budget, allowing for controlled stock policy and incorporating specific plans for resource acquisition and disposition (materials, labour, energy, overheads).

   (iii)   Resource budgets within production centres, by area and level of responsibility.

   (iv)   Budgets of marketing, selling and distribution expense.

   (v)   Budgets of general administrative expense.

   (vi)   Budgets for R&D, including product development.

   (vii)   Profit budgets by areas of profit responsibility (product group, geographical area, etc.).

   (viii)   Capital expenditure budget.

   (ix)   Working capital budgets, including stock, debt management, cash, borrowing capacity.

   (x)   Master budget, with suitably analysed profit and loss account and balance sheet.

(c)   Managers may be reluctant to participate in setting budgets, because 'participation' may not be on an acceptable basis. According to the management style of a business the term may cover almost any degree or lack of consultation.

At one extreme minimal discussion may be used as the basis for an authoritarian, imposed budget. At the other extreme a laissez-faire management style may lead to a lack of interest by or incentive for managers to set budgets which provide real targets for improvement. For participation in budgeting to be successful it must stem from full and frank discussion between managers at all levels. It must be based on accepted areas of responsibility and full knowledge of the objectives to be achieved and of the interaction of one department's activities with those of others. Managers must also be capable of understanding the financial and accounting implications of their actions, and may need to be given training in these subjects.

Finally, any budget will be based on forecasts of future circumstances, and these will often be imperfect. In exercising control against budgets, therefore, it is necessary to judge whether managers' achievements have been satisfactory in relation to the actual circumstances then prevailing. This is not to say that the ultimate profit objective should be abandoned, but that 'participation' should be a continuous activity in modifying detailed targets where necessary in order to approach the achievement of the required profit in a different way.

CHAPTER 5

Budgetary Control and Responsibility Accounting (Questions)

5.1 Budgetary information

Several assumptions are commonly made by accountants when preparing or interpreting budgetary information.

Required

Explain why each of the following five assumptions might be made by accountants when designing a system of budgeting, and set out in each case any arguments which, in your view, raise legitimate doubts about their validity.

(a) Budgetary performance should be reasonably attainable but not too loose.

(b) Participation by managers in the budget-setting process leads to better performance.

(c) Management by exception is the most effective system of routine reporting.

(d) A manager's budget reports should exclude all matters which are not completely under his control.

(e) Budget statements should include only matters which can easily and accurately be measured in monetary terms.

5.2 Inclusion

(a) Discuss the behavioural arguments for and against involving those members of management who are responsible for the implementation of the budget in the annual budget setting process.

(b) Explain how the methods by which annual budgets are formulated might help to overcome behavioural factors likely to limit the efficiency and effectiveness of the budget.

5.3 Arden Engineering Ltd (AAT D95)

Data

Arden Engineering Ltd makes a single product and, for planning purposes, the company breaks its annual budget into 13 four-weekly periods. From information provided by the marketing director, total sales for the year will be 3,296,500 units. This is broken down as follows:

Period	1	2	3	4	Each subsequent period
Unit sales	190,000	228,000	266,000	304,000	256,500

A similar pattern and volume of sales is expected next year. Because of the technical nature of the product, manufacturing has to take place one period prior to sale. In addition, there is a five per cent wastage which is only discovered on completion. This wastage has no monetary value.

Manufacturing labour is employed by the week and the wages cost per four-week period totals £270,000. The production director believes it is possible to manufacture up to 290,000 gross units per period although, because of wastage, good production will be below this figure. Any increase beyond the gross production of 290,000 units will involve paying overtime at a rate equivalent to £1.50 per extra unit produced. The material component of each unit costs £3.50. The only other production cost relates to fixed overheads. For the forthcoming year these are estimated at £6,940,000. Fixed overheads are charged to production on the basis of the gross number of units produced.

Task 1

For the first three periods of the forthcoming year prepare the production budget, in a form suitable for consideration by the production director, on the assumption that all production takes place one period before it is sold. Your budget should show the total units to be produced per period, the production cost per period and the unit cost per period.

Task 2

The production director is concerned that the budget involves overtime payments and suggests this is not necessary.

Two proposals are put forward: that part of the production is sourced from outside suppliers at a unit cost of £5.95 or that production is brought forward to periods when there is surplus capacity.

If production is brought forward, this will involve financing and other costs equivalent to 50p per unit per four-week period.

Required

Evaluate the two proposals given above and show, with supporting workings, the revised production schedule in units and the savings possible from your preferred proposal.

5.4 Alderley Ltd (AAT D96)

Data

You have recently been appointed as the management accountant to Alderley Ltd, a small company manufacturing two products, the Elgar and the Holst. Both products use the same type of material and labour but in different proportions. In the past, the company has had poor control over its working capital. To remedy this, you have recommended to the directors that a budgetary control system be introduced. This proposal has now been agreed.

Because Alderley Ltd's production and sales are spread evenly over the year, it was agreed that the annual budget should be broken down into four periods, each of 13 weeks, and commencing with the 13 weeks ending 4 April 19X7. To help you in this task, the sales and production directors have provided you with the following information.

Marketing and production data

	Elgar	Holst
Budgeted sales for 13 weeks (units)	845	1,235
Material content per unit (kilograms)	7	8
Labour per unit (standard hours)	8	5

Production labour

The 24 production employees work a 37-hour, five-day week and are paid £8 per hour. Any hours in excess of this involve Alderley in paying an overtime premium of 25%. Because of technical problems, which will continue over the next 13 weeks, employees are only able to work at 95% efficiency compared to standard.

Purchasing and opening stocks

The production director believes that raw material will cost £12 per kilogram over the budget period. He also plans to revise the amount of stock being kept. He estimates that the stock levels at the commencement of the budget period will be as follows:

Raw materials	Elgar	Holst
2,328 kilograms	163 units	361 units

Closing stocks

At the end of the 13-week period, closing stocks are planned to change. On the assumption that production and sales volumes for the second budget period will be similar to those in the first period:

♦   raw material stocks should be sufficient for 13 days' production

♦   finished stocks of the Elgar should be equivalent to 6 days' sales volume

♦   finished stocks of the Holst should be equivalent to 14 days' sales volume.

Task 1

Prepare in the form of a statement the following information for the 13-week period to 4 April 19X7:

(a)   the production budget in units for the Elgar and the Holst

(b)   the purchasing budget for Alderley Ltd in units

(c)   the cost of purchases for the period

(d)   the production labour budget for Alderley Ltd in hours

(e)   the cost of production labour for the period.

Note. Assume a five-day week for both sales and production.

Data

The managing director of Alderley Ltd, Alan Dunn, has also only recently been appointed. He is keen to develop the company and has already agreed to two new products being developed. These will be launched in eighteen months' time. While talking to you about the budget, he mentions that the quality of sales forecasting will need to improve if the company is to grow rapidly. Currently, the budgeted sales figure is found by initially adding 5% to the previous year's sales volume and then revising the figure following discussions with the marketing director. He believes this approach is increasingly inadequate and now requires a more systematic approach.

A few days later, Alan Dunn sends you a memo. In that memo, he identifies three possible strategies for increasing sales volume. They are:

- more sales to existing customers

- the development of new markets

- the development of new products.

He asks for your help in forecasting likely sales volumes from these sources.

Task 2

Write a brief memo to Alan Dunn. Your memo should:

(a) identify *four* ways of forecasting future sales volume

(b) show how each of your four ways of forecasting can be applied to *one* of the sales strategies identified by Alan Dunn and justify your choices

(c) give *two* reasons why forecasting methods might not prove to be accurate.

5.5 Pickerings (AAT J97)

Data

The Pickerings Canning Company produces a range of canned savoury and sweet products. The company prepares its budgets annually. The cost accountant has recently left and you, as the assistant cost accountant, have been requested to take over the responsibility of budget preparation. The managers of the company need the information quickly but they realise that the full budget will take too long to prepare. Because of this, a short-term budget for the month of September is requested. Before leaving, the cost accountant provided you with the following information:

♦ the only product which will be produced during the month is Apple Pie Filling and 80,000 cans per month are required by customers

♦ the apples are purchased whole and there is approximately 50% waste in production

♦ the net amount of apple in 1,000 cans is 100kg

♦ at the final stage of the production process 5% of the cans are damaged and they are sold to employees

♦ the labour required to produce 1,000 cans is 6 hours

♦ each employee works 38 hours per week

♦ the employees are currently in dispute with the company and there is 10% absenteeism. This problem is likely to continue for the foreseeable future

♦ the employees are paid £4 per hour

♦ the buyer at the company has provided prices for the apples but these are estimates mainly based on the actual figures for last year

    ♦ the basic price of apples is budgeted at £200 per tonne for August

    ♦ an internal index of apple prices for last year for the same period was:

	19X6
August	*120*
September	*125*

Task 1

For the month of September 19X7:

(a) prepare a materials purchases budget (at basic price)

(b) prepare a labour budget in terms of numbers of employees

(c) assuming the rate of price increase is the same this year as last year, recalculate the cost of materials purchased.

Data

The budget has been discussed with the production manager and he is concerned about two issues, namely:

♦ how useful are the materials price indices supplied by the buyer for budgeting the costs of materials?

♦ given that the wages costs are significant, what information should be supplied daily, weekly and month to control this area?

Task 2

Prepare a memo for the production manager. Your memo should:

(a) address the issues of concern

(b) suggest and justify an alternative method for predicting materials prices.

5.6 George Phillips (AAT D97)

Data

George Phillips makes and sells two types of garden ornament, the Alpha and the Beta. George prepared his 19X8 budget several months ago but since then he has discovered that there is a shortage of raw material used for making the ornaments. As a result, he will only be able to acquire 20,000 kilograms of the raw material for the first 13 weeks of 19X8.

An extract from his original budget is reproduced below.

Sales budget

	Units	Selling price £	Turnover £
Alpha	6,500	36.00	234,000
Beta	7,800	39.00	304,200

Extract from the production budget

	Units produced	Material per unit Kg	Total material Kg
Alpha	6,900	2.0	13,800
Beta	9,000	1.5	13,500
Materials issued to production			27,300

Purchases budget

	Kg	Price per kg £	Total cost £
Materials issued to production	27,300	5.00	136,500
Opening stock	(6,000)	5.00	(30,000)
Closing stock	6,600	5.00	33,000
Purchases	27,900		139,500

Labour budget

	Units produced	Labour hours per unit	Total hours
Alpha	6,900	2.500	17,250
Beta	9,000	2.785	25,065
Labour hours			42,315
Labour cost			£169,260

George also provides you with additional information as follows.

◆   The budget is based on a 13-week period.

◆   Employees work a 35-hour week.

◆   The closing stocks of materials and finished products must be kept to the figures in the original budget.

◆   The original sales budget represents the maximum demand for the Alpha and the Beta in a 13-week period.

Task 1

You are the recently appointed accounting trainee at the company. George Phillips asks you to revise his budget for the first 13 weeks of 19X8 to take account of the shortage of raw materials. You should prepare the budgets for the following.

(a)   Materials purchases

(b)   Materials issued to production

(c)   Sales volume and turnover

(d)   Labour hours and cost

(e)   The number of employees required

Data

On reviewing the revised figures George realises that there are too many employees and he calls a meeting of the managers of the business. During the meeting the following issues are raised.

◆   The production manager does not wish to reduce the number of employees as he will lose key trained staff who may not wish to be re-employed later. He argues that the labour costs are fixed as the employees are not employed on a piece work basis.

◆   In preparing the original budget George had been advised by one of the partners at the firm's auditors that the key factor should be identified before the budget was prepared. He had assumed that sales would be the key factor and therefore the budget had been based on sales; this was invalid since materials are now the limiting factor.

◆   George complains that the original budget took many hours to prepare and he seeks your advice on the benefits of using a relevant spreadsheet package.

Task 2

Prepare a report covering the issues raised by George Phillips and his managers at the meeting.

5.7 Mayfield School (AAT J98)

Data

Jim Smith has recently been appointed as the head teacher of Mayfield School in Midshire. The age of the pupils ranges from 11 years to 18 years. For many years, Midshire County Council was responsible for preparing and reporting on the school budget. From June 19X8, however, these responsibilities passed to the head teacher of Mayfield School.

The last budget statement prepared by Midshire County Council is reproduced below. It covers the ten months to the end of May 19X8 and all figures refer to cash payments made.

Statement of school expenditure against budget: 10 months August 19X7 to May 19X8

	Expenditure to date £	Budget to date £	Under/(over) spend £	Total budget for year £
Teachers – full time	1,680,250	1,682,500	2,250	2,019,000
Teachers – part time	35,238	34,600	(638)	41,520
Other employee expenses	5,792	15,000	9,208	18,000
Administrative staff	69,137	68,450	(687)	82,140
Caretaker and cleaning	49,267	57,205	7,938	68,646
Resources (books etc)	120,673	100,000	(20,673)	120,000
Repairs and maintenance	458	0	(458)	0
Lighting and heating	59,720	66,720	7,000	80,064
Rates	23,826	19,855	(3,971)	23,826
Fixed assets: furniture and equipment	84,721	100,000	15,279	120,000
Stationery, postage and phone	1,945	0	(1,945)	0
Miscellaneous expenses	9,450	6,750	(2,700)	8,100
Total	2,140,477	2,151,080	10,603	2,581,296

Task 1

Write a memo to Jim Smith. You should identify the following.

(a) Four weaknesses of the existing statement as a management report.

(b) An improved outline statement format showing revised column headings and a more meaningful classification of costs which will help Jim Smith to manage his school effectively (figures are not required).

(c) Two advantages of your proposed format over the existing format.

Data

The income of Mayfield School is based on the number of pupils at the school. Jim Smith provides you with the following breakdown of student numbers.

Mayfield School: student numbers as at 31 May 1998

School year	Age range	Current number of pupils
1	11-12	300
2	12-13	350
3	13-14	325
4	14-15	360
5	15-16	380
6	16-17	240
7	17-18	220
Total number of students		2,175

Jim also provides you with the following information relating to existing pupils.

♦   Pupils move up one school year at the end of July.

♦   For those pupils due to enter Year 6, there is an option to leave the school. As a result only 80% of the current Year 5 pupils will go on to enter Year 6.

♦   Of those currently in Year 6, only 95% continue into Year 7.

♦   Pupils currently in Year 7 leave to go on to higher education or employment.

♦   The annual income per pupil is £1,200 in Years 1 to 5 and £1,500 in Years 6 to 7.

The new Year 1 pupils come from the final year at four junior schools. Not all pupils, however, elect to go to Mayfield School. Jim has investigated this matter and derived accurate estimates of the proportion of final year pupils at each of the four junior schools who go on to attend Mayfield School.

The number of pupils in the final year at each of the four junior schools is given below along with Jim's estimate of the proportion likely to choose Mayfield School.

Junior school	Number in final year at 31 May 19X8	Proportion choosing Mayfield School
Ranmoor	60	0.9
Hallamshire	120	0.8
Broomhill	140	0.9
Endcliffe	80	0.5

Task 2

(a)   Forecast the number of pupils and the income of Mayfield School for the year August 19X8 to July 19X9.

(b)   Assuming expenditure next year is 5% more than the current annual budgeted expenditure, calculate the budgeted surplus or deficit of Mayfield School for next year.

CHAPTER 5

Budgetary Control and Responsibility Accounting (Answers)

5.1 Budgetary information

(a) *Setting budgeted performance levels*

When deciding how 'tough' to set budgeted levels of performance it is worth considering the purposes for which standards are set and the functions of budgetary control. These functions include motivating staff, evaluating their performance and helping in planning and controlling the activities of a business.

Taking these three in turn, if standards are set to motivate staff with a view to improving performance, and if these standards are too severe and regarded as unobtainable, then those standards will be ignored and may even have a 'demotivating' effect. If on the other hand the standards set are too loose then the level of performance will drop.

Considering the need to evaluate the performance of managers and their staff such a procedure is obviously meaningless if performance is compared with unrealistic standards. The need for a comparison with 'reasonable' or realistic standards has given rise to the suggestion that traditional variances should be reviewed and re-classified under 'planning and operational' headings. The third function stated, planning and controlling a business, is of prime importance; if planned performance is unrealistic this will lead to problems such as overstocking of raw materials if production levels cannot be achieved, inaccurate cashflow forecasts, incorrect staffing levels, suboptimal resource allocation and many more. The statement, in short, is not so much an assumption as a truism.

The few reservations that might be held include the following:

(i) Who decides what is reasonable, though this is perhaps better dealt with in (b).

(ii) The possible need, for motivating individual staff, for different standards for different employees.

(iii) The need to modify budgeted performance levels, or review actual performance, in the light of changing technology and working conditions.

(b) *Participation*

Participation in the budget-setting process is recommended because the process:

(i) improves initiative, morale and enthusiasm

(ii) produces better and more realistic plans

(iii) helps communication between staff, with managers becoming aware of overall objectives and all employees seeing where they fit into the responsibility structure

(iv) increases co-operation between departments.

It has been discovered that standards set by the employees themselves are inevitably higher than imposed standards and that performance is better also.

One problem encountered by firms attempting to practise participation in budget-setting is the attitude of senior managers who may feel that in doing so they are shedding some of their power or authority. This in turn has been said to give rise to 'pseudo-participation' when participation either corresponds to ratification of top management's decisions or else opinions are solicited and then ignored, procedures which possibly do more harm than good.

Added to this attitude of top management are problems such as:

(i)   time taken to reach communal conclusions

(ii)   the need to reach a balance of opinion and ideas especially if some participators are more forceful than others

(iii)   the feeling by middle management that by participating in budget-setting they are appearing to be on 'both sides of the fence'.

(c)   *Management by exception*

Management by exception is generally held to be an effective system of routine reporting since:

(i)   If operations are working to plan, management do not need to be told; it is only when things deviate from those plans that managers need to be informed and corrective action taken.

(ii)   By only notifying managers of 'exceptional' performance (particularly if some sort of cut-off point is established for what represents exceptional) the amount of paperwork passing across a manager's desk is reduced, thus encouraging action when reports do appear.

(iii)   A generally accepted feature of 'good information' is that it should be brief and relevant. If an information system sifts out the irrelevant and disseminates a reduced amount of relevant information there is a chance that this might be produced more quickly (a third feature of good information).

The problems of such a reporting system are:

(i)   the original standards might be incorrect (in which case no news is not necessarily goods news)

(ii)   the measurement and recording of performance may be inaccurate

(iii)   the reported deviation from planned activity can only be appraised in the light of actual activity (what percentage variation is this) other figures for costs and revenue (how relevant is this figure in the final profit figure) and the previous history of this particular figure (are random variations to be expected and to what extent are they undesirable).

(d)   *Reporting controllable factors only*

The various reasons why a manager's budget reports should exclude matters not under his control include:

(i)   the need for such reports to inform managers of costs and revenues for which they are held responsible

(ii)   the 'demotivating' effect of specifying costs that, given the time span of the report, are not controllable

(iii)   if a report includes some uncontrollable costs, a manager may not feel the need to achieve any targets set out in such a report.

There are however, equally valid reasons for including extra information:

(i)   Such a report is, in part, a means of communication – explaining how a manager's performance affects the company overall.

(ii)   The principle of excluding such information, if taken to extremes, could lead to a very brief report, since the performance of each manager is, to some extent affected by that of several other managers.

(iii)   Treated with discretion additional information could appear on a manager's budget report provided the costs under his control were highlighted.

(e)   *Use of monetary measures*

Because budget statements are part of the financial control system of an organisation it is natural that they are expressed in purely monetary terms. Also, if the objectives of an organisation are considered to be primarily financial it is consistent that targets and budget reports should be presented accordingly. This assertion is linked to the notion that in the end, profit is the ultimate reflection of the success of an organisation and that all other aspects are incorporated in this financial statistic, at least in the long run. Information stated in monetary terms gives an idea of the importance of each feature of a budget and any decisions made during budget-setting are helped if monetary amounts are available.

The inclusion of monetary items only could also be defended on other grounds, such as:

(i)   It is the only common basis on which performance can be analysed, in relation to managers or departments and therefore on which comparisons can be made.

(ii)   Much of the information used is already available within the accounting system for other purposes, for example external reporting.

(iii)   The inclusion of non-monetary measures would be on such an arbitrary basis that its potential value would be doubtful.

(iv)   The production of monetary statements is relatively straightforward and any extension into alternative types of qualitative measure would not be cost effective.

(v)   Managers understand monetary measures, which can, if necessary, be directly related to organisational reward systems.

These assertions depend on monetary measures being relevant and up to date and on an acceptance of an accounting concept of 'objectivity'. More generally, they also depend on the assumption regarding the firm's objectives. The main arguments against the assumption therefore reject this simplistic view both regarding organisational objectives and the nature of performance measurement. The alternative assumption is that aspects of performance related to the achievement of the firm's goals cannot necessarily be measured in monetary terms and therefore different or additional measures should be introduced. The performance for instance of service departments cannot easily be measured in monetary terms and various qualitative measures need to be used.

A related view is that in striving for the monetary objectives, gains are made at the expense of costs, which by their nature are not readily measurable and do not appear in budget statements. The range of 'qualitative' variables which could be introduced vary considerably in their facility for measurement. Items such as labour turnover rates, absenteeism rates and training time can be fairly accurately measured, although their interpretation would be largely subjective. On the other hand, the measurement of attitudes and other interpersonal judgements is severely restricted by the availability of appropriate methods and the interpretation problem is further increased.

Tutorial note

These answers are fuller than could be expected from even the best students. The best approach may be to incorporate salient points from the answers into your own notes.

5.2 Inclusion

(a) The budget-setting process may either include or exclude those members of management who will be responsible for implementing the budget.

The main arguments for and against inclusion are set out below:

For

(i) Participation may increase commitment to the budget.

(ii) Managers may find it easier to communicate budget objectives to other members of staff if they helped to formulate them.

(iii) Motivation may be increased leading to improved performances.

(iv) Involvement in the budget-setting process may increase the awareness of managers and stimulate ideas.

(v) Team spirit may be encouraged.

Against

(i) Bias may creep into the process in order that managers get more easily achievable targets.

(ii) Decisions may be more difficult to reach with the larger number of people involved.

(iii) If participation is pseudo and not real then this is likely to cause more behavioural problems than no participation at all.

On balance there are more points in favour of participation than against and in most organisations it will pay off in improved commitment, human relations and performance. However, individuals vary and much will depend on the personalities and cultures of the staff involved.

(b) Budgets may be set using either an incremental or zero-based approach.

The use of incremental budgeting involves the acceptance of last period's budget as the basis for the next. Increments are then added on or subtracted. It can be argued that this approach is most likely to lead to behavioural problems and a lack of goal congruence. Departmental heads will simply try to increase their allocation from the previous period and fight to get the largest increase.

Zero-based budgeting requires each function to justify its very existence for each new period. The relative importance of each area is constantly re-evaluated and budget allowances given from scratch. This is likely to lessen bias and budgetary slack and encourage deeper thought throughout the organisation.

5.3 Arden Engineering Ltd

Task 1

Workings

	Period 1	Period 2	Period 3	Period 4
Sales	190,000	228,000	266,000	304,000
Good production	228,000	266,000	304,000	
Loss = 5/95 x good production	12,000	14,000	16,000	
Total production	240,000	280,000	320,000	

Over the year sales units equals good units produced = 3,296,500 units.

Gross production is therefore 3,296,500 x (100/95) = 3,470,000 units.

Production overhead = £6,940,000/3,470,000 units = £2 per unit.

Arden Engineering – Production Budget for 3 periods ending....

	Period 1	Period 2	Period 3	Total
Gross production per period	240,000	280,000	320,000	840,000
Good production per period	228,000	266,000	304,000	798,000
	£	£	£	£
Weekly paid labour	270,000	270,000	270,000	810,000
Overtime	0	0	45,000	45,000
Total labour	270,000	270,000	315,000	855,000
Material	840,000	980,000	1,120,000	2,940,000
Direct costs	1,110,000	1,250,000	1,435,000	3,795,000
Production overhead	480,000	560,000	640,000	1,680,000
Production cost	1,590,000	1,810,000	2,075,000	5,475,000
Unit cost (based on good production)	£6.97	£6.80	£6.83	£6.86

Task 2

Workings

The option to purchase from outside the organisation is not viable as the variable cost per unit of good production – even if produced in the overtime period – is only £5.26 per unit. This comprises the £3.50 of material and the £1.50 of labour multiplied by 100/95 to allow for wastage.

Financial costs for the first period comprise 20,000 units of additional production at 50p per unit for two months. For the second period the cost comprises 10,000 units at 50p for one period, a total of £25,000.

Evaluation of revised production schedule

	£
Savings in overtime	45,000
Financing costs	(25,000)
Savings	20,000

	Period 1 £	Period 2 £	Period 3 £
Planned production	240,000	280,000	320,000
Maximum production	290,000	290,000	290,000
(Over)/under capacity	50,000	10,000	(30,000)
Planned production	240,000	280,000	320,000
Change in planned production	20,000	10,000	(30,000)
Revised production schedule	260,000	290,000	290,000

5.4   Alderley Ltd

Task 1

Alderley Ltd Budget Statements 13 weeks to 4 April 19X7

(a)   Production Budget

	Note	Elgar units	Holst units
Budgeted sales volume		845	1,235
Add closing stock		78	266
Less opening stock	1	(163)	(361)
Units of production		760	1,140

(b)	*Material purchases budget*		*Elgar* kg	*Holst* kg	*Total* kg
	Material consumed	2	5,320	9,120	14,440
	Add raw material closing stock	3			2,888
	Less raw material opening stock				(2,328)
	Purchases (kg)				15,000

(c)	*Purchases (£)*	4			£180,000

(d)	*Production labour budget*		*Elgar* hours	*Holst* hours	*Total* hours
	Standard hours produced	5	6,080	5,700	11,780
	Productivity adjustment	6			620
	Total hours employed				12,400
	Normal hours employed	7			11,544
	Overtime hours				856

(e)	*Labour cost*				£
	Normal hours	8			92,352
	Overtime	9			8,560
					100,912

Notes

1   Number of days per period = 13 weeks x 5 days = 65

Stock: Elgar (6/65) x 845 = 78, Holst (14/65) x 1,235 = 266

2   Elgar 760 x 7 = 5,320, Holst 1,140 x 8 = 9,120

3   (13/65) x 14,440 = 2,888

4   15,000 x £12 = £180,000

5   Elgar 760 x 8 hours = 6,080, Holst 1,140 x 5 hours = 5,700

6   (5/95) x 11,780 = 620

7   24 employees x 37 hours x 13 weeks = 11,544

8   11,544 x £8 = £92,352

9   856 x £8 x 125% = £8,560

Task 2

MEMO

To: Alan Dunn   **From:**   Management Accountant

Date: 4 December 19X6

Subject: **Sales forecasting**

(a)   Ways of forecasting sales

Sales forecasts can be built up in several different ways. Where the number of potential customers is small, it is possible to ask them what their likely demand will be next year. Failing that, it is possible to ask for estimates from the sales personnel who deal with the particular customers.

It is also possible to estimate future demand by carrying out market research. This can be via secondary data such as determining the size of the market from published statistics and identifying the number of competitors. Alternatively, it could involve the collecting of primary data either by some form of sampling or by bringing small groups of potential customers together and identifying their needs.

Another approach is to calculate a time series using least squares regression and derived from past sales data.

Some organisations are able to forecast sales by establishing a pattern of demand as changes take place in another economic indicator. There are three forms of indicator. A leading indicator is one which anticipates changes. A coincident indicator follows the general trend while a lagging indicator follows the general trend after a timing delay. House building is often the first industry to be affected by the onset of a recession. If the products of Alderley are sensitive to changes in the state of the general economy, then this could be used to help us forecast demand.

(b)   Applicability

Interviewing customers, either directly or by receiving reports from the sales force, is more likely to be applicable to existing customers although this method might also be feasible if the number of potential new customers is small.

Market research may be the better method of estimating demand if the number of existing or new customers is large. If the new products are so different from existing products that comparisons are impossible, then primary market research may be the only way of beginning to identify the likely demand.

Time series assume that sales demand is a function of time. Based on past data, the technique assumes that past patterns will repeat themselves through time. As such, the technique is likely to be most appropriate where the past has been relatively stable. Because of this, it is more likely to be applicable to existing customers as potential customers are excluded from the original data giving rise to the time series.

Economic indicators can provide useful background information about the likely demand from not only existing customers but also the potential demand in the market as a whole. Therefore, it may be of help in estimating sales demand from new and existing customers.

Page 1/2

(c) *Limitations to the techniques*

Asking existing customers may not always result in accurate information. They may not wish to divulge the information as it might be commercially sensitive. Even if they give our company the information, they may place some orders with competitors. Asking the sales force what the likely demand will be overcomes this problem. Unfortunately, the sales force may be suspicious of the motives for the information and not provide a full answer.

Market research is also not without its limitations. If we are concerned with collecting primary data on a new product, participants in the market research may not be able to fully comprehend the new product and so give misleading information about possible demand. In addition, primary market research often uses relatively small samples and so there is the possibility of statistical error.

Two major limitations of time series are that linear relationships are often assumed and that demand is simply a function of time. It also requires past data – data which is not available if entering into new markets or developing new products.

Economic indicators can be of help in short-term forecasting. However, as they depend on other fairly recent data, they are of less help in longer-term forecasting. As with time series, economic indicators depend on the past repeating itself. This is not always so. Ten years ago, most British holidaymakers booked their holidays in January, enabling packaging tour operators to accurately forecast hotel and flight requirements. Now, many leave the booking of holidays until much later in the year, making accurate forecasting that much more difficult.

Page 2/2

5.5 Pickerings

Task 1

(a) *Materials purchases budget for September 19X7 (to the nearest £)*

	£
September 19X7	3,368

Working

80,000 x 100/95 (damage adjustment) x 100kg/1,000 cans x 100/50 (waste) x £200/tonne

(b) *Monthly labour budget – number of employees*

September 19X7	3.69 – say 4 employees

Working

80,000 cans x 100/95 (damage adjustment) x 6 hours/1,000 cans x 100/90 (absenteeism) x 1/38 (hours per employee) x 1/4 (weeks per month)

(c)   *Materials purchases budget (adjusted for price indices)*

$£$

September 19X7   3,508

Working

Answer "(a)" x 125/120

Task 2

MEMO

To: Production Manager   **Date:**   18 June 19X7

From: Assistant Cost Accountant

Subject: Budgeting for Materials and Labour

The following memo covers the issues raised by yourself and follows the same sequence.

Material prices are usually forecast for the year ahead and a single average value is chosen for convenience. Unfortunately prices of materials in the market will vary so that the average price used may reflect the movement in prices over the period but it is not likely to reflect the prices on a smaller timescale e.g. a month. Therefore the accuracy of prices is weakened as a result. The solution that we chose was to base the price changes on last years' figures, which is an improvement on the use of a single average price. Unfortunately the confidence in these figures may not be high as the price may be affected by Political, Economic, Social and Technological (P.E.S.T.) factors.

As regards an alternative method of predicting prices, we could use time series analysis. This may be a more accurate method as it would take into account trends, seasonal variations and cycles. Again this method would be affected by P.E.S.T. factors but possibly to a lesser extent.

The type of labour information which should be supplied is:

Daily – Attendance, absenteeism, production, damaged goods, productive hours, productivity.

Weekly – Weekly summaries of the daily figures, total wages cost plus comparison with planned figures, labour costs/1,000 cans.

Monthly – Monthly performance reports expressing the weekly figures in monetary terms, including variance analysis. The monthly figures would prove the overall control of the labour costs but any deviation from the plan would be identified from the daily and weekly figures.

5.6   George Phillips

Task 1

(a)   The purchases budget for materials is 20,000 kilograms at £5 per kg – a value of £100,000.

(b)   The next step is to calculate the materials issued to production figure; this is 19,400 kg which is the following.

Purchases	20,000 kg
Opening stock	6,000
Closing stock	(6,600)
Materials issued to production	19,400

(c)   Given the limit on materials purchased and usage, the next step is to decide which products should be produced and sold. This would depend on product contribution per limiting factor; in this case, materials.

	Alpha	*Beta*
Sales price/unit	£36	£39
Materials cost/unit	10	7.50
Labour cost/unit	10	11.14
Variable cost/unit	20	18.64
Contribution/unit	£16	£20.36
Limiting factor (materials)	2 kg	1.5 kg
Contribution/limiting factor	£8	£13.57
Ranking	2	1

Given that 9,000 units of Beta will be produced, requiring 13,500 kg of materials, the balance of materials usage for the Alpha is 5,900 kg, which equates to 2,950 units of product. This represents the decrease in the Alpha production of 3,950 units (6,900 – 2,950). If the closing stock remains the same, the budgeted sales must also be reduced by this amount. Alpha sales will therefore be 6,500 – 3,950 = 2,550 units.

The revised sales budget would be as follows;

	Units	Selling price	Turnover
		£	£
Alpha	2,550	36.00	91,800
Beta	7,800	39.00	304,200
			396,000

(d)   The revised labour budget would be as follows.

Alpha 2,950 units x 2.5 hours =	7,375	hours
Beta (as original labour budget)	25,065	"
Total labour hours	32,440	"
Labour cost (x £4/hour)	£129,760	

(e)   Using a 13 week period and a 35 hour week, 32,440 hours translates into 71.3 employees, a reduction of 21.7.

Task 2

REPORT

To: George Phillips

From: Trainee Accountant   **Date:**   1   March 1998

Subject: Classification of labour costs, key factors and spreadsheet packages.

The following report is in response to your request for advice on the issues raised at your recent management meeting. The report follows the same sequence as the issues raised.

(a) The decision on whether to reduce the workforce or not is a crucial one. The use of standards and estimates of 2.5 hours per unit for the Alpha and 2.785 hours per unit for the Beta, suggests that the labour costs are variable. This would be the case if the employees were employed on a piecework basis but most companies employ labour per week or per period and therefore the labour costs become a fixed cost in the short term. The effect on the cash flow should also be considered, ie the cost of redundancy, the cost of continued employment and the cost of recruitment and training.

For the longer term, all costs are variable and the company would not continue to employ staff if they were surplus to requirements. The production manager has a valid point in that the staff who have been made redundant may not be keen to be re–employed if there is a risk of them being make redundant again. The case for retaining them is also supported by the fact that they are stated to be highly trained staff and the training value lost may take some time to regain. Another factor to be considered would be the cost of recruiting new staff and the costs of training them and the potential increase in reject products. On balance it would probably be preferable to keep the staff as the problem appears to be a short term one.

(b) The importance of identifying key factors or limiting factors in the preparation of budgets should not be undervalued. There are many key factors in an organisation and their ranking may change as time elapses. The key factors in most organisations are sales, stock, materials, space, cash, equipment, trained staff and cost of staff to name a few. It is true that key factors do change over time; the secret is to establish what they are and what the implications are of solving them. For example the company may not have enough machine capacity; this can be solved by buying more machinery, but this decision may well impact on cash flow (insufficient cash to purchase the machinery), and labour (not enough trained staff to run the machine) and sales (the sales will not immediately increase to fill the capacity of the machine). Therefore the identification of key factors is important as is the implications for the company of any change in their ranking.

(c) A relevant package here would be a spreadsheet package incorporating Profit and Loss statement, Balance Sheet and Cash Flow statement. The model could be set up using a data area for the key variables such as material usage per product, price per kilo of material, inflation, payment profiling and so on. The relevant relationships could then be input into the cells of, say, the Profit and Loss schedule, eg sales x selling price per unit. The model could be used to ask 'what if' questions and to illustrate the effect of changes in the figures on the three statements, with the recalculation of the figures being automatic. The figures could also be used to calculate key ratios. Constraints (eg overdraft not to exceed £x) could also be built into the formulae. The benefits of using such a package are significant in terms of time and accuracy, particularly as the costs of such a package are relatively low.

5.7 Mayfield School

MEMO

To: Jim Smith, Head Teacher   **Date:** 17 June 19X8

From: A Technician

Subject: Limitations of existing budget statement and possible improvements.

(a) The existing budget statement suffers from a number of weaknesses.

- there are no actual or budgeted figures for the current month and hence no monthly variances

- in many cases, the budget to date is simply 10/12 of the total budget and so there has been no attempt to realistically profile the budget against likely expenditure

- the actual expenditure is based on cash payments rather than the use of accruals. Cash accounting can give misleading information about expenses to date and funds remaining

- capital expenditure is included as an expense rather than shown as assets, which would then be depreciated over their useful life

- no attempt has been made to forecast the likely year–end result. Many organisations estimate the year–end out–turn by adding expenses to date to likely expenditure to the year–end and comparing this with the annual budget

- the expenditure headings are not grouped into meaningful sub–headings

- the under–/overspend column is misleading for non–accountants with the term 'Cr'.

Page 1/2

(b)   A possible improved statement format would be as follows.

Expense type	Monthly data Actual Budget Variance	Year to date data Actual Budget Variance	Year–end forecast Out–turn Budget Variance
Direct teaching			
Teachers – full-time			
Teachers – part-time			
Other employee expenses			
Resources			
Administration			
Administrative staff			
Stationery, postage and phone			
Property services			
Caretaker and cleaners			
Lighting and heating			
Repairs and maintenance			
Rates			
Other			
Miscellaneous expenses			
TOTAL REVENUE EXPENDITURE			
Fixed assets			
TOTAL CAPITAL EXPENDITURE			

Page 2/2

(c)   Advantages of proposed format

♦   identification of current month's budget and actual expenditure. This allows speedy remedial action and/or early warning of difficulties which would otherwise have been subsumed within the total for the year

♦   the replacement of 'under–/overspend' by the expression 'variance' and for the variances to be followed by 'F' for favourable and 'A' for adverse, making the statement easier to understand

♦   the introduction of an out–turn column which, when measured against the annual budget, will give an estimate of the likely final financial position

♦   the grouping of the expenses into similar categories of expenditure. This enables the main sources of expenditure to be identified and shows any compensating variances. For example, the expenditure on teaching full-time is favourable but this may be due to fewer teachers being employed full-time and more employed part-time as the part-time teacher heading shows an adverse variance.

Task 2

Calculation of number of year 1 pupils

Junior School	*Number in final year*	*Proportion choosing Mayfield School*	*Number choosing Mayfield School*
Ranmoor	60	0.9	54
Hallamshire	120	0.8	96
Broomhill	140	0.9	126
Endcliffe	80	0.5	40
Total choosing Mayfield School			316

(a)   Forecast of pupil numbers and income

Year	*Age range*	*1997/8*	*1998/9*
1	11 – 12	300	316
2	12 – 13	350	300
3	13 – 14	325	350
4	14 – 15	360	325
5	15 – 16	380	325
6	16 – 17	240	304
7	17 – 18	220	228
		2,175	2,185

Note.

Current years 1 – 4 pupils become years 2 – 5 pupils next year.
80% of current year 5 pupils become year 6 pupils next year.
95% of current year 6 pupils become year 7 pupils next year.

Years	*Pupil numbers*	*Annual fee*	*Total income*
1 – 5	1,651	£1,200	£1,981,200
6 – 7	532	£1,500	£798,000
Totals	2,183		£2,779,200

(b)   Budgeted surplus

Income	£2,779,200
Expenditure £2,581,296 x 1.05	£2,710,361
Budgeted surplus	£68,839

CHAPTERS 6 AND 7

Standard Costing and Variance Analysis (Questions)

6.1 Operating statements

Obelix Ltd manufactures a single product for the building trade, the Hodabrix. The budgeted and actual results for 19X6 are shown below.

		Budget		Actual
Production (units)		60,000		62,000
Sales (units)		55,000		59,000
		£		£
Materials	(240,000 kg at £1)	240,000	(250,000 kg)	280,000
Labour	(30,000 hrs at £3)	90,000	(35,000 hrs paid)	84,000
			(34,000 hrs worked)	
Variable production overhead		30,000		37,000
Fixed production overhead		108,000		110,000
		468,000		511,000
Variable selling costs		5,500		4,500
Fixed selling costs		5,500		5,500
		11,000		10,000
Sales revenue		544,500		560,500

There were no opening or closing stocks of raw materials and no opening or closing work in progress. Also there was no opening stock of finished goods due to an unexpected order at the end of last year from a construction firm Cubbix.

Required

You have been asked, as management accountant, to produce:

(a) an operating statement on total absorption costing lines

(b) a revised statement on marginal (or direct) costing lines

(c) a reconciliation of the profit figures shown in (a) and (b).

6.2 Products X and Y

The information shown below is an extract from the previous period's budget and standard cost data for the machining department in a company manufacturing two products. It operates a total absorption standard costing system.

	Product X	Product Y
Budgeted production	6,500 units	4,200 units
Standard machine hours allowed to process each product in the machining department	4 hours	7 hours

The department's overhead is applied to production by means of a standard machine hour absorption rate and this is calculated at the beginning of each period. The variable element of the previous period's absorption rate was £1.50 per standard machine hour and the department's total overheads for that period were budgeted to be £207,750. The budget assumes that one standard machine hour should be produced in one actual hour of machining time.

The actual results in the machining department for the previous period were:

Actual machining time	54,000 hours
Production: Product X	7,200 units
Product Y	4,000 units
Actual overheads incurred: Fixed	£120,550
Variable	£87,600

Required

(a) Calculate the following variances from standard/budgeted cost which occurred in the machining department during the previous period:

(i)   fixed overhead volume variance

(ii) fixed overhead expenditure variance

(iii) variable overhead expenditure variance.

(b) Discuss in detail the possible reasons for the fixed overhead volume variance.

(c) Calculate the machining department's total flexed overhead budget for the actual level of production in the previous period and explain the difference between this total budgeted amount and the total production overhead absorbed by the department in the period.

6.3 Fixed overhead variances (AAT D95)

Data

You are employed as part of the management accounting team in a large industrial company which operates a four-weekly system of management reporting. Your division makes a single product, the Alpha, and, because of the nature of the production process, there is no work in progress at any time.

The group management accountant has completed the calculation of the material and labour standard costing variances for the current period to 1 December but has not had the time to complete any other variances. Details of the variances already calculated are reproduced in the working papers below, along with other standard costing data.

Standard costing and budget data – four weeks ended 1 December

	Quantity	Unit price	Cost per unit
Materials (litres)	40	£4.00	£160
Labour (hours)	10	£8.40	£84
Fixed overhead (hours)	10	£6.70	£67
Standard cost per unit			£311

Budgeted production for the four weeks	Units	Standard unit cost	Standard cost of production
	12,000	£311	£3,732,000

Working papers:

Actual production and expenditure for the four weeks ended 1 December

Units produced	11,200
Cost of 470,000 litres of materials consumed	£1,974,000
Cost of 110,000 labour hours worked	£935,000
Expenditure on fixed overheads	£824,000

Material and labour variances

Material price variance	£94,000 (A)
Material usage variance	£88,000 (A)
Labour rate variance	£11,000 (A)
Labour efficiency variance	£16,800 (F)

Task 1

You have been requested to:

(a)   Calculate the following variances:

   (i)   the fixed overhead expenditure variance

   (ii)   the fixed overhead volume variance

   (iii)   the fixed overhead capacity variance

   (iv)   the fixed overhead efficiency variance.

(b)   Prepare a report for presentation to the production director reconciling the standard cost of production for the period with the actual cost of production.

Task 2

The production director, who has only recently been appointed, is unfamiliar with fixed overhead variances. Because of this, the group management accountant has asked you to prepare a brief memo to the production director.

Required

Your memo should:

(a)   Outline the similarities and differences between fixed overhead variances and other cost variances such as the material and labour variances

(b)   Explain what is meant by the fixed overhead expenditure, volume, capacity and efficiency variances and show, by way of examples, how these can be of help to the production director in the planning and controlling of the division.

6.4   Albion Ltd 2 (AAT D96)

Data

Albion Ltd operates a standard absorption costing system. Standards are established at the beginning of each year. Each week the management accounting section prepares a statement for the production director reconciling the actual cost of production with its standard cost. Standard costing data for week 8 of quarter 4 in the current year is given below.

Standard costing and budget data for week 8 of quarter 4

	Quantity	Unit price	Cost per unit
Material (kilograms)	3	£23.00	£69
Labour (hours)	2	£20.00	£40
Fixed overhead (hours)	2	£60.00	£120
Standard unit cost			£229

Budgeted production for the four weeks	Budgeted units	Standard cost per unit	Standard cost of production
	10,000	£229	£2,290,000

During week 8, production of Xtra totalled 9,000 units and the actual costs for that week were:

Inputs	Units	Total cost
Materials (kilograms)	26,500	£662,500
Labour (hours)	18,400	£349,600
Fixed overheads (hours)	18,400	£1,500,000

Using this data, a colleague has already calculated the fixed overhead variances. These were as follows:

◆   Fixed overhead expenditure (or price) variance   £300,000 adverse

◆   Efficiency (or usage) variance   £24,000 adverse

◆   Capacity variance   £96,000 adverse

Task 1

Your colleague asks you to:

(a)   Calculate the following variances:

    (i)   material price

    (ii)   material usage

    (iii)   labour rate

    (iv)   labour efficiency (sometimes called utilisation).

(b)   Prepare a statement reconciling the actual cost of production with the standard cost of actual production.

Data

The production director of Albion Ltd is concerned that the material price variance may not accurately reflect the efficiency of the company's purchasing department.

Task 2

You have been asked by your finance director to write a *brief* memorandum to the production director. Your memo should:

(a)   explain what variances are attempting to measure *

(b)   list *three* general ways production variances arise other than through errors*

(c)   identify *three* general reasons why there might be errors in reporting variances*

(d)   use your answer to Task 1 (a) to suggest why the production director's concern might be justified.

Note. In parts (a), (b) and (c) of this task, you should restrict your comments to variances in general and not address issues arising from particular types of variances.

6.5   Malton Ltd (AAT J97)

Data

Malton Ltd operates a standard marginal costing system. As the recently appointed management accountant to Malton's Eastern division, you have responsibility for the preparation of that division's monthly cost reports. The standard cost report uses variances to reconcile the actual marginal cost of production to its standard cost.

The Eastern division is managed by Richard Hill. The division only makes one product, the Beta. Budgeted Beta production for May 19X7 was 8,000 units although production was 9,500 units.

In order to prepare the standard cost report for May, you have asked a member of your staff to obtain standard and actual cost details for the month of May. This information is reproduced below.

	Unit standard cost				*Actual details for May*	
	Quantity	*Unit price*	*Cost per beta*		*Quantity*	*Total cost*
		£	£			£
Material	8 litres	20	160	Material	78,000 litres	1,599,000
Labour	4 hours	6	24	Labour	39,000 hours	249,600
Standard marginal cost			184	Total cost		1,848,600

Task 1

(a)   Calculate the following:

   (i)   the material price variance

   (ii)   the material usage variance

   (iii)   the labour rate variance

   (iv)   the labour efficiency variance (sometimes called the utilisation variance).

(b)   Prepare a standard costing statement reconciling the actual marginal cost of production with the standard marginal cost of production.

Data

After Richard Hill has received your standard costing statement, you visit him to discuss the variances and their implications. Richard, however, raises a number of queries with you. He makes the following points:

♦   an index measuring material prices stood at 247.2 for May but at 240.0 when the standard for the material price was set

♦   the Eastern division is budgeted to run at its normal capacity of 8,000 units of production per month but during May it has to manufacture an additional 1,500 Betas to meet a special order agreed at short notice by Malton's sales director

- because of the short notice, the normal supplier of the raw materials was unable to meet the extra demand and so additional materials had to be acquired from another supplier at a price per litre of £22

- this extra material was not up to the normal specification, resulting in 20% of the special purchase being scrapped *prior* to being issued to production

- the work force could only produce the special order on time by working overtime on the 1,500 Betas at a 50% premium.

Task 2

(a) Calculate the amounts within the material price variance, the material usage variance and the labour rate variance which arise from producing the special order.

(b) (i) Estimate the revised standard price for materials based on the change in the material price index.

(ii) For the 8,000 units of normal production, use your answer in (b)(i) to estimate how much of the price variance calculated in Task 1 is caused by the general change in prices.

(c) Using your answers to part (a) and (b) of this Task, prepare a revised standard costing statement. The revised statement should subdivide the variances prepared in Task 1 into those elements controllable by Richard Hill and those elements caused by factors outside his divisional control.

(d) Write a *brief* note to Richard Hill justifying your treatment of the elements you believe are outside his control and suggesting what action should be taken by the company.

6.6 Significant variables

A firm has recently commenced using a standard costing system but the manager is having some difficulty in identifying significant variances (ie. those that require further analysis and investigation).

Required

(a) Describe the factors which determine whether or not a variance is significant.

(b) Suggest ways in which significant variances could be more easily identified.

(c) Explain what changes, if any, there would be to your previous answers if the variances were sub-divided into planning and operational variances.

6.7 Ruggerball Ltd

(a) Ruggerball Ltd does nothing but manufacture rugby balls. As each ball is completed, it is booked out to a subsidiary company, Try Ltd. Ruggerball's budget for the seventh four-weekly control period of its financial year was as follows:

	£	£
Sales (6,000 units at £8 each)		48,000
Variable costs:		
Bladders (6,000 at 50p each)	3,000	
Leather (200 ten hide bales at £76 each)	15,200	
Sundry and packaging materials	1,300	
Direct labour (5,000 hours at 90p per hour)	4,500	
	24,000	
Fixed costs:		
Administrative and establishment expenses	4,239	
Staff and directors' salaries	8,261	
		(36,500)
Budgeted net profit		11,500

During recent power shortages, Ruggerball was only able to manufacture during 60% of the budgeted production hours and was unable to sanction any overtime. Despite this the direct labour force was paid in full for the budgeted hours.

Various other differences from budget occurred and the following are the actual figures for the period:

	£	£
Sales (4,000 units at £9 each)		36,000
Variable costs:		
Bladders (4,000 at 70p each)	2,800	
Leather (100 ten hide bales at £133.33 each)	13,333	
Sundry and packaging materials	867	
Direct labour (5,000 hours at £1 per hour)	5,000	
	22,000	
Fixed costs:		
Administrative and establishment expenses	4,385	
Staff and directors' salaries	8,315	
		(34,700)
Actual net profit		1,300

Required

(i)   Prepare a statement reconciling the budgeted contribution with the actual contribution, stating the variances in the way which you think will be most helpful to management. Present your calculations as schedules with references to the main statement.

(ii)   Comment briefly on any apparent inter-relationships between the variances.

(b)   In the next period, there was an adverse leather usage variance of £600 and a decision needs to be made as to whether to investigate the process to determine whether it is out of control.

On the basis of past experience, the cost of an investigation is estimated at £160 and the cost of correction if the process is out of control is estimated at £350. The probability of it being out of control is estimated at 0.4.

Required

Show calculations to support your decision as to whether or not to investigate the variance.

6.8 Mel Donte

A company has an inspection department in which operatives examine fruit in order to extract blemished input before the fruit is transferred to a processing department.

The input to the inspection department comes from a preparation department where the fruit is washed and trimmed.

Stocks cannot be built up because of the perishable nature of the fruit. This means that the inspection department operations are likely to have some idle time during each working day.

A standard output rate in kilogrammes per hour from the inspection process has been agreed as the target to be aimed for in return for wages paid at a fixed rate per hour irrespective of the actual level of idle time.

The standard data for the inspection department are as follows:

(1)   Standard idle time as a percentage of total hours paid for: 20%

(2)   Standard wage rate per hour: £3.00

(3)   Standard output efficiency is 100%, ie. one standard hour of work is expected in each hour excluding idle time hours.

(4)   Wages are charged to production at a rate per standard hour sufficient to absorb the standard level of idle time.

The labour variance analysis for November for the inspection department was as follows.

Variances	£	Expressed in % terms
Productivity	525 (F)	2.2 (F)
Excess idle time	150 (A)	2.5 (A)
Wage rate	800 (A)	3.3 (A)

The actual data for the inspection department for the three months December to February is as follows.

	Dec	Jan	Feb
Standard hours of output achieved	6,600	6,700	6,800
Labour hours paid for	8,600	8,400	8,900
Idle time hours incurred	1,700	1,200	1,400
Actual wages earned	£26,660	£27,300	£28,925

The labour variances to be calculated in the operation of a standard cost system are as follows.

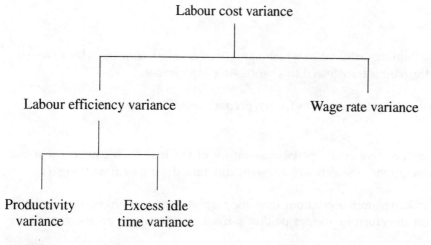

Required

(a) Calculate the labour variances for productivity, excess idle time and rate of pay for each of the months December to February.

(b) In order to highlight the trend and materiality of the variances calculated in (a) above, express them as percentages as follows:

  (i) productivity variance: as a percentage of standard cost of production achieved

  (ii) excess idle time variance: as a percentage of expected idle time

  (iii) wage rate variance: as a percentage of hours paid for at standard rates of pay.

(c) Explain why variance trend and materiality data in percentage terms may provide useful additional control information for management. Comment on the data given for November and calculated for December to February, giving possible explanations for the figures produced.

CHAPTERS 6 AND 7

Standard Costing and Variance Analysis (Answers)

6.1 Operating statements

(a) *Total absorption costing operating statement for the year ended 31 December 19X6*

				£
Budgeted profit (55,000 x £1.90)				104,500
Sales volume variance				7,600 (F)
Standard profit on actual sales				112,100
Sales price variance				(23,600) (A)
				88,500

Cost variances

		F	A	
		£	£	
Materials	– Price		30,000	
	– Usage		2,000	
Labour	– Rate	21,000		
	– Idle time		3,000	
	– Efficiency		9,000	
Variable	– Rate		3,000	
	– Efficiency		3,000	
		21,000	50,000	
Fixed	– Expenditure		2,000	
	– Capacity	14,400		
	– Efficiency		10,800	
		35,400	62,800	
Variable selling	– Expenditure	1,400		
Fixed selling	– Volume	400		
		37,200	62,800	
				(25,600)
Actual profit				62,900

(b)   *Marginal costing operating statement for the year ended 31 December 19X6*

	£	£
Budgeted contribution (55,000 x £3.80)		209,000
Sales volume variance		15,200 (F)
Standard contribution on actual sales		224,200
Sales price variance		(23,600) (A)
		200,600

Cost variances

	£	£
Materials, labour and variable production overhead	(29,000)	
Variable selling expenditure	1,400	
		(27,600)
Actual contribution		173,000

Fixed overheads	*Budget*	*Exp Var*	*Actual*	
	£	£	£	
Production	108,000	2,000	110,000	
Selling	5,500		5,500	
	113,500	2,000	(115,500)
Actual profit				57,500

(c)   *Reconciliation*

The two profit figures can be 'proved' by producing summarised profit and loss accounts.

(i)   *Total absorption profit and loss account*

	£	£
Revenue		560,500
Production costs	511,000	
Closing stock (3,000 @ £7.80)	(23,400)	
	487,600	
Selling costs	10,000	
		(497,600)
Profit		62,900

(ii) *Marginal costing profit and loss account*

	£	£
Revenue		560,500
Variable production costs	401,000	
Closing stock (3,000 @ £6)	(18,000)	
	383,000	
Fixed production costs	110,000	
	493,000	
Selling costs	10,000	
		(503,000)
Profit		57,500

The difference in the two profit figures arises purely as a result of the difference in the two closing stock valuations. In (i) the 3,000 units of closing stock are valued at total absorption cost, £7.80 per Hodabrix, in (ii) they are valued at marginal cost, £6 per Hodabrix. The difference in the profit is the 3,000 units of extra fixed production overhead (£1.80 per unit) carried forward in closing stock under the total absorption costing system.

Workings

(1) *Standard cost card*

		£
Materials	(4 kg at £1/kg)	4.00
Labour	(½ hr at £3/hr)	1.50
Variable overhead	(½ hr at £1/hr)	0.50
Marginal cost of production		6.00
Fixed overhead (½ hr at £3.60/hr)		1.80
Total absorption cost of production		7.80
Variable selling overhead (per unit)		0.10
Fixed selling overhead (per unit)		0.10
		8.00
Standard profit per unit		1.90
Selling price per unit		9.90

(2)   *Sales variances*

	Units	£
Budgeted sales at standard profit	55,000	104,500
Actual sales at standard profit	59,000	112,100
Volume variance	4,000	7,600 F
Actual sales at standard price	59,000	584,100
Actual sales at actual price	59,000	560,500
Price variance		23,600 A

(3)   *Materials variances*

	Kg	£
Actual purchases at actual price	250,000	280,000
Actual purchases at standard price	250,000	250,000
Price variance		30,000 A
Actual purchases at standard price	250,000	250,000
Standard usage at standard price (62,000 x 4 kg x £1)	248,000	248,000
Usage variance	2,000	2,000 A

(4)   *Labour variances*

	Hrs	£
Actual hours paid at actual rate	35,000	84,000
Actual hours at standard price	35,000	105,000
Rate variance		21,000 F
Actual hours paid at standard rate	35,000	105,000
Actual hours worked at standard rate	34,000	102,000
Idle time variance	1,000	3,000 A
Actual hours worked at standard rate	34,000	102,000
Standard hours at standard rate (62,000 x 0.5 x £3)	31,000	93,000
Efficiency variance	3,000	9,000 A

(5)   *Variable overhead variances*

	Hrs	£
Actual hours worked at actual rate	34,000	37,000
Actual hours worked at standard rate	34,000	34,000
Rate variance		3,000 A

Efficiency variance (same number of hours as for labour)
3,000 hours x £1   3,000 A

(6)   *Fixed production overhead variances*

		£
Actual cost		110,000
Budgeted cost		108,000
Expenditure variance (A)		2,000 A

	Hrs	£
Budgeted hours at standard rate	30,000	108,000
Actual hours worked at standard rate	34,000	122,400
Capacity variance (F)	4,000	14,400 F

Efficiency variance (same number of hours as for labour)
3,000 hours x £3.60   10,800 A

(7)   *Variable selling overheads*

	Units	£
Actual sales at actual rate	59,000	4,500
Actual sales at standard rate	59,000	5,900
Expenditure variance		1,400 F

(8)   *Fixed selling overheads*

		£
Budgeted cost		5,500
Actual cost		5,500
Expenditure variance		–

	Units	£
Budgeted sales at standard rate	55,000	5,500
Actual sales at standard rate	59,000	5,900
Volume variance	4,000	400 F

6.2   Products X and Y

(a)   *Fixed overhead volume variance*

		Machine hours
X, 7,200 units x 4 hours		28,800
Y, 4,000 units x 7 hours		28,000
		56,800

		£	
Standard cost of actual production	56,800 x £2.25 (W3)	127,800	
Budgeted fixed overheads (W2)		124,650	
Fixed overhead volume variance		3,150	(F)

Fixed overhead expenditure variance

	£	
Budgeted fixed overheads (W2)	124,650	
Actual fixed overhead expenditure	120,550	
Fixed overhead expenditure variance	4,100	(F)

Variable overhead expenditure variance

		£	
Standard cost of actual production	56,800 x £1.50	85,200	
Actual variable overhead expenditure		87,600	
Variable overhead total cost variance		2,400	(A)

		£	
Standard cost of actual hours worked	54,000 x £1.50	81,000	
Actual variable overhead cost		87,600	
Variable overhead rate (expenditure) variance		6,600	(A)

(b)   *Possible reasons for the fixed overhead volume variance*

(i)   Actual production was 56,800 standard machine hours which was greater than the 55,400 (W1) machine hours budgeted. The increased production may have followed an increase in demand.

(ii)   The efficiency was improved as shown by actual machining time of 54,000 machine hours producing 56,800 standard machine hours.

The improved efficiency could be due to:

(i)   machine operators working harder, or working by more efficient methods

(ii) more effective production scheduling or labour control.

(c)   *Machining department's total flexed overhead budget*

	£
Budgeted fixed overheads (W2)	124,650
Flexed variable overheads 56,800 x £1.50	85,200
	———
Total flexed overhead budget	209,850
	═══

The flexed budget includes fixed overheads at a constant amount but the total production overhead absorbed includes fixed overheads that vary directly with production. The term *flexed budget* can be used in several contrasting (contradictory) ways).

Workings

(1)   *Previous period*

	Machine hours
X, 6,500 units x 4 hours	26,000
Y, 4,200 units x 7 hours	29,400
	———
Budgeted total standard machine hours	55,400
	═══

Budgeted variable overheads 55,400 × £1.50 = £83,100

(2)   *Budgeted fixed overheads*

	£
Total overheads	207,750
Variable overheads (W1)	(83,100)
	———
Fixed overheads	124,650
	═══

(3)   *Budgeted fixed overhead absorption rate*

$$\frac{£124,650}{55,400} = £2.25 \text{ per machine hour}$$

6.3 Fixed overhead variances

Task 1

(a) Calculation of fixed overhead variances:

    (i)   *Fixed overhead expenditure variance*

	£	
Actual overhead	824,000	
Budgeted overhead (12,000 units x £67 per unit)	804,000	
	20,000	(A)

    (ii)   *Fixed overhead volume variance*

	£	
Budgeted overhead (see above)	804,000	
Overhead absorbed (11,200 units produced x £67 per unit)	750,400	
	53,600	(A)

Note. Alternative approach using labour hours.

    (iii)   *Fixed overhead capacity variance*

	Hours	
Budgeted hours (12,000 budgeted units x 10 hours per unit)	120,000	
Actual hours worked	110,000	
Variance in hours	10,000	(A)
Variance in pounds (10,000 hours x £6.70 per hour)	£67,000	(A)

    (iv)   *Fixed overhead efficiency variance*

	Hours	
Actual hours worked	110,000	
Standard hours produced (11,200 units x 10 hours per unit)	112,000	
Variance in hours	2,000	(F)
Variance in pounds (2,000 hours x £6.70 per hour)	£13,400	(F)

(b)   Performance report

Performance Report – X Division four weeks ended 1 December

Issued by: Management Accounting Department

Date: 6 December 19X5   To: Production Director

				£
STANDARD COST OF ACTUAL PRODUCTION (11,200 units)				3,483,200
Material variances:	£			
Price	94,000	(A)		
Usage	88,000	(A)		
	———			
			182,000	(A)
Labour variances:				
Rate	11,000	(A)		
Efficiency	16,800	(F)		
	———			
			5,800	(F)
Fixed overhead variances:				
Expenditure	20,000	(A)		
Capacity	67,000	(A)		
Efficiency	13,400	(F)		
	———			
			73,600	(A)
			———	
ACTUAL COST OF PRODUCTION [1]			3,733,000	

Note

1   Composition of actual cost of actual production

	£
Materials	1,974,000
Labour	935,000
Fixed overheads	824,000
	———
Total	3,733,000

Task 2

MEMO

To: The production director   **Date:**   6 December 19X5

From: Assistant management accountant

Subject: **The meaning of fixed overhead variances**

The fixed overhead expenditure variance is the difference between the actual and budgeted fixed overheads. It is similar to the material price and labour rate variances. Just as they reflect the effect on costs and profit of paying more or less than planned for the resources used, so the fixed overhead expenditure variance reflects paying more or less than planned for the fixed overheads incurred.

It is also possible for material and labour to give rise to material usage and labour efficiency variances whereby more or less resources have been used than should have been for the volume produced. Fixed overheads, however, are a fixed cost that remain constant over the relevant range. As such, the marginal cost is zero and so there cannot be a usage variance in the form of consuming more or less fixed overhead expenditure than planned.

Nevertheless, it is possible to analyse the fixed overheads further where a company such as ours operates a standard absorption costing system. The extent of overheads being under- or over-absorbed is measured by the volume variance. This can be further broken down to show how much of the under- or over-absorbed is due to working the plant more or less than planned – the fixed overhead capacity variance – and how much is due to the speed of production whilst the plant was being worked. This latter variance is known as the fixed overhead efficiency variance. These variances are measuring the extent of overheads being under- or over-absorbed as a result of volume being different from planned – unlike the material usage and labour efficiency variances which measure usage being different from plan *for* the volume achieved.

Because of this, the fixed overhead variances can be of particular help to managers in the division. The expenditure variance highlights the effect on costs and profits of changing input prices, enabling managers to consider other suppliers of the fixed overheads or, if this is not possible, to reconsider the pricing structure of the products manufactured by the division. The volume variance identifies in financial terms the importance of volume on profitability – although the full financial consequence would also include the change in profits resulting from any change in volume. The capacity and efficiency variances give further insight into this. A favourable efficiency variance and an unfavourable capacity variance, for example, might point to an efficient workforce but plant breakdowns.

6.4   Albion Ltd 2

Task 1

Part (a)

(i)   Material price variance: (26,500 x £23) – £662,500 = £53,000 (A)

(ii)   Material usage variance: (27,000 – 26,500) x £23 = £11,500 (F)

(iii)   Labour rate variance: (18,400 x £20) – £349,600 = £18,400 (F)

(iv)   Labour efficiency variance: (18,000 – 18,400) x £20 = £8,000 (A)

Part (b)

Xtra Standard Costing Report – Week 8, quarter 4, 19X6

Issued by: Management Accounting Department

Date: 4 December 19X6	To: Production Director	
	£	£
ACTUAL COST OF PRODUCTION		2,512,100
Material variances:	£	
Price	53,000 (A)	
Usage	11,500 (F)	
	‾‾‾‾‾‾‾	
		41,500 (A)
Labour variances:		
Rate	18,400 (F)	
Efficiency	8,000 (A)	
	‾‾‾‾‾‾‾	
		10,400 (F)
Fixed overhead variances:		
Expenditure	300,000 (A)	
Capacity	96,000 (A)	
Efficiency	24,000 (A)	
	‾‾‾‾‾‾‾	
		420,000 (A)
		‾‾‾‾‾‾‾
STANDARD COST OF PRODUCTION		2,061,000
		═══════

Task 2

MEMO

To: The Production Director   **Date:**   4 December 19X6

From: Assistant Management Accountant

Subject: **Meaning of variances**

(a)   What variances attempt to measure

Practically all organisations need to plan for the future. Planning identifies desired results and how these can be achieved. Two formal mechanisms which help organisations in their planning are budgets and standard costing.

To make planning effective, it is necessary to identify actual results, for these to be compared with the plan and for action to be taken to correct any deviations from the plan. Variances measure these deviations. They do not necessarily identify the reason for the deviation.

(b)   Three broad ways production variances arise

Variances can arise if unit prices are different from planned, if the input usage is different from planned or if the production volume is different from planned.

(c)   General reasons why there might be errors in reporting variances

Errors can occur if the original standard was inappropriate or has become out-of-date. They can also occur if there is a mistake in the recording of the actual results. This might occur if there have been mispostings or if expenses have not been accrued. A further way errors can occur is when a cost centre incurs a variance but this arises from the actions of other departments. For example, the marketing department might give the production department inadequate notice of the need for a particular job. Because of this, the production department may have to pay overtime to its workforce. Although the adverse labour rate variance will be charged against the production department, the error was caused by the marketing department and should have been charged to it.

(d)   The production director's query

There may be grounds for the concern expressed by the production director. The standard price is £23 but the forecast price was £27. The actual price paid in that quarter was £25 (£662,500/26,500). If £27 was the current market price of material X, then the production director has been efficient by acquiring the material for £25 per kilogram. Despite that, the standard costing system will report an adverse price variance because of an inappropriate standard.

6.5   Malton Ltd

Task 1

(a)   Calculation of the material and labour variances

Material variances

	£	
Actual usage at standard price (78,000 litres x £20)	1,560,000	
Actual usage at actual price (given in data)	1,599,000	
Material price variance	39,000	(A)
Standard usage (9,500 units produced x 8 litres)	76,000	
Actual usage (given in task)	78,000	
Excess litres used	2,000	
Material usage variance (£20 x 2,000 litres)	40,000	(A)

Labour variances

	£	
Actual hours at standard rate (39,000 hours x £6)	234,000	
Actual hours at actual rate (given in data)	249,600	
Labour rate variance	15,600	(A)
Standard hours (9,500 units x 4 hours)	38,000	
Actual hours (given in data)	39,000	
Excess hours	1,000	
Labour efficiency variance (£6 x 1,000 hours)	6,000	(A)

Part (b)

Standard marginal costing statement for Beta production – May 19X7	
	£
Actual marginal cost of production (£1,599,000 + £249,600)	1,848,600
Material price variance	39,000 (A)
Material usage variance	40,000 (A)
Labour rate variance	15,600 (A)
Labour efficiency variance	6,000 (A)
Standard marginal cost of production (9,500 units x £184)	1,748,000

Key: A = adverse

Task 2

(a) **Calculation of variances attributable to the special order**

	Litres	
Material purchased (1,500 units x 8 litres x [10/8])	15,000	
Standard usage (1,500 units x 8 litres)	12,000	
Excess usage (litres)	3,000	
Material usage variance (£20 x 3,000 litres)	£60,000	(A)
Material price variance (15,000 litres x [£22 – £20])	£30,000	(A)
Labour rate variance (1,500 x 4 hours x £6 x 50%)	£18,000	(A)

(b) **Revised standard price based on current index**

		£	
(i)	Revised standard price (247.2/240.0) x £20	20.60	
	Original standard (given in task)	20.00	
	Difference	0.60	
(ii)	Effect on original material price variance ([78,000 – 15,000] litres x £0.60)*	37,800	(A)

*Actual purchase = 78,000 litres. Purchases for special order = 15,000 litres.

Part (c)

Revised standard marginal costing statement for Beta production – May 19X7		
	£	£
Actual marginal cost of production		1,848,600
Variances from factors outside departmental control		
Special order		
Material usage variance	(60,000) (A)	
Material price variance	(30,000) (A)	
Labour rate variance	(18,000) (A)	
	(108,000) (A)	
Out of date standard material price	(37,800) (A)	
		(145,800) (A)
Variances under departmental control		
Material price variance (39,000 – 30,000 – 37,800)	28,800 (F)	
Material usage variance (40,000 – 60,000)	20,000 (F)	
Labour rate variance (15,600 – 18,000)	2,400 (F)	
Labour efficiency variance (as above)	(6,000) (A)	
		45,200 (F)
Standard marginal cost of production		1,748,000
Key: A = adverse, F = favourable		

(d)

| **To:** | Richard Hill | **Date:** | 18 June 19X7 |

From:　　The Management Accountant

Subject:　　**Variances arising outside your control**

Justification for showing the variances separately

Within the original divisional adverse variance of £100,600, £108,000 arose because of the acceptance of the special order by Malton's sales director and £37,800 arose because of a general increase in material prices. Although these originated in your division, neither were *caused* by the division. Because you have no responsibility for these variances, you cannot control them and so they are reported separately from those variances you can control and be held responsible for.

Possible action to be taken

The adverse variance arising from the general increase in prices suggests that the standard cost of the materials needs revising. Before doing this, however, the company should check that the index is an appropriate one for the material used in Beta production and that there is not a cheaper and better alternative source of supply.

The adverse variance arising from the special order should first be compared with the overall profitability of that order. If, after charging the variances to the order, it was still profitable then the variances, by ignoring the revenue aspect, might be sending out a false signal. If the adverse variances made the special order unprofitable then the consequences of this should be made known to the sales director to prevent similar losses being incurred in the future. Secondly, it might be useful to discuss with the sales director whether advance warning of extra orders could be given in the future as this would, at least, enable materials to be sourced from the normal supplier at the normal cost.

6.6　Significant variables

(a)　**Factors which determine the significance of variances**

- (i)　*Sign* – adverse variances may be considered important at smaller levels than favourable variances because of their negative effect on profit.

- (ii)　*Monetary amount* – the absolute size of a variance may make it material in the context of the company or department.

- (iii)　*Relative size* – the magnitude of a variance relative to the standard or budget should be considered.

- (iv)　*Trend* – a constant trend of favourable or adverse variances indicates a significant change in the production process, unlike variances which keep changing sign and may be random.

(b) **Identification of significant variances**

    (i)   *£ and % limits* – those variances which exceed a % of standard and/or a monetary amount are investigated.

    (ii)   *Cost benefit test* – investigate only where the expected benefit exceeds the expected cost.

(c) **Planning and operational variances**

This subdivision highlights those variances due to poor budgeting and those which reflect genuine operating performance. Focus would then usually be concentrated on the operational variances as they may represent inefficiencies which should be eliminated.

6.7 Ruggerball Ltd

(a) **Production during power shortages**

    (i)   **Budgeted and actual contributions for period 7**

	£	£	£
Budgeted contribution			24,000
Sales margin variances (W1)		4,000 (F)	
– Price			
– Volume			
Lost through power cuts	9,600		
Gained through labour efficiency	(1,600)		
		8,000 (A)	
			(4,000)
			20,000

	Favourable	Adverse	
Cost variances			
Materials (W2)			
– Price – Bladders		800	
– Leather		5,733	
– Usage – Leather	2,533		
Labour (W3)			
– Rate of pay		500	
– Idle time due to power cuts		1,800	
– Efficiency	300		
	2,833	8,833	6,000
Actual contribution			14,000

Workings

1   Sales margin variances

(Expected production based on reduced hours = 60% × 6,000 = 3,600 balls)

–	Price variance 4,000 at (£9 – £8)	£4,000 (F)
–	Volume variance (6,000 – 4,000) at £4	£8,000 (A)

	£
Lost through power cuts (40% x 6,000) at £4	9,600 (A)
Gained through efficiency (4,000 – 3,600) at £4	1,600 (F)
	8,000 (A)

2   Materials variances

	£
– *Price*	
Actual cost of bladders used	2,800
Standard cost 4,000 at 50p	2,000
	800 (A)
Actual cost of leather used	13,333
Standard cost 100 at £76	7,600
	5,733 (A)
Note. Actual cost of packing materials	867
Standard cost $\frac{4,000}{6,000}$ x £1,300	867
	–

	Bales
– *Usage*	
Actual usage of leather for 4,000 balls	100
Standard usage of leather (4,000 ÷ 6,000) x 200	133 $\frac{1}{3}$
	33 $\frac{1}{3}$
At £76 per bale	£2,533 (F)

3   Labour variances

–	Rate of pay: 5,000 hours at 10p	£500 (A)

–	Idle time due to power cuts
	40% x 5,000 hours = 2,000 hours at 90p £1,800 (A)

–   Efficiency

	Hours
Actual hours (based on reduced time)	3,000
Standard hours for 4,000 units	
(4,000 ÷ 6,000) x 5,000 hours)	3,333
	333
At 90p per hour	£300 (F)

(ii)   Comment

The adverse leather price variance combined with the favourable leather usage variance suggest that the firm may possibly be using a higher grade of leather than that envisaged when the budget was constructed. If this is the case and the higher selling price can be attributed to the better quality leather then the change in policy has resulted in a small gain to the firm (£4,000 + £2,533) – £5,733 = £800

If additionally, the increased labour efficiency was attributable to the higher grade of leather used, then the £1,900 gain shown due to labour efficiency would be a direct consequence of the change in material quality. This illustrates the importance of management flexibility under changing economic circumstances and indicates the problems (and importance) of attributing variances to causes on a total basis, rather than the conventional fragmented approach.

(b)   Investigation decision

The expected cost of investigation is given by:

Cost of investigation + cost of correction when required   =   £(160 + (0.4 × 350))

                                              =   £300

The expected saving to be made would not be greater than 0.4 × £600 = £240

Therefore if expected values are the criterion to be used, this variance is not worth investigating.

6.8   Mel Donte

Part (a)

	Dec	Jan	Feb
Productivity variance			
Actual production in standard hours	6,600	6,700	6,800
Actual hours worked	6,900	7,200	7,500
	300 (A)	500 (A)	700 (A)
x £3.75 per hour	£1,125 (A)	£1,875 (A)	£2,625 (A)
Excess idle time variance			
Actual idle hours	1,700	1,200	1,400
Standard idle hours	1,720	1,680	1,780
	20 (F)	480 (F)	380 (F)
x £3.75 per hour	£75 (F)	£1,800 (F)	£1,425 (F)
Rate of pay variance			
Actual hours paid for	8,600	8,400	8,900
	£	£	£
Standard cost at £3 per hour	25,800	25,200	26,700
Actual wages	26,660	27,300	28,925
	860 (A)	2,100 (A)	2,225 (A)

(b)   Percentage variances

(i)   Productivity $\dfrac{1,125}{6,600\times3.75}\times100$ $\dfrac{1,875}{6,700\times3.75}\times100$ $\dfrac{2,625}{6,800\times3.75}\times100$

= 4.5% A   = 7.5% A   = 10.3% A

(ii)   Excess idle time $\dfrac{20}{1,720}\times100$ $\dfrac{480}{1,680}\times100$ $\dfrac{380}{1,780}\times100$

= 1.2% F   = 28.6% F   = 21.3% F

(iii)   Rate of pay $\dfrac{860}{25,800}\times100$ $\dfrac{2,100}{25,200}\times100$ $\dfrac{2,225}{26,700}\times100$

= 3.3% A   = 8.3% A   = 8.3% A

(c)   An examination of variances expressed in absolute terms may not give much indication of the trend of variations or whether the variances are significant in the context of the total amounts being spent.

By expressing each variance as a percentage of some base, such as the standard cost, then both trend and materiality will become more evident.

Both of these characteristics should be important to management when deciding whether to investigate a variance and the production process which gave rise to it. A discernible trend could suggest either that the standard is wrong or out of date, or that there is a fault on the production process which should be rectified. The materiality of the variance will help to decide whether the benefits of investigation outweigh the costs.

The figures for November to February reveal worsening productivity, a reduction in excess idle time and an increase in wage rates paid.

Whilst many explanations are possible it is likely that these variances are interdependent. In order to improve productivity and cut idle time, wage rates have been raised. However, productivity has not improved and this may be due to other factors outside the control of the workforce. Sub-standard materials could be the cause.

CHAPTER 8

Performance Indicators (Questions)

8.1 Bracknell Investments plc

You are the assistant to the management accountant of Bracknell Investments plc. You have been asked by her to prepare a preliminary memorandum to help her report to the directors on a possible acquisition of two companies in the stationery supply industry, Chasuble Ltd and Prism Ltd.

The only information which you are so far able to obtain is a copy of the latest profit and loss account balance sheet of each company, both for the year ended 30 June 19X6 (see below).

PROFIT AND LOSS ACCOUNTS

	Chasuble Ltd		Prism Ltd	
	£000	£000	£000	£000
Turnover		638		493
Cost of sales		331		297
Gross profit		307		196
Administrative expenses	99		46	
Distribution costs	36		29	
		135		75
Operating profit before tax		172		121
Taxation		21		22
Profit after taxation		151		99
Proposed dividend		50		40
Retained profit for the year		101		59
Retained profit brought forward		60		7
Retained profit carried forward		161		66

BALANCE SHEETS

	Chasuble Ltd		Prism Ltd	
	£000	£000	£000	£000
Fixed assets				
Land and buildings		97		43
Fixtures and equipment		28		17
Motor vehicles		73		51
		198		111
Current assets				
Stocks	60		58	
Debtors	35		43	
Cash at bank	2		–	
	97		101	
Creditors: Amounts falling due within one year				
Trade creditors	24		34	
Proposed dividend	50		40	
Taxation	10		12	
Bank overdraft	–		10	
	84		96	
		13		5
Total assets less current liabilities		211		116
Creditors: Amounts falling due after more than one year				
Debentures		–		20
		211		96
Capital and reserves				
Share capital		50		30
Profit and loss account		161		66
		211		96

Required

Draft a memorandum to the management accountant on the comparative profitability and liquidity of the two companies.

Include in your report:

(a)   appropriate accounting ratios

(b)   brief comments on these ratios

(c)   an indication of possible reasons why one company might be preferable to the other as an investment.

8.2 Flabaga Ltd

The directors of Flabaga Ltd have asked you to report on the draft accounts of the company for the two years ended 30 June 19X1 and 30 June 19X2, which show the following:

TRADING AND PROFIT AND LOSS ACCOUNTS

	19X1		19X2	
	£000	£000	£000	£000
Turnover		6,500		7,800
Less: Cost of sales				
Opening stock	180		220	
Purchases	5,240		6,478	
	5,420		6,698	
Closing stock	(220)		(380)	
		5,200		6,318
Gross profit		1,300		1,482
Less: Administrative expenses	715		936	
Distribution costs	390		468	
		1,105		1,404
Net profit before taxation		195		78
Less: Taxation		14		22
Net profit after taxation		181		56
Less: Dividends paid and proposed		50		20
Retained profit for the year		131		36
Retained profit brought forward		125		256
Retained profit carried forward		256		292

BALANCE SHEETS

	19X1		19X2	
	£000	£000	£000	£000
Fixed assets at net book value		260		281
Current assets				
Stock	220		380	
Debtors	714		1,138	
Cash at bank	21		–	
	955		1,518	
Creditors: Amounts falling due within one year				
Trade creditors	472		713	
Taxation	17		26	
Proposed dividends	40		–	
Bank overdraft	–		178	
	529		917	
Net current assets		426		601
		686		882
Share capital				
Issued and fully paid				
Ordinary shares of £1 each		300		400
15% preference shares of £1 each		50		60
		350		460
Reserves				
Share premium	–		50	
Capital reserve	80		80	
Profit and loss account	256		292	
		336		422
		686		882

Required

Comment critically on the company's results and its liquidity, using whichever accounting and management ratios you consider appropriate.

8.3 Thabwik Ltd

The following summarised balance sheets relate to Thabwik Ltd:

	31.12.X7	31.12.X8
	£000	£000
Freehold property, at cost	300	375
Equipment, at cost less depreciation	324	430
Stock, at cost	130	208
Debtors	56	50
Cash at bank	24	–
	834	1,063
Share capital (£1 shares)	400	500
Share premium	–	20
Revenue reserves	258	296
Creditors	36	70
Taxation	120	110
Proposed dividend	20	35
Bank overdraft	–	32
	834	1,063

The abridged profit and loss accounts were:

	19X7		19X8	
	£000	£000	£000	£000
Turnover		1,500		2,000
Trading profit		250		228
Taxation		(120)		(110)
Profit after tax		130		118
Dividends: Paid	40		45	
Proposed	20		35	
		(60)		(80)
Profits retained		70		38

Note. Thabwik Ltd runs a chain of retail shops. The industry average for profit margins is 8% and for return on capital employed 18%.

Required

(a) Explain in what circumstances a bank overdraft might be regarded as part of capital employed.

(b) Assuming that the bank overdraft is *not* part of capital employed, calculate *five* important ratios for 19X7 and 19X8.

Briefly indicate the usefulness of each ratio and the conclusions which could be drawn from your calculations.

8.4 Minimodels plc

The balance sheet of Minimodels plc, a toy manufacturer, as at 31 December 19X5, was as follows:

	£m	£m
Fixed assets		
Intangible assets – Goodwill		1.9
Tangible assets		12.0
Investments		0.5
		14.4
Current assets		
Stocks	11.9	
Debtors	11.7	
Cash at bank and in hand	0.3	
	23.9	
Creditors: Amounts falling due within one year		
Bank loans and overdrafts	7.2	
Trade creditors	8.9	
Other creditors including taxation and social security	0.4	
Dividends	0.7	
	17.2	
Net current assets		6.7
Total assets less current liabilities		21.1
Creditors: Amounts falling due after more than one year		
Debenture loans		6.0
		15.1

Capital and reserves	£m
Called–up share capital	5.0
Profit and loss account	8.9
	13.9
Minority interest	1.2
	15.1

Turnover during the year 19X5 was £39 million (19X4 £42m). In the first half of 19X6, turnover was £12 million (19X5 £13m).

Cost of sales during 19X5 was £23.4 million (19X4 £24.7m).

Stock at 31 December 19X4 was £2.1 million. Stock is stated at cost (including appropriate production overheads).

Required

(a)   Compute the current ratio of Minimodels plc at 31 December 19X5.

(b)   Briefly, what is the purpose of the current ratio and how may it vary with the nature of the business concerned?

(c)   What subsidiary ratios may usefully be computed which will enable an analyst to form a judgement as to the working capital structure? Illustrate their computation using the balance sheet and other data for Minimodels plc.

(d)   'On the basis that turnover in 19X5 was £39 million, and debtors at 31 December 19X5 £11.7m, the collection period of Minimodels plc is 109.5 days, which is clearly excessive'. Comment on this analysis.

(e)   Comment on the major weakness (apart from debt collection) apparent from the accounts of Minimodels plc.

8.5   Traders plc (AAT D95)

Data

You are the assistant management accountant to Traders plc, a small retailing chain, and you have just left a meeting with the company's managing director who is concerned about the threat posed by the superior profitability of a major competitor, Sellars plc. Sellars have just published their annual report which shows profits of £1,956,760 generated by shareholder's funds of £5,765,000. A board meeting has been called for two weeks' time to discuss the board's development of a strategy to meet this threat. The summarised profit and loss accounts and balance sheets for both companies are reproduced below.

TRADING AND PROFIT AND LOSS ACCOUNTS FOR THE YEAR ENDED 30 JUNE 19X5			*BALANCE SHEETS AS AT 30 JUNE 19X5*		
	Traders plc	Sellars plc		Traders plc	Sellars plc
	£	£		£	£
Turnover	24,000,000	26,800,000	Fixed assets (see note 1)	4,320,000	5,270,000
Cost of sales	18,000,000	19,564,000	Net current assets	1,500,000	1,995,000
Gross profit	6,000,000	7,236,000	Total assets	5,820,000	7,265,000
Administration expenses	4,060,000	4,330,000	Long–term loans		1,500,000
Operating profit	1,940,000	2,906,000		5,820,000	5,765,000
Interest		150,000	Financed by:		
Profit before taxation	1,940,000	2,756,000	Shareholders' funds	5,820,000	5,765,000
Taxation	640,200	799,240			
Profit after taxation	1,299,800	1,956,760			
Dividends	800,000	1,200,000	Number of employees	170	200
Retained profits	499,800	756,760			

Note 1

		Traders plc			**Sellars plc**	
Fixed assets	Cost	Accumulated depreciation	Net book value	Cost	Accumulated depreciation	Net book value
	£	£	£	£	£	£
Land and buildings	5,000,000	1,200,000	3,800,000	12,000,000	7,200,000	4,800,000
Fixtures and fittings	800,000	480,000	320,000	700,000	350,000	350,000
Motor vehicles	400,000	200,000	200,000	600,000	480,000	120,000
Total	6,200,000	1,880,000	4,320,000	13,300,000	8,030,000	5,270,000

	Land and buildings	Fixtures and fittings	Motor vehicles	Land and buildings	Fixtures and fittings	Motor vehicles
Depreciation charge for the year	£100,000	£160,000	£100,000	£240,000	£70,000	£120,000

Task 1

The management accountant of Traders plc has already analysed your company's results focusing on six key ratios. These are:

Return on capital employed (before interest and taxation)	33.33%
Gross profit margin	25%
Net (or sales) margin (before interest and taxation)	8.08%
Asset turnover	4.12 times
Turnover per employee	£141,176
Average age of working capital	30 days

The average age of working capital is defined as $\dfrac{\text{Working capital}}{\text{Cost of sales}} \times 365$

Required

As the assistant management accountant to Traders plc, you are asked to calculate the above ratios for Sellars plc. Present your results in the form of a table alongside the ratios for your own company.

Task 2

The turnover for Traders plc for the year to 30 June 19X4 was £23,000,000. A trade association index of retail prices stood at 224.50 for June 19X4 and 237.90 for June 19X5.

In anticipation of the board meeting, prepare a briefing paper for circulation to the directors of Traders plc.

Your paper should:

(a)   Explain *in outline* the meaning and limitations of each ratio, making use of the given data where possible.

(b)   Comment on any strengths and weaknesses found within Traders plc.

(c)   Use the trade association's statistics to show the percentage growth in Traders' sales volume since last year.

(d)   Suggest two reasons why your estimate of sales volume growth might not be accurate.

8.6   Middle plc (AAT D96)

Data

Middle plc owns two subsidiaries, East Ltd and West Ltd, producing soft drinks. Both companies rent their premises and both use plant of similar size and technology. Middle plc requires the plant in the subsidiaries to be written off over ten years using straight-line depreciation and assuming zero residual values.

East Ltd was established five years ago but West Ltd has only been established for two years. Goods returned by customers generally arise from quality failures and are destroyed. Financial and other data relating to the two companies are reproduced below.

	PROFIT AND LOSS ACCOUNTS YEAR TO 30 NOVEMBER 19X6			*BALANCE SHEETS EXTRACT AT 30 NOVEMBER 19X6*	
	West Ltd	*East Ltd*		*West Ltd*	*East Ltd*
	£000	*£000*		*£000*	*£000*
Turnover	18,000	17,600	Plant	16,000	10,000
Less Returns	90	176	Depreciation to date	3,200	5,000
Net turnover	17,910	17,424	Net book value	12,800	5,000
Material	2,000	2,640	Current assets	4,860	3,000
Labour	4,000	4,840	Current liabilities	(2,320)	(1,500)
Production overheads*	3,000	3,080			
			Net assets	15,340	6,500
Gross profit	8,910	6,864			
Marketing	2,342	1,454			
Research and development	1,650	1,010			
Training	950	450			
Administration	900	1,155			
Operating profit	3,068	2,795			

*includes plant depreciation of £1,600,000 for West Ltd and £1,000,000 for East LtdW

Other data (000s litres)	West Ltd	East Ltd
Gross sales	20,000	22,000
Returns	100	220
Net sales	19,900	21,780
Orders received in year	20,173	22,854

You are employed by Middle plc as a member of a team monitoring the performance of subsidiaries within the group. Middle plc aims to provide its shareholders with the best possible return for their investment and to meet customers' expectations. It does this by comparing the performance of subsidiaries and using the more efficient ones for benchmarking.

Task 1

Your team leader, Angela Wade, has asked you to prepare a report evaluating the performance of West Ltd and East Ltd. Your report should:

(a) calculate and explain the meaning of the following financial ratios for each company:

   (i)   the return on capital employed

   (ii) the asset turnover

   (iii) the sales (or operating profit) margin

(b) calculate the percentage of faulty sales as a measure of the level of customer service for each company

(c) identify one other possible measure of the level of customer service which could be derived from the accounting data

(d) identify *two* limitations to your analysis in part (a), using the data in the accounts.

Data

Peter Smith has recently been appointed as the chief executive to a charity undertaking scientific research. Previously, he had been a marketing manager for many years in a private sector commercial company.

The legal document establishing the charity states that it should operate in an efficient and effective manner. Peter Smith is unsure what these terms mean and has invited you, as a representative of the charity's auditors, to talk to his staff about efficiency and effectiveness in not-for-profit organisations.

Task 2

In preparing for the talk, you are asked to write a *brief* note. In the note you should:

(a) define what is meant by efficiency and effectiveness

(b) identify and justify *one* major way of measuring efficiency in commercial organisations

(c) explain why your chosen measure may not be appropriate in not-for-profit organisations

(d) suggest a substitute measure and comment on its limitations.

8.7 Grand Hotel (AAT D97)

The Grand Hotel is a privately-owned hotel and restaurant located in a major business and tourist centre. Because of this, demand for accommodation is spread evenly throughout the year. However, in order to increase overall demand, the Grand Hotel has recently joined World Rest, an association of similar hotels. World Rest publicises member hotels throughout the world and provides advice and control to ensure common standards amongst its members. In addition, it provides overall performance indicators by location and category of hotel, allowing members to compare their own performance.

You are employed by Green and Co, the Grand Hotel's auditors, and your firm has been asked to calculate the hotel's performance statistics required by World Rest. A colleague informs you that the Grand Hotel:

♦ operates for 365 days of the year

♦ has 80 double or twin bedrooms

♦ charges £80 per night for each bedroom

♦ charges guests separately for any meals taken.

Your colleague also gives you a copy of World Rest's performance indicators' manual. The manual details the performance indicators required and gives guidance on their calculation. The relevant performance indicators and a summary of Grand Hotel's latest set of accounts are reproduced below.

Extract from World Rest's Performance Indicators Manual

Indicator	*Definitions*
Maximum occupancy	Number of days in year × number of bedrooms
Occupancy rate	Annual total of rooms let per night as percentage of maximum occupancy
Gross margin: accommodation	Contribution from accommodation ÷ accommodation turnover
Gross margin: restaurant	Contribution from restaurant ÷ restaurant turnover
Operating profit: hotel	Profit before interest but after all other expenses
Sales margin: hotel	Operating profit ÷ total turnover
Return on capital employed: hotel	Operating profit ÷ net assets
Asset turnover: hotel	Standard definition

GRAND HOTEL

Profit and loss account – 12 months ended 30 November 19X7

	Accommodation £	Restaurant £	Total £
Turnover	1,635,200	630,720	2,265,920
Variable costs	1,308,160	473,040	1,781,200
Contribution	327,040	157,680	484,720

Fixed costs

Depreciation – land and buildings	24,000
Depreciation – fixtures and fittings	29,000
Administration	160,224
Rates and insurance	158,200
Debenture interest	80,000

Profit for the year	33,296

Extract from the balance sheet at 30 November 19X7

	Land and buildings £	Fixtures and fittings £	Total £
Fixed assets			
Net book value	1,200,000	145,000	1,345,000
Net current assets			
Debtors		594,325	
Cash		88,125	
Creditors		(611,250)	
			71,200
Net assets			1,416,200

Task 1

Your colleague asks you to calculate the performance indicators specified in the World Rest Manual for the Grand Hotel using the definitions laid down by World Rest.

Data

A few days later you receive a letter from Claire Hill, the manager of the Grand Hotel. She enclosed a summary sent to her by the World Rest organisation showing the average performance indicators for hotels in similar categories and locations. This is reproduced below.

World Rest Hotel Association Performance Summary	
Location Code B *Category Code 4*	
Occupancy rate	80%
Gross margin – accommodation	22%
Gross margin – restaurant	20%
Sales margin – hotel	10%
Return on capital employed – hotel	20%
Asset turnover – hotel	2 times

In her letter to you, Claire Hill expresses her concern about the performance of the Grand Hotel and provides you with the following information.

♦ The restaurant is currently working at maximum capacity. Any volume improvement must, therefore, come from the accommodation side of the hotel's activities.

♦ It is not possible to change the level of the fixed assets nor the net current assets without adversely affecting the business.

Claire Hill proposes increasing the return on capital employed to 20% by

♦ increasing the occupancy rate to 80% of capacity while maintaining current prices; and

♦ increasing restaurant prices by 5% while decreasing the restaurant's variable costs by 5% without any change in demand.

Task 2

Write a letter to Claire Hill. Your letter should include the following.

(a) Calculate the operating profit required on the existing capital employed to give a 20% return.

(b) Show the revised profit of the Grand Hotel if she achieves *both* her proposed occupancy rate and her proposed changes to the restaurant's pricing and costing structure.

(c) List the following revised performance indicators assuming her proposals are achieved without changing the amount of the capital employed

♦ return on capital employed

♦ asset turnover

♦ sales margin

(d) Use the performance indicators calculated in (c) to suggest

(i) what proportion of the planned increase in profits is due to the increased occupancy rates and what proportion is due to the change in the restaurant's pricing and costing structure

(ii) one possible area of investigation if profits are to be further increased.

8.8   Student Housing Society (AAT J98)

Data

You work as an accounting technician with the Student Housing Society. The Student Housing Society is a registered charity, formed to provide low-cost accommodation for students. The accommodation consists of 100 student bedrooms. The invoiced rent per bedroom is £2,400 per year.

Following the resignation of the previous manager, Helen Brown has recently been appointed as the general manager to the housing society. The society has laid down the following financial objectives for managing the society.

♦   The affairs of the society must be carried out in an efficient and effective manner

♦   The society must attempt to achieve a return on its net assets of between 6% and 8%

♦   The annual operating surplus should be at least 15% but no more than 20% of rents receivable

♦   The general manager should attempt to achieve a 95% occupancy rate

♦   The target average age of rent arrears should be no more than one month

♦   In order to avoid liquidity problems, the year end cash and bank balance should be sufficient to meet the payment of two months' expenses

In a few days time, the Student Housing Society is due to hold its annual general meeting and an extract from the accounts for the year to 31 May 19X8 is reproduced below.

Operating statement for the year ended 31 May 19X8

	£	£
Rent receivable		192,000
Expenses		
Cleaning	16,000	
Lighting and heating	4,800	
Maintenance	11,200	
Rates payable	76,000	
Amortisation	14,000	
Administration costs	58,000	
		(180,000)
Operating surplus		12,000

Balance sheet extract at 31 May 19X8

	Cost £	Accumulated amortisation £	Net book value £
Fixed assets			
Land	200,000	–	200,000
Buildings	700,000	336,000	364,000
	900,000	336,000	564,000
Net current assets			
Debtors (Note)		48,000	
Cash and bank		4,500	
Creditors		(16,500)	
			36,000
Net assets			600,000

Note. Debtors arise entirely from arrears of rent.

Task 1

Helen Brown wishes to know whether or not the charity has achieved the financial objectives laid down and asks you to calculate the following performance indicators in preparation for the annual general meeting.

(a)   The return on net assets

(b)   The operating surplus as a percentage of rents receivable

(c)   The occupancy rate for the society

(d)   The average age of rent arrears in months

(e)   The number of months that expenses could be paid from the cash and bank balance.

Data

On receiving your calculations, Helen Brown discovers that the housing society has failed to meet all its objectives. Helen has previously worked in a commercial organisation and is uncertain how an organisation can be both efficient and effective while restricting the return on net assets and operating surplus margins. She also needs to make proposals at the annual general meeting which will ensure that all of the objectives are met next year. Helen believes it is possible to:

◆   achieve the 95% occupancy rate

◆   reduce the average age of rent arrears to the one month laid down in the objectives.

Helen Brown wants to know the effect on the other performance indicators if these two objectives had been achieved this year. She gives you the following information.

♦ The only marginal or variable costs relate to cleaning, lighting and heating, and maintenance

♦ All other expenses are fixed costs

♦ The creditors entirely relate to rates payable and administration costs

♦ The figure for creditors would not change with any change in occupancy rates.

Task 2

Write a memo to Helen Brown. Your memo should set out the following.

(a) Identify the revised operating surplus if a 95% occupancy rate had been achieved.

(b) Show the value of debtors and cash as a result of achieving the 95% occupancy rate and the one month average age of rent arrears.

(c) Assuming the occupancy rate is 95% and the average age of rent arrears is one month, use your answers to parts (a) and (b) of this task to calculate:

  (i) the revised return on net assets

  (ii) the revised operating surplus as a percentage of rents receivable

  (iii) the number of months that expenses could be paid from the revised cash and bank balance

(d) Briefly explain:

  (i) what is meant by efficiency

  (ii) what is meant by effectiveness

  (iii) why the return on net assets might not be an appropriate measure of efficiency for the housing society.

CHAPTER 8

Performance Indicators (Answers)

8.1 Bracknell Investments plc

Outline answer

Memorandum/addressee/heading etc.

(a) **Ratios**

Profitability			*Chasuble Ltd*	*Prism Ltd*
(i)	Gross profit margin	$\dfrac{\text{GP}}{\text{Sales}}$	$\dfrac{307}{638} = 48.1\%$	$\dfrac{196}{493} = 39.8\%$
(ii)	Net profit margin	$\dfrac{\text{Op profit}}{\text{Sales}}$	$\dfrac{172}{638} = 27.0\%$	$\dfrac{121}{493} = 24.6\%$
(iii)	Asset turnover	$\dfrac{\text{Sales}}{\text{Cap employed}}$	$\dfrac{638}{211} = 3.0$	$\dfrac{493}{116} = 4.25$
(iv)	ROCE	$\dfrac{\text{Op profit}}{\text{Cap employed}}$	$\dfrac{172}{211} = 81.5\%$	$\dfrac{121}{116} = 104.3\%$
(v)	Stock turnover	$\dfrac{\text{Cost of sales}}{\text{Stock}}$	$\dfrac{331}{60} = 5.5$	$\dfrac{297}{58} = 5.1$

Liquidity				
(i)	Current ratio	$\dfrac{\text{CA}}{\text{CL}}$	$\dfrac{97}{84} = 1.2$	$\dfrac{101}{96} = 1.0$
(ii)	Acid test ratio	$\dfrac{\text{CA} - \text{stock}}{\text{CL}}$	$\dfrac{37}{84} = 0.4$	$\dfrac{43}{96} = 0.4$
(ii)	Average debtors' collection period	$\dfrac{\text{Debtors}}{\text{Av daily sales}}$	$\dfrac{35}{1.75} = 20$ days	$\dfrac{43}{1.35} = 32$ days
(iv)	Stock ratio	$\dfrac{\text{Stock}}{\text{CA}}$	$\dfrac{60}{97} = 61.9\%$	$\dfrac{58}{101} = 57.4\%$

(b)   **Comments**

(i)   *Profitability*

Chasuble Ltd ('C') has better GP and NP margins than Prism Ltd ('P'), but P appears to be more efficient at using its assets than C.

Difference in GP margins more marked than in NP margins: C may be better at controlling direct costs than overheads; and P vice versa. More information is needed about comparative volumes of sales and any significant differences in type of products sold.

P has less investment in fixed assets (in particular, cheaper premises), and is better able to use its assets to generate turnover. (Note. This would not be true if the reason for P's low figure of land and buildings is simply that no recent valuation has been carried out.)

With this rate of ROCE P may deliberately be able to take lower, more competitive profit margins. A comparison of selling prices charged for a selection of familiar products would be interesting.

Stock turnover perhaps rather low in both companies, particularly in view of the poor liquidity of both.

(ii)   *Liquidity*

C slightly more liquid than P but not much in it.

Both companies appear to be proposing excessive dividends, not as far as profit available is concerned but through lack of liquid funds.

High ROCEs coupled with low liquidity could indicate that both companies are over-trading, P rather more than C.

Stocks high in both companies relative to working capital: taken together with lowish stock turnover this makes over-trading even more likely.

P in perhaps a worse position than C: current ratio worse, bank overdraft in existence, and longer debtors' collection period.

(c) **Comparison of the two companies as investments**

Both companies are profitable and could benefit from an injection of capital to improve liquidity, and careful management to maintain it.

Chasuble Ltd   –   Higher profit margins

       –   Slightly more liquid

       –   More valuable fixed assets which could perhaps be used to even greater effect

Prism Ltd   –   Better use of assets

       –   Perhaps a better return on a small investment, although greater risk in the first place

8.2 Flabaga Ltd

Ratios

(a) **Profitability**

	19X1	19X2
Gross profit % $\left(\dfrac{GP}{sales} \times 100\%\right)$	$\dfrac{1,300}{6,500} \times 100 = 20\%$	$\dfrac{1,482}{7,800} \times 100 = 19\%$
Net profit % $\left(\dfrac{NPBT}{sales} \times 100\%\right)$	$\dfrac{195}{6,500} \times 100 = 3\%$	$\dfrac{78}{7,800} \times 100 = 1\%$
Asset turnover $\dfrac{sales}{CE}$	$\dfrac{6,500}{686} = 9.5$ times	$\dfrac{7,800}{882} = 8.8$ times
ROCE $\left(\dfrac{NPBT}{CE} \times 100\%\right)$	$\dfrac{195}{686} \times 100 = 28.4\%$	$\dfrac{78}{882} \times 100 = 8.8\%$
Stock turnover (give equal credit for using closing stock) $\left(\dfrac{cost\ of\ sales}{average\ stock}\right)$	$\dfrac{5,200}{200} = 26$ times	$\dfrac{6,318}{300} = 21$ times

(b) **Liquidity**

Current ratio $\dfrac{CA}{CL}$	$\dfrac{955}{529} = 1.8$ times	$\dfrac{1,518}{917} = 1.7$ times
Acid test/quick ratio $\dfrac{CA - stock}{CL}$	$\dfrac{(955 - 220)}{529}$	$\dfrac{(1,518 - 380)}{917}$
	1.4 times	1.2 times

	19X1	*19X2*
Stocks to NCA $\left(\dfrac{\text{Stock}}{\text{NCA}} \times 100\%\right)$	$\dfrac{220}{426} \times 100 = 51.6\%$	$\dfrac{380}{601} \times 100 = 63.2\%$

Average collection period

$$\dfrac{\text{debtors}}{\text{ave daily sales}} \qquad \dfrac{714}{6,500/365} = 40.1 \text{ days} \qquad \dfrac{1,138}{7,800/365} = 53.3 \text{ days}$$

Creditors period

$$\dfrac{\text{creditors}}{\text{ave daily purchases}} \qquad \dfrac{472}{5,240/365} = 32.9 \text{ days} \qquad \dfrac{713}{6,478/365} = 40.2 \text{ days}$$

Comments

(1)   Turnover shows large increase 6,500 to 7,800 – caused by two main factors:

    (a)   reduction in mark-up (GP% 20% to 19%)

    (b)   greater credit facilities given to debtors (collection period 40.1 days to 53.3 days).

(2)   Stock holdings too high in proportion to increase in business:

    (a)   stocks to NCA (51.6% to 63.2%)

    (b)   stock turnover (26 times to 21 times).

(3)   Stock turnover drop might have been caused by:

    (a)   bad debt control (collection period 40.1 days to 53.3 days)

    (b)   bad stock control (stocks to NCA 51.6% to 63.2%)

    (c)   perhaps more extreme than indicated, since mark-down policy should cause increase in stock turnover.

(4)   GP% has dropped by 5% of previous year's level (1%/20%).

NP% has dropped by 66% of previous years level (2%/3%) – indicates overhead expenses have gone out of control, particularly in view of assumed saving in debenture interest.

(5)   ROCE shows fall from 28.4% to 9%, caused more by NP% drop than by asset turnover (9.5 times to 9 times) – indicates company may be using fixed assets relatively efficiently, bearing in mind:

    (a)   re-investment in new assets, which may not be fully on stream yet

    (b)   bad use of stocks and debtors.

(6)   Liquidity

(a)   current ratio dropped (1.8 to 1.6)

(b)   acid test dropped (1.39 to 1.21) less in proportion

(c)   although company less liquid in overall terms, short-term solvency has not suffered as much

(d)   can be demonstrated using creditors payment period ratio (32.9 days to 40.2 days) that company is taking more advantage of credit facilities

(e)   compensates somewhat for bad debtor collection and bad stock control.

8.3   Thabwik Ltd

(a)   The bank overdraft could be regarded as capital employed if it is *effectively long term*. If this is the case the calculation for return on capital employed is:

Note. The overdraft is repayable on demand, therefore strictly speaking a current liability. However, if regularly re-negotiated it becomes long-term finance.

(b)   **Five ratios**

	19X7	*19X8*
Return on capital employed	$\dfrac{250}{658} = 38.0\%$	$\dfrac{228}{816} = 27.9\%$
Asset turnover	$\dfrac{1,500}{658} = 2.28\%$	$\dfrac{2,000}{816} = 2.45\%$
Profit margin	$\dfrac{250}{1,500} = 16.67\%$	$\dfrac{228}{2,000} = 11.4\%$
Liquidity ratio	210:176 1.19:1	258:247 1.04:1
Acid test	80:176 0.45:1	50:247 0.20:1
Dividend cover	$\dfrac{130}{60} = 2.167\%$	$\dfrac{118}{80} = 1.47\%$
Stock turnover	$\dfrac{1,500}{130} = 11$	$\dfrac{2,000}{208} = 9$

Return on capital employed

Usefulness is to check that 'capital' is being profitably employed. Danger is that assets are normally valued at historic cost so that most returns appear better than in fact they are.

As far as Thabwik is concerned, both the 19X7 and 19X8 ratios are well above average; but the reduction from 37.9% to 27.9% would merit enquiry.

Asset turnover

This has actually improved during 19X8 and is above the industry average of 2.25 in both years ($^{18}/8$). It would appear that the company's turnover is reasonable in relation to its assets.

The usefulness of this ratio is to determine whether the assets used are generating sufficient sales.

Profit margin

This is again better than the industry average, but shows an alarming drop from 19X7 to 19X8. This would indicate either an inability to control costs or that gross profit margins have been seriously eroded.

Liquidity ratio/acid test

These ratios indicate the company's ability to meet its short term liabilities out of quickly realisable assets. As this company is a retail store chain, one could imagine that it could convert stock into cash fairly quickly and thus one should not be as alarmed at the low acid ratio as one would be in other types of business.

The expansion programme, which appears to have gone on during the year, has clearly stretched the company considerably. If this has been planned and appropriate overdraft facilities arranged then the company should be viable.

Otherwise the company could well need to arrange long-term finance.

Dividend cover

The usefulness of this ratio is that it indicates to shareholders how safe their dividend is. The greater the cover, the greater the security. The cover for this year seems comparatively low, particularly in view of the heavy investment in plant. The board could well be advised in this situation to reduce the final dividend. This would improve not only the cover but also the liquidity of the company.

Conclusions

Investigate:

(a)   increase in costs

(b)   liquidity

(c)   possibility of reducing dividend.

8.4   Minimodels plc

(a)   Current ratio at 31 December 19X5

$$\frac{\text{Current assets}}{\text{Current liabilities}} = \frac{23.9}{17.2} = 1.39$$

(b)   (i)   Purpose of the current ratio

The *current ratio* is an indicator of the financial soundness and stability of a business. The priority of a business is survival and it cannot survive unless it is able to meet its debts as they become due for payment.

Current assets are those held for conversion into cash in the ordinary course of business. *Current liabilities* are obligations to pay money within 12 months.

By relating those two figures at a particular date one can assess the company's ability to pay debts due within 12 months out of assets which are to be converted into cash in approximately the same time scale.

Current assets include stocks and work in progress which are perhaps the most difficult current asset to convert quickly into cash. It is therefore common to measure the company's immediate ability to pay its debts by computing the *acid test ratio* as follows:

$$\frac{\text{Current assets less stock and work in progress}}{\text{Current liabilities}}$$

Attempts are frequently made to establish a norm for these ratios. For example, what should the current ratio be? It is impossible to state an absolute figure in isolation.

The ratio should be compared year by year within the same company and one would look for a consistent pattern. An industry average would be a useful indicator for a company as it would enable comparison to be made with other companies in the same sector.

Ratios never provide final answers, they can give rise to questions. It is always necessary to relate the figures to previous performance or some external standard.

(ii)   Effect of the nature of the business

The crucial effect of the nature of the business on the current ratio can be illustrated by reference to two elements of working capital.

–   *Stocks*

Manufacturing businesses hold stocks (eg. raw materials, work in progress and finished goods) whereas service companies such as Financial Training tend not to hold stocks.

–　*Debtors*

Businesses who sell for cash (eg. stores and supermarkets) will not have material figures for trade debtors compared with businesses whose sales are principally on credit terms (eg. heavy engineering).

Clearly the current ratios in these types of operation are significantly affected by the nature of the business and this explains why it is necessary to compare current ratios from year to year within the same company or with other companies in the same industry.

(c)　Working capital ratios

It is possible to take an overall view of the level of working capital by computing ratios which link working capital or its constituent elements to other aspects of the business. Having established normal or desired relationships one can monitor deviations from the norm. The object is to establish the causes and effects of these deviations (which may of course be fully justified).

(i)　$\dfrac{\text{Working capital}}{\text{Capital employed}}$ 　　　　　　　　　$\dfrac{6.7}{21.1} = 0.32$

or　$\dfrac{\text{Working capital}}{\text{Tangible fixed assets}}$ 　　　　　$\dfrac{6.7}{12.0} = 0.56$

The implication is that a high proportion of working capital to total capital employed gives the business freedom to adapt to changing circumstances. For example, it might enable a company to boost sales by a temporary reduction of liquidity or to realise assets and invest the proceeds in the most profitable way.

(ii)　Stock turnover ratio

	19X5 £m	19X4 £m
$\dfrac{\text{Cost of sales}}{\text{Stocks and work in progress}}$	$\dfrac{23.4}{11.9} = 2.0$	$\dfrac{24.7}{2.1} = 11.8$

By relating cost of sales to year-end stocks and work in progress, the analyst, who only has access to published information, attempts to assess the effectiveness of the company's control over the stock levels and its ability to generate sales in relation to stocks held.

Published information is deficient here in one principal respect.

No information is disclosed in published accounts about the pattern of sales during the year or about the average level of stocks held during the year. If the business is seasonal it would be helpful to know the average level of stocks held and relate this figure to the cost of goods sold.

(iii)   Average collection period

Sales per day = Sales/Days in year $\dfrac{£39m}{365}$ = £106,850

$\dfrac{\text{Trade debtors}}{\text{Sales per day}}$ $\dfrac{£11.7m}{£106,850}$ = 109.5 days

This ratio, when compared with previous years and with other similar companies, indicates the effectiveness of the company's credit control procedures and adverse movements may suggest the inclusion of bad and doubtful debts in the trade debtors figure. When calculated on the basis of published accounts this ratio requires qualification and these are dealt with in part (d) of this answer.

(d)   Comments on the average collection period

Minimodels plc has a collection period of 109.5 days based on annual turnover £39m and year-end trade debtors £11.7m. This appears to be excessive but like all ratios it must be related to other information. If other toy manufacturers have a similar collection period, Minimodels plc's 109.5 days may appear very long but that may be the norm for that industry.

Ideally the analyst would want more information than is disclosed by published accounts. It would be helpful to know the following details:

(i)   the period of credit offered in the company's terms of trade

(ii)   the analysis of annual turnover between cash sales and credit sales

(iii)   the analysis of annual turnover into monthly/quarterly/half-yearly sales.

If the company is listed on a Stock Exchange, half-yearly sales figures will be announced and quarterly sales figures may also be disclosed by larger groups of companies. It would only be possible as a manager of the business to obtain all the information to enable a proper calculation of the number of days' sales outstanding at the year-end.

This question provides information about the seasonal nature of the company's business; sales in the first half of 19X5 were £13m and doubled in the second half to £26m. For example, if it could be established that the company's normal terms of credit were for example two months and that sales in the fourth quarter of 19X5 were £18m we could recompute the ratio as follows:

Sales per day (over the last quarter) $\dfrac{£18m}{90}$ = £200,000

Collection period $\dfrac{£11.7m}{£200,000}$ = 58.5 days

This calculation demonstrates that the collection period is almost exactly in line with the company's policy whereas using the year-end debtors and *annual* turnover the collection period extends to 109.5 days. This does not mean that credit control is not weak in Minimodels plc, but it is not possible from the published accounts of one year to make a categorical statement about credit control.

(e)   Major weaknesses apparent from the accounts of Minimodels plc

Minimodels plc is a toy manufacturer and one would have expected its stock levels to be relatively low at its year-end because of the seasonal nature of the business. At 31 December 19X4 stocks were valued at £2.1m and one year later they had risen to £11.9m. This occurred in a year when turnover fell from £42m to £39m. One might conclude that the company had been over-producing in 19X5 and the stock/turnover ratio based on year end stocks and the cost of goods sold tends to confirm that conclusion.

One possible explanation for building up stocks at the year-end would be to meet expected demand in the early months of the following year, perhaps to coincide with the launch of a new product or an advertising campaign. However, this is unlikely to be the case with Minimodels plc because its seasonal peak of sales would fall in the final quarter of the year and not in the months of January, February and March.

The question gives a sales figure of £12m for the six months of 19X6. If the cost of producing stock is approximately 60% of selling price (which is the case for both 19X4 and 19X5) the cost of goods sold in the period is £7.2m. This suggests that the stocks valued at £11.97m will easily last the company until the second half of 19X6.

Therefore, it is likely that the company will have to reduce production drastically in 19X6 to avoid holding excessive stocks which are expensive to finance in terms of bank overdraft interest. Redundancies would be an inevitable consequence of major cuts in production and this situation represents a serious threat to the future of the business.

8.5   Traders plc

Task 1

Return on capital employed $\dfrac{£2,906,000}{£7,265,000} \times 100\% = 40\%$

Gross profit margin $\dfrac{£7,236,000}{£26,800,000} \times 100\% = 27\%$

Net margin $\dfrac{£2,906,000}{£26,800,000} \times 100\% = 10.84\%$

Asset turnover $\dfrac{£26,800,000}{£7,265,000} \times 3.69$ times

Turnover per employee $\dfrac{£26,800,000}{200} = £134,000$

Average age of working capital $\dfrac{£1,995,000}{£19,564,000} \times 365 = 37$ days

Comparative performance ratios for 19X5		
	Traders plc	*Sellars plc*
Return on capital employed	33.33%	40.00%
Gross profit margin	25.00%	27.00%
Net (or sales) margin	8.08%	10.84%
Asset turnover	4.12	3.69
Turnover per employee	£141,176	£134,000
Average age of working capital	30 days	37 days

Task 2

(a) and (b) Meaning of the ratios and strengths and weaknesses identified in the analysis

The return on capital employed

The return on capital employed is an overall financial measure of how well the managers of an organisation have used the resources under their control. It is a relative measure which compares the profit generated by management to the total resources they control. On that basis, Sellars appears to have a more efficient management who are able to generate 40p profit for every £1 of financial resource. This compares with only 33.33p per £1 generated by the management of Traders plc. However, the reported difference might result from different accounting policies. For example, both companies appear to be depreciating their land and buildings at 2% per annum based on original cost but Sellars has written off 60% of the cost while Traders have only written off 24%. This suggests that Sellars land and buildings are much older and therefore originally might have cost less. If both companies land and buildings were valued at current costs, it might be that the disparity in performance would be lessened.

The sales margin and asset turnover

The return on capital employed ratio is influenced by two factors; the intensity with which the assets have been used and the margins achieved on sales which have taken place. This is the purpose of the sales margin and the asset turnover ratios. The sales margin ratio identifies profit per pound of sales. The asset turnover ratio shows sales per pound of assets. Either increasing the sales margin – by charging higher prices or reducing costs – or obtaining more sales from the same asset base will improve the overall return on capital employed. Although Sellars is able to squeeze more profit out of each pound of sales than Traders, Traders appears to use its assets more intensively. Care needs to be taken in interpreting these ratios as they may not be independent. An increase in prices – and hence the sales margin – may well lead to a fall-off in sales volume and hence a reduction in the asset turnover. Also the accounting conventions used in valuing the assets might distort the asset turnover ratios whilst different stock valuation and depreciation policies might influence the reported sales margin.

The gross profit margin

The gross profit margin is of particular use in retailing. The gross profit is the difference between the cost of the goods sold and the turnover generated from those sales. From this must be deducted overheads such as light and heating and salaries and wages before determining operating profit. The cost of sales is overwhelmingly a variable cost whilst administrative expenses are predominantly fixed costs. Because of this, the gross profit margin is of particular use in forecasting changes in profitability from changes in sales volume. For example, for every extra pound of sales, Sellars is able to generate 27p extra pre-tax profit whereas our company is only able to generate 25p.

In addition, if both companies have similar pricing policies and range of goods, it might also suggest which company is better able to negotiate favourable terms with suppliers. On that basis, it would appear that Sellars' management are more efficient in negotiating terms with suppliers. On the other hand, it might be that the suppliers terms are very similar but that Traders have lower selling prices as part of its marketing strategy. If that is the case, it might explain why Traders is able to generate more sales per pound of assets employed. To resolve this issue, our company should carry out an analysis of both the pricing policies and the range of goods supplied for each enterprise. This analysis should also consider whether the ratios are influenced by different stock valuation policies in the two companies.

Turnover per employee

The turnover per employee helps to give further insight into how intensively the resources of each company are being used. A particular advantage of the ratio is that it is less influenced by accounting conventions and other distortions. Traders appears to be the more successful of the companies. However, care is required in interpreting the figures as the companies might be operating in different segments of the market requiring different levels of service.

Average age of working capital

Finally, there is the average age of working capital ratio. Working capital represents funds tied up in stocks, debtors and any necessary cash balances less any short-term financing provided by creditors although it is often approximated to current assets less current liabilities. Ideally, there would be no stocks, no debtors and no cash balances with stock being purchased just in time to be sold and sales being for cash which would then be immediately reinvested. This is the logic behind just–in–time stockkeeping.

For our retailing company, profit comes from buying and selling goods, not from holding stocks or cash balances. However, because we do not know exactly what customers require or when they will arrive and, because deliveries can be delayed, we have to hold stocks. Equally, credit may have to be offered and cash kept as a float to enable sales to be made and change given. Working capital control is therefore concerned with minimising funds tied up in net current assets while, at the same time, ensuring sufficient stock, cash and credit facilities are in place to enable trading to take place. This can be achieved by controlling both the levels of current assets and causing suppliers to finance stock holding by the granting of credit.

Some insight into working capital control can be found by calculating the average age of working capital. This ratio identifies how long it takes to convert the purchase of stocks into cash from sales. For our company, this figure is 30 days, a significantly lower figure than the 37 days it takes Sellars and so it appears that Traders' management has a greater control over its working capital. Care needs to be taken in considering what should be an ideal ratio. Reduce it too low, and there may be insufficient stock and other current assets to sustain the volume of trade. Equally, taking too much credit from suppliers may jeopardise relationships and/or cause suppliers to increase prices in compensation. There can also be wider reasons for the difference. Sellars might be deliberately allowing credit to customers in order to generate sales. Likewise, it is possible that it is paying creditors early to gain trade discounts.

(c) **Percentage growth in Traders' sales volume**

Last year £23,000,000 $\times \dfrac{237.9}{224.5}$ = £24,372,829

This year £24,000,000

Growth in current terms (£372,829)

Percentage reduction in sales $\dfrac{£372,829}{£24,372,829} \times 100 = -1.53\%$

(d) **Reasons why estimate of sales growth might not be accurate**

(i) Different product range from trade association.

(ii) Lowering of prices to generate increased market share.

(iii) The index numbers may be a simple average for the whole of the year whereas much of Traders' sales might be seasonal.

8.6 Middle plc

Task 1

To: Angela Wade	**Date:** 4 December 19X6

From: A Technician

Performance Report – West Ltd and East Ltd

(a) **Meaning of financial ratios**

(i) The return on capital employed is an overall measure of the efficiency with which managers have used the resources under their control. In effect, it is measuring the profit per pound of resources. Resources comprise the fixed assets of the organisation plus the current assets less any short term financing of those current assets by current liabilities such as trade creditors.

(ii) The asset turnover attempts to measure the intensity with which an organisation's resources have been used. It is measuring sales per pound of (net) assets.

Page 1 of 2

(iii)   The sales margin measures the profitability per pound of sales. The sales margin is influenced by the level of prices, the extent of marginal costs, the size of fixed costs and the extent to which those fixed costs are spread over volume of sales.

The sales margin and the asset turnover ratio are sub-divisions of the return on capital employed and help identify how an organisation is able to achieve that return.

Financial performance

	Workings for West Ltd	West Ltd	East Ltd
Return on capital employed	3,068/15,340	20.0%	43.0%
Asset turnover	17,910/15,340	1.17	2.68
Sales margin	3,068/17,910	17.1%	16.0%

(b)   Measure of customer service

	Workings for West Ltd	West Ltd	East Ltd
Faulty sales %	100/20,000	0.5%	1.0%

(c)   Further measure of customer service

Three possible measures of customer service are the level of training, the amount of research and development and the timing delay between the receipt of an order and its delivery, in a fault-free condition, to the customer. The time taken for an order to be delivered in each subsidiary is:

	Workings for West Ltd	West Ltd	East Ltd
Days between order and delivery	((20,173 – 19,900)/19,900) x 365	5 days	18 days

(d)   Limitations to the financial analysis

The financial analysis fails to take account of data which is not recorded in the accounts. For example, East Ltd has a poorer record in the current year when providing a service to customers. Not only does it deliver more products of inadequate quality, it also takes much longer to deliver an order once received.

A second limitation to the financial ratios is that it treats all expenses the same in determining performance. From an inspection of the accounts, West Ltd is spending more on research and development and training than East Ltd. Although treated as a revenue for financial accounting purposes, these expenses are effectively investments which may enhance future profitability.

A third limitation which candidates might mention arises from the historical cost principle which underpins the reports. Although both companies have similar plant, East Ltd acquired its plant earlier and at a lower original cost. Because of this, the depreciation charge in the profit and loss account will be lower while, with more accumulated depreciation, the net assets of the business will be smaller. Because of this, East Ltd's return on capital employed will appear larger than the equivalent ratio for West Ltd.

Page 2 of 2

Task 2

Notes on efficiency and effectiveness in not-for-profit organisations

(a)   Definitions of efficiency and effectiveness

In accounting, efficiency is the relationship between inputs and outputs achieved. The fewer the inputs used by an organisation to achieve any given financial output, the more efficient is that organisation.

Effectiveness is the degree to which an objective or target is met.

(b)   Measuring efficiency in commercial organisations

In commercial organisations, efficiency is normally measured by some form of profitability. A profit implies that inputs (expenses) were smaller than outputs (turnover). Often this is extended to recognise that not only does a business incur expenses but also requires other resources in the form of net assets which have an opportunity cost. Because of this, profit is often measured as a relative measure such as return on capital employed. With that ratio, profit is viewed as the output from the resource input of net assets.

(c)   Validity of return on capital employed in not-for-profit organisations

Commercial organisations are assumed to be concerned with maximising their profits. In addition, the amount customers are prepared to pay for the business's products is viewed as a measure of the value of those products.

Not-for-profit organisations such as charities rarely have, as a major objective, the maximisation of profit. Sometimes the beneficiaries of the organisation's output may not be uniquely identifiable – as in most forms of medical research where the beneficiaries will be future generations who cannot pay for the current research activity. Other beneficiaries of not-for-profit organisations do not have the financial resources to make their needs known – as in the case of a charity concerned with the homeless.

(d)   Measures of performance

Because of these differences between not-for-profit organisations and commercial organisations, it is rarely meaningful to measure charities by some form of profit. One way of measuring a charity's performance is to use a physical rather than financial measure of output such as the number of homeless people placed per period and then relate this to either the expenses of running the charity and/or the amount of assets required. What this does not measure is the value of the output. For example, it does not measure the extent of the satisfaction of the homeless on being found accommodation nor the quality of the accommodation. Unlike shoppers in a supermarket, rarely can the homeless take their custom elsewhere because they do not have the financial resources to make this effective.

Scientific research is even more difficult to measure in terms of outputs. Scientific breakthroughs occur only rarely and so are unlikely to be an effective measure of annual performance. One possibility is for a research charity to be audited by other scientists to form a judgement about the quality of the work. Unfortunately, such a process may be extremely subjective. Often there will be little alternative but to use input measures rather than output measures to evaluate performance. An example might be the cost per laboratory hour, but this says nothing about the quality of that laboratory hour.

8.7   Grand Hotel

Task 1

Maximum occupancy (365 days x 80 bedrooms)		29,200 days
Actual occupancy		
Accommodation turnover =	£1,635,200	
Cost per bedroom =	£80	
Number of room–nights sold (£1,635,200 ÷ £80)		20,440
Occupancy rate (20,440 ÷ 29,200) x 100% =		70%
Gross margin: accommodation ((£327,040 ÷ £1,635,200) x 100) =		20%
Gross margin: restaurant ((£157,680 ÷ £630,720) x 100) =		25%
Operating profit (£33,296 + £80,000) =		£113,296
Sales margin (£113,296 ÷ £2,265,920) =		5%
Return on capital employed (£113,296 ÷ £1,416,200) =		8%
Asset turnover (£2,265,920 ÷ £1,416,200)		1.6 times

Task 2

Green and Co
Accountants and Registered Auditors

Claire Hill   3 December 19X7
The Grand Hotel

Dear Ms Hill

Thank you for your recent letter enclosing details of your proposals. I have evaluated these and my comments are detailed below.

(a)   Operating profit to give a 20% return on capital employed

With net assets (= capital employed) of £1,416,200, this implies an operating profit of £283,240.

(b)   Revised profit if plans achieved

	£	£
Increase in occupancy rate		
Revised contribution (£327,040 x (80/70))		373,760
Existing contribution		327,040
Increase in profit		46,720
Change in restaurant prices and costs		
Increase in turnover (£630,720 x 5%)	31,536	
Decrease in variable costs (£473,040 x 5%)	23,652	
		55,188
Increase in profit		101,908
Current operating profit		113,296
Revised profit		215,204

Page 1 of 2

(c) **Revised performance indicators**

Return on capital employed (£215,204/£1,416,200) 15.20%

Revised turnover from accommodation (£1,635,200 x (80/70)) £1,868,800

Revised turnover from restaurant (£630,720 x 105%) £662,256

Revised turnover £2,531,056

Asset turnover (£2,531,056 ÷ £1,416,200) 1.787 times

Sales margin (£215,204 ÷ £2,531,056) 8.50%

(d) **Findings**

The current plan results in an increase in operating profit of £101,908. This almost doubles the return on capital employed to 15.2% but it is still below the 20% average for that type of hotel.

(i) With an increase in contribution of £46,720 coming from the increased occupancy rate, this suggests that 45.8% of the improvement comes from a more intensive use of assets. Similarly with an increase of £55,188 from the change in the restaurant costs and prices, the remainder (54.2%) of the improvement is traceable to improved sales margins in the restaurant.

(ii) Even before the planned changes in the pricing and cost structure, the restaurant was achieving better gross margins than the sector average. With the improvements planned and with full capacity in the restaurant, it is unlikely that additional profit can be generated from that source.

The occupancy rate for the accommodation is planned to be the same as the sector average. However, the 20% gross margin for accommodation is still below the sector average, suggesting some improvement is possible. This should be investigated as an increase in prices with no further change in volume will improve the asset turnover ratio as well as the overall sales margin. Given the circumstances of the hotel, the only other possible area of investigation relates to the fixed overheads. Some of these – such as rates and insurance – are difficult to reduce. However, the level of administration is a possible source of further cost reductions. If the overheads can be reduced, this will have the effect of improving the return on capital employed through improving the sales margin of the hotel.

Yours sincerely

A Technician

Green and Co

8.8   Student Housing Society

Task 1

			Workings	
(a)	Return on net assets		£12,000/£600,000	2.00%
(b)	Operating surplus/rents receivable		£12,000/£192,000	6.25%
(c)	Maximum number of bedrooms	100		
	Number occupied: £192,000/£2,400	80		
	Occupancy rate		80/100	80.00%
(d)	Average age of rent arrears		£48,000/(£192,000 x 12)	3 months
(e)	Total expenses £192,000 – £12,000 =	£180,000		
	Less amortisation	£14,000		
	Expenses involving cash	£166,000		
	Cash available for cash–based expenses		£4,500/£166,000 x 12 = 0.325 month	

Task 2

Workings

		80%	95%
(a)	*Revised operating surplus if 95% occupancy*		
	Activity level	£	£
	Rents receivable	192,000	228,000
	Cleaning	16,000	19,000
	Lighting and heating	4,800	5,700
	Maintenance	11,200	13,300
	Total contribution	160,000	190,000
	Rates payable	76,000	76,000
	Amortisation	14,000	14,000
	Administration costs	58,000	58,000
	Operating surplus	12,000	42,000

(b)	*Revised value of debtors = £228,000/12 =*	£19,000
	Revised cash and bank balance:	£
	Decrease in debtors = £48,000 – £19,000	29,000
	Increase in contribution	30,000
	Existing cash balance	4,500
		63,500

(c)	*Revised performance indicators*	
	Net assets:	
	Fixed assets	564,000
	Debtors	19,000
	Cash and bank	63,500
	Creditors	(16,500)
	Total net assets	630,000

(i)	Revised return on net assets = £42,000/£630,000	6.67%
(ii)	Revised operating surplus/rents receivable = £42,000/£228,000 =	18.42%
(iii)	Total expenses less amortisation = £228,000 – £42,000 – £14,000 =	£172,000
	Cash available for cash–based expenses = £63,500/£172,000 x 12 =	4.4 months

---

MEMO

To:	Helen Brown	**Date:**	17 June 19X8

From: The Accounting Technician

Subject: **Achieving the Society's objectives**

(a) If the Society had been able to achieve a 95% occupancy rate, the operating surplus would have been £42,000. This would have been the result of an increased turnover of £228,000.

(b) This increased turnover coupled with the reduction in the rent arrears would have caused debtors to fall to £19,000 and cash to increase to £63,500.

(c) The revised performance indicators would have been the following.

    (i)   return on net assets   6.67%

    (ii)   operating surplus/rents receivable   18.42%

    (iii)   cash available to pay cash–based expenses   4.4 months

(d) *Efficiency, effectiveness and the return on net assets*

    (i)   *Efficiency* is the relationship between inputs and the benefits achieved from those inputs and is generally measured in financial terms. The most obvious measure is profit related to capital employed (net assets).

    (ii)   *Effectiveness* is the degree to which an objective or target is met.

    (iii)   Commercial organisations often strive to maximise their profit from the resources under their control. This is often measured by the *return on net assets*.

            Charities generally have a different objective. In the case of the housing society, its objective will be to provide for the accommodation needs of students. By focusing on students it denies itself the opportunity of using the resources to generate greater profits, perhaps by using the accommodation as a hotel for tourists. Because of this, using the return on net assets may not be an adequate measure of either efficiency or effectiveness.

CHAPTERS 9 AND 10

Cost Reduction, Quality and Value Enhancement (Questions)

9.1 Quality circles

(a) What are quality circles?

(b) What are the advantages that quality circles can bring to an organisation?

(c) What are the pitfalls that can occur with quality circles?

9.2 PQR plc

PQR plc operates a chain of hotels. Its strategy has been to provide medium-priced accommodation for business people during the week and for families at weekends. The market has become increasingly competitive and PQR plc has decided to change its strategy. In future it will provide 'a high-quality service for the discerning guest'.

Required

(a) Explain the relevance of a programme of 'total quality management' for PQR plc in the implementation of its new strategy.

(b) Discuss the contribution that PQR plc's management accountant could make to the new strategy.

9.3 Local Engineering Ltd (AAT J96)

Data

You are employed as the assistant management accountant with Local Engineering Ltd, a company which designs and makes a single product, the X4, used in the telecommunications industry. The company has a goods received store which employs staff who carry out random checks to ensure materials are of the correct specification. In addition to the random checks, a standard allowance is made for failures due to faulty materials at the completion stage and the normal practice is to charge the cost of any remedial work required to the cost of production for the month. Once delivered to the customer, any faults discovered in the X4 during its warranty period become an expense of the customer support department.

At the end of each month, management reports are prepared for the Board of Directors. These identify the cost of running the stores and the number of issues, the cost of production and the number of units manufactured, and the cost of customer support.

Jane Greenwood, Local Engineering's management accountant, has just returned from a board meeting called to discuss a letter the company recently received from Universal Telecom, Local Engineering's largest customer. In the letter, Universal Telecom explained that it was determined to maintain its position as a world-class provider of telecommunication services and that there was serious concern about the quality of the units delivered by your company. At the meeting, Local Engineering Ltd's board responded by agreeing to establish a company-wide policy of implementing a Total Quality Management (TQM) programme, commencing with a revised model of the X4. Design work on the new model is scheduled to commence in six months' time.

One aspect of this will involve the management accounting department collecting the *cost of quality*. This is defined as the total of all costs incurred in preventing defects plus those costs involved in remedying defects once they have occurred. It is a single figure measuring all the explicit costs – that is, those costs collected within the accounting system – attributable to producing output that is not within its specification.

Task 1

As a first step towards the implementation of TQM, a meeting of the senior staff in the management accounting department has been called to discuss the role the department can play in making TQM a success. Jane Greenwood has asked you to prepare a *brief* background paper for the meeting.

Required

Your paper should:

(a) Explain in outline what is meant by Total Quality Management.

(b) Briefly discuss why the current accounting system fails to highlight the *cost of quality*.

(c) Identify *four* general categories (or classifications) of Local Engineering's activities where expenditure making up the explicit *cost of quality* will be found.

(d) Give *one* example of a cost found within each category.

(e) Give *one* example of a *cost of quality* not normally identified by the accounting system.

Data

Local Engineering Ltd has capacity to produce no more than 1,000 X4s per month and currently is able to sell all production immediately at a unit selling price of £1,250. A major component of the X4 is a complex circuit board. Spot checks are made on these boards by a team of specialist employees when they are received into stores. In May, 100 units were found to be faulty. Good components are then issued to production along with other material.

Upon completion, each X4 is tested. If there is a fault, this involves further remedial work prior to dispatch to customers. For the month of May, 45 units of the X4 had to be reworked because of subsequent faults discovered in the circuit boards. This remedial work cost an additional £13,500 in labour charges.

Should a fault occur after delivery to the customer, Local Engineering is able to call upon a team of self-employed engineers to rectify the fault as part of its customer support function. The cost of the remedial work by the self-employed engineers carried out in May – and the number of times they were used – is shown as contractors under customer support.

Extract from the accounting records of Local Engineering Ltd for the month of May

Stores			Production		
Purchases	Units	£		Units	£
Printed circuits	1,000	120,000	Printed circuits	900	108,000
Less returns	(100)	(12,000)	Other material		121,500
Net cost	900	108,000	Labour		193,500
Other material		121,500	Direct production overhead		450,000
Total purchases issued to production		229,500	Cost of production		873,000
Other direct stores costs					
Goods received, labour costs and rent		54,000	*Customer support*		
Inspection costs		10,000	Direct costs		36,000
Cost of returns	100	4,500	Contractors	54	24,300
Cost of stores		68,500			60,300

Task 2

As part of the continuing development of Total Quality Management, you are asked by Jane Greenwood to calculate:

(a)   the explicit *cost of quality* for Local Engineering Ltd for the month of May

(b)   a further *cost of quality* not reported in the above account records.

Cost Reduction, Quality and Value Enhancement (Answers)

9.1 Quality circles

(a)   Quality circles are small groups of staff (5–10) established to focus on all aspects of quality related to their work and to recommend and implement improvements. Members of quality circles are volunteers and unpaid, although meetings will generally take place in company time. They will have a leader who is either elected or appointed. Normally the members of a quality circle are drawn from the same area of work. However a number of firms have recognised that many quality improvement opportunities lie outside the natural work group and have created quality circles which comprise staff from different work areas. Some companies have even established quality circles which include customer and supplier representatives.

The successful implementation of quality circles requires commitment from top management in terms of financing, launching and supporting the scheme and the organisation itself must be committed to improving quality in all aspects of its operation. Participants must be properly trained in the principles of quality circles and the way they are supposed to work.

In many cases, the members of a quality circle will set their own agenda – being closest to the work process, they understand the problems best. However, they can also be asked to address issues specifically identified by management. Although established to address issues of quality, this task will inevitably lead circles to make recommendations about improving working practices, productivity, working grievances etc.

(b)   Quality circles can result in:

   (i)   a new culture in the organisation in which everyone understands the critical importance of quality to the commercial success of the operation

   (ii)   great improvements in quality with resultant improvement in customer satisfaction

   (iii)   greater 'empowerment' of people further down the organisations

   (iv)   improvement in morale as staff feel that they can influence and improve the quality of *their* product

   (v)   reduced labour turnover as a result of improved motivation

   (vi)   reductions in cost

   (vii)   improvements in productivity

   (viii)   elimination of wasteful procedures and reduction in layers of bureaucracy

(ix) constant stimulation and a desire to see quality continually improve

(x) greater understanding of the objectives and problems within the organisation as a whole.

(c) Introducing quality circles is not easy because it requires changes in traditional management and supervisory attitudes and practices as well as a different approach by the staff themselves (particularly in traditionally heavily-unionised organisations).

Particular pitfalls can be:

(i) lack of commitment and understanding of purpose by senior management

(ii) resistance to the concept by middle managers and supervisors who see QCs as a threat to their traditional role

(iii) inadequate initial training and a failure to recognise that follow-up training may well be required

(iv) constant failure to implement any of the proposals arising from quality circles leading to demoralisation and demotivation among the staff

(v) failure to establish a proper system and set of rules at the outset under which the quality will work

(vi) failure to provide the information and support necessary for members to solve problems

(vii) empire-building by those with overall responsibility for quality circles so that they begin to conflict with the traditional management structures and processes

(viii) failure to measure the impact and effectiveness of quality circles on defect rates, productivity, wastage, grievances etc.

(ix) staff perception of QCs as another way of undermining their traditional roles and responsibilities.

9.2 PQR plc

(a) Since the hotel is implementing a new strategy, there will need to be a commitment from the management to carry this through. Total Quality Management (TQM) can be described as the continuous improvement in quality, productivity and effectiveness obtained by establishing management responsibility for processes as well as outputs. In this, every process has an identified process owner and every person in an entity operates within a process and contributes to its improvement. The steps in the process of quality management are:

(i) establishing standards of quality for a product or service

(ii) establishing procedures or production methods which ought to ensure that these required standards are met in an agreed proportion of cases

(iii) monitoring actual quality

(iv) taking control action when actual quality falls below standard.

The company is planning to upgrade the hotels from medium-priced accommodation to a service providing high quality for a discerning clientele. This will have many implications for the management and staff of the hotels. The service offered to the 'discerning guest' will be particularly important and this will require significant changes in the management and staff of the hotel.

This change will mean a change of culture for the hotel and it will be necessary to change the attitudes as well as the duties and responsibilities of the staff. Senior management commitment is necessary to implement this programme and employees must be involved in the improvement process. The numbers of staff may need to be increased substantially to provide the expected level of service within the hotels and a greater number of managers will be needed to ensure that the quality of service is improved and monitored. Training is necessary to optimise the improvement process and ensure that tasks are standardised to minimise variation. In addition, areas of responsibility will need to be identified and a manager allocated for each. By adopting a policy of TQM, the firm will create an environment in which quality is given priority. The management and staff must also be organised to implement the quality which is essential in an hotel for discerning guests.

(b)   To enable the firm to change its overall strategy, the management accountant should assist in the planning, the decision-making process and the implementation of the plans. Once the establishing of standards has been defined, the emphasis on monitoring quality should become part of the control process within the hotel. The management accountant should take control action when actual quality falls below standard. The concern with quality must be reflected in the reports produced by the management accountant. The reports will also need to provide information regarding factors, such as the level of customer complaints. In addition, the hotel management may encourage the setting up of quality circles and the accounting staff would participate in this.

To enable the firm to reach the expected outcome from the change in strategy, the management will need assistance in producing budgets. Regular reports will help monitor the differences between actual and budgeted expenditure and revenue.

The management accountant will participate in the many important decisions which will arise in the management of the hotel. He/she will be responsible for the data and financial information which will form the basis for these decisions and assist in the decision process. Finally, the management accountant will assist in the implementation of the decisions.

9.3 Local Engineering Ltd

Task 1

Total Quality Management and the Cost of Quality

From: The Assistant Management Accountant   **Date:**   June 19X6

To: Jane Greenwood

(a)   The meaning of Total Quality Management

Total Quality Management is both a philosophy and a series of techniques or programmes. As a philosophy, it is concerned with developing or maintaining a strategic advantage over competitors by profitably meeting the needs of customers. This it does by taking a customer-centred rather than a production-centred approach and meeting their needs in terms of price, quality and timing. In turn, this involves a programme of continuous improvement and the development of commitment and continuous learning throughout the whole organisation. It manifests itself in reduced lead times for new product development and minimising the response time to satisfy the customer as when Just in Time deliveries are provided.

One particular goal of TQM is zero defects. Although not always achievable, by aiming for that goal, the quality to the customer can be improved. Rather than measuring defects as a percentage of production, the aim is to reduce this to parts-per-million (PPM). Prior to the development of TQM, quality was achieved by regular inspection at the various stages of production. But this acceptance of failure rates required the carrying of larger volumes of stock to enable faulty material to be replaced without hindering production. This, in turn, required greater storage space and more complex production scheduling as faulty production was reworked. None of these expenses added value to the product as seen by the customer. A major facet of TQM is therefore to 'design in' quality from the beginning rather than meet the later expense of 'inspecting in' quality.

(b)   Failure of the accounting system to highlight the *cost of quality*

This has implications for the accounting system. Traditionally, failure rates, scrap and reworking have been subsumed within the costs of production by assigning 'normal' loss to good production while other aspects of poor quality were accounted for in either production or marketing overheads. The result has been that the costs of (poor) quality were not only accepted as being inevitable but also they failed to be highlighted for management's attention. In addition, many costs were hidden in traditional accounting reports with their emphasis on volume and decreasing unit costs. Such reports tended to ignore the hidden but real costs of excessive stock levels and the facilities necessary for storing that stock.

Directly identifying the cost of quality in management reports would draw management's attention to these non-value added expenses. By highlighting the costs, the magnitude could be shown and, hopefully, this would enable alternative, effective approaches, such as built-in quality at the design stage, to be developed.

Page 1 of 2

(c) and (d) Explicit costs of quality

There are four recognised categories making up the *cost of quality* which are identifiable within an accounting system. These are outlined below.

Cost of prevention

These are costs incurred to prevent the production of faulty output. They include the cost of equipment to manufacture higher quality products, the cost of training, the cost of improved product design and the cost of enhanced preventive maintenance programmes.

Appraisal costs

Appraisal costs relate to those costs incurred in actually detecting products or inputs which do not conform to specification. Examples are the cost of inspecting deliveries and the cost of inspection production during the manufacturing process.

Internal failure costs

These costs refer to the expenses involved when a substandard unit of production is identified before its delivery to a customer. Examples include scrap, reworking and hold-ups to production caused by faulty products.

External failure costs

External failure costs are costs of below specification products which are only discovered after delivery to the customer. They include the cost of returning the faulty products to the manufacturer, travel costs of inspectors if an on-site visit is required and the incurring of liability claims.

(e) Quality costs not identified by the accounting system

Quality costs which often cannot be identified from the accounting system tend to be of two forms. The first are those unrecorded, opportunity costs such as the loss of a customer as a result of faulty deliveries. The second are those difficult to measure costs within the organisation such as disruption resulting from stock-outs arising from faulty purchases which tend to be subsumed within other account headings.

Page 2 of 2

Task 2

(a)

Explicit cost of quality	£
Store inspection costs	10,000
Cost of returns	4,500
Production reworking	13,500
Customer support	24,300
	52,300

(b)

Implicit cost of quality	Unit £
Labour	200
Printed circuit board	120
Other material	135
Marginal costs	455
Selling price	1,250
Unit contribution	795
Lost production	100
Total lost contribution	**£79,500**

Workings

	£		
		£	
Labour	193,500	*Printed circuit board*	
Less Reworking	(13,500)	Cost of 1,000 units	120,000
	_____	Unit cost	120
Zero defect cost 900 units	180,000		
	_____	*Other material*	
Unit cost (180,000/900)	£200	Cost of 900 units	£121,500
		Unit cost	£135

CHAPTER 11

Case Studies (Questions)

Unit 7 Case Study 11.1: Cam Car Company (AAT J97)

Data

The Cam Car Company is a multinational manufacturer of motor vehicles. It operates two divisions, one producing cars and the other producing vans. You are employed as a management accountant in the van division. The labour content for each type of vehicle is very similar although the material content of a car is much greater than that of a van. Both divisions apply straight-line depreciation to fixed assets.

You have been asked to prepare information to be used in the company's annual wage negotiations. Each year, the van employee representatives make comparisons with the car division and one of your tasks is to calculate performance indictors for your division. Financial and other information relating to both divisions is reproduced below along with some of the relevant performance indicators for the car division.

Balance sheet extracts at 31 May 19X7

	Van division			**Car division**		
	Cost	Depreciation to date	Net	Cost	Depreciation to date	Net
	£m	£m	£m	£m	£m	£m
Buildings at cost	500	400	100	1,200	240	960
Plant and machinery at cost	400	320	80	800	240	560
	900	720	180	2,000	480	1,520
Stock		60			210	
Trade debtors		210			285	
Cash		(140)			150	
Trade creditors		(30)			(265)	
			100			380
Net assets			280			1,900

Profit and loss accounts for year to 31 May 19X7

	Van division		Car division	
	£m	£m	£m	£m
Turnover		420		1,140
Materials and bought–in components	95		790	
Production labour	110		138	
Other production expenses	26		32	
Depreciation – buildings	10		24	
Depreciation – plant and machinery	40		80	
Administrative expenses	27		28	
		308		1,092
Profit		112		48

Other information

	Van division	Car division
Vehicles produced	50,000	84,000
Number of production employees	10,000	12,000

Yearly performance indicators for the car division

Return on capital employed	2.53%	Profit margin	4.21%
Asset turnover	0.6 times	Profit per employee	£4,000
Wages per employee	£11,500	Output per employee	7 vehicles
Production labour cost per unit	£1,643	Added value per employee	£29,167

Task 1

You have been asked to calculate the yearly performance indicators for the van division and to present them in a table with the comparable figures for the car division.

Data

Shortly after preparing the performance indicators, you receive a telephone call from Peter Ross, a member of the management team. Peter explains that the employee representatives of the van division wish to negotiate an increase in wages. The representatives are arguing that employees in the van division are paid less than the equivalent staff in the car division despite the van division being more profitable. In addition, the representatives state that the productivity is higher than in the car division. Peter explains that he is not an accountant. He is not clear how productivity is measured nor what is meant by added value.

Task 2

You are asked to write a memo to Peter Ross. The memo should:

(a)   briefly explain what is meant by

      (i)   productivity

      (ii)   added value

(b)   identify those performance indicators that could be used by the employees of the van division to justify their claims in terms of

      (i)   profitability

      (ii)   productivity

(c)   give *one* example from the performance indicators that could be used to counter those claims and use the financial data given in Task 1 to identify one possible limitation to the indicator

(d)   use *both* the return on capital employed *and* the added value per employee to show why the indicators calculated in Task 1 might be overstated.

Unit 7 Case Study 11.2: Debussy Ltd (AAT D97)

Data

You have recently accepted an appointment as the accountant to Debussy Limited, a small family firm manufacturing a specialised fertiliser. The fertiliser is produced using expensive ovens which need to be kept at a constant temperature at all times, even when not being used. Because of this, the power which provides the heating does not vary with changes in production output and so its costs are viewed as being fixed.

The managing director, Claude Debussy, is concerned that the existing accounting system is not providing adequate information for him to run the business. By way of example, he shows you the accounts for the year ended 30 November 19X7. An extract from those accounts showing budgeted and actual results is reproduced below.

Extract from the Profit and Loss Account of Debussy Ltd for the year ended 30 November 19X7

	Annual budget		Annual results		Quarter 4 budget		Quarter 4 results	
Units produced (tonnes)	12,000		13,000		3,000		2,400	
	£	£	£	£	£	£	£	£
Material		144,000		188,500		36,000		35,280
Labour		192,000		227,500		48,000		42,240
Fixed overheads:								
Lease of machinery	60,000		60,000		15,000		15,000	
Rent	40,000		40,000		10,000		10,000	
Rates	56,000		64,000		14,000		16,000	
Insurance	48,000		52,000		12,000		13,000	
Power	120,000		140,000		30,000		36,000	
		324,000		356,000		81,000		90,000
Total expenses		660,000		772,000		165,000		167,520

Claude Debussy draws your attention to the high level of fixed overheads and how these are absorbed using labour hours.

'I do not fully understand the fixed overhead figures for the fourth quarter' he explained. 'The way they are presented in the accounts does not help me to plan and control the business. It is no good blaming the production workers for the increase in fixed overheads as we have been paying them £8 per hour – the same amount as agreed in the budget – and they have never worked any overtime.'

Claude Debussy turns to you for advice. He is particularly interested in understanding why the fixed overheads have increased in the fourth quarter despite production falling. He is also interested in knowing how many labour hours were planned to be worked and how many hours were actually worked in that quarter.

Task 1

(a)   For the fourth quarter, calculate the following information for Claude Debussy:

      (i)   the labour hours budgeted to be worked

      (ii)   the labour hours actually worked

      (iii)   the budgeted hours per tonne of fertiliser

      (iv)   the actual hours per tonne of fertiliser

(b)   Calculate the following variances for the fourth quarter:

      (i)   the fixed overhead expenditure variance (sometimes known as the price variance)

      (ii)   the fixed overhead volume variance

      (iii)   the fixed overhead capacity variance

      (iv)   the fixed overhead efficiency variance (sometimes known as the usage variance)

      (*Note.* You should base your calculations on the total amount of fixed overheads and not the individual elements.)

Data

Claude Debussy is unfamiliar with standard costing, although he believes the actual fixed overheads for the year are higher than budgeted because more tonnes of fertiliser have been produced. He would like to use standard costing to control fixed overheads, but is uncertain what is meant by the fixed overhead variances you have prepared.

Task 2

Write a memo to Claude Debussy explaining the following.

(a)   Briefly comment on his explanation for the increase in fixed overheads for the year.

(b)   For each of the following three variances, give *one* possible reason they might have occurred:

    ◆   the fixed overhead expenditure (or price) variance

    ◆   the fixed overhead capacity variance

    ◆   the fixed overhead efficiency (or usage) variance

Data

On receiving your memo, Claude Debussy tells you that the annual budgeted fixed overheads have, in the past, simply been apportioned equally over the four quarters. However, the expenditure on power varies between quarters in a regular way depending on the outside temperature. The seasonsl variations, based on many years' experience, are as follows.

	1ˢᵗ *quarter*	2ⁿᵈ *quarter*	3ʳᵈ *quarter*	4ᵗʰ *quarter*
Seasonal variations for power costs	+5%	–10%	–20%	+25%

Claude Debussy believes that it would be more meaningfull if the budgeted expenditure on power reflected thse seasonal variations, but he is uncertain how this would affect the variances calculated in Task 1(b).

Task 3

Prepare notes for Claude Debussy as follows.

(a)   Use the seasonal variations to calculate the revised power budget for the four quarters of the year to 30 November 19X7.

(b)   Briefly discuss whether or not the revised power budget for the fourth quarter should be used for calculating the fixed overhead expenditure (or price) and volume variances for that quarter.

Unit 7 Case Study 11.3: Hampstead plc (AAT J98)

Data

You are employed as the assistant management accountant in the group accountant's office of Hampstead plc. Hampstead recently acquired Finchley Ltd, a small company making a specialist product called the Alpha. Standard marginal costing is used by all the companies within the group and, from 1 August 19X8, Finchley Ltd will also be required to use standard marginal costing in its management reports. Part of your job is to manage the implementation of standard marginal costing at Finchley Ltd.

John Wade, the managing director of Finchley, is not clear how the change will help him as a manager. He has always found Finchley's existing absorption costing system sufficient. By way of example, he shows you a summary of its management accounts for the three months to 31 May 19X8. These are reproduced below.

Statement of budgeted and actual cost of Alpha Production – 3 months ended 31 May 19X8

	Actual		Budget		Variance
Alpha production (units)	10,000		12,000		
	Inputs	£	Inputs	£	£
Materials	32,000 metres	377,600	36,000 metres	432,000	54,400
Labour	70,000 hours	422,800	72,000 hours	450,000	27,200
Fixed overhead absorbed		330,000		396,000	66,000
Fixed overhead unabsorbed		75,000		0	(75,000)
		1,205,400		1,278,000	72,600

John Wade is not convinced that standard marginal costing will help him to manage Finchley. 'My current system tells me all I need to know', he said. 'As you can see, we are £72,600 below budget which is really excellent given that we lost production as a result of a serious machine breakdown.'

To help John Wade understand the benefits of standard marginal costing, you agree to prepare a statement for the three months ended 31 May 19X8 reconciling the standard cost of production to the actual cost of production.

Task 1

(a)   Use the budget data to determine the following.

    (i)   The standard marginal cost per Alpha.

    (ii)   The standard cost of actual Alpha production for the three months to 31 May 19X8.

(b)   Calculate the following variances.

    (i)   Material price variance

    (ii)   Material usage variance

    (iii)   Labour rate variance

    (iv)   Labour efficiency variance

    (v)   Fixed overhead expenditure variance.

(c)   Write a short memo to John Wade as follows.

(i)   Include a statement reconciling the actual cost of production to the standard cost of production.

(ii)   Give two reasons why your variances might differ from those in his original management accounting statement despite using the same basic data.

(iii)   Briefly discuss one further reason why your reconciliation statement provides improved management information.

Data

On receiving your memo, John Wade informs you of the following.

♦   the machine breakdown resulted in the workforce having to be paid for 12,000 hours even though no production took place.

♦   an index of material prices stood at 466.70 when the budget was prepared but at 420.03 when the material was purchased.

Task 2

Using this new information, prepare a revised statement reconciling the standard cost of production to the actual cost of production. Your statement should subdivide the following.

♦   both the labour variances into those parts arising from the machine breakdown and those parts arising from normal production.

♦   the material price variance into that part due to the change in the index and that part arising for other reasons.

Data

Barnet Ltd is another small company owned by Hampstead plc. Barnet operates a job costing system making a specialist, expensive piece of hospital equipment.

Existing system

Currently, employees are assigned to individual jobs and materials are requisitioned from stores as needed. The standard and actual costs of labour and materials are recorded for each job. These job costs are totalled to produce the marginal cost of production. Fixed production costs – including the cost of storekeeping and inspection of deliveries and finished equipment – are then added to determine the standard and actual cost of production. Any costs of remedial work are included in the materials and labour for each job.

Proposed system

Carol Johnson, the chief executive of Barnet, has recently been to a seminar on modern manufacturing techniques. As a result, she is considering introducing Just-in-Time stock deliveries and Total Quality Management. Barnet would offer suppliers a long-term contract at a fixed price but suppliers would have to guarantee the quality of their materials.

In addition, she proposes that the workforce is organised as a single team with flexible work practices. This would mean employees helping each other as necessary, with no employee being allocated a particular job. If a job was delayed, the workforce would work overtime without payment in order for the job to be completed on time. In exchange, employees would be guaranteed a fixed weekly wage and time off when production was slack to make up for any overtime incurred.

Cost of quality

Carol has asked to meet you to discuss the implications of her proposals on the existing accounting system. She is particularly concerned to monitor the cost of quality. This is defined as the total of all costs incurred in preventing defects plus those costs involved in remedying defects once they have occurred. It is a single figure measuring all the explicit costs of quality – that is, those costs collected within the accounting system.

Task 3

In preparation for the meeting, produce brief notes covering the following.

(a)   Identify four general headings (or classifications) which make up the cost of quality.

(b)   Give one example of a type of cost likely to be found within each category.

(c)   Assuming Carol Johnson's proposals are accepted, state, with reasons, whether or not:

    (i)   a standard marginal costing system would still be of help to the managers

    (ii)   it would still be meaningful to collect costs by each individual job.

(d)   Identify one cost saving in Carol Johnson's proposals which would *not* be recorded in the existing costing system.

Unit 8 Case Study 11.4: Club Atlantic (AAT D96)

Data

Club Atlantic is an all-weather holiday complex providing holidays throughout the year. The fee charged to guests is fully inclusive of accommodation and all meals. However, because the holiday industry is so competitive, Club Atlantic is only able to generate profits by maintaining strict financial control of all activities.

The club's restaurant is one area where there is a constant need to monitor costs. Susan Green is the manager of the restaurant. At the beginning of each year, she is given an annual budget which is then broken down into months. Each month, she receives a statement monitoring actual costs against the annual budget and highlighting any variances. The statement for the month ended 31 October 19X6 is reproduced below along with a list of assumptions.

Club Atlantic Restaurant Performance Statement – Month to 31 October 19X6

	Actual	Budget	Variance (Over)/under
Number of guest days	11,160	9,600	(1,560)
	£	£	£
Food	20,500	20,160	(340)
Cleaning materials	2,232	1,920	(312)
Heat, light and power	2,050	2,400	350
Catering wages	8,400	7,200	(1,200)
Rent, rates, insurance and depreciation	1,860	1,800	(60)
	35,042	33,480	(1,562)

Assumptions

(a) The budget has been calculated on the basis of a 30-day calendar month with the cost of rents, rates, insurance and depreciation being an apportionment of the fixed annual charge.

(b) The budgeted catering wages assume:

    (i) there is one member of the catering staff for every forty guests staying at the complex

    (ii) the daily cost of a member of the catering staff is £30.

(c) All other budgeted costs are variable costs based on the number of guest days.

Task 1

Using the data above, prepare a revised performance statement using flexible budgeting. Your statement should show both the revised budget and the revised variances.

Data

Club Atlantic uses the existing budgets and performance statements to motivate its managers as well as for financial control. If managers keep expenses below budget, they receive a bonus in addition to their salaries. A colleague of Susan is Brian Hilton. Brian is in charge of the swimming pool and golf course, both of which have high levels of fixed costs. Each month, he manages to keep expenses below budget and, in return, enjoys regular bonuses. Under the current reporting system, Susan Green only rarely receives a bonus.

At a recent meeting with Club Atlantic's directors, Susan Green expressed concern that the performance statement was not a valid reflection of her management of the restaurant. You are currently employed by Hall and Co, the club's auditors, and the directors of Club Atlantic have asked you to advise them whether there is any justification for Susan Green's concern.

At the meeting with the club's directors, you were asked the following questions:

(a)   Do budgets motivate managers to achieve objectives?

(b)   Does motivating managers lead to improved performance?

(c)   Does the current method of reporting performance motivate Susan Green and Brian Hilton to be more efficient?

Task 2

Write a *brief* letter to the directors of Club Atlantic addressing their questions and justifying your answers.

Note. You should make use of the data given in this task plus your findings from Task 1.

Unit 8 Case Study 11.5: Eskafield Industrial Museum
(AAT D97)

Data

Eskafield Industrial Museum opened ten years ago and soon became a market leader with many working exhibits. In the early years there was a rapid growth in the number of visitors. However, with no further investment in new exhibits, this growth has not been maintained in recent years.

Two years ago, John Derbyshire was appointed as the museum's chief executive. His initial task was to increase the number of visitors to the museum and, following his appointment, he has made several improvements to make the museum more successful.

Another of John's tasks is to provide effective financial management. This year, the museum's Board of Management has asked him to take full responsibility for producing the 19X8 budget. One of his first tasks is to prepare estimates of the number of visitors next year. John had previously played only a limited role in budget preparation and so he turns to you, an accounting technician, for advice.

He provides you with the following information.

♦ previous budgets had assumed a 10% growth in attendance but this has been inaccurate.

♦ very little is known about the visitors to the museum.

♦ the museum keeps details of the number of visitors by quarter but this has never been analysed.

♦ the number of visitors per quarter for the last two years is as follows.

Year	Quarter	Number of visitors
19X6	1	5,800
	2	9,000
	3	6,000
	4	14,400
19X7	1	6,600
	2	9,800
	3	6,800
	4 (estimate)	15,200

Task 1

(a) Calculate the *centred four-point moving average trend* figures and the seasonal variations.

(b) Construct a graph showing the trend line and actual number of visitors, by quarter, for presentation to the Board of Management.

(c) Estimate the forecast number of visitors for each quarter of 19X8, assuming that there are the same trend and seasonal variations for 19X8.

(d) Prepare notes on forecasting for John Derbyshire. Your notes should:

(i) identify two ways to improve the forecasting of visitor numbers and highlight any limitations to your proposals

(ii) explain why telephone sampling might be preferable to using postal questionnaires

(iii) explain how the concept of the product life cycle could be applied to the museum.

Data

Shortly after receiving your notes, John Derbyshire contacts you. He explains that he had prepared a draft budget for the Board of Management based on the estimate numbers for 19X8. This had been prepared on the basis that:

♦   most of the museum's expenses such as salaries and rates are fixed costs

♦   the museum has always budgeted for a deficit

♦   the 19X8 deficit will be £35,000.

At the meeting with the Board of Management, John was congratulated on bringing the deficit down from £41,000 in 19X6 to £37,000 (latest estimate) in 19X7. However the Board of Management raised two issues, as follows.

♦   They felt that the planned deficit of £35,000 should be reduced to £29,000 as this would represent a greater commitment.

♦   They queried why the budget had been prepared without any consultation with the museum staff, ie a top–down approach.

Task 2

Draft a memo to John Derbyshire. Your memo should cover the following.

(a)   Discuss the motivational implications of imposing the budget reduction from £35,000 to £29,000.

(b)   Consider the arguments for and against using a top-down budgeting approach for the museum.

Unit 8 Case Study 11.6: Vecstar Ltd (AAT J98)

Data

Vecstar Ltd produces and sells a single product, the Alpha. The company uses an accounting software package which calculates variances by comparing the fixed budget for the year against actual expenditure. For accounting purposes, the company divides its year into 13, four-weekly periods. The report for the four weeks ended 29 May 19X8 is reproduced below.

Vecstar Ltd Performance Report for four weeks ended 29 May 19X8

	Actual	Budget	Variance	
Units produced	60,000	48,000	12,000	F
	£	£	£	
Variable costs				
Material	18,546	12,480	6,066	A
Labour	7,200	5,760	1,440	A
Semi-variable costs				
Power	900	1,060	160	F
Maintenance	1,600	1,680	80	F
Fixed costs				
Supervision	3,400	3,440	40	F
Rent and insurance	2,050	1,820	230	A
Depreciation	4,000	4,000		
Total	37,696	30,240	7,456	A

Key: A: adverse, F: favourable

You are employed as an accounting technician by Green and Co, the auditors to Vecstar Ltd. On a recent visit to Vecstar, you suggested to James Close, the company's managing director, that the variances calculated by the software package are likely to be misleading and that a system of flexible budgeting would produce more meaningful management information.

James tells you that the following assumptions were made when preparing the budget.

♦ the four-weekly fixed cost of power was estimated at £100 and the addition cost of power per Alpha produced was estimated at 2p.

♦ the fixed cost of maintenance was estimated at £1,200 per four weeks and 1p per Alpha produced.

♦ the annual fixed overhead absorption rate is 20p per Alpha. This was derived by adding the budgeted fixed costs to the fixed element of the budgeted semi-variable costs and dividing by the normal annual production.

Task 1

(a)   Prepare a flexible budget statement for the four weeks to 29 May 19X8.

(b)   Estimate the normal *annual* production of Alphas used to determine the fixed overhead absorption rate.

Data

When you present James Close with the revised budget, he writes to tell you that he cannot understand why some budgeted costs have changed but others have remained the same as in the original fixed budget. In addition, he is concerned that the budgeted cost data becomes increasingly inaccurate, the closer the accounting period is to the year end. By way of example, he gives you the following general indices of production costs.

◆ Index when budget is prepared	160.00
◆ Index at commencement of accounting year	162.40
◆ Average index for four weeks ended 26 June 19X8 (estimated)	165.12

Finally, James is disappointed that the revised report no longer highlights the variations in the units produced between original budget and actual. For May 19X8, production increased by 25 per cent from 48,000 to 60,000 units but this has been largely ignored.

Task 2

Prepare a letter to James Close, covering the following.

(a)   *Briefly* explain why, in the flexible budget, some budgeted costs have remained the same while others have altered.

(b)   Estimate the *total cost* of producing 62,000 Alphas in the four weeks to 26 June using your answer in Task 1 *and* the indices given above.

(c)   Give *one* possible reason why the index used may not be an appropriate one for Vecstar Ltd.

(d)   Suggest *one* way of expressing in a meaningful form for management the variation between original budgeted units and actual units produced.

CHAPTER 11

Case Studies (Answers)

Unit 7 Case Study 11.1: The Cam Car Company

Task 1

The Cam Car Company	Workings	*Yearly performance statistics* Van division	Car division
Return on capital employed	£112m/£280m	40.00%	2.53%
Profit margin	£112m/£420m	26.67%	4.21%
Asset turnover	£420m/£280m	1.5 times	0.6 times
Profit per employee	£112m/10,000	£11,200	£4,000
Wages per employee	£110m/10,000	£11,000	£11,500
Output (vehicles) per employee	50,000/10,000	5	7
Labour cost per vehicle	£110m/50,000	£2,200	£1,643
Added value per employee	(£420m – £95m)/10,000	£32,500	£29,167

Task 2

```
                              MEMORANDUM

To:        Peter Ross

From:      The Management Accountant

Subject:   Wage negotiations and performance      Date:     18 June 19X7
```

(a)   *The meaning of productivity and added value*

Productivity is a ratio of input to output. Normally, this is expressed in physical terms such as hours of labour to units produced. However, sometimes productivity is expressed in financial terms where unit information is either not available or not appropriate.

Companies buy in raw materials and services. They then convert these to finished products by adding labour and overheads. These are then sold, hopefully at a profit. Through these stages, the worth or value attached to the original raw materials is increased. Added value measures the overall increase in value added to those original raw materials by the actions of the organisation. In that sense, it is a monetary measure of the skills added by the organisation. Formally, added value is defined as the difference between sales value and the cost of bought-in material and services. (An alternative definition is conversion costs plus profit.) Often this is expressed as a relative measure by dividing by the number of employees.

(b)   *Performance indication supporting the employees' claims*

Profitability
Return on capital employed
Profit margin
Profit per employee
Wages per employee

Productivity
Productivity
Added value per employee

(c) *Performance indicators questioning the employees' claims*

Although the wages paid to the employees in the van division are lower than those paid to those in the car division, what matters to the company is labour cost per unit. Each employee of the van division only produces 5 vehicles per annum whereas the output per employee in the car division is 7. In addition, the labour cost per vehicle is higher for vans than for cars.

The employee representatives might argue that these indicators result from the van division having a smaller and older investment in building, plant and machinery. With more modern and more efficient equipment output per employee is likely to be higher.

(d) *Possible overstatement of performance statistics*

The depreciation for land and buildings in the profit and loss account is 2% of the original cost for both divisions. For plant and machinery, it is 10% in both cases. Given straight-line depreciation this suggests the following average ages of fixed assets.

		Van division		Car division	
		Buildings	*Plant*	*Buildings*	*Plant*
Cost	(a)	£500m	£400m	£1,200m	£800m
Depreciation this year	(b)	£10m	£40m	£24m	£80m
Depreciation rate	(b)/(a)	2%	10%	2%	10%
Accumulated depreciation	(c)	£400m	£320m	£240m	£240m
Average age of assets (years)	(c)/(b)	40	8	10	3

The van division's fixed assets are considerably older than those for the car division. Both divisions record their fixed assets as historical cost and this may cause the value or replacement cost of the assets to be understated. This is likely to apply more to the van division as its fixed assets are significantly older. The result is that the capital employed is likely to be understated and, with understated depreciation, profit will be overstated. The overall return on capital employed is therefore likely to be overstated compared with that in the car division.

In addition, the added value of the car division is less simple because it buys more of its components from outside suppliers rather than because its activities are less valuable.

Page 2/2

Unit 7 Case Study 11.2: Debussy Ltd

Task 1

(a) *Labour hours*

		Budgeted	Actual
Labour cost		£48,000	£42,240
Budgeted and actual rate		£8	£8
(i) and (ii) Labour hours (labour cost ÷ £8)		6,000	5,280
Tonnes produced		3,000	2,400
(iii) and (iv) Hours per tonne (labour hours ÷ tonnes produced)		2	2.2

(b) *Fixed overhead variances*

Workings

Budgeted fixed overheads	£81,000
Budgeted tonnes	3,000
Budgeted fixed overhead per tonne (£81,000 ÷ 3,000)	£27.00
Budgeted labour hours	6,000
Budgeted fixed overhead per labour hour	£13.50

(i)	Actual cost of fixed overheads	£90,000	
	Budgeted cost of fixed overheads	£81,000	
	Fixed overhead expenditure variance	£9,000	(Adverse)
(ii)	Budgeted tonnes	3,000	
	Actual tonnes	2,400	
	Volume variance (tonnes)	600	(Adverse)
	Fixed overhead volume variance [600 x £27.00]	£16,200	(Adverse)
	Alternative answer		
	Budgeted hours (3,000 tonnes x 2 hours)	6,000	
	Actual hours produced (2,400 x 2 hours)	4,800	
	Volume variance (hours)	1,200	(Adverse)
	Fixed overhead volume variance (1,200 x £13.50)	£16,200	(Adverse)
(iii)	Budgeted hours	6,000	
	Actual hours worked	5,280	
	Capacity variance (hours)	720	(Adverse)
	Fixed overhead capacity variance (720 x £13.50)	£9,720	(Adverse)
(iv)	Actual hours worked	5,280	
	Actual hours produced (2,400 tonnes x 2 hours)	4,800	
	Efficiency variance (hours)	480	(Adverse)
	Fixed overhead efficiency variance (480 x £13.50)	£6,480	(Adverse)

Task 2

MEMO

To: Claude Debussy   **Date:**   3 December 19X7

From: The Company Accountant

Subject: **Fixed overhead variances**

(a)   *Fixed overhead costs and changes in activity*

Fixed overheads are fixed in the sense that they do not vary with changes in output over the relevant range. Instead, they tend to vary with time. The longer the time period, the greater the cost. Examples include rent and rates, which have to be paid irrespective of the number of tonnes of fertiliser made. Because of this, it is inappropriate to excuse automatically the increase in fixed costs simply because volume has increased. Fixed costs, however, are only fixed over the 'relevant range'. For a taxi with five passenger seats, the relevant range would be from one to five passengers resulting in a sixth passenger requiring an additional taxi. Providing Debussy Ltd's production for the year has not exceeded this relevant range, then fixed costs should not have increased as a result of volume increases. Any increase must be due to the fixed overheads costing more than budgeted.

(b)   *Possible reasons for the fixed overhead variances*

Fixed overhead expenditure variance

Inflation
Non–standard supplier for power and insurance
Inappropriate standard

Fixed overhead capacity variance

Reduced demand compared with budget
Inappropriate standard

Fixed overhead efficiency variance

Poor quality materials slowing down production
Workforce working slower than normal
Inappropriate standard

Task 3

The notes should include the following:

(a)   *Revised quarterly power budgets*

	Quarter 1	Quarter 2	Quarter 3	Quarter 4
Seasonal variation (%)	+ 5%	– 10%	– 20%	+ 25%
Current budget	£30,000	£30,000	£30,000	£30,000
Seasonal variation	+ £1,500	– £3,000	– £6,000	+ £7,500
Revised budget	£31,500	£27,000	£24,000	£37,500

(b)   *Use in variance analysis*

Although the power budget does not vary with changes in volume, it does vary with the different outside temperatures of each quarter. Allowing for these seasonal variations will give a more accurate budget figure against which to compare actual costs for control purposes. For example, the existing system shows an adverse expenditure variance for power of £6,000 but with the revised variance this becomes a favourable variance of £1,500. Allowing for the extra £7,500 of expenditure on power causes the budget for quarter 4 to increase by that amount to £88,500.

There is, however, a problem in using the revised budget of £88,500 when calculating the fixed overhead volume variance. Using that figure to calculate fixed overhead absorption rates will cause the volume variance to appear larger than before while reducing any variances in quarters when the seasonal variation is negative. This will result in the same volume variance in tonnes having different monetary values in different quarters and this is likely to be misleading to managers. Given that the seasonal variations will balance out over the four quarters, it would seem reasonable to calculate the volume variance using annual fixed overhead absorption rates.

Unit 7 Case Study 11.3: Hampstead plc

Workings	Standard		Actual	
Metres per Alpha	36,000/12,000 =	3.00	32,000/10,000=	3.20
Cost per metre	£432,000/36,000 =	£12.00	£377,600/32,000 =	£11.80
Labour hours per Alpha	72,000/12,000 =	6.00	70,000/10,000 =	7.00
Cost per hour	£450,000/72,000 =	£6.25	£422,800/70,000 =	£6.04

Task 1

(a) *Standard data*

(i) *Standard marginal cost*

	Units	Cost per unit of input	Cost £
Material (metres)	3	£12.00	36.00
Labour	6	£6.25	37.50
Total			73.50

(ii) *Standard cost of production*

	Units	Unit standard cost	Total standard cost £
Standard cost for 3 months	10,000	£73.50	735,000
Add fixed costs			396,000
			1,131,000

(b) *Calculation of variances*

(i) *Material price variance*

Standard price	£12.00	
Actual price	£11.80	
Difference	£0.20	(F)
Actual material used (metres)	32,000	
Material price variance = 32,000 x 20p	£6,400	(F)

(ii) *Material usage variance*

Standard usage (metres) = 10,000 x 3 metres	30,000	
Actual usage (metres)	32,000	
Difference (metres)	2,000	(A)
Material usage variance = 2,000 x £12.00	£24,000	(A)

(iii) *Labour rate variance*

Standard rate	£6.25	
Actual rate	£6.04	
Difference	£0.21	(F)
Actual hours worked	70,000	
Labour rate variance = 70,000 x 21p	£14,700	(F)

(iv) *Labour efficiency variance*

Standard usage (hours) = 10,000 x 6 hours	60,000	
Actual usage (hours)	70,000	
Difference (hours)	10,000	(A)
Labour efficiency variance = 10,000 x £6.25	£62,500	(A)

(v) *Fixed overhead expenditure variance*

Fixed overhead absorbed	£330,000	
Fixed overhead unabsorbed	£75,000	
Total actual cost of fixed overhead	£405,000	
Standard cost of fixed overhead	£396,000	
Fixed overhead expenditure variance	£9,000	(A)

(c)

MEMO

To: John Wade   **Date:**   17 June 19X8

From: The Assistant Management Accountant

Subject: **Revised management information**

Enclosed below is a statement reconciling the actual cost of production for the three months to 31 May 19X8 to how much is should have cost (its standard cost).

(i) *Reconciliation Statement – 3 months ended 31 May 19X8*

	£	
Actual cost of production	1,205,400	
Material price variance	6,400	(F)
Material usage variance	24,000	(A)
Labour rate variance	14,700	(F)
Labour efficiency variance	62,500	(A)
Fixed overhead expenditure variance	9,000	(A)
Standard cost of production	1,131,000	

Key: F = Favourable, A = Adverse

(ii) *Reasons why the variances differ from the original variances*

The original variances compared a budgeted output of 12,000 Alphas with an actual output of 10,000 Alphas. It therefore did not compare like with like. As a result, had actual output been nil then the favourable variances would have been even greater for materials and labour.

Page 1/2

Secondly, the variances were simply the difference between the budgeted cost and the actual cost. They did not differentiate between variations in input costs and variations in usage.

The revised statement:

♦ is based on the standard cost of the actual production of 10,000 Alphas

♦ differentiates between variations due to input prices being different from planned and the usage of inputs being different from planned.

(iii) *Improved management information*

The revised statement provides more meaningful information because of the following.

♦ It compares like with like based on the actual production achieved

♦ It highlights the major areas giving rise to any differences between planned and actual cost

♦ It allows management by exception

♦ The original statement conveyed the wrong message. It implied that the overall variance was favourable

♦ It shows a change in expenditure as being the only reason why fixed costs can change.

Page 2/2

Task 2

Workings

Subdivision of labour efficiency variance

Actual hours worked	70,000	
Unproductive hours due to machine breakdown	12,000	
Hours employed on production	58,000	
Standard hours produced	60,000	
Difference (hours)	2,000	(F)

	£	
Labour efficiency variance = 2,000 x £6.25	12,500	(F)
Machine breakdown – 12,000 x £6.25	75,000	(A)
Total	62,500	(A)

Subdivision of labour rate variance

	£	
Due to machine breakdown – 12,000 x 21p	2,520	(F)
Due to normal working = 58,000 x 21p	12,180	(F)
Total = 70,000 x 21p	14,700	(F)

Subdivision of material price variance

Change in index ((420.03/466.70) – 1)	– 10%	
Existing standard	£12.00	
Revised standard = £12.00 x 90%	£10.80	
	£	
Due to index (£12.00 – £10.80) x 32,000	38,400	(F)
Due to normal purchases = (£10.80 – £11.80) x 32,000	32,000	(A)
Total	6,400	(F)

Reconciliation statement – 3 months ended 31 May 19X8

	£		£	
Actual cost of production			1,205,400	
Variances arising from normal production				
Material price variance	32,000	(A)		
Material usage variance	24,000	(A)		
Labour rate variance	12,180	(F)		
Labour efficiency variance	12,500	(F)		
Fixed overhead expenditure variance	9,000	(A)		(A)
			40,320	
Variances arising from the machine breakdown				
Labour rate variance	2,520	(F)		
Labour efficiency variance	75,000	(A)		(A)
			72,480	
Variance arising from the change in material prices				
Material price variance			38,400	(F)
Standard cost of production			1,131,000	

Task 3

(a) *Four general headings making up the cost of quality*

Cost of prevention, appraisal costs, internal failure costs, external failure costs

(b) *Examples of types of cost found in each category*

Cost of prevention: training costs, cost of improved product design, cost of higher quality equipment, cost of enhanced preventative maintenance programmes.

Appraisal costs: cost of inspecting raw materials, cost of inspecting during and after manufacture.

Internal failure costs: cost of scrapped production, cost of rectification, cost of delays in production.

External failure costs: cost of returning faulty goods, repair costs, liability claims.

(c)   *Implications for existing accounting system*

(i)   If there are fixed price contracts with guaranteed levels of quality then there are likely to be few, if any, material price and usage variances. With the cost of labour effectively becoming a fixed cost, the actual unit cost of labour will simply depend on the volume produced. It will, therefore, be possible to calculate efficiency variances but these will not be true variances because they will not reflect costs saved or excess wages paid. Labour rate variances are also likely to be minimal if there is a guaranteed weekly wage. There is, therefore, less need for a standard costing system as variances are likely to be both small (or non–existent) and, even if incurred, non–controllable.

(ii) With flexible work practices, it would be extremely difficult to capture actual labour costs by individual job. Only material costs could be collectable in the normal way. It therefore seems that it will no longer be possible to collect the full marginal cost by individual job.

(d)   A cost saving not normally recorded in the existing costing system

With the introduction of Just–in–Time stock–keeping, there will be a saving from no longer having money tied up in keeping high levels of stock. This information is not normally captured by a standard costing system.

Unit 8 Case Study 11.4: Club Atlantic

Task 1

Club Atlantic Restaurant Performance Statement – Month to 31 October 19X6

	Note	Actual	Flexed budget	Variance
Number of guest days		11,160	11,160	
		£	£	£
Food	1	20,500	23,436	2,936 (F)
Cleaning materials	2	2,232	2,232	0
Heat, light and power	3	2,050	2,790	740 (F)
Catering staff wages	4	8,400	8,370	30 (A)
Rent, rates, insurance and depreciation	5	1,860	1,860	0
		35,042	38,688	3,646 (F)

Notes

1   £20,160/9,600 = £2.10 per guest day; £2.10 × 11,160 = £23,436
2   £1,920/9,600 = 20p per guest day; 20p × 11,160 = £2,232
3   £2,400/9,600 = 25p per guest day; 25p × 11,160 = £2,790
4   (11,160/40) × £30 = £8,370
5   Rent, rates etc per day = £1,800/30 = £60 per day; £60 × 31 days = £1,860

Task 2

Hall and Company
Accountants and Registered Auditors

The Directors
Club Atlantic

4 December 19X6

Dear Sirs,

Following our recent meeting, I enclose my comments on the questions you raised.

(a)   *Do budgets motivate managers to achieve objectives?*

Motivation is the amount of effort a manager applies to achieving the goals of the organisation. For budgets to motivate requires the following:

♦   Managers need to know the goals of Club Atlantic
♦   Budgets need to be consistent with these goals
♦   Managers must want to achieve these goals and believe the goals are achievable
♦   Managers must feel they can influence the achievement of goals
♦   Achieving goals should provide a challenge
♦   Equitable rewards, either of a financial or non–financial nature, should be offered.

Page 1/2

(b)   *Do budgets lead to improved performance by managers?*

Even if managers are motivated, this will not automatically lead to improved performance. To achieve improved performance depends on the ability of the individual manager. In turn, this depends on other factors such as training, education and managerial skills. Sometimes there is also an element of luck.

(c)   *Does the current method of reporting motivate managers to be more efficient?*

Two issues need to be addressed before a judgement can be made about efficiency. The first is whether the existing performance statements are a valid measure of efficiency, the second is the effect of those statements on the behaviour of managers.

The current performance statement measures actual performance against a fixed budget. This is unlikely to be a valid standard when there are many variable costs, as in the restaurant. Brian Hilton's activities are mainly fixed costs and so, with increased volume, he will appear to be more in control of his expenses. This may result in Susan Green feeling the system is unfair and her failure to be motivated.

As mentioned earlier budgets need to provide a challenge if they are to encourage motivation. Up to a point, budgets should be demanding but if too demanding, managers might feel they are unachievable (this may be Susan Green's response). If budgets are demanding, there will inevitably be adverse variances from time to time. If Brian Hilton never reports adverse variances, it may be that the budget targets are set too low to motivate.

Yours sincerely,

A Technician

Page 2/2

Unit 8 Case Study 11.5: Eskafield Industrial Museum

Task 1

(a)   *Centred four–point moving average trend figures*

Year	Quarter	Visitors	Moving annual total	Moving average	Centred average (trend)	Seasonal variations
19X6	1	5,800				
	2	9,000				
			35,200	8,800		
	3	6,000			8,900	−2,900
			36,000	9,000		
	4	14,400			9,100	+5,300
			36,800	9,200		
19X7	1	6,600			9,300	−2,700
			37,600	9,400		
	2	9,800			9,500	+300
			38,400	9,600		
	3	6,800				
	4	15,200				

Total = 0

(b)

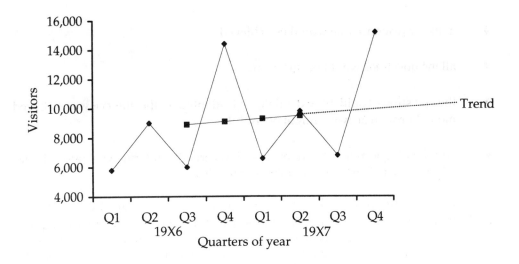

(c)   The figures should be:

19X8	Quarter	1	10,100 − 2,700 = 7,400
		2	10,300 + 300 = 10,600
		3	10,500 − 2,900 = 7,600
		4	10,700 + 5,300 = 16,000

(d)   The notes should include the following:

(i)   A number of methods could be used to forecast visitor numbers: they could be internal or external, primary or secondary. However, the initial step would need to be the gathering of the data which would be used as input.

Internal sources could be extracted from whatever information is currently being gathered eg visitor numbers by quarter; these could be further analysed by month, week or date. This internal data could be analysed using time series analysis in order to establish a trend, as in Task 1. However, this method assumes that the past will be repeated and ignores random and cyclical fluctuations. It also ignores the product life cycle, which again follows a trend.

External information would need to be sourced from past, current, or potential visitors.

Primary and secondary sourcing of data could be used in forecasting; some primary sources are outlined above. Secondary sources would include: leisure–based data, tourist data, industry data, etc. However this data would tend to be less useful in forecasting, as it is not likely to be focused on the industry or on the location required.

(ii)   Both methods would use random or selective sampling. However, telephone sampling would be preferred for the following reasons:

◆   telephone sampling would tend to avoid misunderstandings by clarifying the questions

◆   a higher response rate would be achieved

◆   all the questions would be answered

◆   the questions could be extended and adapted if the interviewer believed more thorough answers might be useful

◆   additional questions could be asked where the interviewee raises issues which were not considered in the original design.

(iii)   The concept of the product life cycle of start–up, growth, maturity and decline could be applied to any area, including a museum. The start–up phase requires investment; this would have been the situation several years ago when the museum was first opened, the investment being in working exhibits, marketing, staff etc. The next phase would have been the growth phase, with the rapid growth in visitors reflecting this. They would have been attracted to the museum by investment in marketing, special offer tickets, special weekend attractions, etc. The maturity stage would be reflected in the number of visitors reaching a peak and levelling off. The final phase would be that of decline which appears to have been the case in recent years.

To achieve sustained growth, there would need to be investment every year, so that each investment would have its own product life cycle which would overlap with the previous investment resulting in sustained growth. It can be seen that with the recent investment, the museum has completed the start–up phase and is now at the beginning of the growth phase after years of decline.

Task 2

MEMO

To: John Derbyshire **Date:** 3 December 19X7

From: Accounting Technician

Subject: **Motivational issues**

(a) *Motivational implications of imposing the budget reduction from £35,000 to £29,000*

Budgets are usually the best estimates of the figures for an organisation when they are submitted to management. However, in some cases, there will be an amount of slack built in, ie additional expenses or reduced income in order to improve the chances of meeting the budget. Top management need to identify this slack so they can make an estimate of what it is, then ask the manager for a reduction. Where slack has not been built in, this request would tend to demotivate the managers as the whole budgeting process will have to be started again and expenses reduced to the levels required. As a result, the manager will not be inclined to own the budget because it has been imposed.

The size of the reduction will also have an affect on morale, with a small reduction having a minor effect and a large reduction, as in this case, having a larger effect.

The reduction to £29,000 appears to have been made for political reasons and not realistic reasons, therefore the effect on the managers is likely to be negative.

(b) *Arguments for and against using a top–down budgeting approach for the museum*

Top–down budgeting is the name given to an approach where the manager decides what the budget should be and then issues it to the staff of the organisation. There is no discussion of the figures.

Bottom–up budgeting is where all the staff of the organisation are involved in the budgeting process and they all participate in the preparation of it.

Top–down budgeting is generally used in start–up situations and with small organisations, whereas bottom-up budgeting is used in more mature organisations, of medium to large size.

For the Eskafield Museum a bottom–up approach is preferable as it combines participation with motivation and results in a budget which is believed in.

Unit 8: Case Study 11.6: Vecstar Ltd

Task 1

(a)

Vecstar Ltd Flexible budget and variances – 4 weeks ended 29 May 19X8

	Note	Actual	Flexible budget	Variance	
Units produced		60,000	60,000	Nil	
		£	£	£	
Material	1	18,546	15,600	2,946	(A)
Labour	2	7,200	7,200		
Power	3	900	1,300	400	(F)
Maintenance	4	1,600	1,800	200	(F)
Supervision		3,400	3,440	40	(F)
Rent and insurance		2,050	1,820	230	(A)
Depreciation		4,000	4,000		
Total		37,696	35,160	2,536	(A)

Notes

1 Material: £12,480 x 60/48 = £15,600
2 Labour: £5,760 x 60/48 = £7,200
3 Power: £100 x (60,000 x 2p) = £1,300
4 Maintenance: £1,200 + (60,000 x 1p) = £1,800

(b)

Fixed costs	£
Power	100
Maintenance	1,200
Supervision	3,440
Rent and insurance	1,820
Depreciation	4,000
	10,560

Fixed overhead absorption rate	£0.20
Normal activity per 4 week period in units (£10,560/20p)	52,800
Annual normal activity in units 52,800 units x 13	686,400

Green and Co
Auditors and Registered Accountants
High Street, Anytown

17 June 19X8

James Close
Managing Director
Vecstar Ltd
New Street
Anytown

Dear Mr Close

Thank you for your recent letter raising queries about the flexible budget prepared for Vecstar Ltd.

(a)   The reason why some budgeted costs have remained the same while others have changed arises from the different ways costs change as activity changes. The original budget was a fixed budget, ie it compared an original plan with actual performance. The flexible budget shows what the original budget would have been had the budgeted volume been the same as that actually achieved. Over the *relevant range* fixed costs, such as rent, remain the same irrespective of changes in volume. Because of this, fixed costs will appear the same in both budgets. Variable costs, such as materials, will change with changes in production. Because the actual production for the four weeks to 29 May was greater than the budgeted production, it is inevitable that more variable costs will be incurred solely as a result of flexing the budget. This explains why the variable costs in the flexible budget differ from those in the original budget. Semi–variable costs comprise an element of fixed cost and an element of variable cost. The budgeted semi–variable costs will change because the higher production involves more of the variable element being incurred.

(b)   *Estimated cost of Alpha production – 4 weeks ended 26 June 19X8*

Budgeted cost of material and labour for 48,000 Alphas.

	£
Materials	12,480
Labour	5,760
Total	18,240

	£
Unit cost of materials and labour £18,240/48,000	0.38
Add budgeted marginal cost of power per unit	0.02
Add budgeted marginal cost of maintenance per unit	0.01
Unit variable cost	0.41

	£
Total variable cost £0.41 x 62,000	25,420
Add fixed costs	10,560
Budgeted cost of producing 62,000 Alphas	35,980
Revised, indexed budgeted cost 165.12/160.00 x £35,980	£37,131

Page 1/2

(c)   Care needs to be used in interpreting the estimated cost of £37,131. First, the index may not be appropriate to the inputs required for Alpha production. Secondly, it is unlikely to affect all inputs equally. For example wages are probably negotiated on an annual, rather than a monthly, basis. Thirdly, the index may not be representative of all regions within a country. This would particularly apply to the cost of wages and rent.

(d)   One of the outcomes of changing from a fixed to a flexible budget is that the difference between the original and the actual units produced is not highlighted, hence your disappointment at the increased production not being shown. One way in which this could be rectified would be to value the difference in production in terms of cost, margin or over-absorbed overheads, ie by multiplying the difference in units by the production cost, the margin or the fixed production overheads. These proposals would be more meaningful by placing a value on the difference in units.

Yours sincerely,

A Technician

Green and Co

Page 2/2

CHAPTER 12

Mock Central Assessments (Questions)

Unit 7: Mock Central Assessment

Time allowed – 3 hours plus 15 minutes reading time.
This central assessment is in two sections.
You are reminded that competence must be achieved in EACH section. You should therefore attempt and aim to complete EVERY task in EACH section.
You are advised to spend approximately 95 minutes on Section 1 and 85 minutes on Section 2.
All essential workings should be included within your answers, where appropriate.

SECTION 1

Data

Pronto Ltd was recently established in the UK to assemble cars. All parts are sent directly to the UK in the form of a kit by Pronto's owner from its headquarters in a country called Erehwon.

The contract between Pronto and its owner is a fixed price contract per kit and the contract specifies zero faults in all of the parts. This fixed price was used to establish the standard cost per kit. Despite this, the managing director of Pronto, Richard Jones, is concerned to receive the following statement from the management accounting department where you are employed as an accounting technician.

	September 19X8	October 19X8	November 19X8
Kits delivered	2,000	2,100	2,050
Actual cost invoiced	£12,059,535	£11,385,495	£10,848,600
Unit cost per kit to nearest £	£6,030	£5,422	£5,292

Richard Jones cannot understand why, with a fixed price contract and guaranteed quality, the unit cost should vary over the three months. He provides you with the following information:

♦ the contract's cost was fixed in Erehwon dollars of $54,243 per kit

♦ there has been no change in the agreed cost of the parts and no other costs incurred.

On further investigation you discover that the exchange rate between the UK pound and the Erehwon dollar was as follows:

At time of contract	September 19X8	October 19X8	November 19X8
$9.80	$9.00	$10.00	$10.25

Task 1.1

(a)   Prepare a memo to Richard Jones. Your memo should include a calculation of:

      (i)   the UK cost per kit at the time the contract was agreed

      (ii)   the UK cost of the kits delivered using the exchange rates given for each of the three
           months

      (iii)   the price variance due to exchange rate differences for each of the three months

      (iv)   any usage variance in each of the three months, assuming no other reason for the
           price variance

(b)   Briefly discuss whether price variances due to exchange rate differences should be
      excluded from any standard costing report prepared for the production manager of
      Pronto Ltd.

Data

Pronto uses a highly mechanised and computerised moving assembly line known as a track to
build the cars. Although individual employees are assigned to particular parts of the track, they
work in teams. If the production of cars slows below the speed of the track, teams help each
other to maintain the speed of the track and the production of cars. Because of this approach:

◆   labour is viewed as a fixed cost

◆   machine hours (the hours that the track is in use) are used to charge overheads to
      production.

For the week ended 28 November 19X8, the management accounting department has prepared a
statement of budgeted and actual fixed overhead for Richard Jones. This is reproduced below.

Pronto Ltd: Budgeted and actual fixed overheads – week ended 28 November 19X8		
	Budget	Actual
Car production	560 cars	500 cars
Machine (or track) hours of production	140 hours	126 hours
Fixed overheads:	£	£
Rent and rates	16,000	16,000
Maintenance and depreciation	10,000	13,000
Power	75,000	71,000
Labour	739,000	742,000
	840,000	842,000

Task 1.2

Richard Jones finds that the statement is not particularly helpful as it does not give him sufficient information to manage the company. He asks for your help.

In preparation for a meeting with Richard Jones:

(a)   calculate:

      (i)   budgeted overheads per machine (or track) hour

      (ii)   budgeted number of cars produced per machine (or track) hour

      (iii)   standard hours of actual production

(b)   calculate the following variances using the information identified in (a):

      (i)   fixed overhead expenditure variance

      (ii)   fixed overhead volume variance

      (iii)   fixed overhead efficiency variance

      (iv)   fixed overhead capacity variance

(c)   Prepare a statement for the week ended 28 November 19X8 reconciling the fixed overheads incurred to the fixed overheads absorbed in production.

SECTION 2

Data

You are employed by Micro Circuits Ltd as a financial analyst reporting to Angela Frear, the Director of Corporate Strategy. One of your responsibilities is to monitor the performance of subsidiaries within the group. Financial and other data relating to subsidiary A is reproduced below.

SUBSIDIARY A				

Profit and loss account year to 30 November 19X8 | **Extract from balance sheet at 30 November 19X8**

Profit and loss account	£000	£000	Balance sheet extract	£000 Land and buildings	£000 Plant and machinery	£000 Total
Sales		4,000	Fixed assets			
Less returns		100	Cost	2,000	2,500	4,500
Turnover[1]		3,900	Additions	–	1,800	1,800
				2,000	4,300	6,300
Material	230					
Labour	400		Accumulated depreciation	160	1,700	1,860
Production overheads[2]	300					
Cost of production	930			1,840	2,600	4,440
Opening finished stock	50		Raw material stock		15	
Closing finished stock	(140)		Finished goods stock		140	
Cost of sales		840			155	
Gross profit		3,060	Debtors		325	
Marketing	500		Cash and bank		40	
Customer support	400		Creditors		(85)	
Research and development	750					435
Training	140		Net assets			4,875
Administration	295					
		2,085				
Operating profit		975				

Other information

Notes

1   *Analysis of turnover*

	£000		£000
Regular customers	3,120	New products	1,560
New customers	780	Existing products	2,340
	3,900		3,900

2   *Production overheads include £37,200 of reworked faulty production.*

3   **Orders received in the year totalled £4,550,000.**

Task 2.1

Angela Frear asks you to calculate the following performance indicators in preparation for a board meeting:

(a)   the return on capital employed

(b)   the asset turnover

(c)   the sales (or operating profit) margin

(d)   the average age of debtors in months

(e)   the average age of finished stock in months.

Data

One of the issues to be discussed at the board meeting is the usefulness of performance indicators. Angela Frear has recently attended a conference on creating and enhancing value.

Three criticisms were made of financial performance indicators:

♦ They could give misleading signals

♦ They could be manipulated

♦ They focus on the short term and do not take account of other key, non–financial performance indicators.

At the conference, Angela was introduced to the idea of the balanced scorecard. The balanced scorecard looks at performance measurement from four perspectives:

The financial perspective
This is concerned with satisfying shareholders. Examples include the return on capital employed and sales margin.

The customer perspective
This asks how customers view the business and is concerned with measures of customer satisfaction. Examples include speed of delivery and customer loyalty.

The internal perspective
This looks at the quality of the company's output in terms of technical excellence and customer needs. Examples would be striving towards total quality management and flexible production as well as unit cost.

The innovation and learning perspective
This is concerned with the continual improvement of existing products and the ability to develop new products as customers' needs change. An example would be the percentage of turnover attributable to new products.

Task 2.2

Angela Frear asks you to prepare briefing notes for the board meeting. Using the data from Task 1 where necessary, your notes should:

(a)   suggest *one* reason why the return on capital employed calculated in Task 1 might be misleading

(b)   identify *one* way of manipulating the sales (or operating profit) margin

(c)   calculate the average delay in fulfilling orders

(d)   identify *one* other possible measure of customer satisfaction other than the delay in fulfilling orders

(e)   calculate *two* indicators which may help to measure performance from an internal perspective

(f)   calculate *one* performance indicator which would help to measure the innovation and learning perspective.

Unit 8: Mock Central Assessment

Time allowed: 3 hours plus 15 minutes reading time.
This central assessment is in two sections.
You are reminded that competence must be achieved in EACH section. You should therefore attempt and aim to complete EVERY task in EACH section.
You are advised to spend approximately 75 minutes on Section 1 and 105 minutes on Section 2.
All essential workings should be included within your answer, where appropriate.

SECTION 1

Data

Amber Ltd is a subsidiary of Colour plc and makes a single product, the Delta. Budgets are prepared by dividing the accounting year into 13 periods, each of four weeks. Amber's policy is to avoid overtime payments wherever possible and this was one of the assumptions built into the preparation of Amber's budget for this year. However, some overtime payments have been necessary.

Helen Roy, Amber's finance director, has recently carried out an investigation and discovered why overtime has been paid. She found that the labour hours available over each four–week period were more than sufficient to meet the four–weekly production targets. However, *within* any four–week period, production levels could vary considerably. As a result, in some weeks, overtime had to be paid.

You are employed in the management accounting section of Colour plc as an assistant to Helen Roy. Although Helen did not have the next period's *production* volumes analysed by individual week, she was able to explain the problem by showing you the forecast *sales* of Deltas over each of the next four weeks. These are reproduced below.

Week	1	2	3	4
Forecast *sales* of Deltas (units)	23,520	27,440	28,420	32,340

Helen Roy also gives the following information.

♦ Amber's maximum production capacity per week before overtime and rejections is 30,400 Deltas.

♦ For technical reasons, production has to take place at least one week before it is sold.

♦ At present, all production takes place exactly one week before it is sold.

♦ Sales cannot be delayed to a subsequent week.

♦ The weekly fixed cost of wages before overtime is £21,280.

♦ Overtime is equivalent to £2 per unit produced in excess of 30,400 Deltas.

♦ The cost of material per Delta is £5.

♦   There is a 2% rejection rate in the manufacture of Deltas. Rejected Deltas are only discovered on completion and have no monetary value.

♦   Budgeted fixed production overheads for the year are estimated to be £3,792,825. These are absorbed on the basis of an estimated annual production before rejections of 1,685,700 Deltas.

Task 1.1

Helen Roy asks you to prepare Amber's *weekly* production budgets for weeks 1 to 3 on the current basis that all production takes place exactly one week before it is sold. The budget should identify:

(a)   the number of Deltas to be produced in each of the three weeks

(b)   the cost of any overtime paid

(c)   the cost of production for each of the three weeks, including fixed production overheads.

Data

You give Helen Roy Amber's production budget for the next three weeks. She now tells you that it may be possible to save at least some of the overtime payments by manufacturing some Deltas in advance of the normal production schedule. However, any Deltas made earlier than one week before being sold will incur financing costs of 20p per Delta per week.

Task 1.2

Helen Roy asks you to calculate:

(a)   the number of Deltas to be produced in each of the three weeks if the overall costs are to be minimised

(b)   the net savings if your revised production plan in (a) is accepted.

SECTION 2

Data

Colour plc has two more subsidiaries, Red Ltd and Green Ltd. Red Ltd makes only one product, a part only used by Green Ltd. Because Green is the only customer and there is no market price for the part, the part is sold to Green at cost.

Last year, Red prepared two provisional budgets because Green was not certain how many parts it would buy from Red in the current year. These two budgets are reproduced below.

Red Ltd provisional budgets 12 months to 30 November 19X8		
Volume (units)	18,000	20,000
	£	£
Material	180,000	200,000
Labour	308,000	340,000
Power and maintenance	33,000	35,000
Rent, insurance and depreciation	98,000	98,000
Total cost	619,000	673,000

Shortly afterwards, Green told Red that it needed 20,000 parts over the year to 30 November 19X8. Red's budget for the year was then based on that level of production.

During the financial year, Green Ltd only bought 19,500 parts. Red's performance statement for the year to 30 November 19X8 is reproduced below.

Red Ltd performance statement – year to 30 November 19X8				
	Budget	*Actual*	*Variances*	
Volume (units)	20,000	19,500		
	£	£	£	
Material	200,000	197,000	3,000	(F)
Labour	340,000	331,000	9,000	(F)
Power and maintenance	35,000	35,000	–	
Rent, insurance and depreciation	98,000	97,500	500	(F)
Total cost	673,000	660,500	12,500	(F)

Key: (F) = favourable, (A) = adverse

Task 2.1

(a) Using the data in the provisional budgets, calculate the fixed and variable cost elements within each of the expenditure headings.

(b) Using the data in the performance statement and your solution to part (a), prepare a revised performance statement using flexible budgeting. Your statement should show both the revised budget and the variances.

Data

Colour plc is about to introduce performance–related payments for all senior managers in the three subsidiaries. The purpose is to motivate senior managers to improve performance.

For Red Ltd, the additional payments will be based on two factors:

♦   achieving or exceeding annual budgeted volumes of production set by the Board of Directors of Colour plc at the beginning of the year

♦   keeping unit costs below budget

Tony Brown, the managing director of Red Ltd, is about to call a meeting of his senior managers to discuss the implications of the proposals. He is not certain that performance–related pay will automatically lead to improved performance in the subsidiaries. Even if it does, he is not certain that performance–related pay will help *his* subsidiary improve performance.

Task 2.2

Write a memo to Tony Brown. Your memo should identify:

(a)   *three* general conditions necessary for performance–related pay to lead to improved performance

(b)   *two* reasons why the particular scheme might not be appropriate to the senior management of Red Ltd

(c)   *one* example where it would be possible for the managers of Red Ltd to misuse the proposed system by achieving performance–related pay without extra effort on their part.

CHAPTER 12

Mock Central Assessments (Answers)

Unit 7: Mock Central Assessment

SECTION 1

Task 1.1

MEMO

To: Richard Jones   **Date:** 2 December 19X8

From: Accounting Technician

Subject: **Variances in kit costs**

(a) (i) The standard cost per kit was based on an exchange rate of $9.80 to the pound. Because of this, the UK standard cost became £5,535 ($54,243/9.80). The detailed costs and variances are calculated below.

Month	Workings	September	October	November
Number of kits		2,000	2,100	2,050
Contract cost in $	number of kits x $54,243	$108,486,000	$113,910,300	$111,198,150
Exchange rate		$9.00	$10.00	$10.25
		£	£	£
(ii) Contract cost in £	$ cost/exchange rate	12,054,000	11,391,030	10,848,600
Standard cost	Cost in Erehwon $/$9.8	11,070,000	11,623,500	11,346,750
(iii) Price variance		984,000 (A)	232,470 (F)	498,150 (F)
Cost in £	as above	12,054,000	11,391,030	10,848,600
Actual cost	given in task	12,059,535	11,385,495	10,848,600
(iv) Usage variance		5,535 (A)	5,535 (F)	nil

(b) The price variances due to exchange rate differences are unlikely to be of help to the production manager of Pronto Ltd as they are not controllable by him and should, therefore, be excluded.

Task 1.2

(a) *Budgeted data*

    (i)   Budgeted overheads per machine (or track) hours £840,000/140 = £6,000 per hour.

    (ii)   Budgeted number of cars produced per machine (or track) hour = 560/140 = 4 per hour.

    (iii)   Standard hours of production = 500/4 = 125 hours.

(b) *Variances*

    (i)   Fixed overhead expenditure variance = £840,000 – £842,000 = £2,000 (Adverse).

    (ii)   Fixed overhead volume variance = (125 hours – 140 hours) x £6,000 = £90,000 (Adverse).

    (iii)   Fixed overhead efficiency variance = (125 hours – 126 hours) x £6,000 = £6,000 (Adverse).

    (iv)   Fixed overhead capacity variance = (126 hours – 140 hours) x £6,000 = £84,000 (Adverse).

(c)

Reconciliation statement between fixed overheads incurred and fixed overheads absorbed week ended 28 November 19X8		
	£	
Fixed overheads incurred	842,000	
Expenditure variance	2,000	(A)
Efficiency variance	6,000	(A)
Capacity variance	84,000	(A)
Fixed overheads absorbed 125 x £6,000	750,000	

SECTION 2

Task 2.1

(a)	Return on capital employed	£975/£4,875 x 100	20%
(b)	Asset turnover	£3,900/£4,875	0.8 times
(c)	Sales (or operating profit) margin	£975/£3,900 x 100	25%
(d)	Average age of debtors	(£325/£3,900) x 12	1 month
(e)	Average age of finished stock	(£140/£840) x 12	2 months

Task 2.2

Briefing notes considering the use of wider performance indicators

Prepared for Angela Frear
Prepared by Financial Analyst
Date: 2 December 19X8

(a)   Return on capital employed

The return on capital employed might be misleading for a number of reasons. A great deal of the overheads are discretionary costs, that is they could be reduced without immediately affecting output. However marketing, customer support, research and development, and training could all be viewed as investments in the future even though they are treated as revenue expenditure for accounting purposes. Without these expenses, the return on capital employed would have looked much higher.

(b)   Manipulation of the sales margin

It is possible to manipulate the sales margin in a number of ways. The obvious ones are to reduce expenditure on the discretionary costs identified in (a). Other ways include choosing a longer time period over which to depreciate the assets and choosing a different way of valuing stock if this gave a higher closing stock figure. All of these would show short–term improvements although probably at the expense of long–term viability.

(c)   Average delay in fulfilling orders

	£
Orders during the year	4,550,000
Turnover during the year	3,900,000
	─────
Unfulfilled orders	650,000
	─────
Average delay = (650/3,900) x 12	2 months

Page 1 of 2

525

(d)   Other measures of customer satisfaction

There are at least two other possible measures of customer satisfaction:

♦   Repeat custom (£3,120/£3,900) x 100 = 80%.

♦   The amount of customer support per customer or per £ of sales.

(e)   Internal perspective indicators

There are a number of indicators which would support the performance of the company from an internal perspective. One would be the level of training as a percentage of manufacturing cost. There are, however, two which can be measured directly. These are:

♦   The percentage of returns (100/4,000) x 100 = 2.5%.

♦   The percentage of reworking (37.2/930) x 100 = 4%.

The objective should be for these to be as small as possible – unlike the amount of training.

(f)   Innovation and learning

Two possible measures are:

♦   The percentage of turnover derived from new products (£1,560/£3,900) = 40%.

♦   The amount spent on research and development, perhaps expressed as a percentage of sales or production costs.

Page 2 of 2

Unit 8: Mock Central Assessment

SECTION 1

Task 1.1

Amber Ltd production budget for next three weeks

	Week	1	2	3	4
	Sales (units)	23,520	27,440	28,420	32,340
	Good production required (units)	27,440	28,420	32,340	
	Loss = 2/98 x good production	560	580	660	
(a)	Gross production required (units)	28,000	29,000	33,000	
		£	£	£	
	Weekly paid labour	21,280	21,280	21,280	
(b)	Overtime (33,000 – 30,400) x £2			5,200	
	Total labour cost	21,280	21,280	26,480	
	Material [1]	140,000	145,000	165,000	
	Production overhead [2]	63,000	65,250	74,250	
(c)	Cost of production	224,280	231,530	265,730	

Notes:

1   Gross production volume x £5

2   Production overhead per gross unit = £3,792,825/1,685,700 = £2.25

    Production overhead per week = gross production volume x £2.25

Task 1.2

+--+

Amber Ltd Revised production budget and savings for next three weeks

		Week	1	2	3
		Planned production units (gross)	28,000	29,000	33,000
		Maximum production possible	30,400	30,400	30,400
		Surplus/(deficit)	2,400	1,400	(2,600)
		Planned production units (gross)	28,000	29,000	33,000
		Change in planned production	1,200	1,400	(2,600)
(a)		Revised production plan (units)	29,200	30,400	30,400

				£	£
		Savings			
		Overtime saved			5,200
		Finance cost week 1: (20p x 1,200 units x 2 weeks)		480	
		Finance cost week 2: (20p x 1,400 units x 1 week)		280	
					760
(b)		Net savings			4,440

+--+

SECTION 2

Task 2.1

(a)

Red Ltd – Analysis of fixed and variable costs

	First budget	Second budget	Change in volume	Unit variable cost	Total variable cost	Fixed cost
	a	b	$c = a-b$	$d = c/2,000$	$e = d \times 20,000$	$f = b-e$
Volume (units)	18,000	20,000	2,000			
	£	£	£	£	£	£
Material	180,000	200,000	20,000	10	200,000	nil
Labour	308,000	340,000	32,000	16	320,000	20,000
Power and maintenance	33,000	35,000	2,000	1	20,000	15,000
Rent, insurance and depreciation	98,000	98,000	nil	nil	nil	98,000
Total cost	619,000	673,000	54,000	27	540,000	133,000

(b)

	Unit variable cost	Total variable cost	Fixed cost	Flexed budget	Actual cost	Variance
	£	£	£	£	£	£
Material	10	195,000		195,000	197,000	2,000 (A)
Labour	16	312,000	20,000	332,000	331,000	1,000 (F)
Power and maintenance	1	19,500	15,000	34,500	35,000	500 (A)
Rent, insurance and depreciation	nil		98,000	98,000	97,500	500 (F)
Total cost				659,500	660,500	1,000 (A)

Red Ltd – Revised performance statement – year to 30 November 1998

Key: (A) = Adverse, (F) = Favourable

Task 2.2

MEMO

To: Tony Brown **Date:** 2 December 19X8

From: Accounting technician

Subject: **Performance–related pay**

(a) In order for performance–related pay to lead to improved performance, a number of conditions are necessary.

♦ Managers need to know the objectives of the whole organisation.

♦ Budgets need to be consistent with those objectives.

♦ Managers must want to achieve those objectives.

♦ Managers must feel that the objectives are achievable.

♦ Managers must feel they can influence the achievement of the objectives.

♦ The objectives should provide a challenge.

♦ The level of rewards – both financial and non–financial – should be sufficient to help motivate managers.

♦ Managers need to have the appropriate skills to achieve improved performance.

Page 1/2

(b)   Given these conditions, it is not clear that the proposed scheme of performance–related pay will lead to improved performance.

♦   The level of production is not under the control of Red's managers. It is dictated by the needs of the Green subsidiary.

♦   One measure of performance is profit. Under the present accounting system, any profit generated for Colour plc by Red Ltd is reported in Green's performance as the part is sold at cost.

♦   Some of the expenditure incurred by Red Ltd such as rent and insurance may not be controllable by its managers.

(c)   The proposed scheme is possibly open to misuse by the managers of Red Ltd.

♦   By simply focusing on costs, the managers of Red Ltd might use inferior materials.

♦   If Green requires a higher volume of parts from Red, then unit cost will fall because of the element of fixed costs being spread over a larger volume. The managers of Red Ltd will, therefore, achieve an increase in their pay even though this will not have involved any effort on their part.

Page 2/2

Index

STUDY PACK REVIEW FORM

We hope that you have found this Study Pack stimulating and useful and that you now feel confident and well prepared for your Central Assessments in Units 7 and 8.

We would be grateful if you could take a few moments to complete the questionnaire below, so we can assess how well our material meets the needs of students. There's a prize for four lucky students who fill in one of these forms from across the AAT range and are lucky enough to be selected!

	Excellent	Adequate	Poor
Range of coverage by questions			
Appropriateness of coverage to Central Assessment once sat			
Presentation			
Level of accuracy			

Did you spot any errors or ambiguities? Please let us have the details below.

Thank you for your feedback.

Please return this form to:

AAT review forms
Profex Publishing
1 High Street
Maidenhead
Berkshire SL6 1JN

Or e-mail your comments to: profex@clara.co.uk